Homemade

Homemade

learn to make your own everyday items

Published by the Reader's Digest Association, Inc.
London • New York • Sydney • Montreal

HOMEMADE

Consultant Georgina Bitcon
Food Recipes Kim Gayton Elliott
Beauty Products Jay Ansell, Beth Kalet
Home Remedies Debra Gordon
Cleaning Products Steven Schwartz
House, Garden and Pet Products
   Delilah Smittle
Editorial Project Manager Deborah Nixon
Senior Editor Jessica Cox
Copyeditors Georgina Bitcon, Kirsten
   Colvin, Janine Flew, Katri Hilden
Designer Susanne Geppert
Cover Design Kylie Mulquin
Senior Production Controller
   Monique Tesoriero

FOR VIVAT DIRECT

Editorial Director Julian Browne
Art Director Anne-Marie Bulat
Managing Editor Nina Hathway
Trade Books Editor Penny Craig
Picture Resource Manager Sarah
   Stewart-Richardson
Pre-press Technical Manager
   Dean Russell
Production Controller Jan Bucil
Product Production Manager
   Claudette Bramble

Note to Readers The information in this book has been carefully researched and all efforts have been made to ensure its accuracy and safety. The publisher and the individual contributors do not assume any responsibility for any injuries suffered or damages or losses incurred as a result of following the instructions in this book. Before taking any action based on information in this book, study it carefully and make sure that you understand it fully. Observe all warnings. Test any new or unusual repair or cleaning method before applying it broadly, or on a highly visible area or a valuable item.

This paperback edition published in 2012 in the United Kingdom by Vivat Direct Limited (t/a Reader's Digest), 157 Edgware Road, London W2 2HR

First published in 2010

Homemade is owned and under licence from The Reader's Digest Association, Inc. All rights reserved.

Adapted from *Homemade: how to make hundreds of everyday products fast, fresh and more naturally* published by The Reader's Digest Association, Inc., USA, in 2007. This edition first published by Reader's Digest (Australia) Pty Limited in 2010

We are committed both to the quality of our products and the service we provide to our customers. We value your comments so please do contact us on **0871 351 1000** or via our website at **www.readersdigest.co.uk**

If you have any comments or suggestions about the content of our books you can contact us at **gbeditorial@readersdigest.co.uk**

Printed and bound in China

Concept code US4581/IC
Product code 400-603-UP0000-1
ISBN 978 1 78020 131 3

The Magic of Homemade

Many of us have a similar shopping ritual. Once a week we go to the supermarket, grab a trolley and load up with a box of this and a bottle or a carton of that. If you also add visits to your local convenience store for extra supplies, it's a whole lot of shopping – and spending – week after week after week.

But what do we get with all these packaged products? We get reliability and convenience, and we get choices – supermarket aisles are packed with mind-boggling variations of the same product. But that's not all we get. Many everyday food items are filled with unwanted chemicals and preservatives, and goods come with wasteful packaging. You also get to see your name-brand products on TV – but it's your money that pays for all those advertisements.

All of this is modern life, but when a window cleaner comes with 'citrus orange' or 'mountain berry' varieties, or a kitchen bench cleaner is produced in five different 'natural fragrances' to try and get our attention, consumerism seems to be getting out of control.

You do, however, have options. You can make your own alternative versions of hundreds of items that you buy at the supermarket, and they will be cheaper, healthier and effective. That is exactly what *Homemade* is all about. In this book, you'll find more than 700 recipes for substitutes for the most common items bought in shops. And they are not just for food items. Beauty products, toiletries, pet supplies, cleaning and garden products and even everyday medicines can be made at home, easily, quickly and effectively.

You will not only save a lot of money, but also have great fun and get a real sense of pride from making these easy and clever recipes. You'll love the quality, you'll love the savings and, most of all, you'll love the feeling of accomplishment.

The Editors
Reader's Digest Books

Contents

Introduction

Part 1 22 In the Kitchen

The Joy of Homemade Living

Picking up a bottle of shampoo or jar of mayonnaise at the supermarket is not that much trouble – and in the grand scheme of things neither seems particularly expensive. And if you are buying a name brand, you can feel relatively confident that you are getting products of reliably consistent quality that will do the job – a shampoo that cleans your hair with lots of bubbly lather or a condiment that will add a creamy tang to your sandwiches and salads. Multinational food and home products corporations are adept at putting out innocuous uniform products with a long shelf life and eye-pleasing packaging.

So why bother to make them yourself? There are many reasons that we'll explore on the following pages. The recipes that we provide are not 'replication' recipes. We don't claim to have the formula for a famous brand cleanser or a secret herbs-and-spices mix. Our versions of everyday products won't smell or look like many of the name-brand products they are replacing. But rest assured that they work – and work terrifically well.

The Rewards of Making It Yourself

There are many good reasons and real, tangible benefits to making common household products yourself. In many cases, you'll find that the quality of the homemade product is superior to the equivalent shop-bought item. You'll not only save money, but when you make something yourself, you know exactly what goes into it. You'll know for sure that it contains no questionable extenders, stabilisers or other artificial ingredients, and you can also adjust the recipe to meet your own needs or tastes. Not only that, when you make something yourself, you create a lot less waste, so you can feel good about doing your bit to help the environment. And ultimately, you gain a reward that can't be duplicated by anything that you buy – a great feeling of personal satisfaction that you actually made the product yourself.

Saving Money

Don't overlook the savings when you make something yourself, because the more you make, the more you save! Every time you buy a bottle of tomato sauce, a cream for an itch or liver treats for your dog, only a small percentage of the money goes to cover the cost of making the product. Indeed, if you leave out the cost of manufacturing, the ingredients in most products account for only a tiny fraction of the total. The rest covers the costs of advertising, packaging, shipping, overheads and the retailer's bottom line.

Healthier and More Natural

A commercial product may need to survive weeks or months from the time it is manufactured until it is finally picked up and used. Depending on the product, it could be pumped full of stabilisers, plasticisers, extenders, fillers and other chemicals. Some additives are there to facilitate the manufacturing process, making the product move faster, release from a mould easier or create less interference to the smooth flow of production. Other artificial ingredients are added to help the item withstand heat and cold and to be less likely to clump, precipitate or adhere to packaging.

Still other chemicals are used to cut the cost of using natural ingredients. Why use expensive, perishable, real strawberries when you can add a few pinches of a chemical compound that simulates their smell and taste? Most things that you make yourself are likely to be more natural and healthy for you than manufactured products – whether it's a food, a beauty product or a cleaning compound. And in the case of food, it's going to taste a lot fresher.

Suit Your Own Needs

Another great advantage of making products yourself is that you can customise them to be just the way you want them. If you like your moisturiser to be fresh smelling and restorative without being greasy and overwhelmingly perfumy, it can be. If you like your chocolate biscuits to be extra chocolatey, they can be. If you want your spaghetti sauce tangier, your soup thicker, your mustard spicier, or if the doctor told you to cut back on the salt or sugar, you can. Nearly all the recipes in this book are flexible and can be adjusted to suit you. Experiment until you get a product just the way you like it.

Make Less Waste

When making your own staples, you'll reduce the amount of waste and rubbish you produce. You won't be throwing away packaging and you'll be reusing jars, bottles and other containers. You'll also cut waste by making things in batches that you use up without throwing anything out if it goes bad. For cleaning, laundering and polishing, you will also be using compounds that are much gentler and less damaging to surfaces and fabrics – and to drains. So when you make it yourself, you'll be doing your bit for the environment.

Creating Your Own Food Products

The recipes in Part 1 of this book cover some 350 commonly purchased food products that you can make in your own kitchen. There are recipes for making items to stock your pantry, refrigerator and freezer – or for creating fast on-the-spot replacements for such items. And there are recipes for many foods that you would normally buy already prepared – spending a great deal of money in the process. All told, they cover condiments, seasonings, sauces, pickled and preserved foods, baked goods, snack foods, drinks, take-away foods, confectionery, ice cream and other sweets. You don't need a large kitchen or a whole battery of equipment, but certain well-designed tools will make your work in the kitchen go faster and more smoothly. See page 14 for a listing of the pots, pans and other gear for food preparation and cooking that make life in the kitchen easier.

Before You Start ...

Take stock of your pots and pans. You want your pots and pans to conduct heat evenly, and you want at least one pan with a non-stick coating for low-fat cooking. Here are your choices:

❖ Cast-iron cookware heats slowly and evenly, but it is porous, absorbs flavours and reacts badly to acidic foods.

❖ Enamelled cast iron has all the advantages of cast iron, plus it is non-reactive, but it is heavy to lift.

❖ Aluminium cookware conducts heat well, but reacts badly with acidic food.

❖ Anodised aluminium is heavier and less prone to warping. Its surface finish makes it less reactive than plain aluminium.

❖ Stainless steel metal pots are made of several metals fused together to take advantage of each one's properties – copper for even heat and stainless steel for easy cleaning, for example.

❖ Tin-lined copper pots cook as well as other pans; but need to be polished and regularly re-tinned on the inside.

Check out your large appliances. Use an oven thermometer to check that your oven actually registers the heat it is set for. If it is only 5 to 10 degrees off, you can compensate by setting it higher or lower than the recipe requires. More than 10 degrees off, and it may need recalibrating. Check the temperatures of your freezer and refrigerator with a refrigerator thermometer. The freezer should read −18°C and the refrigerator 5°C.

Evaluate your freezer space. Making your own food is most efficient when you do it in batches large enough to last for a while. When you make a large pot of stock, for example, freeze some of it in ice cube trays and the rest in 1 cup (250 ml) or 2 cup (500 ml) containers. If you put the frozen stock cubes in a freezer bag, you will find it easy to add a little stock to a sauce or gravy to make it more flavoursome. Save larger containers for making soups and stews that call for homemade stock. You also need space for containers of Brilliant Basic Mince (page 166), which gives you a head start on many fast dinners. Use plastic containers or heavy-duty plastic self-sealing bags. Extra pancakes, scones or muffins can also be frozen in freezer bags to make speedy breakfasts or snacks. Freezing the best seasonal produce at its peak will require room, too.

As a Precaution ...

* When bottling, sterilise jars and use only fresh seals.
* If you are worried about salmonella, cook eggs at 72°C for a minute or two to be safe.
* Label and date everything that you freeze or bottle.
* If anything has an 'off' colour or odour, discard it immediately.

When You Are Finished ...

Store leftover foods in covered containers or plastic bags and put in the refrigerator right away. Never leave cooked meat, poultry or fish at room temperature for more than 2 hours. Foods in a slow cooker are kept at 74°C, just hot enough to kill harmful bacteria.

A well-equipped kitchen

When making the food recipes in this book, you don't need any specialised kitchen equipment beyond what you would ordinarily use for preparing meals. Here is a list of recommended items.

Pots and Pans
25 cm frying pan with a tight-fitting lid
18 cm frying pan
3 litre saucepan with a tight-fitting lid
1 litre saucepan with a tight-fitting lid
4 to 5 litre Dutch oven or heavy casserole
15 litre stock pot/pasta pot
Roasting pan, 33 x 23 x 5 cm with rack
Grill pan with rack

Baking Equipment
2 baking sheets
1 Swiss-roll tin
Loaf tin, 23 x 12 x 8 cm
1 litre microwave-safe casserole
2 litre microwave-safe casserole
3 nesting mixing bowls
2 six-hole muffin pans
20 cm or 23 cm cake tins
20 cm or 23 cm pie tins
2 wire cooling racks

Knives
20 to 25 cm chef's knife
5 to 10 cm paring knife
23 to 25 cm serrated bread knife
15 cm utility knife

Small Appliances
Blender or food processor
Coffee maker
Ice-cream maker (optional)
Microwave oven
Slow cooker
Waffle iron (optional)

Accessories
Bottle opener
Can opener
Citrus juicer
Colander
Corkscrew
Cutting board
Egg slice
Expandable steamer
Flour sifter
Funnels
Grater
Kettle
Knife sharpener
Ladle
Long-handled spoon
Measuring cups
Measuring spoons
Pastry blender
Pepper grinder
Rolling pin
Rubber spatulas
Salad spinner
Scales
Sieves
Slotted spoon
Sugar thermometer
Tongs
Vegetable peeler
Whisks
Wooden spoons

Creating Health and Beauty Products

Part 2 of this book covers more than 200 homemade beauty and health products, and food and health products for your pets. You may at first be sceptical about making your own cosmetics or home remedies. Commercial over-the-counter medications and beauty products are expensive (and well advertised) and promise so much that you may feel reluctant to compete – or to compromise your skin, hair or health, or that of your pet.

You should have no such trepidations. Both home remedies and homemade beauty products have a long and honoured tradition. In the case of homemade beauty products, it's best to start slowly – with a single moisturiser, for example, and see how it feels and smells on your skin. Try treating your hair after a shampoo with a vinegar hair rinse. Then try one of the facial masks and a toner. Little by little, you will be won over to using these fresh, natural products and want to make more and more of them on a regular basis.

Being able to create your own home remedies instantly is reassuring. You don't have to run to the chemist or call the doctor every time you or another family member feels a little unwell. In this book, you'll find more than 100 remedies for everyday ailments. Remember, however, that home remedies do not take the place of conventional medicine – they complement it. If you don't respond to a home remedy, see a doctor and let the doctor know how you have treated yourself.

Making your own pet supplies gives you control over the quality of the food and care that your animals receive. Making non-toxic flea dips and ear oils, for example, will keep your dogs and cats healthy and make them less dangerous to the people who pet them. Commercial flea collars are poisonous to people, too, remember.

Before You Start ...

Follow the recipe closely. Read the recipes carefully and don't be tempted to use more of any ingredient than what is specified. Make sure you know the difference between regular oils and essential oils. Regular, or 'fixed', oils, such as olive or canola oil, are the non-volatile mostly seed-derived oils that we use for cooking, while essential oils, such as geranium, lavender or lemon oils, are highly concentrated volatile distillations of leaves and flowers. They are called 'essential' because they capture the essence of the plant. Most essential oils must be diluted in a fixed oil before they are applied to the skin. In this case, the fixed oil is known as a carrier oil. You need very little essential oil in each recipe – to conserve your supply, keep them in a cool, dark place, but not in the refrigerator.

Source your ingredients. You can buy the ingredients for most home remedies and beauty products in health-food shops, the supermarket, chemists or online. Ideally, grow and dry your own herbs. You can buy seeds or seedlings for many fresh herbs at garden centres and nurseries; plant them in a sunny spot.

The ingredients for pet foods and care products are available in supermarkets, pet shops, health-food shops or garden centres. None are particularly exotic or difficult to locate.

Take care with equipment. Although you use ordinary cookware to make home remedies or beauty products, it is best to keep this equipment separate from your regular kitchenware to avoid contaminating foodstuffs. A list of the items you may need is provided in the table opposite. Making pet products doesn't involve any special equipment other than what you probably already have in your kitchen.

Equipment for home remedies and beauty products

To make either beauty or health products:
You will need non-reactive equipment to protect your health or beauty products from chemical changes in colour and odour. That means avoiding uncoated aluminium, iron or copper cookware.

❖ Glass, stainless steel or enamelled double boiler
❖ Set of non-reactive mixing bowls
❖ Stainless steel or ceramic funnel
❖ Stainless steel measuring and stirring spoons
❖ Wooden stirring and mashing spoons
❖ Stainless steel or ceramic lemon squeezer
❖ Kettle
❖ Ceramic tea bowls and cups
❖ Tea strainer
❖ Sugar thermometer

Select safe storage jars and dispensers. Look for small opaque jars with wide mouths and tight-fitting lids for storing your beauty creams or skin ointments. Because they have no preservatives, they need to be kept away from light and air. Tinted or coloured glass – amber, white or blue – protects creams from light. Keeping a cream in a small container that it fills almost completely protects the cream from air. When you use up half a jar of cream, decant the remaining cream into a smaller jar to protect it further. Tight-fitting lids are important to keep out air and prevent evaporation. Cork lids are too porous to be safe.

You'll also need spray bottles and 500 ml bottles with tight lids. You can probably reuse many of the jars you need from your regular kitchen and bathroom supplies. Sterilise any storage jars before you use them. Wash plastic spray bottles thoroughly in soap and hot water, rinse thoroughly, and let them air-dry.

As a Precaution ...

❖ If you are taking prescription medication, talk to your doctor about possible interactions between it and any herbs or essential oils suggested in this book.
❖ If you have allergic reactions to any foods or medications, consult your doctor before taking any home remedy that might contain the allergen.

- ❖ If you are pregnant, don't take any herbal medications without consulting your doctor.
- ❖ Although side effects from using natural cosmetics are uncommon, allergic reactions can occur in susceptible people. If you have a reaction, stop using the product immediately.
- ❖ When planning to use a herb or product that is new to you, patch-test it first. Rub the herb against the tender skin on the underside of your arm right above the elbow or in the elbow crease. Wait overnight. If redness or irritation occur, don't use it.
- ❖ Check with a doctor before using products with essential oils if you have a chronic or acute disorder such as heart disease, epilepsy, asthma, diabetes or kidney disease, or if you are pregnant. Keep containers sealed and out of reach of children.
- ❖ If an essential oil is accidentally swallowed, do not induce vomiting. Call a poison hotline or get the person to an emergency department immediately.

When You Are Finished ...

Be sure to label each new jar or bottle of a product as you fill it. Write the product's name and the date of preparation. If you give a homemade beauty product as a gift, list its ingredients as well (you don't want to inadvertently cause an allergic reaction).

Store natural products in a cool, dark, dry place, and check them often. Heat, moisture, light and contact with air can all cause deterioration. In summer, the refrigerator is probably the safest place to store homemade beauty products (away from young children). Inspect them regularly to be sure that they have not lost their potency. If a product is discoloured or has a funny smell, discard it and make a new batch.

Making Products for the House and Garden

Part 3 of this book covers more than 100 useful household and gardening products – including cleaning and polishing compounds, glue and craft supplies, indoor and outdoor pest repellents, weed killers, fertilisers and soil conditioners – even houseplant food and whitewash. Having simple, non-toxic aids and remedies for house and garden makes maintenance chores much more pleasant – and much, much cheaper.

Whether you are dealing with a cleanser, a polish, a bleach, a weed spray or an insecticide, the problem with some commercial products is that they may contain harsh and toxic chemicals that may be hard on grime, tarnish, stains and bugs, but they are also hard on furniture, floors, clothes and shrubs – and hard on your skin, eyes and lungs as well.

The good news is that there are many inexpensive, time-proven products that will help your garden to flourish and your house to sparkle, smell good and gleam invitingly without such effects. You probably already have most of the ingredients for these homemade products on hand. Try making one of the cleaning recipes and using it. It won't take long or cost much money. Expect to be happily surprised.

Once you discover that there are easy, inexpensive ways to foil the pests that have plagued your woollens in the past, you won't find putting away winter clothes so onerous. Keeping ants and cockroaches out of the cupboards is not a problem either when you get out the borax.

And as you find inexpensive, non-toxic ways to keep pests out of the garden, you may finally be able to grow the herbs and vegetables that you have dreamed about.

Before You Start ...

Find your ingredients. None of the ingredients required is particularly exotic. If you don't already have them at home, you can buy most of them at your supermarket or hardware store.

❖ Get the largest, cheapest sizes of bicarbonate of soda, cider vinegar and white vinegar available. You don't need giant sizes of chlorine bleach or ammonia, however, because the recipes that do use them call for very little of either.

❖ You'll find borax and washing soda among the detergents in a supermarket.

❖ Look for castile soap, glycerine and essential oils at health-food shops and on many Internet sites.

❖ Inexpensive house brands of methylated spirits are readily available from any supermarket.

❖ Boiled linseed oil and materials needed for paints and finishes are available at paint, art supply or hardware stores. You can find equipment and wax for candle-making at craft stores.

❖ Another useful traditional cleaning-compound ingredient is pure soap flakes. If you can't find a box of soap flakes, it is very simple to make your own soap flakes by simply lightly grating a bar of pure soap on a coarse grater.

Make garden potting easier. You need some large containers for mixing soil and making compost tea. You can use plastic rubbish bins or find large buckets at cleaning supply stores. If you have unusually clayey, sandy or other problematic soil, it's best to test the soil before adjusting it with homemade nutrients. To get your soil tested, ask at your local garden centre or look on the Internet for a service in your area.

Devise a potting table – a place to take care of your container plants, and where you can keep extra pots, homemade fertilisers and pesticides, potting soil and other supplies. The table should be waist high and have shelves above for storing fertilisers and pesticides out of reach of children, and shelves below for large containers of compost, vermiculite or sand. You can make your gardening workstation in the garage or on a covered veranda.

As a Precaution ...

- ❖ Never combine chlorine bleach and ammonia. They can form a noxious gas if mixed.
- ❖ Label cleaning compounds, pesticides, compost teas and other fertilisers, and keep the containers out of reach of children.
- ❖ Wear appropriate vinyl gloves to protect your hands when mixing and using household and gardening products.
- ❖ If an essential oil is accidentally swallowed, don't induce vomiting. Call a poison hotline or rush the patient to emergency.

When You Are Finished ...

Most of the household and gardening products in this book are best prepared just before you use them so that you get the maximum potency and best results. Most are simple enough to whip up in a few minutes. But as the recipes advise, you can store some products, such as scouring powders and some cleaning and bug-control compounds, for periods ranging from a few days up to a couple of weeks. When you do, be sure to put them in tightly closed labelled and dated jars or spray bottles.

Recycle rags and spray bottles

There are many simple ways to keep down the cost of household supplies:
❖ One is to recycle worn or outgrown family clothing as rags for cleaning, polishing and crafts. Cloth nappies make famously good rags. Old cotton T-shirts and underpants are also good candidates. Well-worn terry-towelling cloths absorb water better than anything. Best of all, they can be tossed in the washing machine and reused.
❖ Also, finish cleaning windows with old newspaper. It's not only cheaper but gives a better result, so you may never buy paper towels again (at least for cleaning) or expensive disposable cloths.
❖ Wash out old empty spray bottles and reuse them for your homemade household or gardening products. (If you do need to buy some, try a garden centre or a cleaning supply store; they are listed in the phone book and online.)

Part 1

In the Kitchen

Breakfast Cereals

Muesli ❖ Fruit and Nut Cereal ❖ Crunchy Toasted Muesli ❖ Porridge Mix

Condiments and Spreads

Ketchup ❖ Seafood Cocktail Sauce ❖ Mustard ❖ Classic Mayonnaise ❖ Aïoli (Garlic Mayonnaise) ❖ Tartare Sauce ❖ Spicy Tomato Salsa ❖ Tomato Passata ❖ Mint Sauce ❖ Salsa Verde ❖ Plum Sauce ❖ Sweet Chilli Sauce ❖ Peanut Butter

Salad Dressings

Classic Vinaigrette ❖ Herb Vinaigrette ❖ Walnut Vinaigrette ❖ Garlic Vinaigrette ❖ Balsamic Vinaigrette ❖ Raspberry Vinaigrette ❖ Herb Dressing Mix ❖ Herb Dressing ❖ Thai Salad Dressing ❖ Ranch Dressing Mix ❖ Ranch Dressing ❖ Blue Cheese Dressing ❖ Light Blue Cheese Dressing ❖ French Dressing ❖ Italian Dressing ❖ Thousand Island Dressing

Seasonings

Bouquet Garni ❖ Fines Herbes ❖ Herbes de Provence ❖ Italian Herb Blend ❖ Chicken Seasoning Mix ❖ Chilli Powder ❖ Cajun Seasoning Mix ❖ Laksa Paste ❖ Chermoula ❖ Caribbean Spicy Meat Rub ❖ Curry Powder ❖ Green Curry Paste ❖ Red Curry Paste

Marinades

Red Wine Marinade ❖ Mustard Marinade ❖ Lemon Herb Marinade ❖ Orange Ginger Marinade ❖ Soy and Sesame Marinade

Cooking Stocks

Beef Stock ❖ Chicken Stock ❖ Fish Stock ❖ Vegetable Stock

Sauces

Barbecue Sauce ❖ Gravy ❖ Satay Sauce ❖ Sweet and Sour Sauce ❖ Mushroom Wine Sauce ❖ Béarnaise Sauce ❖ Hollandaise Sauce ❖ Basic White Sauce ❖ Cheese Sauce ❖ Dijon Mustard Sauce ❖ Mushroom Sauce

Dessert Sauces

Blueberry Syrup ❖ Apple Sauce ❖ Mango and Passionfruit Sauce ❖ Raspberry Sauce ❖ Custard ❖ Fruit Coulis ❖ Butterscotch Sauce ❖ Chocolate Sauce ❖ Caramel Sauce

Dry Mixes

Pancake and Waffle Mix ❖ Basic Cake Mix

Pasta

Simple Fresh Pasta ❖ Luxury Fresh Pasta ❖ Superfast Fresh Pasta

Pantry Staples

Nowhere do the benefits of making your own pay off more generously than in the kitchen, especially in making replacements for the cereals, condiments, salad dressings, seasonings, sauces and mixes that line your pantry shelves.

To give them an almost indefinite shelf life, these manufactured staples are more likely than any other food products to be packed with fillers, preservatives, stabilisers and other unnatural ingredients. In this chapter, you will not only learn how easy it is to make your own all-natural versions of these staples but also discover how much better a homemade creation tastes.

Homemade stock has real flavour. And there is nothing like freshly ground peanut butter that melts in your mouth or fresh pasta so delectably light that it makes any sauce seem tastier.

None of the staple items here have the extraordinary shelf life of manufactured products. But you will find healthy, nutty breakfast cereals that will keep their fresh taste for weeks, as well as everyday condiments, ranging from peanut butter and mustard that will last for months to fresh salsas that are best eaten in a day or two. Most salad dressings and both savoury and sweet sauces are also best if used right away – keep them in the fridge for a couple of days – and there are salad dressing mixes you can prepare ahead of time.

Most herbs, seasonings and dry mixes will keep for weeks or months, as will fresh pasta and stocks if frozen.

Breakfast Cereals

Muesli

2 cups (200 g) rolled oats
¼ cup (30 g) sunflower seeds
¼ cup (25 g) flaked almonds
¼ cup (25 g) wheatgerm
⅓ cup (55 g) finely chopped
  dates
2 tablespoons oat bran
1 cup (40 g) wheat bran flakes
¼ cup (30 g) raisins
1 tablespoon sugar (optional)

Makes 3½ cups
(about 7 servings)

This traditional cereal is full of healthy grains, seeds, nuts and fruit, plus it's dry-roasted without oil so it will stay fresh for longer. Packaged versions are quite pricey and not nearly as tasty.

1 Preheat the oven to 180°C (Gas 4). In a 30 x 25 cm roasting tin, combine the oats, sunflower seeds and almonds. Roast for 10 to 15 minutes, until the almonds are almost golden. Remove the roasted mix to a separate bowl. Add the wheatgerm to the roasting tin and roast for 5 minutes, making sure it doesn't burn.
2 In a large bowl, combine the dates and oat bran, and stir to coat the dates with the bran. Add the roasted oats mixture and wheatgerm, then add the wheat bran flakes, raisins and sugar, if using. Stir to combine all the ingredients.
3 Place the muesli in an airtight container or a self-sealing plastic bag. Label, date and store in a cool, dry place for up to 2 months.

Fruit and Nut Cereal

2 cups (200 g) instant
  porridge oats
1 cup (50 g) crumbled
  wheat cereal biscuits,
  or shredded wheat
1 cup (75 g) wheat bran
  or bran cereal
1 cup (90 g) wheatgerm
1 cup (100–150 g) unsalted
  walnuts, almonds, pecans
  or cashew nuts
½ cup (80 g) chopped pitted
  dates
1 cup (175 g) chopped dried
  prunes, apricots, pears,
  apples or bananas
1 cup (125 g) raisins
1 cup (100 g) skim milk
  powder

Makes about 9 cups
(about 18 servings)

Packed with protein and high in complex carbohydrates, this tasty mix will keep you full until lunchtime.

1 In a large bowl, combine the oats, crumbled wheat biscuits, wheat bran, wheatgerm and nuts. Add the dates and dried fruit, then toss to combine the ingredients and coat the fruit with the oat mixture. Add the raisins and milk powder, then stir to combine all the ingredients.
2 Place the cereal in an airtight container or self-sealing plastic bag. Label, date and store for up to 2 months in the refrigerator.

Crunchy Toasted Muesli

cooking spray
4 cups (400 g) rolled oats
½ cup (20 g) wheat bran flakes
½ cup (20 g) barley flakes
1 cup (155 g) roughly chopped almonds
½ cup (115 g) firmly packed soft brown sugar
1 teaspoon salt
1 teaspoon ground cinnamon
¼ cup (60 ml) apple juice concentrate (available at health-food shops)
2 tablespoons butter, melted
2 tablespoons vegetable oil
2 tablespoons honey
1 teaspoon vanilla extract
finely grated zest of 1 orange
1 cup (100 g) dried cranberries
1 cup (125 g) raisins

Makes 7 cups
(about 14 servings)

Packed with nutrition and taste, this toasted muesli is the ultimate combination. Eat it with milk for breakfast; sprinkle it on fruit, yogurt or ice cream; incorporate it into crumble toppings for fruit cobblers – or just grab a handful for a healthy, energy-boosting snack. To cut the cost of homemade muesli, check out the bulk aisles of health-food shops or supermarkets.

1 Preheat the oven to 150°C (Gas 2). Lightly coat a shallow 30 x 25 cm baking tin with the cooking spray and set aside.
2 In a large bowl, combine the rolled oats, wheat bran flakes, barley flakes, almonds, sugar, salt and cinnamon; set aside. In a small bowl, whisk together the apple juice concentrate, butter, oil, honey, vanilla extract, orange zest and ¼ cup (60 ml) water. Pour the juice mixture over the oat mixture and stir to combine the ingredients. Spread the mixture evenly in the prepared tin.
3 Bake, stirring every 15 minutes, for about 1 hour, until golden and slightly crunchy.
4 Remove the tin to a rack to cool completely, about 1 hour. When cooled, stir in the cranberries and raisins. Label, date and store in an airtight container for up to 1 week.

Porridge Mix

6 cups (600 g) instant porridge oats
1⅓ cups (135 g) milk powder
1 cup (175 g) chopped dried apples, apricots, bananas, prunes, raisins or mixed berries
¼ cup (55 g) sugar
¼ cup (45 g) firmly packed soft brown sugar
1 tablespoon ground cinnamon
1 teaspoon salt
¼ teaspoon ground cloves

Makes 8 cups
(about 16 servings)

Ready-to-eat flavoured porridge mixes are perfect for those busy mornings when you need a healthy breakfast in a hurry. However, the shop-bought mixes aren't cheap, so whip up your own and vary it to suit your family's tastes.

1 In a large bowl, combine all the ingredients and stir until well blended.
2 Store the porridge mix in an airtight container or self-sealing plastic bag. Label, date and store in a cool, dry place for up to 6 months.
To use: Shake the mix well before using. In a saucepan, bring ½ cup (125 ml) water to a boil. Slowly stir in ½ cup of porridge mix. Reduce the heat and cook, stirring, for 1 minute. Remove the saucepan from the heat, cover, and let stand for 1 minute more or until porridge reaches the desired consistency.

Condiments and Spreads

Ketchup

3 kg tomatoes, peeled, cored
and chopped
1 large brown onion, chopped
1 large red capsicum (pepper),
cored, seeded and chopped
1½ teaspoons celery seeds
1 teaspoon mustard seeds
1 teaspoon whole allspice
1 cinnamon stick
1¼ cups (285 g) firmly packed
soft brown sugar
1 tablespoon salt
1½ cups (375 ml) cider vinegar
1 tablespoon paprika

Makes 6 cups (1.5 litres)

Forget about buying this staple condiment – homemade sauce is much tastier and an inspired way to use up extra tomatoes at the end of summer.

1 In a very large, non-metallic stockpot or saucepan, combine the tomatoes, onion and capsicum, then cook over medium heat until soft. Press the vegetables through a food mill (mouli) or sieve to make a purée. Return purée to saucepan.
2 Over high heat, boil the purée for about 1 hour, until it is thick and has reduced by half.
3 Cut a 10 cm square of muslin (cheesecloth). Place the celery seeds, mustard seeds, allspice and cinnamon stick in the centre of the cloth, gather up the corners to form a bag, then secure with kitchen string. Add the spice bag, brown sugar and salt to the tomato mixture. Over low heat, cook the mixture gently for 25 minutes, stirring frequently.
4 Stir in the vinegar and paprika. Continue to cook, stirring frequently, until the mixture is thick.
5 Spoon the ketchup into three sterilised 500 ml jars, leaving a 3 cm space between the top of the ketchup and the rim of the jar. Wipe the rims, cover and leave for 10 minutes in boiling water (see Safe Bottling and Preserving, page 72). Cool and test for airtight seals. Label, date and store in a cool, dark place for up to a year; the ketchup will be ready to eat in 1 week. Once a jar has been opened, store in the refrigerator.

Seafood Cocktail Sauce

1 cup (250 ml) Ketchup
(above)
1 tablespoon horseradish
1 tablespoon lemon juice
½ teaspoon worcestershire
sauce
¼ teaspoon hot chilli sauce,
or more to taste

Makes about 1 cup (250 ml)

This classic sauce adds zest to tasty prawns. It's cheaper than bottled cocktail sauce, and you can mix the ingredients to suit your taste. To turn up the heat, add more horseradish or hot chilli sauce.

1 In a small, non-metallic bowl, combine all the ingredients and stir until well blended. Cover the bowl and refrigerate for at least 1 hour before serving.
2 Store in an airtight container in the refrigerator for up to 1 month.

Mustard

⅓ cup (45 g) yellow mustard
  seeds
3 tablespoons mustard powder
½ cup (125 ml) cider vinegar
½ cup (125 ml) stout or dark
  beer
2 cloves garlic, crushed
⅓ cup (80 g) firmly packed
  soft brown sugar
¾ teaspoon salt
½ teaspoon ground ginger
¼ teaspoon ground allspice

Makes about 2 cups (500 ml)

This versatile condiment is easy to make and can be adjusted to your tastes. The basic mix includes 2 to 3 tablespoons of liquid (vinegar, wine, water, flat beer) and about 3 tablespoons mustard powder. You could also add ground turmeric (for a traditional yellow tint), chopped fresh garlic, dried tarragon, sugar or honey, salt and more. Use it to spice up hot dogs, hamburgers or sandwiches, or brush over meats before grilling or roasting.

1 In a small bowl, combine the mustard seeds, mustard powder and cider vinegar. Cover the bowl with plastic wrap and let the mustard mixture stand at room temperature for 3 hours.
2 In a small saucepan, combine the stout, garlic, brown sugar, salt, ginger and allspice. Stir in the mustard mixture. Over medium heat, bring the mixture to a boil; reduce heat to low and simmer for 5 minutes, stirring occasionally.
3 Spoon the mustard into a hot, clean canning jar and seal tightly. Leave the mustard to cool to room temperature before using. Store in a cool, dark place. Once a jar has been opened, store in the refrigerator.

Classic Mayonnaise

4 egg yolks
1 tablespoon white wine
  vinegar
1½ cups (375 ml) vegetable oil
  or a combination of vegetable
  and extra virgin olive oils
1 pinch ground white pepper

Makes about 2 cups (500 g)

Homemade mayonnaise is a tasty addition to most salads and sandwiches. You can experiment with the flavour by using different oils and lemon juice instead of the vinegar. You could also try cayenne pepper in place of the white pepper.

1 In a food processor or blender, process the egg yolks, vinegar and 2 tablespoons water until just combined. With the motor running, drizzle in the oil very slowly so that the mixture emulsifies; if the oil is added too quickly, it will remain a thin, liquid dressing.
2 Stir in the white pepper. Cool quickly and store in the refrigerator for up to 5 days.

Aïoli (Garlic Mayonnaise)

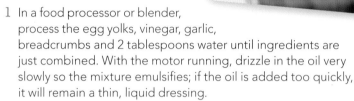

4 egg yolks

1 tablespoon white wine
vinegar

1 clove garlic, crushed

½ cup (40 g) fresh white
breadcrumbs

1½ cups (375 ml) extra virgin
olive oil

1 pinch ground cayenne
pepper

Makes 3 cups (750 g)

Traditionally served with
poached fish, aïoli can also
be used as a dip for fresh
vegetables or seafood, or as
a salad dressing. Homemade
aïoli is delicious and much
better value than the shop-
bought variety.

1 In a food processor or blender,
process the egg yolks, vinegar, garlic,
breadcrumbs and 2 tablespoons water until ingredients are
just combined. With the motor running, drizzle in the oil very
slowly so the mixture emulsifies; if the oil is added too quickly,
it will remain a thin, liquid dressing.

2 Stir in the cayenne pepper. Cool quickly and store in the
refrigerator for up to 5 days.

A safer way to make mayonnaise

Raw eggs may contain the bacterium
salmonella, which can cause illness and
is particularly dangerous for pregnant
women, very young children, the elderly
and anyone who has a serious illness.
To reduce the risk of contamination
from salmonella, you should boil the
mayonnaise. Transfer the blended dressing
to the top of a double boiler and cook until
a thermometer placed in the mayonnaise
registers 75°C. Cool the sauce quickly and
store in the refrigerator for up to 5 days.

Tartare Sauce

½ cup (125 g) Classic
Mayonnaise (page 29)

½ cup (125 ml) reduced-fat
sour cream

6 spring onions, finely chopped

¼ cup (60 g) chopped Sweet
Pickles (page 67)

2 tablespoons lemon juice

1 tablespoon capers, rinsed
and squeezed dry

1 tablespoon finely chopped
fresh parsley

1 tablespoon dijon mustard

Makes 1¼ cups (310 g)

When you have tasted a homemade version of this
classic fish accompaniment, you won't waste your
money on shop-bought tartare sauce.

1 In a bowl, combine all the ingredients and stir until they
are well blended.

2 Cover the bowl and refrigerate for 2 hours or overnight
before using. Store in the refrigerator for up to 5 days.

Spicy Tomato Salsa

3 tomatoes, cored, seeded
  and chopped
3 small spring onions,
  trimmed and roughly
  chopped
1 jalapeño pepper, cored,
  seeded and finely chopped
  (wear gloves when handling;
  they burn)
1 clove garlic, crushed
¾ teaspoon salt
⅓ cup (10 g) roughly chopped
  fresh coriander leaves

Makes 3½ cups (875 g)

A staple of Mexican cuisine, salsa is now popular
everywhere. The spiciness can vary from very mild
to tongue-burning hot, depending on the variety and
quantity of chillies used. The zesty mix in this basic
recipe is not just for tortilla dipping; you can also
dollop it on grilled chicken breasts, firm fish, in beef
fajitas or omelettes.

1 In a large, non-metallic bowl, combine the tomatoes, spring
  onions, jalapeño pepper, garlic and salt, then stir until well
  blended. Let the salsa stand for 1 hour to allow the flavours
  to mellow.
2 Just before serving, add the chopped coriander and stir. Serve
  immediately or store in the refrigerator for up to 2 days.

Tomato Passata

1 kg tomatoes (about 10),
  halved
2 tablespoons olive oil
1 onion, finely chopped
salt and freshly ground black
  pepper

Makes 2½ cups (625 g)

Try this rich sauce over freshly cooked pasta, as a base
for chilli con carne or veal parmigiana, or smear it over
a pizza base before adding the topping.

1 In a very large, non-metallic stockpot or saucepan, cook the
  tomatoes, covered, over medium heat for 10 minutes. Press the
  tomatoes through a food mill (mouli) or sieve to make a purée.
  Discard the skins and seeds.
2 In a large saucepan, heat the oil. Add the onion and cook
  over medium heat, stirring, until the onion is translucent but
  not brown. Add the tomato purée and simmer for about
  30 minutes, until the sauce thickens. Season to taste. Store
  in an airtight container in the refrigerator for up to 1 week,
  or freeze for up to 3 months.

Mint Sauce

1 cup (250 ml) malt vinegar
2 tablespoons sugar, plus more
  to taste
4 cups (200 g) finely chopped
  fresh mint, firmly packed
5 drops green food colouring
  (optional)

Makes about 1 cup (250 ml)

This simple mint sauce can be cooked in next to no time
and is the perfect accompaniment to roast lamb.

1 In a small saucepan, bring the vinegar to a simmer over
  medium heat, then add the sugar and mint. Simmer for
  20 minutes, until well infused. Add more sugar for a sweeter
  sauce, or add water to reduce the intensity. Remove from heat.
2 Add food colouring, if using. Pour the sauce into a hot, clean
  jar and seal tightly. Leave to cool to room temperature, then
  use immediately, or store in the refrigerator for up to 1 month.

Salsa Verde

⅔ cup (12 g) flat-leaf parsley
⅔ cup (20 g) fresh basil leaves
1 clove garlic, halved
3 tablespoons capers, rinsed
  and squeezed dry
2 tablespoons chopped
  anchovies
¼ cup (60 ml) red wine
  vinegar
⅓ cup (80 ml) extra virgin
  olive oil
½ teaspoon dijon mustard
freshly ground black pepper,
  to taste

Makes about 1 cup (250 ml)

This homemade green salsa – a mixture of fresh herbs, garlic, capers and salty anchovies – is sensational with seafood.

1 In a food processor or blender, process the parsley, basil, garlic, capers and anchovies until smooth.
2 Stir in the vinegar, olive oil and mustard. Add the pepper. Serve immediately or store in the refrigerator for up to 2 days.

Plum Sauce

1.5 kg plums, washed, stalks
  removed
2 cups (500 ml) white wine
  vinegar
1½ cups (345 g) firmly packed
  soft brown sugar
½ teaspoon salt
½ teaspoon freshly ground
  black pepper
½ teaspoon ground cayenne
  pepper
2 cinnamon sticks
2 star-anise
2 teaspoons ground cloves
5 cm piece fresh ginger, grated

Makes about 3 cups (750 ml)

You'll never purchase plum sauce again once you've tasted this spicy homemade alternative. It will keep for months in a cool, dark place.

1 In a large, heavy-based saucepan, combine all the ingredients and stir over a medium heat, without boiling, until the sugar is completely dissolved.
2 Bring to a boil and simmer, uncovered and stirring occasionally, for about 20 minutes, until the fruit is soft and pulpy and the stones have loosened.
3 Push the mixture through a food mill (mouli) or coarse sieve, then discard the stones and other spices. Return the sauce to the saucepan and simmer again, until it thickens to the desired consistency.
4 Spoon the sauce into three warm, sterilised, wide-mouthed, 250 ml jars, leaving a 6 mm space between the top of the sauce and the rim of the jar. Wipe the rims, cover and leave for 10 minutes in boiling water (see Safe Bottling and Preserving, page 72). Label, date and store the jars of sauce in a cool, dark place; the sauce will be ready to eat in 2 weeks.

Sweet Chilli Sauce

1 red chilli, thinly sliced
2 teaspoons arrowroot
⅓ cup (80 ml) lime juice
2 tablespoons rice vinegar
1 tablespoon soft brown sugar
2 teaspoons fish sauce

Makes about ½ cup (125 ml)

It doesn't take long to make a small batch of this sauce fresh for your next meal. If you don't need the whole quantity, try freezing it; using arrowroot as a thickener will ensure it thaws well.

In a small saucepan, combine the chilli and arrowroot. Slowly stir in the lime juice, vinegar, brown sugar and fish sauce, until well combined. Over medium–high heat, bring the mixture to a boil, until thickened. Remove from the heat and leave to cool to room temperature. Use immediately, or freeze in an airtight container for up to 1 month.

Peanut Butter

4 cups (650 g) salted,
   dry-roasted peanuts
1 tablespoon plus 1 teaspoon
   safflower or other mild-
   flavoured vegetable oil

Makes 1 cup (250 g)

This family favourite can really eat up your budget. Surprisingly, making your own peanut butter in bulk is cheaper, not to mention healthier.

For smooth style: Using a food processor or blender, and working in batches, process the peanuts and the oil until the desired consistency is reached. Stop and scrape down the sides of the bowl as needed.

For chunky style: Using a food processor or blender, roughly chop about one-third of the peanuts; set aside. Working in batches, process the remaining peanuts with the oil until the desired consistency is reached. Scrape down the sides of the container as needed. Stir in the chopped peanuts.

To store: Scrape the peanut butter into a clean container with an airtight lid. Store in the refrigerator for up to 1 month but no longer – without preservatives, the oil can turn rancid.

VARIATION
Replace the peanuts with salted, dry-roasted almonds, hazelnuts or cashew nuts for luxurious nut butters.

About peanut butter

Peanut butter is an excellent source of protein, fibre and B vitamins. These days, peanut butter is a staple of most average households, but in its early years it was mostly only eaten by the wealthy people who frequented health spas. Peanut butter was initially marketed as a protein source for vegetarians.

Salad Dressings

Classic Vinaigrette

¼ cup (60 ml) extra virgin
  or virgin olive oil
1 tablespoon vinegar (such
  as white wine, red wine
  or tarragon) or fresh
  lemon juice
½ teaspoon salt
freshly ground black pepper,
  to taste

Makes ¼ cup (60 ml)

This classic salad dressing can be whipped up just before serving, then used over fresh salad greens. All the ingredients are pantry staples, so it's a quick and easy gourmet touch that's not costly.

In a small, non-metallic bowl, whisk together all the ingredients until well blended. Use immediately.

Herb Vinaigrette

¼ cup (60 ml) extra virgin
  or virgin olive oil
1 tablespoon vinegar (such
  as white wine, red wine
  or tarragon) or fresh
  lemon juice
1 tablespoon finely chopped
  fresh herbs, such as
  tarragon, basil, chives
  or parsley
½ teaspoon salt
freshly ground black pepper,
  to taste

Makes about ¼ cup (60 ml)

The fresh herbs in this vinaigrette add zest that you will never find in a bottled version.

In a small, non-metallic bowl, whisk together all the ingredients until well blended. Use immediately.

Walnut Vinaigrette

¼ cup (60 ml) walnut oil
2–3 tablespoons red wine
  vinegar
freshly ground black pepper

Makes about ¼ cup (60 ml)

Make a special bottle of walnut oil go further by using it in this tasty vinaigrette.

In a small, non-metallic bowl, whisk together all the ingredients until well blended. Use immediately.

Garlic Vinaigrette

¼ cup (60 ml) extra virgin
  or virgin olive oil
1 tablespoon vinegar (such
  as white wine, red wine
  or tarragon) or fresh
  lemon juice
1 clove garlic, crushed
½ teaspoon salt
freshly ground black pepper,
  to taste

Makes about ¼ cup (60 ml)

Try experimenting with different vinegars and/or lemon juice to vary the taste of this dressing.

In a small, non-metallic bowl, whisk together all the ingredients until well blended. Use immediately.

Balsamic Vinaigrette

¼ cup (60 ml) extra virgin
  or virgin olive oil
1 tablespoon balsamic vinegar
1 tablespoon finely chopped
  fresh basil
½ teaspoon salt
freshly ground black pepper,
  to taste

Makes about ¼ cup (60 ml)

Use the best balsamic vinegar and olive oil that you can afford for this dressing.

In a small, non-metallic bowl, whisk together all the ingredients until well blended. Use immediately.

Flavouring oils with herbs

Surprisingly easy to make, flavoured oils pack a powerful flavour punch in salads. They make fabulous gifts, too, but make them in small quantities because they are perishable. The best choices for flavourings are lower-moisture herbs, such as rosemary, thyme or sage, or spices such as coriander seeds or chillies.

❖ **To make a flavoured oil**, all you need are several sprigs of fresh herbs or whole spices and enough olive oil to fill the bottles.

1 Spread the herbs or spices on a clean work surface. Using a rolling pin, gently press down on the herbs or spices to lightly bruise them.

2 In a small saucepan over low heat, warm the olive oil. Add the herbs or spices and let them steep for several minutes. Using a slotted spoon, transfer the herbs or spices to sterilised bottles, distributing them equally. Pour the warm oil on top of the herbs or spices, leaving a 1 cm space between the top of the oil and the rim of the bottle. Wipe the rims, cover tightly and refrigerate for at least 2 days to allow the herbs or spices to infuse the oil.

3 Strain the oil into a new set of sterilised bottles, adding a fresh herb sprig or whole spice to each bottle. Wipe the rims, cover, label and date. Store the flavoured oil in the refrigerator for up to 1 month. Keep refrigerated after the oil is opened.

Make your own croutons

A wonderful way to use up stale bread, croutons are so easy to prepare that it makes no sense to spend money on ready-made ones that have been sitting on the shelf.

Cut slices of day-old bread into 1 cm cubes. In a large frying pan over medium heat, heat some extra virgin olive oil. Add the bread cubes and sauté, stirring constantly, until the cubes are well coated, golden in colour and crisp. Transfer the cubes to paper towels and let drain. Add to salads or float on soups. Store the croutons in airtight containers.

To add more flavour to your croutons, first sauté some garlic slices, sprigs of fresh herbs or even whole chillies in the olive oil. Remove and discard the flavourings before adding the bread cubes to the flavoured oil, and sautéing as above.

Raspberry Vinaigrette

2 x 340 g jars raspberry preserves, seedless if available
1¼ cups (275 g) sugar
⅓ cup (50 g) chopped red onion
¼ cup (60 ml) balsamic vinegar
1 tablespoon dried tarragon
1 tablespoon curry powder
1 teaspoon ground white pepper
1 teaspoon freshly ground black pepper
1 cup (250 ml) extra virgin or virgin olive oil

Makes about 4 cups (1 litre)

Sweet, tart and tangy, this dressing will quickly become a family favourite. Homemade not only tastes better, but it's a fraction of the price of the bottled version.

1 In a large, non-metallic saucepan over high heat, combine the raspberry preserves and ¾ cup (165 g) of the sugar and bring to a boil. Remove the saucepan from the heat and let cool slightly. Pour the raspberry mixture into a food processor or blender. Add the onion, vinegar, tarragon, curry powder, white pepper, black pepper, the remaining sugar and ¼ cup (60 ml) water.

2 Cover and process, adding the olive oil in a slow, steady stream, until the ingredients are well blended. Use immediately, or store in an airtight container in the refrigerator for up to 1 week. Bring to room temperature and whisk vigorously before using.

Flavouring vinegars with herbs

It's easy to make your own herb-flavoured vinegars – they add a subtle taste to salads, especially those simply dressed with oil and vinegar. But remember, the higher quality vinegar you use, the better the result.

To make flavoured vinegar, you only need:

❖ Several sprigs of fresh herbs
❖ Sterilised bottles with screwtop lids
❖ Good-quality vinegar to fill the desired number of bottles. Here's how to proceed:

1 Spread the herbs on a clean work surface. Using a rolling pin, gently press down on the herbs to bruise them lightly. Place 1 sprig in each bottle.

2 In a large, non-metallic saucepan over high heat, bring the vinegar to a boil. Using a funnel, pour the hot vinegar over the herb sprigs in each bottle. Cover the bottles and place them on a sunny windowsill for at least 2 weeks to allow the herbs to infuse. Turn each bottle daily.

3 Place a fresh herb sprig into each of a new set of sterilised bottles. Strain the vinegar, discarding the old herbs. Pour the flavoured vinegar into the bottles over the fresh herb sprigs. Cover, label and date. Store the flavoured vinegar in a cool, dark place for up to 1 year; it will be ready to use in 2 weeks. Store the flavoured vinegar in the refrigerator after opening. The plain vinegar does not need refrigeration.

Herb Dressing Mix

4 tablespoons dried parsley
3 tablespoons dried oregano
3 tablespoons dried basil
3 tablespoons dried marjoram
¼ cup (55 g) sugar
2 tablespoons fennel seeds, crushed
2 tablespoons mustard powder
1 tablespoon freshly ground black pepper

Makes 2 cups (150 g)

All the taste and no preservatives required! Keep this mix on hand to make a Herb Dressing (page 38) that's suited to your taste.

1 In a large jar, combine all the ingredients. Seal the jar and shake until all the herbs are well mixed.
2 Store in a cool, dry, dark place for up to 6 weeks.

Herb Dressing

2 tablespoons Herb Dressing
Mix (page 37)
1½ cups (375 ml) warm water
2 tablespoons olive oil
100 ml white or tarragon
vinegar
2 cloves garlic, crushed

Makes 2 cups (500 ml)

You can adjust the strength of this mouth-watering dressing by increasing or decreasing the amount of Herb Dressing Mix you use.

1 In a small, non-metallic bowl, whisk together all the ingredients until well blended. Let the dressing stand at room temperature for 30 minutes; whisk vigorously again and use.
2 Store the dressing in an airtight jar or bottle in the refrigerator for up to 1 week.

Thai Salad Dressing

1 tablespoon peanut or
sunflower oil
2 red chillies, finely chopped
(wear gloves when handling;
they burn)
1 tablespoon grated fresh
ginger
1 lemongrass stem, white part
only, finely chopped
2 cloves garlic, finely chopped
¼ cup (60 ml) lime juice
1 tablespoon fish sauce
1 teaspoon soft brown sugar

Makes about ⅓ cup (80 ml)

This zesty sauce is the one to dress a traditional Thai beef salad, or more contemporary salad combinations, such as seafood, salad leaves and fresh herbs.

1 Heat the oil in a large, non-stick frying pan over medium heat, then add the chillies, ginger, lemongrass and garlic. Cook for 1 minute, stirring.
2 Remove from the heat and allow to cool slightly. In a small bowl, combine the lime juice, fish sauce and sugar. Add the chilli mixture and stir until well combined. Use immediately.

Ranch Dressing Mix

2½ tablespoons onion flakes
1 tablespoon dried parsley
2 teaspoons paprika
2 teaspoons sugar
2 teaspoons salt
2 teaspoons freshly ground
black pepper
1½ teaspoons garlic powder

Makes about ¼ cup (20 g)

This mix makes it easy to whip up Ranch Dressing on demand, for tossing through salads, dipping with crudités or soothing the heat of spicy chicken wings.

1 In a small, airtight container, combine all the ingredients. Cover and shake vigorously until well blended.
2 Store in a cool, dry, dark place for up to 1 year.

Ranch Dressing

1 quantity Ranch Dressing
  Mix (page 38)
1 cup (250 g) mayonnaise
1 cup (250 ml) buttermilk
  or low-fat natural yogurt

Makes about 2 cups (500 g)

To make a lower-fat version of this dressing, substitute low-fat mayonnaise for the regular mayonnaise. Buttermilk is made from skim milk, so it is already low in fat and kilojoules. Instead of buttermilk, use runny, low-fat natural yogurt. If you'd like a thicker consistency for dipping, use sour cream.

In a small, non-metallic bowl, whisk together all the ingredients until the dressing is smooth and creamy.

Blue Cheese Dressing

1½ cups (375 g) mayonnaise
½ cup (125 ml) sour cream
¼ cup (60 ml) cider vinegar
4 teaspoons sugar
½ teaspoon mustard powder
1 teaspoon crushed garlic
2 teaspoons finely chopped
  onion
1 cup (125 g) crumbled blue
  cheese

Makes about 2 cups (500 g)

You can make this tangy treat or any of the following prepared salad dressings from scratch and keep them on hand in the refrigerator. They are all easy to make and cost a lot less than their commercial counterparts.

In a small, non-metallic bowl, combine all the ingredients except the blue cheese. Whisk to blend until the dressing is smooth and creamy. Gently stir in the blue cheese. Cover the bowl and refrigerate for at least 2 hours before serving. Store, covered, in the refrigerator.

Light Blue Cheese Dressing

½ cup (125 g) low-fat
  mayonnaise
2 tablespoons skim milk
1 tablespoon lemon juice
½ teaspoon sugar
1 teaspoon crushed garlic
¼ teaspoon mustard powder
½ cup (60 g) crumbled blue
  cheese

Makes about 1 cup (250 g)

Rich, creamy and loaded with flavour – you'd never guess this is a low-fat dressing.

In a small, non-metallic bowl, combine all the ingredients except the blue cheese. Whisk to blend until the dressing is smooth and creamy. Gently stir in the blue cheese. Cover the bowl and refrigerate for at least 2 hours before serving. Store, covered in the refrigerator.

French Dressing

1 cup (250 ml) Ketchup
  (page 28)
½ cup (125 g) low-fat
  mayonnaise
3 tablespoons cider vinegar
3 tablespoons honey
2 tablespoons water
1 tablespoon olive oil
1 teaspoon lemon juice
½ teaspoon mustard powder
¼ teaspoon salt

Makes 2½ cups (625 ml)

You probably have all the ingredients for this creamy dressing in your pantry. It takes just a few minutes to prepare and is more delicious than the bottled variety.

In a food processor or blender, process all the ingredients until the dressing is well blended, smooth and creamy. Store in an airtight container in the refrigerator.

Italian Dressing

¼ cup (60 ml) extra virgin
  or virgin olive oil
¼ cup (60 ml) red wine
  vinegar
1 clove garlic, crushed
1 teaspoon finely chopped
  onion
½ teaspoon mustard powder
½ teaspoon celery seeds
½ teaspoon paprika
¼ teaspoon Italian Herb Blend
  (page 42)
2–4 tablespoons sugar

Makes about ⅔ cup (170 ml)

Nothing tastes better – or is more pleasing to the wallet – than homemade Italian dressing.

In a small, airtight container, combine all the ingredients. Cover and shake vigorously until all the ingredients are well blended. Use immediately or store in the refrigerator overnight.

Thousand Island Dressing

2 cups (500 g) Classic
  Mayonnaise (page 29)
¼ cup (60 ml) hot chilli sauce
¼ cup (60 g) chopped Sweet
  Pickles (page 67) or similar
  cucumber pickle

Makes 2½ cups (625 ml)

For a lighter version of this dressing, substitute low-fat mayonnaise or low-fat natural yogurt for the regular mayonnaise. Using homemade mayonnaise will please both your palate and your budget.

1 In a small, non-metallic bowl, whisk together all the ingredients until the dressing is well blended and creamy.
2 Store in an airtight container in the refrigerator.

Seasonings

Bouquet Garni

1 bay leaf
2 sprigs parsley
1 sprig thyme

This famous combination uses either fresh herb sprigs or dried leaves. Use it for soups, stews and casseroles.

1 Cut a piece of muslin (cheesecloth) about 10 cm square. Lay the herbs in the centre of the muslin, then bring the corners of the cloth together to form a bundle around the herbs. Tie the top of the bundle with kitchen string.
2 Add the herb bundle to a soup or stew. Once the cooking has finished, remove the bundle and discard.

Fines Herbes

4 tablespoons dried parsley
1 tablespoon dried tarragon
1 tablespoon dried chervil
1 tablespoon dried chives

This classic blend of four herbs enhances the flavour of fish, poultry, egg dishes or cooked vegetables.

1 In a self-sealing plastic bag or airtight container, combine all the herbs. Shake until the herbs are well blended.
2 Label, date and store in a dry place at room temperature. Use within 3 months.

How to dry herbs

Drying fresh herbs that you have grown yourself will really save you money. For best flavour, try to use dried herbs within 4 to 6 months after preserving them. Once dried, crumble the leaves with your hands, so they are ready to be used in recipes.

❖ **Air-drying** Pick fresh herbs. Gather the herbs in bunches and tie each bunch of stems with string, leaving a long end. Using the long end, hang the herb bunches upside down in a cool, dry place until they are completely dried.

❖ **Drying in an oven** Preheat an electric oven to 50°C. Preheat a gas oven to 100°C (Gas ½), then turn off the oven. Spread the herbs in a single layer over a baking tray with a rim, then place in the oven until the herbs are completely dried, about 50 minutes.

Herbes de Provence

1½ tablespoons dried oregano
3 teaspoons dried basil
3 teaspoons dried marjoram
3 teaspoons dried thyme
1½ teaspoons dried mint
1½ teaspoons dried rosemary
1½ teaspoons dried sage
1 teaspoon fennel seeds

This popular French herb mixture can be sprinkled over meats, fish or poultry before grilling; stirred into rice or couscous; added to omelettes or scrambled eggs; or whisked together with oil and vinegar for a herbed salad dressing.

1 In a mortar, blender or food processor, crush or pulse all the herbs together until they reach the desired consistency.
2 Place the herb mixture in a self-sealing plastic bag or airtight container, label and date. Keep in a dry place at room temperature. Use within 3 months.

Italian Herb Blend

6 tablespoons dried basil
3 tablespoons dried oregano
2 tablespoons dried parsley
2 tablespoons dried thyme
1 teaspoon dried garlic

This well-loved herb mix is almost essential in pasta dishes and sprinkled on pizza. It is also delicious with chicken or firm fish.

1 In a self-sealing plastic bag or airtight container, combine all the ingredients. Shake until all the herbs are well blended.
2 Label, date and store in a dry place at room temperature. Use within 3 months.

Chicken Seasoning Mix

2 cups (300 g) plain flour, sifted
1 tablespoon paprika
2 teaspoons dried marjoram
2 teaspoons dried thyme
2 teaspoons onion powder
2 teaspoons garlic powder
1 teaspoon dried rosemary
½ teaspoon salt
¼ teaspoon freshly ground black pepper

Makes enough to coat 20 pork chops or four whole chickens

This is a fabulous addition to fried or baked chicken and pork recipes.

1 In a self-sealing plastic bag or airtight container, combine all the ingredients. Shake until all the ingredients are well blended.
2 Label, date and store in a cool, dry place for up to 6 months.

Make it a gift

Jars of herb mixtures are always welcome in a cook's home. You can make herb or spice bags with muslin (cheesecloth) tied with string, then place the bags in a glass jar – all the cook needs to do is pull out a bag and pop it into whatever's cooking to add extra flavour.

Freezing herbs

Freezing herbs protects their flavour even more than drying them, in the opinion of many knowledgeable cooks. You can freeze herbs as whole sprigs or as chopped leaves frozen in an ice cube.

❖ **Whole sprigs** Wash and spin-dry sprigs of bushy herbs using a salad spinner. Pack in self-sealing freezer bags, label, date and freeze. Remove leaves as needed, returning the sprigs to the bags, then resealing and refreezing them.

❖ **Chopped leaves in ice cubes** Chop leaves of fresh herbs, such as chives, parsley or basil. Place 1 tablespoon of the chopped herb into each container of an ice-cube tray. Pour just enough water into each container to cover the herbs. Place in the freezer until well frozen. Pop out the frozen herb cubes, place in self-sealing freezer bags, label, date and freeze. When using those herbs in a recipe, just add the cube and let it melt.

Chilli Powder

3 tablespoons chilli powder
  or paprika
1 tablespoon ground cumin
1 teaspoon ground turmeric
1 teaspoon dried oregano
1 teaspoon garlic powder
¼–1 teaspoon ground cayenne
  pepper
¼ teaspoon salt
¼ teaspoon freshly ground
  black pepper

Makes about ¼ cup (30 g)

You don't have to pay fancy prices for fancy spice mixes. Make your own, then slowly start adding a little more of one ingredient or a little less of another until you have your own favourite blend. You can adapt this recipe to your own taste: make it hotter by adding more cayenne pepper, then add more or less of each spice.

1 In an airtight container, combine all the ingredients. Shake until all the spices are well blended.
2 Label, date and store in a cool, dark place for up to 6 months.

Cajun Seasoning Mix

⅔ cup (65 g) ground cayenne
  pepper
½ cup (156 g) salt
¼ cup (20 g) garlic powder
¼ cup (20 g) onion powder
¼ cup (20 g) chilli powder
2 tablespoons freshly ground
  black pepper

Makes about 2 cups (350 g)

Sprinkle this spice sensation over popcorn, hot chips, chicken pieces or use it in Cajun dishes.

1 Combine all the ingredients in an airtight container. Shake until all the spices are well blended.
2 Label, date and store in a cool, dark place for up to 6 months.

Laksa Paste

1 onion, roughly chopped
4 cloves garlic
2 tablespoons finely chopped
fresh ginger
2 stems lemongrass, white
part only, roughly chopped
3 red birdseye chillies,
roughly chopped
6 macadamia nuts or toasted
candlenuts
2 teaspoons shrimp paste
1 teaspoon ground turmeric
1 teaspoon ground cumin
2 teaspoons ground coriander
10–12 Vietnamese mint leaves
1 cup (50 g) roughly chopped
fresh coriander (leaves,
stems and roots)
4 kaffir lime leaves, finely
chopped
¼ cup (60 ml) vegetable oil,
plus extra for storage

Makes about 1 cup (250 g)

Keep this spicy paste in the fridge, so you can whip
up your favourite laksa recipe in less time than it takes
to get to your local takeaway.

1 Process all the ingredients in a food processor or blender
until a paste forms.
2 Put the paste into a sterilised jar and drizzle over a little extra
oil until the surface of the paste is covered, then seal with a
tight-fitting lid. Keep the paste in the refrigerator for up to
1 month or divide the paste into ¼ cup portions (the amount
required in most laksa recipes to serve 4) and freeze for up
to 6 months.

Chermoula

½ cup (15 g) fresh coriander
leaves, finely chopped
½ cup (10 g) fresh parsley,
finely chopped
1 small red onion, finely
chopped
2 cloves garlic, crushed
1 teaspoon ground cumin
1 teaspoon ground paprika
1 teaspoon ground turmeric
1 teaspoon chilli powder
½ cup (125 ml) olive oil
2 tablespoons lemon juice

Makes about 1 cup (250 g)

This Moroccan herb and spice mixture can be used
as a marinade for meat, poultry and fish. It can also
be applied to meat as a paste, which will form a crust
during cooking.

In a bowl, combine the coriander, parsley, onion, garlic, cumin,
paprika, turmeric and chilli powder. Add the olive oil and lemon
juice, then stir until well combined.

Caribbean Spicy Meat Rub

3 tablespoons soft brown
   sugar
2 tablespoons paprika
2 teaspoons mustard powder
2 teaspoons garlic salt
1½ teaspoons dried basil
1 teaspoon ground coriander
1 teaspoon dried savory
1 teaspoon dried thyme
1 teaspoon freshly ground
   black pepper
1 teaspoon ground cumin
1 bay leaf, crushed

Makes about ½ cup (85 g)

A pungent sweet, spicy blend to rub onto just about any kind of meat before grilling, this mix can also be added to sauces and stews. Alternatively, stir 4 tablespoons of the rub into 2 tablespoons vegetable oil and heat just until the aromas are released, then add to any marinade for tougher cuts of meat.

1 Combine all the ingredients in an airtight container. Shake until all the ingredients are well blended.
2 Label, date and store in a cool, dark place for up to 6 months.

Curry Powder

3 tablespoons ground
   coriander
2 tablespoons ground turmeric
2 teaspoons ground cumin
2 teaspoons ground ginger
2 teaspoons ground allspice
1 teaspoon ground cinnamon
1 teaspoon ground celery seed
1 teaspoon ground black
   pepper
¼ teaspoon ground cayenne
   pepper

Makes about ½ cup (60 g)

Try making this basic recipe, then experiment each time you make it to find a blend that's perfect for you by adding or subtracting one of the following: cumin seeds, ground turmeric, black peppercorns, fennel seeds, cayenne pepper, ground coriander, ground cinnamon, nutmeg or mace, ground cloves, tamarind paste or cardamom seeds.

1 Combine all the ingredients in an airtight container. Shake until all the spices are well blended.
2 Label, date and store in a cool, dark place for up to 6 months.

Green Curry Paste

4 French shallots, chopped
1 teaspoon shrimp or anchovy
   paste
3 cloves garlic, quartered
2 dried kaffir lime leaves,
   crushed, or 1 teaspoon
   lime zest
10 cm-long piece lemongrass
   stem, inner stalk chopped
1 tablespoon coriander seeds
1 tablespoon thinly sliced
   fresh ginger
1 teaspoon freshly grated
   nutmeg
1 teaspoon cumin seeds
1 teaspoon white peppercorns
6 green chillies, seeded
   and quartered
3–4 tablespoons coconut cream

Makes about ¾ cup (290 g)

This recipe and the one that follows are two staples of Thai cooking. You'll be surprised how often you'll reach for these pastes to add a little exotic flavour to your meals. You can find many of the ingredients at specialty Asian food shops. Stir this paste into poultry or vegetable dishes, or add it to more delicately flavoured meat dishes. To release the flavours, sauté the paste in a little vegetable oil before using.

1 In a food processor or blender, process all the ingredients until well blended and smooth.
2 Use the paste at once or place in an airtight container, cover with vegetable oil and store in the refrigerator for up to 4 days. Alternatively, pack the paste into an ice-cube tray, freeze, pop out the paste cubes and store in a self-sealing, freezer-safe plastic bag in the freezer. Use the cubes as needed in recipes.

Red Curry Paste

1 tablespoon coriander seeds
3–6 red chillies, stem removed
   but not seeded
4 French shallots, quartered
1 red onion, cut into eighths
4 cloves garlic, quartered
10 cm-long piece lemongrass
   stem, inner stalk chopped
¼ cup (7 g) fresh coriander
   leaves
2 kaffir lime leaves, finely
   chopped
zest of 2 limes
1 teaspoon freshly grated
   nutmeg
1 teaspoon cumin seeds
1 teaspoon white peppercorns
2 teaspoons shrimp or
   anchovy paste

Makes about 1 cup (290 g)

You can adjust the heat of this spicy Thai delight by adding or subtracting the fresh red chillies. As with the Green Curry Paste (above), sautéing the paste in a little oil before using it will fully release the flavours.

1 In a frying pan over medium–high heat, toast the coriander seeds for about 30 seconds. In a food processor or blender, process the toasted coriander seeds, chillies, shallots, onion, garlic, lemongrass, coriander leaves, kaffir lime leaves, zest, nutmeg, cumin seeds and white peppercorns until all the ingredients are well blended.
2 In a frying pan over medium–low heat, dry-roast the shrimp or anchovy paste for 2 to 3 minutes, stirring constantly. Add to the chilli mixture and process until smooth. Use the paste at once, or place in an airtight container, cover with vegetable oil and store in the refrigerator for up to 2 weeks.

Marinades

Red Wine Marinade

¼ cup (60 ml) dry red wine
2 French shallots, chopped
2 tablespoons balsamic
  vinegar
½ teaspoon dried rosemary
2 tablespoons olive oil
2 cloves garlic, crushed
½ teaspoon salt
½ teaspoon freshly ground
  black pepper

There's no need to buy an expensive packaged marinade when you can easily make one. The purpose of any marinade is twofold: an acid, such as lemon juice or vinegar, breaks down the fibres in tough pieces of meat, while the seasonings infuse the meat with piquant flavour. Try marinating chunks of beef or lamb in this rich-tasting marinade before grilling them on skewers.

In a small, non-metallic bowl, stir together all the ingredients until well blended. Pour the marinade into a large, self-sealing bag and add the lamb or beef to be marinated. Place the bag in the refrigerator for at least 4 hours or overnight.

Mustard Marinade

⅓ cup (80 ml) lemon juice
2 French shallots, chopped
2 tablespoons soy sauce
2 tablespoons dijon mustard
2 tablespoons olive oil
¼ teaspoon hot chilli sauce

Use this tasty mixture to marinate boneless, skinless chicken breasts, either for grilling or cutting into cubes to thread on skewers.

In a small, non-metallic bowl, stir together all the ingredients until well blended. Pour the marinade into a large, self-sealing bag and add the poultry to be marinated. Place the bag in the refrigerator and store for at least 4 hours or overnight.

Make your own tenderising meat marinades

These marinades not only add flavour but will also tenderise the meat.

❖ **Beer** Place the meat in a non-metallic dish, pour a bottle of beer over it and place it in the refrigerator for 1 hour, or overnight, turning it once or twice. If you're slow-cooking the meat (the best method for tough cuts), use beer as part of the cooking liquid.

❖ **Natural yogurt** Yogurt is great when used as a marinade, especially for lamb and chicken.

❖ **Lemon juice** If you grow your own lemons, you have a terrific tenderiser for nothing! Lemon juice breaks down tough fibres quickly and easily – and adds a bright citrus taste.

❖ **Vinegar** Soak a tough piece of meat in 1 or 2 cups of vinegar overnight in the refrigerator to tenderise it. Try different vinegars with different meats to find out which combinations you prefer.

Lemon Herb Marinade

¼ cup (60 ml) vegetable oil
1 teaspoon grated lemon zest
¼ cup (60 ml) lemon juice
2 cloves garlic, crushed
1 teaspoon dried rosemary
½ teaspoon dried thyme
½ teaspoon salt
¼ teaspoon freshly ground
    black pepper

Makes about ½ cup (125 ml)

This Greek-style marinade is lovely with lamb chops and great with chicken. It's easy, inexpensive and delicious.

In a small, non-metallic bowl, stir together all the ingredients until well blended. Pour the marinade into a large, self-sealing bag and add the lamb or poultry to be marinated. Place the bag in the refrigerator for at least 4 hours.

Orange Ginger Marinade

¼ cup (60 ml) soy sauce
2 French shallots, chopped
⅓ cup (90 ml) orange juice
2 teaspoons grated fresh
    ginger
2 tablespoons olive oil
2 tablespoons grated orange
    zest
1 clove garlic, crushed

Makes about 200 ml

Lend a sweet, tangy flavour to scallops, prawns or fish with this easy-to-make mixture, which rivals any prepared marinade.

In a small, non-metallic bowl, stir together all the ingredients until well blended. Pour the marinade into a large, self-sealing bag and add the seafood to be marinated. Place the bag in the refrigerator for 30 minutes to 1 hour.

Soy and Sesame Marinade

¼ cup (60 ml) lemon juice
½ teaspoon salt
2 tablespoons sesame oil
1 large clove garlic, crushed
1 tablespoon soy sauce

Makes about ½ cup (125 ml)

Sensational with prawns, this marinade is also good with chicken or rump steak. Compare your own version with the ingredients in the bottled ones and you'll be glad you saved the money. If salt is an issue, use salt-reduced soy sauce.

In a small, non-metallic bowl, stir together all the ingredients until well blended. Pour the marinade into a self-sealing bag and add the seafood, meat or poultry to be marinated. Place the bag in the refrigerator for at least 1 hour.

VARIATIONS
Teriyaki Marinade: In a small, non-metallic bowl, stir together ¼ cup (60 ml) soy sauce, 2 tablespoons mirin or rice vinegar, 2 tablespoons honey, 1 small finely chopped garlic clove and ¾ teaspoon ground ginger until well blended. Use as above.

Cooking Stocks

Beef Stock

1.8 kg meaty beef bones, including marrow and shin bones or knucklebones
2 onions, thickly sliced
2 carrots, thickly sliced
2 celery stalks with leaves, sliced
6 sprigs fresh parsley
2 small bay leaves
1 sprig fresh thyme, or ½ teaspoon dried thyme
10 black peppercorns
1 tablespoon salt

Makes 12 cups (3 litres)

At the heart of every great soup is a great stock. Although shop-bought stocks are convenient, they never have as much flavour as those you make yourself. Plus, when you make your own, you know exactly what goes into it – and what doesn't. When you buy the beef for this rich-tasting stock, ask the butcher to break up the bones into pieces small enough to fit into your stockpot or largest saucepan.

1 Preheat the oven to 200°C (Gas 6). Place the bones, onions and carrots in a roasting tin, then roast for 30 to 45 minutes, until the bones turn a rich brown.
2 Transfer the mixture to a stockpot or very large saucepan. Add the celery, parsley, bay leaves, thyme, peppercorns and salt. Add enough water (about 5 litres) to cover the mixture.
3 Add a little water to the roasting tin and stir to loosen any browned bits. Pour the liquid and bits into the stockpot.
4 Place the stockpot over medium–high heat, then slowly bring the mixture to a boil, using a slotted spoon to skim off any fat or scum that rises to the surface. Reduce the heat, partly cover the pot and simmer gently for 3 to 4 hours.
5 Line a fine sieve with muslin (cheesecloth) and set it over a large bowl. Slowly pour the stock through the sieve; discard the solids. Let the stock cool to room temperature. Pour the stock into serving-sized, airtight containers; cover, label and date. Store in the refrigerator for 1 week, or freeze for up to 6 months. If fat congeals on top of the stock while refrigerated or frozen, remove and discard before using the stock.

Make your own stock cubes

While stock (boullion) cubes are convenient, you don't have to buy them. When cooking a pot of stock, cook the liquid down to 2 cups (500 ml) – it will be thick and intense in both flavour and colour. Let the reduced stock cool completely, then pour it into ice-cube trays and place the trays in the freezer. When the stock cubes are solid, remove them from the trays, wrap each in foil and store them in a labelled, dated, self-sealing freezer bag. Each cube, diluted, will make 1 cup (250 ml) of stock.

Chicken Stock

2.5 kg whole stewing hen,
   or 900 g chicken wing tips,
   necks and backs
3 celery stalks, sliced
1 large carrot, sliced
1 large onion, quartered
1 leek, white part only, halved
   lengthwise, cleaned and
   sliced
6 sprigs fresh parsley
½ teaspoon dried thyme
1 bay leaf
1 teaspoon salt
½ teaspoon black peppercorns

Makes 8 cups (2 litres)

As an alternative to chicken, use the same technique to make turkey stock with Christmas leftovers.

1 In a stockpot or very large saucepan, combine all the ingredients. Add enough water to cover the mixture. Bring slowly to a boil over medium–low heat, using a slotted spoon to skim off any fat or scum that rises to the surface.
2 Reduce the heat, partly cover the pot and gently simmer the stock for about 3 hours, until the stock is well flavoured. The longer you simmer the stock, the richer the flavour.
3 Line a fine sieve with muslin (cheesecloth) and set it over a large bowl. Slowly pour the stock through the sieve; discard the solids. Let the stock cool to room temperature. Pour the stock into serving-sized, airtight containers; cover, label and date. Store in the refrigerator for 1 week, or freeze for up to 6 months. If fat congeals on top of the stock while refrigerated or frozen, remove and discard before using the stock.

Fish Stock

700 g whole white-fleshed fish,
   such as cod, snapper or
   haddock, cleaned and scaled
1–2 celery stalks, sliced
1 small onion, sliced
1 cup (250 ml) white wine,
   or the juice of 1 lemon
3 sprigs fresh parsley
1 sprig fresh thyme or
   ½ teaspoon dried thyme
1 small bay leaf
½ teaspoon salt
½ teaspoon black peppercorns

Makes 6 cups (1.5 litres)

An elegant base for seafood soups and stews, this delicately flavoured stock can also be used as a poaching liquid for whole fish. Be careful not to overcook fish stock; too much cooking destroys the complex flavour and can give it a bitter edge. After making the stock, use the cooked fish in salads or a fish pie.

1 Cut off the fish head, slit open the fish and remove the bones. In a large saucepan, combine the fish fillets, head and bones. Add the remaining ingredients and 6–8 cups (1.5–2 litres) water. Bring the mixture to a boil over medium–high heat, using a slotted spoon to skim off any fat or scum that rises to the surface.
2 Reduce the heat to very low and barely simmer the stock, uncovered, for about 5 minutes, until the fish fillets are just cooked. Using a slotted spoon, lift out the fish fillets and set aside to drain.
3 Simmer the stock for a further 15 minutes.
4 Line a fine sieve with muslin (cheesecloth) and set it over a large bowl. Slowly pour the stock through the sieve; discard the solids. Let the stock cool to room temperature. Pour the stock into serving-sized, airtight containers; cover, label and date. Store in the refrigerator for 1 week, or freeze for up to 6 months.

Clarifying stock

The best-quality stock is beautifully clear. This is achieved by clarifying the liquid after cooking. There are two methods for clarifying stock: the first will yield fairly clear results; the second method, very clear.

❖ **Straining** Line a fine sieve with muslin (cheesecloth) and pour the stock through; this will remove any small solids floating in the stock.

❖ **Eggwhite method** Separate 2 eggs and whisk together the whites. Crush the eggshells and add to the stock with the eggwhites. Leaving the lid off, slowly bring to a simmer. When the eggwhites begin to set, remove the stock from the heat. Pour the stock through a sieve or colander lined with muslin (cheesecloth) into a large bowl; any floating solids or particles will be trapped in the cooked eggwhites. Discard the whites and shells.

Vegetable Stock

¼ cup (60 g) unsalted butter
5 onions, chopped
2 leeks, white part only, halved lengthwise and sliced
2 cloves garlic
4 carrots, chopped
4 celery stalks with leaves, chopped
6–8 dried mushrooms, such as porcini
1 small bunch fresh parsley
1 sprig fresh thyme, or ½ teaspoon dried thyme
1 tablespoon salt
½ teaspoon ground allspice
pinch of mace or nutmeg
1 tablespoon red wine vinegar (optional)
1 fresh red chilli, halved and seeded (optional); wear gloves when handling – they burn

Makes about 12 cups (3 litres)

Homemade vegetable stock is very economical and a creative way to use up vegetable peelings, leftover vegetables or the parts that are full of nutrition yet not generally served, such as mushroom stems, celery tops, and broccoli and cauliflower stalks.

1 In a stockpot or very large saucepan, melt the butter over medium heat. Add the onions, leeks and garlic and sauté for 5 to 8 minutes, until the onions are golden. Add the carrots, celery, mushrooms, parsley, thyme, salt, allspice, mace or nutmeg and 16 cups (4 litres) cold water.

2 Bring the mixture slowly to a boil, using a slotted spoon to skim off any fat or scum that rises to the surface. Reduce the heat, partly cover the pot, then simmer gently for 2 hours, adding more water as needed to maintain the level at about 12 cups (3 litres). Add the vinegar and chilli, if using, then simmer for 30 minutes longer.

3 Line a fine sieve with muslin (cheesecloth) and set it over a large bowl. Slowly pour the stock through the sieve, gently pressing with a wooden spoon to squeeze all the liquid from the solids; discard the solids and the chilli. If desired, clarify the stock (see Clarifying Stock, above). If a thicker stock is desired, do not discard the solids after straining; purée about ½ cup of the cooked vegetables and stir the purée back into the stock. Let the stock cool to room temperature. Pour the stock into serving-sized, airtight containers; cover, label and date. Store in the refrigerator for 1 week, or freeze for up to 6 months.

Sauces

Barbecue Sauce

1 onion, chopped
¼ cup (60 ml) vegetable oil
1 cup (250 ml) Ketchup
  (page 28) or Tomato Passata
  (page 31)
2 tablespoons worcestershire
  sauce
2 tablespoons sugar
¼ cup (60 ml) cider vinegar
2 tablespoons mustard
1 teaspoon salt
½ teaspoon freshly ground
  black pepper

Makes about 2½ cups (625 ml)

Great with beef, chicken or pork, this homemade sauce is not only cheaper than bottled ones, but can also be customised to suit your family's taste.

1 In a non-metallic saucepan over low heat, combine all the ingredients and ¾ cup (185 ml) water. Simmer, uncovered, fo 20 minutes, then remove from the heat and allow to cool.
2 Store in an airtight container in the refrigerator for up to 1 week, or freeze for up to 6 months.

Gravy

¼ cup (60 ml) pan drippings
  from roast meat or poultry
melted butter, as needed
2 cups (500 ml) Beef Stock
  (page 49) or Chicken Stock
  (page 50)
¼ cup (35 g) plain flour
salt and freshly ground black
  pepper, to taste

Makes 2 cups (500 ml)

Real gravy, made using the drippings from roasted meat or poultry, is the finishing touch for any roast, especially when you use homemade stock. You can also use shop-bought stock, but the flavour will be less intense.

1 Pour the drippings into a large frying pan and set aside; if needed, add some melted butter to make up the full amount.
2 Place the roasting tin with the remaining drippings over medium heat. Stir in the stock and simmer, stirring to loosen any browned bits on the bottom of the tin, about 1 minute.
3 Place the frying pan over medium heat and heat the drippings for 1 minute. Blend in the flour and cook, whisking, until the flour is a nutty brown, 1 to 2 minutes. Gradually add the stock, whisking constantly, then cook until the mixture boils and thickens.
4 Reduce the heat to medium–low and simmer, stirring occasionally, for a further 2 to 3 minutes. Add salt and pepper. If the gravy is lumpier than desired, strain it through a sieve. Transfer to a heated gravy boat and serve immediately.

Note: For extra flavour, add chopped fresh or dried herbs to the stock; try rosemary for lamb and tarragon for chicken.

Satay Sauce

⅓ cup (90 g) crunchy Peanut
   Butter (page 33)
1 teaspoon salt-reduced
   soy sauce
1 teaspoon honey
1 teaspoon rice vinegar
   or cider vinegar
1 large clove garlic, peeled
1 spring onion, chopped
⅓ cup (80 ml) reduced-fat
   coconut milk
1 tablespoon Sweet Chilli
   Sauce (page 33)

Makes about 1 cup (250 ml)

Full of flavour, this rich, creamy sauce is robust enough
to take on meat, tofu and vegetable skewers.

In a food processor or blender, process all the ingredients
until almost smooth.

Sweet and Sour Sauce

30 g glacé ginger, drained
   (reserve the syrup) and
   finely grated
3 teaspoons syrup from
   the ginger
2 small canned pineapple
   rings, drained and finely
   chopped
2 tablespoons soft brown
   sugar
pinch of ground cayenne
   pepper
3 teaspoons rice vinegar,
   white wine vinegar or cider
   vinegar
salt and freshly ground black
   pepper, to taste
1½ teaspoons arrowroot

Makes about 1 cup (250 ml)

Try this sauce poured over cooked beef, fish, chicken
or pork, or use it for dipping.

1 In a saucepan, combine all the ingredients except the
   arrowroot. Add ⅔ cup (170 ml) water. Bring the mixture to
   a boil over medium heat, stirring often. Reduce the heat
   to low and simmer for 5 minutes.
2 Blend the arrowroot with 2 teaspoons cold water, then
   stir into the sauce. Return the sauce to a boil, stirring
   continuously, until it thickens and becomes clear.

Mushroom Wine Sauce

¼ cup (60 g) unsalted butter

50 g dry-cured ham, such as Virginia, chopped

1 onion, chopped

1 carrot, thinly sliced

¼ cup (35 g) plain flour

3 cups (750 ml) Beef Stock (page 49)

1½ cups (375 ml) Chicken Stock (page 50)

2 tablespoons tomato paste

½ teaspoon salt

¼ teaspoon dried thyme

¼ teaspoon freshly ground black pepper

3 tablespoons butter, extra

2 French shallots, finely chopped

225 g button, shiitake or portobello mushrooms, thinly sliced

⅔ cup (170 ml) dry red wine

Makes 3½ cups (875 ml)

Many a steak lover considers this sauce the perfect accompaniment, but it is equally good with veal or chicken. Shop-bought mushroom gravy just doesn't come close, either in taste or economy.

1 In a large, heavy-based saucepan, melt the butter over medium heat. Add the ham and cook, stirring frequently, until lightly golden, about 8 minutes. Add the onion and sauté for 5 minutes, until soft. Add the carrot and cook for another 5 minutes, until tender.

2 Sprinkle the flour over the mixture and stir until blended. Gradually add the beef and chicken stocks, stirring constantly. Add the tomato paste, salt, thyme and pepper. Cook, stirring frequently and skimming off any scum that rises to the surface, for about 30 minutes, until the sauce thickens and thickly coats the back of a spoon. Strain the sauce through a sieve and discard the solids.

3 In a large frying pan over medium heat, melt the extra butter. Add the shallots and cook until soft. Add the mushrooms and cook until tender. Pour in the wine, increase the heat and boil, uncovered, until the liquid is reduced by half.

4 Add the mushroom mixture to the sauce, stirring until the ingredients are well blended.

How to clarify butter

Clarified butter is essential for making certain sauces, such as hollandaise, and for dipping artichoke leaves or steamed lobster into. By clarifying butter, you are removing the milk solids, leaving a clear, golden, rich oil. In a small saucepan over very low heat, melt ½ cup (125 g) butter. When the butter has completely liquified but not yet begun to cook, remove the saucepan from the heat and let the butter stand until the white milk solids sink to the bottom. Place a piece of muslin (cheesecloth) over a small glass bowl. Carefully pour the golden-yellow liquid butter into the bowl through the muslin; be careful to stop pouring when the white solids begin to move. Remove the muslin. Cover the clarified butter and store in the refrigerator until required.

Béarnaise Sauce

⅓ cup (10 g) chopped fresh
    tarragon
2 tablespoons white wine
    vinegar
1 tablespoon finely chopped
    French shallot
2 egg yolks
¼ teaspoon salt
½ cup (125 ml) clarified
    unsalted butter (see How
    to Clarify Butter, opposite),
    liquid but not hot
pinch of ground white pepper

Makes 1 cup (250 ml)

Egg-based sauces add immediate elegance to almost any meal. This Béarnaise sauce and the Hollandaise that follows are among the most refined. Once made with raw eggs (or eggs only lightly cooked in a double boiler), these recipes cook the eggs enough to remove any fear of salmonella contamination. Slow and steady is the rule when cooking egg sauces – or you may scramble your culinary plans. Béarnaise is the sauce served with fillet mignon in fine restaurants for sky-high prices, and jars sold in specialty food stores just don't measure up.

1 In a small saucepan, combine the tarragon, vinegar and shallot. Cook over medium–high heat for 1 to 2 minutes, then remove from the heat and leave to cool.
2 In a 4 cup (1 litre) saucepan, combine the egg yolks, salt, tarragon mixture and 2 tablespoons water. Bring to a boil over medium–high heat, whisking constantly.
3 Remove the saucepan from the heat. The mixture will begin to curdle, but continue whisking until the mixture becomes smooth. Stir in the clarified butter, 1 tablespoon at a time. Add the pepper and stir until smooth.

Hollandaise Sauce

2 egg yolks
¼ teaspoon salt
1 tablespoon lemon juice
½ cup (125 ml) clarified
    unsalted butter (see How
    to Clarify Butter, opposite),
    liquid but not hot
pinch of ground white pepper

Makes 1 cup (250 ml)

There is simply no comparison to homemade hollandaise. It's essential for dishes such as eggs benedict and eggs florentine, and superb drizzled over fresh steamed asparagus, broccoli, cauliflower or poached fish.

1 In a 4 cup (1 litre) saucepan, combine the egg yolks, salt, lemon juice and 2 tablespoons water. Bring to a boil over medium–high heat, whisking constantly.
2 Remove the saucepan from the heat. The mixture will begin to curdle, but continue whisking until the mixture becomes smooth. Stir in the clarified butter, 1 tablespoon at a time. Add the pepper and stir until smooth.

Basic White Sauce

1 tablespoon butter
1 tablespoon plain flour
1 cup (250 ml) hot milk
¼ teaspoon salt
pinch of ground white or
    freshly ground black pepper

Makes 1 cup (250 ml)

Thin, medium or thick, white sauce is the most versatile of all sauces and can be adapted to suit many dishes. Thin white sauce serves as a base for creamy soups or stews; medium white sauce is added to casseroles and creamed vegetable mixtures or used as a base for other sauces; thick white sauce works as a binder or a base for dishes such as soufflés or croquettes. Making your own white sauce, starting with this basic version, allows you to make all kinds of other recipes, such as the three that follow.

1 In a small heavy-based saucepan, melt the butter over low heat. Add the flour and cook, whisking constantly, for 2 to 3 minutes, until the mixture is smooth; do not let the flour brown. Gradually stir in the milk.
2 Increase the heat to medium and cook, stirring constantly, for 3 to 5 minutes, until the sauce is thickened and smooth, and no raw flour taste remains. Remove the saucepan from the heat and stir in the salt and pepper.
3 To store, lay plastic wrap directly on the surface of the sauce to prevent a skin forming. Allow the sauce to cool to room temperature, then refrigerate until needed. Reheat the sauce in the top of a double boiler.

Cheese Sauce

1 tablespoon butter or
    margarine
1 tablespoon plain flour
½ teaspoon mustard powder
1 cup (250 ml) hot milk
½–¾ cup (60–90 g) grated
    cheddar
¼ teaspoon salt
pinch of ground white or
    freshly ground black pepper

Makes 1¼ cups (310 ml)

Remember that you can choose the kind of cheese to use in this sauce. Cheddar is the classic variety, but there are many other possibilities. Pour the sauce over potatoes or steamed vegetables for a simple starter dish.

1 In a small heavy-based saucepan, melt the butter over low heat. Add the flour and mustard powder and cook, whisking constantly, for 2 to 3 minutes, until the mixture is smooth; do not let the flour brown. Gradually stir in the milk.
2 Increase the heat to medium and cook, stirring constantly, for 3 to 5 mintues, until the sauce is thickened and smooth, and no raw flour taste remains. Remove the saucepan from the heat and stir in the cheese, salt and pepper.
3 To store, lay plastic wrap directly on the surface of the sauce to prevent a skin forming. Allow the sauce to cool to room temperature, then refrigerate until needed. Reheat the sauce in the top of a double boiler.

Dijon Mustard Sauce

1 tablespoon butter or
   margarine
1 tablespoon plain flour
1 cup (250 ml) hot milk
2 tablespoons dijon mustard
1 teaspoon white wine vinegar
¼ teaspoon salt
pinch of ground white or
   freshly ground black pepper

Makes 1 cup (250 ml)

This tangy condiment is wonderful with ham, or poached
or grilled fish.

1 In a small heavy-based saucepan, melt the butter over
   low heat. Add the flour and cook, whisking constantly, for
   2 to 3 minutes, until the mixture is smooth; do not let the
   flour brown. Gradually stir in the milk.
2 Increase the heat to medium and cook, stirring constantly,
   for 3 to 5 minutes, until the sauce is thickened and smooth,
   and no raw flour taste remains. Remove the saucepan from
   the heat and stir in the mustard, vinegar, salt and pepper.
3 To store, lay plastic wrap directly on the surface of the sauce
   to prevent a skin forming. Allow the sauce to cool to room
   temperature, then refrigerate until needed. Reheat the
   sauce in the top of a double boiler.

Mushroom Sauce

3 tablespoons butter or
   margarine
½ cup (45 g) chopped
   mushrooms
1 tablespoon plain flour
1 cup hot milk (250 ml)
   or Beef Stock (page 49)
¼ teaspoon salt
pinch of ground white or
   freshly ground black pepper

Makes 1 cup (250 ml)

Serve this creamy mushroom sauce with roast meat
or poultry, or use it in casseroles. It's a far cry from
canned mushroom soup or sauces!

1 In a small frying pan, melt 2 tablespoons of the butter over
   medium heat. Add the mushrooms and sauté for 3 minutes,
   then remove from the heat and set aside.
2 In a small heavy-based saucepan, melt the remaining
   1 tablespoon butter over low heat. Add the flour and cook,
   whisking constantly, for 2 to 3 minutes, until smooth; do not
   let the flour brown. Gradually stir in the milk or, if a darker
   sauce is desired, the stock. Increase the heat to medium and
   cook, stirring constantly, for 3 to 5 minutes, until the sauce is
   thickened and smooth, and no raw flour taste remains.
3 Remove the saucepan from the heat and stir in the
   mushrooms, salt and pepper.
4 To store, lay plastic wrap directly on the surface of the
   sauce to prevent a skin forming. Allow the sauce to cool
   to room temperature, then refrigerate until needed.
   Reheat the sauce in the top of a double boiler.

Dessert Sauces

Blueberry Syrup

4 cups (600 g) blueberries,
   fresh or frozen
2 thin strips lemon zest
3 cups (660 g) sugar
1 tablespoon lemon juice

Makes 3½ cups (875 ml)

This fresh syrup is a perfect match for bread-and-butter pudding, ice cream or pancakes.

1 In a large saucepan, crush the berries using a wooden spoon. Add the lemon zest and 1 cup (250 ml) water. Over medium heat, bring the mixture to a simmer. Reduce the heat to low and cook, uncovered, for 5 minutes without simmering.
2 Line a colander or large sieve with muslin (cheesecloth) and set it over a large bowl. Pour the berry mixture into the colander, squeezing the muslin to extract all the juice; there should be about 2 cups (500 ml) blueberry juice. Discard the solids.
3 In a saucepan over medium–high heat, combine the sugar and another 2 cups (500 ml) water. Bring to a boil, stirring until the sugar has dissolved. Continue boiling, without stirring, until a sugar thermometer reads 125°C.
4 Add the blueberry mixture and boil, uncovered, for 1 minute. Remove from the heat and let cool, then stir in the lemon juice. Store in an airtight container in the refrigerator for up to 1 month.

Apple sauce

3 small cooking apples, peeled,
   cored and sliced
¼ teaspoon ground allspice
2 teaspoons soft brown sugar
2 tablespoons lemon juice

Makes about 1 cup (250 ml)

Keep this versatile sauce on hand to serve with ice cream or yogurt for dessert – but remember it's also a great match with pork for a main meal.

1 In a small saucepan, combine the apples, allspice, sugar, lemon juice and 1 tablespoon water. Cover and cook over low heat for about 30 minutes, until soft and pulpy.
2 Remove from the heat and mash with a fork. For a finer texture, cool the sauce, then purée it in a food processor or blender.

Mango and Passionfruit Sauce

1 large mango, stoned, peeled
   and roughly chopped
½ cup (125 ml) passionfruit
   pulp (from 6–8 fruit)

Makes 1 cup (250 ml)

The only ingredients in this delicious sauce are fresh fruit. No canned sauce can come close for pure taste.

1 In a food processor or blender, purée the mango and passionfruit pulp until smooth.
2 Chill before serving. Store in an airtight container in the refrigerator for up to 2 days.

Raspberry Sauce

½ cup (110 g) sugar
2 tablespoons orange-flavoured
  liqueur
2 cups (250 g) raspberries,
  fresh or frozen

Makes about ¾ cup (185 ml)

Simple and sensational, this sauce is quick to make and inexpensive when raspberries are in season. It will quickly become a family favourite, served over fruit salad or ice cream.

1 In a small saucepan, bring the sugar and ½ cup (125 ml) water to a boil. Remove from the heat and let the syrup cool.
2 Add the liqueur and raspberries, then stir gently; let stand for 2 minutes. Pour through a sieve into a bowl, pressing to remove the seeds; discard the solids.
3 Chill before serving. Store in an airtight container in the refrigerator for up to 2 days.

Custard

1½ cups (375 ml) milk
¼ cup (55 g) sugar
pinch of salt
3 egg yolks, lightly beaten
¾ teaspoon vanilla extract

Makes about 1½ cups (375 ml)

Forget thick, gluggy, shop-bought custard – enjoy this classic creamy sauce with its hint of vanilla, also known as crème anglaise.

1 In a saucepan over low heat, combine the milk, sugar and salt, and heat just until small bubbles appear on the surface. In a bowl, whisk ¼ cup (60 ml) of the milk mixture into the egg yolks, then stir the mixture back into the saucepan. Cook over low heat, whisking constantly, for about 10 minutes, until the mixture coats the back of a spoon.
2 Remove the saucepan from the heat and strain the mixture through a sieve into a bowl. Stir in the vanilla. Let the sauce cool to room temperature, then cover and refrigerate until ready to serve.

Fruit Coulis

2 cups (250 g) berries, fresh
  or frozen
sugar, to taste

Makes about 1 cup (250 ml)

Here is a versatile sauce that you can whip up to take advantage of berries in season – or less costly frozen ones the rest of the year. You can use raspberries, blueberries, blackberries or strawberries. You can also use fresh peaches or apricots – just lightly poach them before puréeing.

1 Rinse and drain the berries thoroughly (frozen berries do not require rinsing). In a food processor or blender, purée the berries until smooth. If desired, add a little sugar while puréeing.
2 Press the mixture through a sieve into a bowl; discard any solids or seeds. Taste and add more sugar if desired.
3 Chill before serving. Store in an airtight container in the refrigerator for up to 2 days.

Butterscotch Sauce

1½ cups 375 g unsalted butter
1½ cups (345 g) firmly packed
   soft brown sugar
pinch of salt
1 cup (250 ml) thick cream
1 teaspoon vanilla extract

Makes about 2½ cups (625 ml)

Once you've tried this delicious sauce warm over ice cream in summer or sticky date pudding in winter, you'll never buy the commercial variety again.

1 In a small saucepan over low heat, melt the butter. Add the sugar, salt and cream, and stir until the sugar has dissolved. Simmer for 8 to 10 minutes, stirring continuously so that the sugar doesn't crystallise. Remove the saucepan from the heat and stir in the vanilla.
2 Serve warm or cold. Can be refrigerated in a covered container for up to 1 week.

Chocolate Sauce

2 tablespoons good-quality
   cocoa powder, such as Dutch
   processed
½ cup (125 g) unsalted butter
1½ cups (225 g) chopped dark
   chocolate (85 per cent cocoa)
⅔ cup (100 g) chopped dark
   chocolate (70 per cent cocoa)
1 cup (230 g) firmly packed
   soft brown sugar
¾ cup (165 g) sugar
½ cup (125 ml) light corn
   syrup or glucose syrup
¼ teaspoon salt
1 teaspoon vanilla extract

Makes about 2½ cups (625 ml)

Quality cocoa powder and dark chocolate make for a decadent sauce that can't be matched at any price.

1 In a glass cup, combine the cocoa powder and 3 tablespoons cold water and stir until completely dissolved. In the top of a double boiler, melt the butter over low heat. Add the cocoa mixture and all the chocolate, then stir in 1 cup (250 ml) boiling water, both types of sugar, the corn syrup and salt.
2 Remove the top of the double boiler, place over medium heat and bring the mixture to a boil; boil, uncovered, for 5 minutes (or for 7 minutes for a thicker sauce that will harden when it comes into contact with ice cream).
3 Remove the saucepan from the heat and let the sauce cool to room temperature, then stir in the vanilla.

Caramel Sauce

2 tablespoons unsalted butter
⅓ cup (60 g) soft brown sugar
3 tablespoons cream

Makes about ⅔ cup (170 ml)

This recipe is great for last-minute guests; in less than 10 minutes you can transform just three ingredients into a real crowd-pleaser.

1 In a small saucepan, slowly melt the butter over medium heat. Add the sugar and stir for about 2 minutes, until it has dissolved. Add the cream and simmer the mixture gently for about 3 minutes, stirring frequently, until it turns a caramel colour. Remove from the heat and serve.

Dry Mixes

Pancake and Waffle Mix

6 cups (900 g) plain flour
(or half plain flour and
half wholemeal flour)
3½ tablespoons baking powder
1 cup (100 g) skim milk powder
1 tablespoon salt
1 cup (200 g) solid vegetable
shortening, such as Copha
or Trex

Makes about 8 cups (1.2 kg)

This mix will quickly make these favourite treats – see
Pancakes and Waffles (page 142).

1 In a large bowl, sift together the flour, baking powder, milk
powder and salt, then stir until well blended.
2 Add the vegetable shortening and, using a pastry blender
tool or two knives, 'cut' the shortening into the flour mixture,
until it resembles coarse crumbs.
3 Put the mix in a self-sealing bag. Label, date and refrigerate
for up to 6 weeks.

Basic Cake Mix

8 cups (1.2 kg) plain flour
6 cups (1.3 kg) sugar
¼ cup (50 g) baking powder
1½ teaspoons salt
2¼ cups (450 g) solid vegetable
shortening, such as Copha
or Trex

Makes about 16 cups (3 kg)

Even if you don't usually use packet cake mix, it pays
to keep this homemade mix on hand. It can be stored
for 10 to 12 weeks and makes about 16 cups, enough for
several cakes. Use it to create the delectable Spice Cake
(page 116) and Chocolate Cake (page 117). Using those
recipes as a guide, you can easily develop your own to
make your family's favourite cakes.

1 In a large bowl, sift together the flour, sugar, baking powder
and salt, then stir until well blended.
2 Add the vegetable shortening and, using a pastry blender
tool or two knives, 'cut' the shortening into the flour mixture,
until it resembles very coarse crumbs.
3 Place the mix in a large, airtight container or a self-sealing
plastic bag. Label, date and store the mix in a cool, dry place
or in the refrigerator for 10 to 12 weeks.

Make your own real vanilla extract

Every kitchen needs a bottle of
vanilla extract, so why not make
your own? Vanilla is one of the
most used flavourings, but as
you know, real vanilla extract
is not an inexpensive purchase.
While imitation vanilla extract
is less expensive, you pay the
price in the loss of that real
vanilla flavour.

1 Place a vanilla bean in a small,
clean screw-top jar.
2 Pour 3 tablespoons plain
vodka over the vanilla bean.

Close the lid tightly and let
the mixture stand for about
4 weeks.
3 Discard the vanilla bean from
the infused vodka before
using the extract.

Pasta

Simple Fresh Pasta

3 eggs
2 cups (300 g) plain flour

Makes 4 to 6 servings of
spaghetti or linguine, or enough
sheets for a large lasagne

Fresh pasta is quite easy to make, cooks more quickly
than dried pasta, and is light and delicious. There are
three steps to making fresh pasta: (1) mixing together
a dough; (2) rolling the dough out and cutting it; and
(3) cooking it. You can mix the dough by hand or in
a food processor. This is the simplest recipe: the eggs
provide enough moisture to form a dough.

1 In a large bowl, beat the eggs. Sift in the flour, stirring
constantly, until a soft dough forms.
2 On a lightly floured surface, knead the dough until it is smooth
and elastic.
3 Roll out and cut the dough by hand or with a pasta machine
(see Rolling and Cutting Fresh Pasta, opposite).
4 To cook, bring a large pot of lightly salted water to a boil.
Add the pasta. Fresh pasta cooks very quickly – thin strands
may be cooked by the time they float to the surface of the
water; other varieties will cook in about 1 to 2 minutes, while
ravioli will cook in 6 minutes.

Luxury Fresh Pasta

2 cups (300 g) plain flour
2 large eggs
2 teaspoons olive oil
2 tablespoons water
½ teaspoon salt

Makes 4 to 6 servings
of spaghetti or linguine,
or enough sheets for a
large lasagne

This dough contains olive oil and water, which makes
it a little easier to handle.

1 On a lightly floured surface, pour the flour in a mound. Using
your hands, make a well in the centre of the mound.
2 In a small bowl, stir together the eggs, olive oil and water.
Slowly pour the egg mixture into the flour well; sprinkle with
the salt.
3 Carefully push the flour from around the edges into the well,
stirring with your fingers to form a batter. Continue adding
flour to the well until the mixture forms a soft dough.
4 Knead the dough for at least 5 minutes, until it is smooth and
elastic. Cover the dough with an inverted bowl or plastic wrap,
then let it rest for 1 hour before rolling.
5 Roll out and cut the dough by hand or with a pasta machine
(see Rolling and Cutting Fresh Pasta, opposite).
6 To cook, bring a large pot of lightly salted water to a boil.
Add the pasta. Fresh pasta cooks very quickly – thin strands
may be cooked by the time they float to the surface of the
water; other varieties will cook in about 1 to 2 minutes, while
ravioli will cook in 6 minutes.

Rolling and cutting fresh pasta

It's easy to make pasta, either by hand or with a pasta machine.

❖ **By hand** On a lightly floured surface, using a long, thin rolling pin, roll out one piece of dough to a 1–2 mm thick, 50 x 35 cm rectangle. Lightly flour the top of the dough to prevent sticking. Fold the rectangle of dough in half lengthwise, then fold it again; you should have a 12.5 x 35 cm rectangle – do not press the dough together. Using a very sharp knife or pastry wheel – and a ruler or straightedge if needed – cut the sheet of dough into strips. Carefully unfold the strips and either hang them gently on a drying rack or lay them flat on tea towels. Let dry for 1 to 2 hours. Fresh pasta must air-dry before cooking or it will become gluey when boiled.

❖ **Using a pasta machine** Following the manufacturer's directions, pass the dough several times through the machine's rollers to knead it and make it elastic. With each pass, set the rollers closer together, until the pasta is thin enough to cut. Set the machine to cut the desired shapes and cut. Let the pasta dry on a drying rack or flat on tea towels for 1 to 2 hours.

Superfast Fresh Pasta

2¼ cups (335 g) plain flour
2 eggs
¼ cup (125 ml) water
1 tablespoon olive oil
1 teaspoon salt

Makes 4 to 6 servings of spaghetti or linguine, or enough sheets for a large lasagne

You can make quick work of mixing pasta dough if you use a food processor instead of your hands.

1 Fit a food processor with a plastic dough blade or a metal chopping blade. Add all the ingredients and process for 20 to 30 seconds, until the dough rides up in the centre.
2 On a lightly floured surface, knead the dough for about 5 minutes, until it is smooth and elastic. Cover the dough with plastic wrap and let it sit for 30 minutes before rolling.
3 Roll out and cut the dough by hand or with a pasta machine (see Rolling and Cutting Fresh Pasta, above).
4 To cook, bring a large pot of lightly salted water to the boil. Add the pasta. Fresh pasta cooks very quickly – thin strands may be cooked by the time they float to the surface of the water; other varieties will cook in about 1 to 2 minutes, while ravioli will cook in 6 minutes.

Storing fresh pasta

Let the pasta dry for several hours, or until it is dry but not brittle. For long strands of pasta (fettuccine or linguine, for example), when the dough has dried slightly but is still pliable, gently wrap a loose bunch around your fingers to form a 'nest'. Place the nest in a cool, dry place to dry completely. For large lasagne sheets, allow each to dry completely. Then stack the pieces between sheets of wax paper. Store cut pasta in self-sealing plastic bags or airtight containers in the refrigerator for up to 1 week, or freeze for up to 1 month.

Pickles and Relishes

Chilli Jam ❖ Dill Pickles ❖ Sweet Pickles ❖
Pickled Gherkins ❖ Piccalilli ❖ Tomato Relish
❖ Pickled Cauliflower Florets ❖ Pickled Onions ❖
Red Onion Relish ❖ Pickled Spiced Plums ❖
Roasted Red Capsicums in Oil ❖
Oven-dried Tomatoes

Chutneys

Mango Chutney ❖ Spicy Tomato Chutney ❖
Green Tomato Chutney ❖ Lemon Lime Chutney

Jams, Jellies and Marmalades

Dried-apricot Jam ❖ Lemony Fig Jam ❖
Pear Jam ❖ Peach Jam ❖ Melon Ginger Jam ❖
Strawberry Jam ❖ Three-berry Jam ❖ Apple
Ginger Jelly ❖ Quince Jelly ❖ Mint Jelly ❖
Seville Orange Marmalade ❖ Citrus Marmalade

Frozen Vegetables

Asparagus ❖ Beetroot ❖ Broad Beans ❖
Broccoli and Cauliflower ❖ Brussels Sprouts ❖
Capsicums (Peppers) ❖ Carrots ❖ Green Beans
❖ Mushrooms ❖ Peas ❖ Pumpkin and Sweet
Potato ❖ Sweet Corn ❖ Mixed Vegetables

Frozen Fruit

Apples ❖ Apricots ❖ Blackberries ❖ Blueberries
❖ Cherries ❖ Mangoes ❖ Peaches and Plums ❖
Raspberries ❖ Redcurrants and Blackcurrants
❖ Strawberries

Pickled, Preserved and Frozen Foods

Whether you grow your own fruit and vegetables, or like to buy produce when it's in season and at its best, the recipes in this chapter will help you take advantage of nature's seasonal abundance.

Tomatoes, capsicums (peppers), cucumbers, corn, peaches and other fresh produce flood fruit stands, roadside stalls and supermarket shelves when they are at their seasonal peak and, following the simple law of supply and demand, the price is at its lowest. Indeed, you can often get a case of tomatoes or peaches for what you would pay for a handful at another time of year.

   If you buy fresh vegetables and fruit at their peak and when their prices are most reasonable, you can freeze them and enjoy them throughout the year. All the instructions you need are in this chapter. Freezing is incredibly simple. With only a bit more effort, you can make your own unbelievably tasty pickles, relishes and chutneys. And if you also make your own jellies and jams, you will not only save money, but also have ready-made presents for friends and neighbours as well.

Pickles and Relishes

Chilli Jam

250 g capsicums (peppers),
  halved, cored and seeded
2½ long red chillies, roughly
  chopped
¼ cup (60 ml) olive oil
1 small onion, finely chopped
2 cloves garlic, finely chopped
1 tablespoon grated palm
  sugar
1 tablespoon fish sauce
2 teaspoons tamarind paste
1 tablespoon finely chopped
  fresh coriander leaves
1 tablespoon finely chopped
  fresh mint

Makes about 1 cup (300 g)

Serve a bowl of this tasty savoury jam with barbecued food or a dollop on a pan-fried chicken breast.

1 Place the capsicums under a hot grill, skin side up, for about 10 minutes, until the skins are charred. Transfer the hot capsicums to a large heatproof bowl, cover with plastic wrap and cool for about 10 minutes, until safe to handle. Peel off the skins, then roughly chop the flesh. In a food processor, purée the capsicums and chillies until smooth.

2 In a small saucepan, heat the oil over medium heat. Add the onion and cook for 1 to 2 minutes, until softened. Add the garlic and cook for 30 seconds.

3 Add the capsicum-chilli mixture, palm sugar, fish sauce and tamarind, then cook for 10 minutes over low heat, stirring occasionally. Stir the coriander and mint through, then let cool to room temperature; use immediately or store in an airtight container in the refrigerator for up to 2 weeks.

Dill Pickles

1.8 kg small to medium
  (10–13 cm long) pickling
  cucumbers
4 cloves garlic
8 sprigs fresh dill
4 teaspoons mustard seeds
3 tablespoons salt
1 tablespoon sugar
1½ cups (375 ml) vinegar

FOR THE SOAKING BRINE
⅓ cup (100 g) salt
8 cups (2 litres) hot water

Makes two 1 litre jars

Enjoy these as a snack, on an antipasto platter or sliced in hamburgers.

1 Scrub the cucumbers. To make the soaking brine, combine the salt and water in a large, non-metallic bowl. Stir until the salt has dissolved completely. Add the cucumbers to the brine and leave to soak overnight.

2 Drain the cucumbers and discard the soaking brine. Pack the cucumbers, standing on end, into two sterilised 1 litre canning jars. In each jar, place 2 garlic cloves, 4 dill sprigs and 2 teaspoons mustard seeds.

3 In a large, non-metallic saucepan, combine the 3 tablespoons salt, the sugar, vinegar and 3 cups (750 ml) water, then bring the mixture to a boil. Pour the hot brine over the cucumbers in the jars, dividing it equally.

4 Wipe the rims, cover and process for 20 minutes in boiling water (see Safe Bottling and Preserving, page 72). When cool, label, date and store in a cool, dark place for 4 to 6 weeks. Once a jar has been opened, store in the refrigerator.

Sweet Pickles

30 small to medium pickling
  cucumbers, scrubbed and
  thinly sliced
8 large onions, halved
  lengthwise and thinly sliced
  crosswise
1 red capsicum (pepper),
  chopped
½ cup (150 g) pickling salt
4 cups (about 800 g) crushed
  ice
4 cups (1 litre) white vinegar
4½ cups (1 kg) sugar
2 tablespoons mustard seeds
2 teaspoons celery seeds
1 tablespoon ground turmeric
1 teaspoon ground ginger
1 teaspoon black peppercorns

Makes eight 500 ml jars

These pickles go well with corned beef sandwiches. It's
best to use pickling salt; it keeps the pickles green, while
natural anti-caking agents keep the liquid clear.

1 In a very large colander set over a larger bowl or saucepan,
  combine the cucumber slices, onions and capsicum. Sprinkle
  the mixture with the pickling salt and toss well. Cover the
  vegetables with a 5 cm layer of crushed ice. Refrigerate for
  3 to 4 hours, adding more ice as needed.
2 In a very large, heavy-based, non-metallic saucepan, bring
  the vinegar, sugar, mustard seeds, celery seeds, turmeric,
  ginger and peppercorns to a boil over medium heat. Boil
  for 10 minutes, then stir in the cucumber mixture and return
  just to a boil.
3 Ladle the vegetables and liquid into eight sterilised 500 ml
  canning jars, leaving a 6 mm space between the top of the
  pickles and the rim of the jar. Run a long, thin spatula around
  the inside of the jars to release any trapped air bubbles.
4 Wipe the rims, cover and process for 10 minutes in boiling
  water (see Safe Bottling and Preserving, page 72). When cool,
  label, date and store in a cool, dark place for 4 to 6 weeks.
  Once a jar has been opened, store in the refrigerator.

Pickled Gherkins

600 g (about 120) French
  gherkins or baby pickling
  cucumbers, scrubbed
1½ cups (450 g) pickling salt,
  plus 1–2 tablespoons extra,
  to taste
30 peppercorns – white, green
  or multicoloured
6 small bay leaves
18 sprigs fresh tarragon
4–6 cups (1–1½ litres) white
  wine vinegar
4½ cups (1 kg) sugar

Makes six 1 litre jars

These tiny pickles, also called cornichons, are
traditionally served with pâtés and terrines.

1 In a large, non-metallic bowl, sprinkle the gherkins with the
  1½ cups salt. Loosely cover and let stand for 24 hours.
2 Drain the gherkins and discard the brine. Pack the gherkins,
  standing on end, into six warm, sterilised, wide-mouthed, 1 litre
  canning jars, leaving a 6 mm space at the top of the jar. In each
  jar, place 5 peppercorns, 1 bay leaf and 2 tarragon sprigs.
3 Meanwhile, in a large, heavy-based, non-metallic saucepan,
  combine the vinegar, sugar and remaining tarragon sprigs.
  Bring the mixture to a boil over high heat. Pour the mixture
  over the gherkins to cover. Cover the jars and stand overnight.
4 Drain the vinegar from the jars into a large, non-metallic
  saucepan. Stir in the remaining salt and, over high heat, bring
  the mixture to a boil. Remove the pan from the heat and let
  the brine cool. Pour the cooled brine over the pickles in the
  jars, dividing it equally.
5 Wipe the rims, cover and process for 15 minutes in boiling
  water (see Safe Bottling and Preserving, page 72). When cool,
  label, date and store in a cool, dark place for 4 to 6 weeks.
  Once a jar has been opened, store in the refrigerator.

Piccalilli

FOR THE VEGETABLES

⅓ cup (100 g) salt

500 g baby onions, peeled

675 g cauliflower florets, cut into smaller florets

500 g pickling cucumbers, or regular cucumbers quartered lengthwise and diced

500 g green beans, topped and tailed, then halved

3 small red chillies, thinly sliced

FOR THE SAUCE

1 cup (220 g) sugar

¾ cup (110 g) plain flour

2 teaspoons allspice

2 tablespoons ground ginger

2 tablespoons mild curry powder

2 teaspoons ground turmeric

2 tablespoons mustard powder

½ teaspoon ground cayenne pepper

5 cups (1.25 litres) white or cider vinegar

2 tablespoons black peppercorns

Makes four 250 ml jars

The name 'piccalilli' probably comes from its chief components: vegetable pickle and red-hot chilli. It is splendid served with cold meats.

1 In a large, heavy-based, non-metallic saucepan or stockpot, bring the salt and 5 cups (1.25 litres) water to a boil. Add the prepared vegetables and chillies, then reduce heat to low and cook for 5 minutes. Pour into a colander, rinse well under cold water, then drain thoroughly on paper towels or a clean tea towel.

2 Meanwhile, to make the sauce for the pickle, combine the sugar, flour, allspice, ground ginger, curry powder, turmeric, mustard powder and cayenne pepper in a bowl. Add 3–4 tablespoons of the vinegar and mix to form a thick paste.

3 Put the spice paste, peppercorns and the remaining vinegar in a large, non-metallic saucepan and bring to a boil, stirring continuously. Reduce the heat and continue to cook, stirring continuously, for 3–5 minutes, until the sauce thickens. Remove the pan from the heat and leave to cool, stirring occasionally to prevent a skin forming.

4 Put the drained vegetables in a large bowl, add the sauce and mix together. Cover the bowl and leave to stand for 24 hours.

5 The following day, stir the piccalilli again to coat the vegetables evenly, then spoon into four sterilised, wide-mouthed, 250 ml canning jars. Wipe the rims, cover and process for 15 minutes in boiling water (see Safe Bottling and Preserving, page 72). When cool, label, date and store in a cool, dark place for 2 to 3 months. Once a jar has been opened, store in the refrigerator.

In preserving, acid content is crucial

Jams, jellies, marmalades, chutneys and pickles – basically any fruit, mixture or preserve with a high enough acid content to inhibit the growth of micro-organisms – can be safely bottled with a hot-water bath (page 72). Low-acid vegetables – every type other than tomatoes, which are actually a fruit – should be frozen for storage or bottled with a pressure cooker unless you are pickling them. Pickling vegetables in vinegar adds enough acidity to allow for safe hot-water processing.

Tomato Relish

2 kg tomatoes, skinned and
finely chopped
3 large onions, finely chopped
1½ tablespoons salt
3 large celery stalks, finely
chopped
1 red capsicum (pepper), finely
chopped
2¼ cups (500 g) sugar
1 tablespoon mustard seeds
1¾ cups (440 ml) vinegar

Makes four
250 ml jars

Use this versatile relish to accompany cold meats
or salad, or spread it on sandwiches.

1 In a bowl, combine the tomatoes and onions, then sprinkle
   with the salt and leave overnight. The next day, pour the
   mixture into a colander and leave to drain for 5–6 hours.
2 In a bowl, combine the celery, capsicum, sugar, mustard seeds
   and vinegar. Stir in the tomato mixture. Spoon the relish into
   four warm, sterilised, wide-mouthed, 250 ml jars. Label, date
   and store in the refrigerator for up to 1 month.

Pickled Cauliflower Florets

1 large cauliflower, cut into
florets
white vinegar, to cover
the cauliflower
1 tablespoon salt
1 tablespoon white
peppercorns
1 tablespoon soft brown sugar
1 capsicum (pepper), finely
sliced
6 small dried red chillies

Makes two 1 litre jars

This is a traditional addition to any antipasto plate.

1 In a large, non-metallic saucepan or stockpot, place the
   cauliflower florets and pour in enough vinegar to cover.
   Add the salt, peppercorns and sugar and bring the mixture
   to a boil over high heat.
2 Add the capsicum and boil for 1 minute. Using a slotted
   spoon, transfer the cauliflower to two warm, sterilised,
   wide-mouthed 1 litre jars, reserving the brine. Pack the
   cauliflower firmly into the jars, dividing the capsicum strips
   between them. Add 3 chillies to each jar.
3 Pour the hot brine over the vegetables in the jars until the
   cauliflower is completely covered, leaving a 6 mm space
   between the top of the brine and the rim of the jars. Wipe
   the rims, cover and process for 20 minutes in boiling water
   (see Safe Bottling and Preserving, page 72). Cool, label, date
   and store in a cool, dark place for 4 to 6 weeks; the cauliflower
   will be ready to eat in 2 weeks. Once a jar has been opened,
   store in the refrigerator.

Pickled Onions

1.8 kg small white pickling onions

½ cup (150 g) pickling salt

8 black peppercorns

4 red chillies (wear gloves when handling; they burn)

4 bay leaves

4 cups (1 litre) cider vinegar

Makes four 1 litre jars

These bitey onions are a tasty appetiser or a match for blue cheese.

1 Place the onions in a large, heatproof, non-metallic bowl. Pour enough boiling water over them to cover. Let stand for 5 minutes, then drain. Trim the root end and the crowns of the onions; the peels should slip off easily. Do not remove too many onion layers.

2 Place the peeled onions in a large bowl and cover with cold water. Add the salt and mix well, then let stand overnight.

3 Drain the onions. Using a large slotted spoon, transfer the onions to four warm, sterilised, wide-mouthed 1 litre jars. To each jar, add 2 peppercorns, 1 chilli and 1 bay leaf.

4 In a large, non-metallic saucepan, bring the vinegar to a boil over high heat. Immediately pour the hot vinegar over the onions in the jars to cover them, leaving a 3 mm space between the top of the vinegar and the rim of the jars.

5 Wipe the rims, cover and process for 10 minutes in boiling water (see Safe Bottling and Preserving, page 72). Cool, label, date and store in a cool, dark place; the onions will be ready to eat in 4 weeks. Once a jar has been opened, store in the refrigerator.

Red Onion Relish

¼ cup (60 ml) olive oil
900 g red onions, sliced
½ cup (110 g) sugar
1 teaspoon salt
½ teaspoon freshly ground
black pepper
4 tablespoons balsamic or
sherry vinegar
1 cup (250 ml) red wine

Makes two 500 ml jars

A noteworthy accompaniment to almost any variety of cheese, this red onion treat is cheaper and tastier when made at home.

1 In a large, non-metallic saucepan, heat the olive oil over medium heat. Add the onions and cook for about 20 minutes, stirring occasionally.
2 Stir the sugar, salt and pepper into the onions. Reduce the heat to low, cover the saucepan, and cook very gently for 10 minutes; if the heat is too high, use a heat diffuser.
3 Add the vinegar and wine, then cook, uncovered and stirring at regular intervals, for 20 to 30 minutes, until the mixture has the consistency of chutney. Skim off and discard any foam that forms during cooking.
4 Ladle the relish into two warm, sterilised, wide-mouthed 500 ml jars, leaving a 3 mm space between the top of the relish and the rim of the jar.
5 Wipe the rims, cover and process for 10 minutes in boiling water (see Safe Bottling and Preserving, page 72). Cool, label, date and store in a cool, dark place; the onion relish will be ready to eat in 4 weeks. Once a jar has been opened, store in the refrigerator.

Pickled Spiced Plums

1⅗ cups (360 g) sugar
1 cup (250 ml) cider vinegar
4 cinnamon sticks, broken
1 tablespoon whole cloves
1 tablespoon black
peppercorns
2–3 strips orange zest
900 g small, firm red or purple
plums, scrubbed

Makes two 1 litre jars

Enjoy the enticing spices of these aromatic plums – the perfect partner to roast pork or lamb.

1 In a saucepan, combine the sugar and 2⅔ cups (670 ml) water. Bring to a boil over medium–high heat, stirring to dissolve the sugar. Reduce the heat and simmer for 10 minutes.
2 Stir in the vinegar, cinnamon sticks, cloves, peppercorns and orange zest. Cover the pan and gently simmer for 15 minutes.
3 Using a sterilised skewer, prick each plum in several places. Divide the plums between two warm, sterilised, wide-mouthed, 1 litre jars. Pour the hot, spiced syrup over the plums to cover them, leaving a 3 mm space between the top of the syrup and the rim of the jars.
4 Wipe the rims of the jars, cover and process for 25 minutes in boiling water (see Safe Bottling and Preserving, page 72). Cool, label, date and store in a cool, dark place; the plums will be ready to eat in 4 weeks. Once a jar has been opened, store in the refrigerator.

Safe bottling and preserving

Pickling and preserving your food extends its shelf-life by ridding it of micro-organisms and discouraging their growth. A simple way to do this is with a 'hot water bath', where food is processed at a high enough temperature for a long enough time to knock out bugs. To prevent a fresh batch of bugs creeping in, it is essential that our freshly preserved or pickled goods go straight into jars that have just been sterilised, which again is very easy to do. You can buy preserving kits, or put one together yourself. Here's what you need to do.

❖ **You will need:**
- 1 large, deep, heavy-based, non-metallic saucepan or stockpot with a tight-fitting lid
- 1 wire rack or basket to fit the saucepan
- Glass jars and lids (the jars and metal screw bands to hold the lids in place can be reused; new lids must be used every time)
- Tongs (to transfer hot jars)
- Additional wire racks for cooling the jars

❖ **Here is how to proceed:**
1 Start by sterilising all the jars. Wash them in hot, soapy water, rinse thoroughly and place in a saucepan of boiling water that covers the jars by 2–3 cm; boil for 10 minutes. Remove the saucepan from the heat, but let the jars sit in the water until ready to use.
2 Prepare the lids following the manufacturer's directions.
3 Once the food is cooked, remove the cooking saucepan from the heat. Carefully remove the jars from the hot water and place on a wooden chopping board (placing them straight on a cold workbench could cause them to crack). Ladle the food into the warm, clean jars, leaving a 3–6 mm space between the top of the food and the rim of the jar as specified in the recipe. Run a sterilised spatula around the inside of the jar to remove any large air bubbles.
4 Using a clean, damp cloth, wipe the rims of each jar. Following the manufacturer's directions, apply the lids and screw bands.
5 Place a wire rack in the processing saucepan and fill halfway with hot water. Place the filled jars on the rack, then add boiling water (pour around the jars, not directly on them) until they are covered by at least 2–3 cm of boiling water. Cover the saucepan.

Set the saucepan over high heat and bring the water to a boil; begin timing when the water comes to a rolling boil. Process for the time specified in the recipe.
6 When the processing time has been reached, use the tongs to transfer the jars from the saucepan to a second wire rack and let the jars cool completely; be sure to leave space between the jars on the rack. Let the jars stand for 12 to 24 hours.
7 Gently press the centre of each lid: if the depression in the centre holds, the seal is good, so you can remove the screw band and store the jar; if the depression does not hold, the seal is not good and you should store the jar in the refrigerator and use the food immediately.
8 Label and date each jar. Store in a dark, cool (4°C to 15°C) storage space; check the seals periodically and just before opening. Any jar that leaks, or food that smells or looks questionable when opened, should be discarded. Never taste food to check for freshness.

Roasted Red Capsicums in Oil

1.8 kg (about 8 medium) firm
   red capsicums (peppers),
   halved, cored and seeded
2 tablespoons coriander seeds
1 tablespoon peppercorns
5 cloves garlic
5 bay leaves
olive oil, to cover

Makes three 500 ml jars

Colourful and luscious, these capsicums (peppers) are a must for any antipasto platter and make a superb snack on crusty bread.

1 Place the capsicums under a hot grill, skin side up, for about 10 minutes, until the skins are charred. Transfer the hot capsicums to a large heatproof bowl, cover with plastic wrap and cool for about 10 minutes, until safe to handle. Peel the skins, then thickly slice the capsicums.

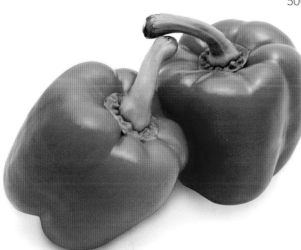

2 Transfer the capsicums to three warm, sterilised, wide-mouthed, 500 ml jars, dividing them equally. Add some of the coriander seeds, peppercorns, garlic and bay leaves to each jar, dividing them equally and arranging capsicums and spices attractively.

3 Pour olive oil into each jar to cover the capsicums, leaving a 6 mm space between the top of the oil and the rim of the jars. Using a sterilised skewer, expel any air bubbles from the oil. Wipe the rims of the jars, cover and store in the refrigerator for up to 1 month; the capsicums will be ready to eat within a few days.

Oven-dried Tomatoes

1.8 kg roma or large cherry
   tomatoes, halved
¼ cup (75 g) pickling salt
¼ teaspoon freshly ground
   black pepper
2 tablespoons dried marjoram
olive oil, to cover

Makes two 500 ml jars

Oven drying is an easy, relatively quick way to preserve garden-fresh tomatoes.

1 Preheat the oven to very low, just below 100°C (Gas ½).

2 Using a teaspoon, remove the seeds but not the fibrous tissue from the tomato halves. Line a baking tray with foil. Place the tomatoes, cut side up, on the baking tray and sprinkle them with the salt, pepper and marjoram. Place the baking tray in the oven and bake for 12 to 24 hours; check periodically to be sure the tomatoes are drying, not cooking. As they dry, the tomatoes will slowly darken and wrinkle. Small tomatoes may take only 12 hours to dry; large tomatoes may take as long as 24 hours.

3 Spoon the tomatoes into two warm, sterilised, 500 ml jars. Pour olive oil over the tomatoes to cover, leaving a 3 mm space between the top of the oil and the rim of the jar. Wipe the rims of the jars, cover and cool. Label, date and store in the refrigerator for up to 1 month.

Chutneys

Mango Chutney

2.25 kg green mangoes (4–5),
  stoned, peeled and chopped
1 teaspoon pickling salt
1¼ cups (310 ml) cider vinegar
1¼ cups (310 ml) non-alcoholic
  apple cider, or apple juice
1 tablespoon chopped fresh
  ginger
2 teaspoons ground cayenne
  pepper
1 large onion, chopped
1½ cups (345 g) firmly packed
  soft brown sugar

Makes six 250 ml jars

The pungent flavour of fresh ginger and the heat of
cayenne pepper combine in this classic companion to
spicy curries.

1 In a large, non-metallic bowl, sprinkle the mangoes with the
  salt. Set aside for 24 hours.
2 Rinse the mangoes under cold, running water, then drain
  thoroughly and place in a very large, heavy-based, non-metallic
  saucepan. Add the vinegar, apple cider, ginger, cayenne pepper,
  onion and sugar. Simmer the mixture, uncovered, over low
  heat for 30 to 40 minutes.
3 Spoon the chutney into six warm, sterilised, wide-mouthed
  250 ml jars, leaving a 3 mm space between the top of the
  chutney and the rim of the jar. Wipe the rims, cover the jars
  and process for 10 minutes in boiling water (see Safe Bottling
  and Preserving, page 72). Cool, label, date and store in a cool,
  dark place; the chutney will be ready to eat in 4 weeks. Once
  a jar has been opened, store in the refrigerator.

Spicy Tomato Chutney

2.25 kg tomatoes
5 onions, chopped
3 cloves garlic, crushed
2 tablespoons mustard powder
1 tablespoon salt
1 tablespoon chopped fresh
  ginger
1 tablespoon cumin seeds
2 teaspoons ground turmeric
1 teaspoon mustard seeds
1 teaspoon ground cayenne
  pepper
1 cup (250 ml) cider vinegar

Makes eight 250 ml jars

Turmeric, cumin, mustard and cayenne pepper all add
spice to this intense, easy-to-make chutney. Stir a dollop
into curry as it is cooking to add even more flavour,
then serve the chutney on the side for extra spice.

1 In a very large, heavy-based, non-metallic saucepan, combine
  all the ingredients. Bring the mixture to a boil over medium–
  high heat; reduce the heat to low and gently simmer, uncovered
  and stirring occasionally, for 50 to 60 minutes, until thickened.
2 Spoon the chutney into eight warm, sterilised, wide-mouthed
  250 ml jars, leaving a 6 mm space between the top of the
  chutney and the rim of the jar. Wipe the rims, cover the jars
  and process for 10 minutes in boiling water (see Safe Bottling
  and Preserving, page 72). Cool, label, date and store in a cool,
  dark place; the chutney will be ready to eat in 4 weeks. Once
  a jar has been opened, store in the refrigerator.

Green Tomato Chutney

1.8 kg green tomatoes, chopped
2 onions, chopped
1 large green apple, peeled,
  cored and chopped
¾ cup (90 g) raisins
1 teaspoon salt
1 teaspoon ground allspice
1 teaspoon curry powder
½ teaspoon ground cayenne
  pepper
1 cup (230 g) firmly packed
  soft brown sugar
2 cups (500 ml) cider vinegar

Makes six 250 ml jars

If it looks like all your tomatoes will ripen at once, harvest some green ones now and put up a few jars of this tasty condiment.

1 In a very large, heavy-based, non-metallic saucepan, combine all the ingredients. Over low heat, bring the mixture to a simmer and gently cook, uncovered, for about 45 minutes, until thickened. Stir occasionally to prevent the chutney burning; remove from the heat if the chutney begins to dry out.

2 Spoon the chutney into six warm, sterilised, wide-mouthed, 250 ml jars, leaving a 6 mm space between the top of the chutney and the rim of the jar. Wipe the rims, cover the jars and process for 10 minutes in boiling water (see Safe Bottling and Preserving, page 72). Cool, label, date and store in a cool, dark place; the chutney will be ready to eat in 4 weeks. Once a jar has been opened, store in the refrigerator.

Lemon Lime Chutney

4 large lemons, washed and
  wiped
2 limes, washed and wiped
2 onions, chopped
1 teaspoon salt
2½ cups (625 ml) cider vinegar
¾ cup (90 g) raisins
1 tablespoon mustard seeds
1 teaspoon ground ginger
½ teaspoon ground cayenne
  pepper
2 cups (440 g) sugar

Makes five 250 ml jars

This citrus sensation is superb with mildly spiced couscous and lamb. It's an expensive luxury when shop-bought, but an inexpensive treat when you make it at home.

1 Finely chop the whole lemons and limes, including the skin, and remove any seeds. In a large bowl, combine the chopped lemons, limes and onions. Sprinkle the mixture with the salt, then set aside for 12 hours.

2 Pour the lemon mixture and all the juices into a large, heavy-based, non-metallic saucepan. Bring the mixture to a simmer over medium heat, then gently cook, uncovered, until the fruit is soft. Stir in the vinegar, raisins, mustard seeds, ginger, cayenne pepper and sugar. Increase the heat and bring the mixture to a boil; reduce the heat and simmer, uncovered, for about 45 minutes, until thickened.

3 Spoon the chutney into five warm, sterilised, wide-mouthed, 250 ml jars, leaving a 6 mm space between the top of the chutney and the rim of the jar. Wipe the rims, cover and process for 10 minutes in boiling water (see Safe Bottling and Preserving, page 72). Cool, label, date and store the jars in a cool, dark place; the chutney will be ready to eat in 4 weeks. Once a jar has been opened, store in the refrigerator.

Jams, Jellies and Marmalades

Dried-apricot Jam

2½ cups (450 g) dried apricots
3½ cups (875 ml) orange juice
¾ cup (165 g) sugar
1 tablespoon lemon juice
½ teaspoon ground cinnamon
¼ teaspoon ground ginger

Makes four 250 ml jars

Buy dried apricots in bulk at health food shops, or look for them on sale and stock up. Using dried apricots intensifies the flavour, giving you a superior jam at a reasonable price.

1 In a very large, heavy-based, non-metallic saucepan or stockpot, combine the apricots, orange juice and sugar. Bring the mixture to a boil over medium–high heat; reduce the heat, cover the saucepan and simmer for 30 minutes.
2 Stir in the lemon juice, cinnamon and ginger. Remove the pan from the heat and let the mixture cool to room temperature.
3 Transfer the mixture to a food processor or blender and purée. Spoon the purée into four warm, sterilised, wide-mouthed 250 ml jars, leaving a 6 mm space between the top of the jam and the rim of the jar. Wipe the rims, cover and process for 10 minutes in boiling water (see Safe Bottling and Preserving, page 72). Cool, label, date and store in a cool, dark place; the jam will be ready to eat in 2 weeks. Once a jar has been opened, store in the refrigerator.

The trio of good jamming ingredients

To make a great jam, jelly or marmalade, you need three components to work in harmony: acid, pectin and sugar. If the proportions of each or any one of these is off, you may not be happy with the results.

❖ **Acid** Added to the mixture as citrus juice (usually lemon) or tartaric acid, this improves both the taste and appearance of the finished product, and in conjunction with pectin, helps the mixture to gel.

❖ **Pectin** Most fruits contain some amount of pectin naturally and it is released when the fruit is boiled, but not all fruits are created equal. Apples are known for their pectin, so they are sometimes added in one form or another to fruits that are lower in pectin to help them gel. Currants and red plums are also high-pectin fruits; moderate-pectin fruits include apricots, blueberries, peaches and raspberries. Pectin is also found in peels (particularly citrus) and seeds, so these are sometimes included in part of a recipe to release their pectin during cooking. Pectin is also available in powdered form (check out health-food shops and larger supermarkets) and in liquid form in some countries. If you make jams regularly, it is prudent to keep some pectin on hand, just in case your jam, marmalade or jelly is not setting. Always follow the manufacturer's directions carefully.

❖ **Sugar** Another factor in gelling, sugar also helps to preserve the fruit. It really brings out the flavour of the fruit, in addition to adding sweetness and countering any bitterness.

Lemony Fig Jam

2¾ cups (500 g) dried figs,
  washed and roughly chopped
3 cups (660 g) sugar
zest and juice of 2 lemons
½ cup (80 g) pine nuts, lightly
  toasted

Makes three 250 ml jars

The tart lemons set off the sweet figs in this distinctively different jam. It makes a lovely gift without needing to go to an expensive food specialty store.

1 In a bowl, combine the figs and 4 cups (1 litre) water. Cover and let stand for 12 hours or overnight.
2 Transfer the figs and soaking water to a very large, heavy-based, non-metallic saucepan or stockpot. Bring the mixture to a boil over high heat; reduce the heat to low and simmer for 35 minutes.
3 Add the sugar, lemon zest and juice and stir until the sugar has dissolved. Return the mixture to a boil, then reduce the heat slightly and cook for 10 to 15 minutes, until the jam thickens. Using a slotted spoon, skim off any foam that rises to the surface. Add the pine nuts and stir until well combined.
4 Remove the saucepan from the heat and stir to distribute the fruit and nuts evenly. Spoon the hot jam into three warm, sterilised, wide-mouthed 250 ml jars, leaving a 6 mm space between the top of the jam and the rim of the jar. Wipe the rims, cover and process for 10 minutes in boiling water (see Safe Bottling and Preserving, page 72). Cool, label, date and store in a cool, dark place; the jam will be ready to eat in 2 weeks. Once a jar has been opened, store in the refrigerator.

Pear Jam

8 cups (about 2.5 kg) peeled,
  cored and chopped pears
4 cups (880 g) sugar
1 teaspoon ground cinnamon
¼ teaspoon ground cloves

Makes six 250 ml jars

Jazzed up with cinnamon and cloves, this spicy jam can be made for very little money, and doesn't require any pectin to thicken it.

1 In a very large, heavy-based, non-metallic saucepan or stockpot, combine all the ingredients. Simmer the mixture, uncovered, over medium–low heat for 1½ to 2 hours, until thickened. Occasionally stir the mixture while it cooks, increasing the frequency of stirring as the mixture thickens.
2 Remove the saucepan from the heat; skim off any foam that rises to the surface. Spoon the hot jam into six warm, sterilised, wide-mouthed, 250 ml jars, leaving a 6 mm space between the top of the jam and the rim of the jar. Wipe the rims, cover and process for 10 minutes in boiling water (see Safe Bottling and Preserving, page 72). Cool, label, date and store in a cool, dark place. Once a jar has been opened, store in the refrigerator.

Peach Jam

1 kg peaches (about 4)
3 strips (1 cm x 5 cm) orange zest
⅔ cup (170 ml) fresh orange juice
⅔ cup (170 ml) unsweetened white grape juice
⅔ cup (155 g) firmly packed soft brown sugar
1 tablespoon lemon juice
¼ teaspoon ground ginger

Makes six 250 ml jars

The natural sweetness of peaches means you don't need to add much sugar. Peaches are cheap in summer, so buy them in season and put up enough jars for the year.

1 In a very large, heavy-based, non-metallic saucepan or stockpot, bring 8–10 cups (2–2.5 litres) water to a boil over medium–high heat. Add the peaches, two at a time, and boil for 30 seconds. Using a slotted spoon, transfer the peaches to a colander and rinse with cold water; the skins should slide off easily. Peel, stone and roughly chop the peaches.

2 Place the chopped peaches in a large, heavy-based, non-metallic saucepan or stockpot with the orange zest and juice, grape juice, sugar, lemon juice and ginger. Slowly bring the mixture to a boil over medium heat. Boil, stirring frequently, for about 30 minutes, until the jam thickens.

3 Remove the saucepan from the heat and stir to distribute the fruit evenly; skim off any foam that rises to the surface, then remove and discard the orange zest. Spoon the hot jam into six warm, sterilised, wide-mouthed, 250 ml jars, leaving a 6 mm space between the top of the jam and the rim of the jar. Wipe the rims, cover and process for 10 minutes in boiling water (see Safe Bottling and Preserving, page 72). Cool, label, date and store in a cool, dark place. Once a jar has been opened, store in the refrigerator.

Melon Ginger Jam

6¼ cups (1 kg) peeled, seeded and finely chopped jam melon
1 cup (220 g) glacé ginger, diced, or 100 g peeled, finely chopped fresh ginger
4½ cups (1 kg) sugar
juice of 6 lemons
¼ teaspoon ground cayenne pepper

Makes four 250 ml jars

This recipe uses the low-sugar jam melon, the variety traditionally used in jam, rather than eaten fresh. You won't often find these in the shops, but you can grow it from seed; alternatively, use casaba or honeydew melon.

1 In a non-metallic bowl, combine the melon, ginger and sugar, then leave overnight.

2 Place the melon mixture in a very large, heavy-based, non-metallic saucepan or stockpot and boil until it is transparent. Add the lemon juice and cayenne pepper, then continue to boil for 5 to 10 minutes, until the jam reaches the gelling point (see Has It Gelled Yet? page 81). Using a slotted spoon, skim off any foam that rises to the surface.

3 Remove the saucepan from the heat. Spoon the hot jam into four warm, sterilised, wide-mouthed, 250 ml jars, leaving a 6 mm space between the top of the jam and the rim. Wipe the rims, cover and process for 10 minutes in boiling water (see Safe Bottling and Preserving, page 72). Cool, label, date and store in a cool, dark place; the jam will be ready to eat in 2 weeks. Once a jar has been opened, store in the refrigerator.

Strawberry Jam

4 cups (600 g) strawberries,
washed and hulled
¼ cup (60 ml) lemon juice
1 packet (about 50 g)
powdered fruit pectin
7 cups (1.5 kg) sugar

Makes eight 250 ml jars

The price of this dainty fruit goes way down in summer.
Look for the ripest, reddest berries for the best flavour.

1 Place the strawberries in a bowl and crush them, using a potato
masher. You should have about 4 cups of crushed berries.
2 Transfer the crushed berries to a very large, heavy-based,
non-metallic saucepan or stockpot and add the lemon juice.
Stir in the pectin, checking the manufacturer's directions to
make sure that one packet of pectin is appropriate for 4 cups
of strawberries. Bring the mixture to a boil over high heat,
stirring occasionally, then add the sugar and stir until dissolved.
Boil, stirring constantly, for 1 minute.
3 Remove the saucepan from the heat. Using a slotted spoon,
skim off any foam that rises to the surface.
4 Spoon the hot jam into eight warm, sterilised, wide-mouthed,
250 ml jars, leaving a 6 mm space between the top of the jam
and the rim of the jar. Wipe the rims, cover and process for
10 minutes in boiling water (see Safe Bottling and Preserving,
page 72). Cool, label, date and store in a cool, dark place;
the jam will be ready to eat in 2 weeks. Once a jar has been
opened, store in the refrigerator.

Three-berry Jam

4 cups (620 g) blueberries,
fresh or frozen
2½ cups (310 g) raspberries,
fresh or frozen
2½ cups (375 g) strawberries,
fresh or frozen
¼ cup (60 ml) lemon juice
2 packets (50 g each) powdered
fruit pectin
11 cups (2.4 kg) sugar

Makes six 500 ml jars

This sweet salute to summer makes the most of berries
in season. Combining three berries makes a deliciously
different jam, and so much cheaper than shop-bought.

1 In a very large, heavy-based, non-metallic saucepan or
stockpot, combine the blueberries, raspberries, strawberries
and lemon juice. Slightly crush the fruit using the back of a
wooden spoon. Stir in the pectin, checking the manufacturer's
directions to ensure that two packets of pectin is appropriate
for the quantity and type of berries. Bring the mixture to a boil
over high heat, stirring constantly.
2 Add the sugar, return the mixture to a boil, then boil for
1 minute, stirring constantly. Remove the saucepan from the
heat; skim off any foam that rises to the surface.
3 Spoon the hot jam into six warm, sterilised, wide-mouthed,
500 ml jars, leaving a 6 mm space between the top of the jam
and the rim of the jar. Wipe the rims, cover and process for
15 minutes in boiling water (see Safe Bottling and Preserving,
page 72). Cool, label, date and store in a cool, dark place.
Once a jar has been opened, store in the refrigerator.

Apple Ginger Jelly

2.5 kg green apples (8–10),
 roughly chopped, core and
 peel intact
½ cup (125 ml) lemon juice
3 cm piece fresh ginger, peeled
 and bruised
sugar

Makes five 250 ml jars

Although you remove the solids later, the naturally rich pectin in the apple seeds means you don't need to add commercial pectin to this delicious jelly.

1 In a very large, heavy-based, non-metallic saucepan or stockpot, combine the apples, lemon juice, ginger and 6 cups (1.5 litres) water. Bring the mixture to a simmer over medium heat, then simmer for 25 to 30 minutes, until the fruit is very soft.

2 Strain the apple mixture through a wet jelly bag overnight (see A Bag to Give You Perfectly Clear Jelly, page 82).

3 Measure the juice; to each 1 cup (250 ml) juice, you'll need ¾ cup (165 g) sugar. In a large, non-metallic saucepan over medium–high heat, bring the apple juice to a boil; add the appropriate amount of sugar and stir until the sugar has dissolved. Slightly reduce the heat and gently boil the mixture for 5 to 10 minutes, until the jelly reaches the gelling point (see Has It Gelled Yet?, opposite). Using a slotted spoon, skim off any foam that rises to the surface.

4 Remove the saucepan from the heat. Spoon the hot jelly into five warm, sterilised, wide-mouthed, 250 ml jars, leaving a 6 mm space between the top of the jelly and the rim of the jar. Wipe the rims, cover and process for 10 minutes in boiling water (see Safe Bottling and Preserving, page 72). Cool, label, date and store in a cool, dark place; the jelly will be ready to eat in 2 weeks. Once a jar has been opened, store in the refrigerator.

Quince Jelly

2 kg just-ripe quinces
   (about 6), scrubbed and
   cut into eighths
juice of 2 lemons, or
   2 teaspoons citric acid
sugar

Makes two 500 ml jars

These fruit turn from green to bright yellow when fully ripe. Too astringent to eat raw, they're at their best when cooked into an apple pie or savoured as quince jelly.

1   In a very large, heavy-based, non-metallic saucepan or stockpot, combine the quinces, lemon juice or citric acid and 8 cups (2 litres) water. Simmer until tender, then strain through a jelly bag for 15 minutes (see A Bag to Give You Perfectly Clear Jelly, page 82). Return the pulp to the pan with the remaining water and simmer for another 30 minutes. Strain. Mix the two batches of juice together and measure this.
2   Return to the pan with 3⅔ cups (800 g) sugar for every 4 cups (1 litre) of juice. Stir until boiling point is reached, then keep boiling until the mixture reaches setting point. Remove the saucepan from the heat; skim off any foam that rises to the surface. Spoon the hot jelly into two warm, sterilised, wide-mouthed 500 ml jars, leaving a 6 mm space between the top of the jelly and the rim of the jar. Wipe the rims, cover and process for 10 minutes in boiling water (see Safe Bottling and Preserving, page 72). Cool, label, date and store in a cool, dark place. Once a jar has been opened, store in the refrigerator.

Has it gelled yet?

The crucial moment in jam- and jelly-making is the temperature at which the mixture gels and no longer needs to be cooked. To determine that 'gelling point', most cooking experts recommend that you use a sugar thermometer, but the plate method works well, too.
❖ **Thermometer** Determine the gelling point for your altitude.

Hold a sugar thermometer vertically in a pot of boiling water. Read the temperature at eye level and add 5°C for the gelling point. From sea level to about 300 metres above, the boiling point should be 100°C and the gelling point is 105°C.
❖ **Plate method** At the point indicated in the recipe, remove the saucepan from the heat

and drop a teaspoonful of the jam or jelly onto a small, cold plate. Lightly press the jam or jelly with a fingertip – the surface should wrinkle, which indicates that it has begun to gel. If the jam or jelly is still too liquid or does not pass the press test, return the saucepan to the heat and cook a few minutes longer, then retest.

Mint Jelly

1 cup (20 g) tightly packed
  fresh mint leaves
½ cup (125 ml) cider vinegar
3½ cups (770 g) sugar
1 packet (about 50 g)
  powdered pectin
5 drops green food colouring

Makes three or four
250 ml jars

The classic, emerald-green accompaniment to lamb,
this jelly makes an eye-catching gift. You can make
your own very inexpensively, particularly if you have
a patch of mint.

1 Wash the mint, remove the stems and coarsely chop the
  leaves. Place in a very large, heavy-based, non-metallic
  saucepan or stockpot with the vinegar, sugar and 1 cup
  (250 ml) water. Stir in the pectin, checking the manufacturer's
  directions to make sure that one packet of pectin is
  appropriate for this quantity of jelly.
2 Over high heat, bring the mixture to a boil, stirring constantly.
  Remove the saucepan from the heat and add the food
  colouring. Place back over the heat, return to a boil, then
  boil for 30 seconds. Remove from the heat and strain the
  mixture through two layers of muslin (cheesecloth).
3 Spoon the hot jelly into three or four warm, sterilised,
  wide-mouthed, 250 ml jars, leaving a 6 mm space
  between the top of the jelly and the rim of the jar.
  Wipe the rims, cover and process for 10 minutes
  in boiling water (see Safe Bottling and Preserving,
  page 72). Cool, label, date and store in a cool,
  dark place. Once a jar has been opened, store
  in the refrigerator.

A bag to give you perfectly clear jelly

Jelly is meant to be crystal clear, unlike
jams and marmalades, so removing even
the tiniest solid particles is crucial to
achieving perfect results. Fortunately,
there is equipment to facilitate the desired
finished product: a jelly bag.

  Cone-shaped with a hanging handle, a
jelly bag forces the solids out of the jelly
mixture over a period of time (generally
12 hours or overnight). After boiling the

fruit with the liquid, dampen the jelly
bag and hang it over a large, non-metallic
bowl or saucepan. Pour the boiled fruit
and liquid through, then let it stand for
the specified amount of time. The weight
of the fruit solids will be enough to press
down and push out the liquid; don't
squeeze the bag to extrude more liquid
or you may make the jelly cloudy.

How to make perfect marmalade

A dose of patience and careful attention to stirring are the two qualities needed to make marmalade – the first so you don't try to hurry the process, and the second to avoid scorching the fruit or syrup and tainting the finished taste. Unlike clear jelly, or thicker jam with puréed or chunks of fruit, marmalade is a thick syrup with bits of fruit that are cooked until they are almost translucent.

Seville Orange Marmalade

1 kg (4–6) Seville oranges, washed
juice of 3 lemons
8 cups (1.8 kg) sugar
¼ cup (90 ml) Scotch whisky (optional)

Makes eight 250 ml jars

This is what most people think of when they hear the word 'marmalade'. If Seville oranges are difficult to find, substitute any firm, thin-skinned variety, such as Valencia. Here, the pectin in the orange seeds helps the marmalade set.

1 Using a sharp knife, cut the oranges crosswise into thin slices, catching any juice and reserving the seeds. Combine the oranges with their juice in a large bowl with 4 cups (1 litre) water. Tie the reserved seeds up in a bag of muslin (cheesecloth) and add it to the bowl. Cover the bowl and let the orange mixture stand in a cool place for 18 hours.

2 Transfer the orange mixture to a very large, heavy-based, non-metallic saucepan or stockpot and add the lemon juice. Simmer the mixture, uncovered, over medium–low heat for 20 to 30 minutes, until the orange zest is tender.

3 Add the sugar and stir until it has dissolved. Bring the mixture to a boil and cook for 30 to 40 minutes, until the marmalade has reached the gelling point (see Has It Gelled Yet?, page 81). Using a slotted spoon, skim off any foam that rises to the surface.

4 Remove the saucepan from the heat, then stir to distribute the fruit evenly. Spoon the hot marmalade into eight warm, sterilised, wide-mouthed, 250 ml jars, leaving a 6 mm space between the top of the marmalade and the rim of the jar. Wipe the rims, cover and process for 10 minutes in boiling water (see Safe Bottling and Preserving, page 72). Cool, label, date and store in a cool, dark place; the marmalade will be ready to eat in 2 weeks. Once a jar has been opened, store in the refrigerator.

Citrus Marmalade

1 large grapefruit, washed
1 large orange, washed
1 large lemon, washed
12 cups (2.6 kg) sugar

Makes eight 250 ml jars

Popularity and tradition marry in this bright marmalade, composed of grapefruit, orange and lemon. Be sure to leave enough time, as it needs to stand for two 12 hour (or overnight) periods for the flavours to develop.

1 Using a sharp knife, cut the grapefruit, orange and lemon crosswise into thin slices, then cut each slice into quarters. Remove the seeds and tie in a bag of muslin (cheesecloth).
2 Combine the fruit, bag of seeds and 3 cups (750 ml) water in a very large, heavy-based, non-metallic saucepan or stockpot. Bring the mixture to a boil and cook for 10 minutes. Remove the saucepan from the heat, cover and let stand in a cool place for 12 hours.
3 Return the mixture to a boil over high heat; reduce the heat to medium and cook for about 40 minutes, until the zests are tender. Remove the pan from the heat, cover and let stand in a cool place for a further 12 hours.
4 Reheat the mixture over medium heat. Add the sugar and stir until the sugar has dissolved. Return the mixture to a boil and cook for 20 to 30 minutes, until the marmalade has reached the gelling point (see Has It Gelled Yet?, page 81). Using a slotted spoon, skim off any foam that rises to the surface.
5 Remove the saucepan from the heat, then stir to distribute the fruit evenly. Spoon the hot marmalade into eight warm, sterilised, wide-mouthed, 250 ml jars, leaving a 6 mm space between the top of the marmalade and the rim of the jar. Wipe the rims, cover and process for 10 minutes in boiling water (see Safe Bottling and Preserving, page 72). Cool, label, date and store in a cool, dark place; the marmalade will be ready to eat in 2 weeks. Once a jar has been opened, store in the refrigerator.

Frozen Vegetables

Freeze vegetables in self-sealing freezer bags that you have labelled and dated with a permanent marker; be sure to expel any excess air from the bag before sealing. Once the vegetables have thawed, do not refreeze.

Asparagus

1–1.3 kg fresh yields 4 cups frozen

Wash, trim and cut into 5 cm pieces. Sort the asparagus according to the thickness of the spears; water-blanch thin spears for 2 minutes, and thick spears for 4 minutes. Rinse briefly under cold water and drain thoroughly. Pack, seal, label, date and freeze.

Beetroot

1–1.3 kg fresh yields 4 cups frozen

Wash and trim, leaving 3 cm stems (be careful not to pierce the skins). Sort according to size and cook small beetroot in boiling water for 25 to 30 minutes, and large ones for 45 to 50 minutes, until tender when pierced with a fork. Drain and cool. Peel off the skins and slice or cube the flesh, as desired. Pack, seal, label, date and freeze.

Broad Beans

1 kg fresh yields 4 cups frozen

Shell young, tender beans and discard any damaged ones. Water-blanch small beans for 1 minute, medium beans for 2 minutes and large beans for 3 minutes. Cool quickly and drain thoroughly. Pack, seal, label, date and freeze.

How to blanch vegetables

You can blanch vegetables with either boiling water or steam. Which method you use – and the time required to do it – depends on the vegetable involved.

❖ Water-blanching Bring at least 12 cups (3 litres) water to a boil in a large saucepan. Place 500 g prepared vegetable pieces in a wire-mesh basket and plunge into the boiling water. When the water returns to a boil, cook the vegetables for the time required. Lift the basket and place it into a large bowl of cold or ice water to cool; change the water or add ice to keep the water cold. Drain completely.

❖ Steam-blanching Place the prepared vegetables in a single layer inside a steamer basket in a large saucepan containing 5 cm of boiling water. Cover and steam the vegetables for the time required. Cool, but don't rinse the vegetables.

Broccoli and Cauliflower

900 g–1 kg fresh yields 4 cups frozen

Wash and peel the stalks if woody. Cut the stalks and florets into 4 cm pieces. Steam-blanch for 5 minutes. Cool quickly and drain thoroughly. Pack, seal, label, date and freeze.

Brussels Sprouts

900 g–1 kg fresh yields 4 cups frozen

Trim off coarse leaves and stems, then sort by size. Water-blanch small sprouts for 3 minutes, large sprouts for 5 minutes. Cool quickly and drain thoroughly. Pack, seal, label, date and freeze.

Capsicums (Peppers)

1.3 kg fresh yields 4 cups frozen

Cut out the stems and any seeds. Halve or cut the capsicums into slices or rings. Blanch the halves for 2 minutes, and slices and rings for 1 minute. Cool quickly and drain thoroughly. Pack, seal, label, date and freeze.

Carrots

1–1.3 kg fresh yields 4 cups frozen

Wash, trim and, if desired, cut into 5 cm pieces or 5 cm slices. Blanch whole carrots for 5 minutes, slices for 2 minutes. Rinse briefly under cold water and drain thoroughly. Pack, seal, label, date and freeze.

Green Beans

800 g–1 kg fresh yields 4 cups frozen

Wash, then trim tops and any blemishes. Small green beans may be water-blanched whole; cut the larger beans into 5 cm pieces. Blanch whole beans for 3 minutes, pieces for 2 minutes. Cool quickly and drain thoroughly. Pack, seal, label, date and freeze.

Mushrooms

450 g–1 kg fresh yields 4 cups frozen

Wipe with a damp cloth to remove any dirt; do not peel or rinse.
Button varieties: Spread whole, raw mushrooms on a baking tray and place in the freezer. When they are hard, pack, seal, label, date and freeze.
Wild mushrooms (portobello, shiitake): Slice and sauté in butter. Pour the mushrooms with the cooking liquid into individual bags. Seal, label, date and freeze.

Peas

1 kg fresh yields 4 cups frozen

Peas: Shell the peas, discarding any damaged ones; water-blanch for 1½ minutes. Cool quickly and drain thoroughly. Pack, seal, label, date and freeze.

Sugar snap or snow peas (mangetout): String the pods and water-blanch for 2 minutes. Cool quickly and drain thoroughly. Pack, seal, label, date and freeze.

Pumpkin and Sweet Potato

1.3 kg fresh yields 4 cups frozen purée

Wash, peel and cut in half; remove any seeds and strings. Cut into slices or cubes, then steam-blanch until tender. Mash and let cool completely. Pack in plastic dishes (leaving a 1 cm space at the top), then seal, label, date and freeze.

Sweet Corn

1 kg fresh kernels yields 4 cups frozen

Ears: Use young cobs only; remove the husks and silks. Water-blanch for 4 minutes. Cool quickly and drain well. Individually wrap each ear in freezer paper or foil, moulding it to the shape of the ear, so it is airtight. Pack several together in a freezer bag, expelling as much air as possible.

Kernels: Blanch the ears as above and cool completely. Using a very sharp knife, cut the kernels off the cobs and separate into meal-sized portions. Pack, seal, label, date and freeze.

Mixed Vegetables

Mix together family favourites, such as peas and corn, peas and beans, or a stir-fry such as broccoli, carrot, baby corn, beans, mushrooms and red capsicum.

Chop larger vegetables or cut them into bite-sized pieces. Blanch according to directions for each individual vegetable, noting that a shorter blanching time may be required for smaller piece size. When they are cool, mix the vegetables and pack in plastic freezer bags in meal-sized quantities. Seal, label, date and freeze.

Frozen Fruit

Use only unblemished fruit and keep the handling time to a minimum (fruit tends to brown when handled). To stop cut fruit turning brown, follow the 'dipping' instructions. Be sure to expel any excess air before sealing the freezer bags. Thaw frozen fruit in the bag in the refrigerator for several hours, or place the bag in a bowl of cool water for 30 minutes.

Apples

1–1.3 kg fresh yields 4 cups prepared

Peel, core and slice the apples. Dip and drain the slices thoroughly. Arrange in a single layer on a baking tray and freeze until just firm. Pack, seal, label, date and freeze.

Apricots

600–700 g fresh yields 4 cups prepared

Halve and stone the apricots, then slice if desired. Dip and drain the halves or slices thoroughly. Arrange in a single layer on a baking tray and freeze until just firm. Pack, seal, label, date and freeze.

Blackberries

450 g fresh yields 4 cups prepared

Remove the stems and leaves. Dip and drain the berries thoroughly. Arrange in a single layer on a baking tray and freeze until just firm. Pack, seal, label, date and freeze.

Blueberries

450–700 g fresh yields 4 cups prepared

Remove any stems. Dip and drain the berries thoroughly. Arrange in a single layer on a baking tray and freeze until just firm. Pack, seal, label, date and freeze.

Cherries

900 g–1.3 kg fresh yields 4 cups prepared

Stem and pit the cherries. Dip and drain thoroughly. Arrange in a single layer on a baking tray and freeze until just firm. Pack, seal, label, date and freeze.

Mangoes

1–1.3 kg fresh yields 4 cups prepared

Halve and stone the mangoes, then slice if desired. Dip and drain the halves or slices thoroughly. Arrange in a single layer on a baking tray and freeze until just firm. Pack, seal, label, date and freeze.

Peaches and Plums

900 g–1.3 kg fresh yields 4 cups prepared

Halve and stone the fruit, then slice, if desired. Dip and drain the slices or halves thoroughly. Arrange in a single layer on a baking tray and freeze until just firm. Pack, seal, label, date and freeze.

Raspberries

450 g fresh yields 4 cups prepared

Remove the stems and leaves. Dip and drain the berries thoroughly. Arrange in a single layer on a baking tray and freeze until just firm. Pack, seal, label, date and freeze.

Redcurrants and Blackcurrants

450–700 g fresh yields 4 cups prepared

Remove any stems. Dip and drain the currants thoroughly. Arrange in a single layer on a baking tray and freeze until just firm. Pack, seal, label, date and freeze.

Strawberries

600 g fresh yields 4 cups frozen

Remove the leaves and hull the strawberries; slice or leave whole. Dip and drain the berries thoroughly. Arrange in a single layer on a baking tray and freeze until just firm. Pack, seal, label, date and freeze.

How to prepare fruit for freezing

'Dipping' cut fruit before freezing stops it browning. When working, keep fresh fruit in a bowl of acidulated water (about 8 cups/ 2 litres water with 1½ tablespoons of lemon juice or mild vinegar added). After dipping, drain the fruit on paper towels to remove as much moisture as possible. This prevents ice from forming around the pieces and stops them sticking together.

Quick Breads

Beer Bread ❖ Cheese and Parsley Bread ❖ Corn Bread ❖ Cheese Bread ❖ Irish Soda Bread ❖ Olive and Sun-dried Tomato Bread ❖ Sesame Pumpkin Bread ❖ Banana Nut Bread ❖ Carrot Bread ❖ Pecan Bread ❖ Zucchini Bread

Yeast Breads

French Bread ❖ Multigrain Bread ❖ Soy and Linseed Bread ❖ Focaccia ❖ Challah ❖ Brioche ❖ Cinnamon–Raisin Swirl Bread ❖ Pita Bread ❖ Sourdough Bread

Muffins

Apple and Raisin Muffins ❖ Choc-chip Muffins ❖ Blueberry Muffins ❖ Bran Muffins ❖ Herb and Bacon Muffins ❖ Cheese and Cranberry Muffins

Rolls

Potato Dinner Rolls ❖ Bagels ❖ Soda Bread Rolls ❖ Cinnamon Scrolls ❖ Hot Cross Buns ❖ Sticky Buns

Cakes

Spice Cake ❖ Chocolate Cake ❖ Rich Dark Fruit Cake ❖ Butter Cake ❖ Angel Cake ❖ Banana Cake ❖ Orange Cake ❖ Cheesecake with Strawberry Glaze ❖ Cupcakes ❖ Vanilla Icing ❖ Chocolate Ganache Icing ❖ Chocolate Buttercream Icing ❖ Simple Glaze Icing ❖ Cream Cheese Icing

Pies and Meringues

Basic Double Crust Pie Pastry ❖ Basic Single Crust Pie Pastry ❖ Puff Pastry ❖ Shortcrust Pastry ❖ Custard Pie ❖ Perfect Apple Pie ❖ Meringue Shells ❖ Pavlova

Biscuits, Slices and Brownies

Chocolate Chip Cookies ❖ Anzac Biscuits ❖ Peanut Butter Biscuits ❖ Coconut Macaroons ❖ Gingersnaps ❖ Digestive Biscuits ❖ Shortbread ❖ Refrigerator Biscuits ❖ Brownies ❖ Chocolate Caramel Slice ❖ Friands

Baked Goods You Can Make

Nothing can compare to the aroma – or taste – of freshly baked bread from your own kitchen. But with the abundance of supermarket bread, it is not a pleasure that we encounter that often anymore.

The sad truth of the matter is that many of those packaged and wrapped breads, rolls, muffins, cakes, pies and biscuits that you find in the typical supermarket may be made from bleached flour – flour that has been stripped of most of its healthy nutrients and fibre. These have often been replaced with additives and preservatives to give the product a longer shelf life.

If your baking has been limited to the occasional pie or birthday cake, you will be pleasantly surprised at how easy, fast and economical it is to make your own everyday baked goods such as bread, rolls and muffins. You will discover not only how much better they taste, but also the enormous variety of savoury and sweet baked bread products you can serve, fresh and additive-free, to your family. The same is true of the really sweet baked goodies – there's an ample selection of cakes, pies and biscuits on the following pages. Some of the cakes can be made in almost no time using the cake mix from Chapter 1, and you can make pies with handmade pastry that is flaky, with a rich flavour that complements any filling.

Quick Breads

Beer Bread

2½ cups (375 g) plain flour
2 tablespoons sugar
2 teaspoons baking powder
1 teaspoon salt
1 cup (250 ml) beer
¼ cup (60 g) plus 2 tablespoons
butter, melted

Makes 1 loaf

The type of beer used will affect the flavour of the bread. Use a light lager for a mild taste – or be bold with a stout (such as Guinness) for a richer, darker flavour.

1 Preheat the oven to 180°C (Gas 4). Lightly grease a 20 x 10 cm loaf tin and line it with baking paper.
2 In a large bowl, sift together the flour, sugar, baking powder and salt. Add the beer and the ¼ cup (60 ml) melted butter, and stir until a soft dough forms.
3 Spoon the dough into the loaf tin and brush the remaining 2 tablespoons of melted butter over the top of the loaf. Bake until the loaf is golden brown and sounds hollow when tapped, 40 to 45 minutes. Turn the loaf out onto a wire rack to cool.

Cheese and Parsley Bread

2 cups (300 g) wholemeal flour
1 teaspoon baking powder
1 teaspoon bicarbonate of soda
¾ cup (90 g) grated cheddar
or ¼ cup (25 g) grated
parmesan
¼ cup (5 g) fresh parsley
1 teaspoon salt
¾ cup (185 ml) milk or
buttermilk

Makes 1 loaf (8 wedges)

Golden, crusty, savoury – this loaf is essentially a big scone and totally irresistible. Quick breads such as this are best eaten on the day they are made.

1 Preheat the oven to 230°C (Gas 8). In a food processor, place the flour, baking powder, bicarbonate of soda, all but 1 tablespoon of the cheese, the parsley and salt. Process until the cheese crumbles into the flour and the parsley is finely chopped.
2 Add the milk or buttermilk all at once, and process just until a soft dough forms, about 5 seconds.
3 Lightly flour a work surface and a baking tray. Turn the dough out onto the work surface and knead gently. Transfer to the baking tray and form into a round loaf. Using a sharp knife, cut the dough almost through into 8 wedge-shaped pieces. Sprinkle the wedges with the remaining tablespoon of cheese.
4 Bake until the loaf is puffed and brown, 20 to 25 minutes. Remove the loaf from the oven, wrap it in a clean lint-free tea towel, and let it cool slightly. Cut through the marked wedges of the bread to serve.

Corn Bread

1½ cups (225 g) plain flour
1¼ cups (185 g) polenta
　(cornmeal)
4 teaspoons baking powder
2 tablespoons sugar
1 teaspoon salt
1 egg
1¼ cups (310 ml) cold milk
¼ cup (60 ml) vegetable oil

Makes 1 loaf (about 9 squares)

This beautiful yellow bread is a wholesome and tasty addition to any meal. Polenta is also known as cornmeal.

1　Preheat the oven to 200°C (Gas 6). Lightly grease a 20 cm square cake tin.
2　In a large bowl, sift together the dry ingredients. In a smaller bowl, combine the egg, milk and oil, then beat until well blended. Make a well in the centre of the dry ingredients. Pour in the milk mixture all at once and, using a fork, stir just until the wet and dry ingredients are blended – do not overmix.
3　Pour the batter into the cake tin and bake until the bread pulls away slightly from the sides of the tin and is lightly browned, 20 to 25 minutes.
4　Transfer the tin to a wire rack and let the bread cool for 10 minutes. Cut into large squares and serve warm.

VARIATION

Corn muffins: Prepare the batter as above, but pour into well-greased or paper-lined muffin cups. Bake until the muffins are lightly browned and springy to the touch, 17 to 20 minutes.

Cheese Bread

2 cups (300 g) plain flour
1 teaspoon baking powder
1 tablespoon sugar
1 teaspoon salt
⅓ cup (90 g) butter, chopped
1 cup (125 g) grated sharp
　cheddar
1 cup (250 ml) milk
1 large egg
1 cup (135 g) grated zucchini
　(courgette), squeezed dry
　in a tea towel to remove
　excess moisture
1 tablespoon grated onion
1 teaspoon dijon mustard

Makes 1 loaf

Use this recipe to make a loaf or muffins – either version is a splendid backdrop to cream cheese, smoked salmon and a few capers. Toasted slices of this bread are delicious with a hearty soup.

1　Preheat the oven to 190°C (Gas 5). Lightly grease a 20 x 10 cm loaf tin.
2　In a large bowl, sift together the flour, baking powder, sugar and salt. Using a pastry blender or two knives, 'cut' in the butter until the mixture resembles coarse crumbs. Stir in the cheese.
3　In a bowl, combine the milk and egg, and beat until well blended. Stir in the zucchini, onion and mustard. Add the milk mixture to the dry ingredients. Using a fork, stir just until all the ingredients are moistened and the dough holds together; do not overmix or the bread may be too heavy.
4　Spoon the dough into the loaf tin. Bake until the bread is well risen and brown, and a skewer inserted into the centre of the loaf comes out clean, 40–45 minutes.
5　Transfer to a wire rack to cool in the tin for 10 minutes, then remove the bread from the tin and let it cool completely.

Irish Soda Bread

4 cups (600 g) plain flour
3 tablespoons sugar
3 teaspoons baking powder
1 teaspoon salt
¾ teaspoon bicarbonate of soda
⅓ cup (90 g) cold butter or
    margarine
1½ cups (225 g) currants
    or raisins
1 tablespoon caraway seeds
2 eggs, lightly beaten
1½ cups (375 ml) buttermilk

Makes 1 loaf

This easy-to-make bread can be topped with a sprinkling of seeds or oatmeal, and is a wonderful accompaniment to stews and hearty soups.

1 Preheat the oven to 180°C (Gas 4). In a large bowl, sift together the flour, sugar, baking powder, salt and bicarbonate of soda. Using a pastry blender or two knives, 'cut' in the butter until the mixture resembles coarse crumbs. Stir in the currants or raisins and caraway seeds.

2 Set aside 1 tablespoon of the beaten egg. In a bowl, combine the buttermilk and remaining eggs and stir until well blended. Make a well in the centre of the flour mixture. Pour the buttermilk mixture into the well and stir just until the flour is moistened and a sticky dough forms.

3 Flour a work surface well. Turn the dough out onto the work surface and, using well-floured hands, knead about 10 times. Shape the dough into a round loaf.

4 Lightly grease a 23 cm round cake tin. Place the loaf in the tin. Using a sharp knife, cut a cross, 5 mm deep, in the top centre of the loaf. Brush the loaf with the reserved egg.

5 Bake until a skewer inserted near the centre of the loaf comes out clean, about 1 hour and 20 minutes. If the top of the loaf browns too quickly, cover loosely with foil for the final 20 minutes of baking time. Transfer to a wire rack and cool in the tin for 10 minutes, then turn out the loaf and leave on the rack to cool completely.

If you run out of buttermilk

If a recipe calls for 1 cup (250 ml) buttermilk and you don't have any on hand, pour 1 tablespoon white vinegar or lemon juice into a 1 cup (250 ml) measure and add enough regular milk to make 1 cup. Or simply substitute 1 cup (250 g) natural yogurt.

Olive and Sun-dried Tomato Bread

2 eggs
⅔ cup (170 ml) milk
2 cups (300 g) plain flour
2 teaspoons baking powder
1 teaspoon sea salt
3 tablespoons oil drained
  from the sun-dried tomatoes,
  or olive oil
½ cup (70 g) black olives in oil,
  drained, pitted and slivered
½ cup (75 g) sun-dried
  tomatoes packed in oil,
  drained and sliced
1 tablespoon finely chopped
  fresh basil or marjoram

Makes 1 loaf

You can almost taste the Mediterranean when you bite into this peasant-style bread, with its strong flavours and chewy texture. Plain or toasted, this recipe is a good accompaniment to a bowl of soup.

1 Preheat the oven to 200°C (Gas 6). Lightly grease a 20 cm spring-form tin.
2 Place the eggs and milk in a food processor or blender. Process just until combined. Sift together the flour and baking powder and add to the milk mixture. Process for 2 minutes; add the salt and oil and process for 1 minute more. Using a spoon, stir in the olives, sun-dried tomatoes and basil or marjoram.
3 Pour the batter into the spring-form tin and bake until a skewer inserted into the bread comes out clean, about 30 minutes.
4 Transfer the tin to a wire rack and let the bread cool slightly. Remove the outer ring of the tin and serve the bread warm.

Sesame Pumpkin Bread

4 cups (600 g) plain flour
¼ cup (55 g) sugar
4 teaspoons baking powder
1 teaspoon salt
1 cup (250 ml) milk, plus
  2 tablespoons extra
1 egg
1 cup (250 g) mashed pumpkin
⅓ cup (90 g) butter, melted
1 tablespoon sesame seeds

Makes 1 loaf

You can boil, steam or bake pumpkin to make the mash used in this recipe. Butternut, jap, kent and Queensland blue are all suitable types of pumpkin.

1 Preheat the oven to 220°C (Gas 7). Lightly grease and flour a baking tray. In a large bowl, sift together the flour, sugar, baking powder and salt.
2 In a bowl, combine the 1 cup (250 ml) milk and the egg; beat until well blended. Stir in the mashed pumpkin and butter. Make a well in the centre of the dry ingredients; pour in the pumpkin mixture and, using a fork, stir until well blended.
3 Lightly flour a work surface. Turn the dough out onto the work surface and knead lightly until smooth, about 4 to 5 minutes. Shape into a round loaf and transfer to the baking tray. Using a sharp knife, cut a cross into the top of the loaf. Brush lightly with the remaining 2 tablespoons milk, then sprinkle with the sesame seeds.
4 Bake for 25 minutes, then reduce the oven temperature to 190°C (Gas 5). Bake until the loaf sounds hollow when tapped, about 15 minutes longer. Transfer the loaf to a wire rack to cool.

Banana Nut Bread

½ cup (60 g) walnuts or
    pecans
1¾ cups (260 g) plain flour
1½ teaspoons baking powder
½ teaspoon bicarbonate of soda
½ teaspoon salt
½ teaspoon ground cinnamon
¼ teaspoon ground allspice or
    mixed spice
½ cup (125 g) butter, at room
    temperature
⅓ cup (80 g) firmly packed
    soft brown sugar
½ cup (110 g) sugar
2 eggs
1 cup (240 g) mashed ripe
    banana
⅓ cup (80 ml) buttermilk or
    natural yogurt
¼ teaspoon almond extract
1 cup (125 g) sultanas

Makes 1 loaf

This luscious loaf is a good way to use up over-ripe bananas. It's delicious for brunch or teatime, and is particularly good when toasted and slathered with butter. You can double or triple the recipe and freeze the extra loaves for later.

1 Preheat the oven to 180°C (Gas 4). Lightly grease a 23 x 13 cm loaf tin; lightly dust the tin with flour.
2 Spread the walnuts or pecans in a dish or cake tin and toast in the oven, uncovered, until lightly browned, about 7 minutes. Let the nuts cool, then coarsely chop and set aside.
3 In a bowl, combine the flour, baking powder, bicarbonate of soda, salt, cinnamon and allspice or mixed spice; stir until the ingredients are well blended.
4 In a large bowl, beat the butter until it is creamed, using electric beaters on medium speed. Gradually add both sugars, beating well after each addition. Add the eggs, one at a time, beating well after each addition. Add the flour mixture, a little at a time, beating only enough to incorporate the flour. The batter will not be smooth.
5 In a small bowl, combine the mashed banana, buttermilk and almond extract; stir until blended. Pour the banana mixture into the batter, stir, then fold in the raisins and toasted nuts.
6 Pour and scrape the batter into the loaf tin. Bake until a skewer inserted into the centre of the loaf comes out clean, 50 to 55 minutes. Transfer the tin to a wire rack and let the bread cool in the tin for 10 minutes. Using a knife or spatula, loosen the edges of the bread from the sides of the tin and carefully remove the bread from the tin. Let the bread cool completely on the rack.

If you run out of baking powder

If a recipe calls for 1 teaspoon baking powder and you don't have any on hand, combine ¼ teaspoon bicarbonate of soda with ½ teaspoon cream of tartar.

Carrot Bread

1¾ cups (260 g) plain flour
2½ teaspoons baking powder
½ teaspoon salt
¼ teaspoon ground cardamom
¼ teaspoon ground ginger
¼ teaspoon ground allspice
or mixed spice
½ cup (125 g) butter, at room
temperature
⅔ cup (140 g) sugar
2 eggs
1½ cups (235 g) firmly packed
coarsely grated peeled carrot
½ cup (125 ml) orange juice

Makes 1 loaf

The spicy goodness of this bread brings to mind carrot cake, without the high price. Serve it with tea or coffee or as a dessert.

1 Preheat the oven to 180°C (Gas 4). Lightly grease a 23 x 13 cm loaf tin; lightly dust the tin with flour.
2 In a bowl, combine the flour, baking powder, salt, cardamom, ginger and allspice or mixed spice; stir until the ingredients are well blended.
3 In a large bowl, beat the butter until it is creamed, using electric beaters on medium speed. Gradually add the sugar, beating well after each addition. Add the eggs, one at a time, beating well after each addition. Add the flour mixture, a little at a time, beating only enough to incorporate each addition of flour. The batter will not be smooth.
4 In a small bowl, mix together the carrot and orange juice. Pour the mixture into the batter and stir until well blended.
5 Pour the batter into the loaf tin. Bake until a skewer inserted into the centre of the loaf comes out clean, about 1 hour. Transfer the tin to a wire rack and let the bread cool in the tin for 10 minutes. Using a knife or spatula, loosen the edges of the bread and carefully turn out the loaf. Let the bread cool completely on the rack.

Pecan Bread

2 cups (300 g) plain flour
2 teaspoons baking powder
1 teaspoon salt
¾ cup (90 g) coarsely chopped
pecans
⅓ cup (80 g) firmly packed
soft brown sugar
1 cup (250 ml) milk
1 egg
3 tablespoons butter, melted

Makes 1 loaf

This nutty bread is excellent served with fruit and soft cheeses after a meal.

1 Preheat the oven to 180°C (Gas 4). Lightly grease a 20 x 10 cm loaf tin.
2 In a large bowl, sift together the flour, baking powder and salt. Stir in the pecans and sugar. In a bowl, beat the milk and egg until well combined. Stir in the melted butter.
3 Make a well in the centre of the flour mixture. Pour the milk mixture into the well and, using a fork, stir the ingredients just until they are all moistened and the dough holds together; do not overmix.
4 Spoon the dough into the loaf tin. Bake until a skewer inserted into the centre of the loaf comes out clean, 45 to 50 minutes.
5 Transfer the tin to a wire rack and let the bread cool 10 minutes, then remove the bread from the tin and let it cool completely.

Zucchini Bread

1 cup (120 g) chopped pecans
1¾ cups (260 g) plain flour
1½ teaspoons baking powder
½ teaspoon salt
½ teaspoon bicarbonate of soda
1 teaspoon ground cinnamon
½ cup (125 g) butter, at room
    temperature
¾ cup (165 g) sugar
2 eggs
1½ cups (200 g) grated
    zucchini (courgette),
    squeezed to remove excess
    moisture
⅓ cup (80 ml) buttermilk or
    natural yogurt
¼ teaspoon almond extract
    (optional)

Makes 1 loaf

Zucchini has little flavour on its own but it helps to keep the bread moist. You can double or triple the recipe and freeze the extra loaves.

1 Preheat the oven to 180°C (Gas 4). Lightly grease a 23 x 13 cm loaf tin; lightly dust the tin with flour.
2 Spread the pecans in a pie dish or cake tin and toast in the oven, uncovered, until lightly browned, about 7 minutes. Let the nuts cool, then coarsely chop and set aside.
3 In a bowl, combine the flour, baking powder, salt, bicarbonate of soda and cinnamon; stir until well blended.
4 In a large bowl, beat the butter until it is creamed, using electric beaters on medium speed. Gradually add the sugar, beating well after each addition. Add the eggs, one at a time, beating well after each addition. Add the flour mixture, a little at a time, beating only enough to incorporate the flour. The batter will not be smooth.
5 In a small bowl, combine the zucchini, buttermilk and almond extract, if using; stir until blended. Stir the zucchini mixture into the batter, then fold in the reserved toasted nuts.
6 Pour and scrape the batter into the loaf tin. Bake until a skewer inserted into the centre of the loaf comes out clean, about 1 hour. Transfer the tin to a wire rack and let the bread cool in the tin for 10 minutes. Using a knife or spatula, loosen the edges of the bread and carefully turn out the loaf. Let the bread cool completely on the rack.

Yeast Breads

French Bread

7 g packet dry yeast
1½ cups (375 ml) warm water
    (about 45°C)
1 tablespoon sugar
2 teaspoons salt
1 tablespoon butter, melted
4 cups (600 g) plain flour,
    plus extra for sprinkling
polenta (cornmeal), for
    sprinkling

Makes 2 loaves

Many meals can be finished off with a loaf of French bread to sop up the gravy, hold the cheese or complement the salad. Nothing is better, but unfortunately, nothing goes stale more quickly, so making your own not only saves money but also ensures a fresh, crusty loaf. Unusually, this recipe doesn't require kneading.

1   In a large bowl, combine the yeast with ½ cup (125 ml) of the water and stir until the yeast is dissolved. Add the sugar, salt, butter and remaining water and stir until all the ingredients are well blended. Add the flour and stir until the dough is smooth; do not knead. Cover the bowl and let the dough rise in a warm place until doubled in size, about 1 hour.

2   Lightly flour a work surface. Divide the dough in half; let the dough rest again for 10 minutes. Using a lightly floured rolling pin, roll one dough half into a 25 x 20 cm rectangle. Beginning on a long side, roll up the dough, in Swiss-roll fashion; pinch the edges to seal the loaf. Repeat with the remaining dough half.

4   Lightly grease a baking tray and sprinkle it with polenta. Place the loaves, seam side down, on the baking tray; sprinkle the tops with additional polenta. Cover the loaves and let them rise in a warm place until doubled in size, about 45 minutes.

5   Preheat the oven to 200°C (Gas 6). Using a sharp knife, make five diagonal cuts across the top of each loaf. Bake the loaves until lightly browned, 20 to 30 minutes. Transfer the loaves to wire racks to cool.

Making yeast breads is easier than you think

One of the absolute best aromas in the world is that of fresh homebaked bread. You may have shied away from yeast breads in the past, thinking that yeast would be difficult to work with. Not at all. Just follow the packet directions and you'll be turning out perfect loaves in no time. If you enjoy the aroma and the price of homemade bread, but time is a factor, you may want to invest in a bread machine. Most recipes can be converted for a machine.

Multigrain Bread

2 teaspoons sugar

½ cup (125 ml) lukewarm
water (about 45°C)

two 7 g packets dry yeast

1¼–1½ cups (185–225 g)
plain flour, plus extra for
sprinkling

1 cup (150 g) wholemeal flour

1 cup (100 g) rye flour

⅓ cup (50 g) sifted stone-
ground yellow or white
polenta (cornmeal)

¼ cup (20 g) wheat bran

¼ cup (25 g) wheatgerm

1 cup (250 ml) buttermilk
or natural yogurt

3 tablespoons butter, melted

1½ teaspoons salt

Makes 1 loaf

Wholemeal flour, rye flour, stone-ground polenta, wheat bran, wheatgerm and buttermilk form this hearty, wholesome bread that your family will rave about. Your wallet will be pretty happy with it, too.

1 In a large bowl, combine the sugar, water and yeast. Stir until the solids are dissolved. Let stand until the mixture is bubbly, about 10 minutes.

2 In another large bowl, combine 1¼ cups (185 g) of the plain flour with the wholemeal and rye flours, polenta, wheat bran and wheatgerm.

3 Place the buttermilk, butter and salt in a small saucepan and gently heat until the mixture is lukewarm.

4 Pour the buttermilk mixture into the yeast mixture. Using a wooden spoon or an electric mixer with the dough hook attached, beat at medium speed, adding the flour mixture 1 cup at a time, until the dough is soft but manageable; beat in the remaining ¼ cup (35 g) of plain flour if needed to reach the desired consistency. Continue to beat until the dough is smooth and elastic, 7 to 8 minutes. If mixing by hand, knead on a floured work surface for 8 to 10 minutes.

5 Generously butter a large bowl. Shape the dough into a ball and place it in the bowl, turning it until it is completely coated with butter. Cover the bowl with a tea towel and let the dough rise in a warm place until doubled in size, 1½ to 2 hours.

6 Lightly grease a 23 x 13 cm loaf tin; lightly flour a work surface. Punch down the dough and turn it out onto the work surface. Knead gently for 2 minutes. Shape the dough into a loaf, place it in the loaf tin, cover and leave to rise again until doubled in size, about 1 hour.

7 Preheat the oven to 190°C (Gas 5). Bake until the loaf is golden brown and sounds hollow when tapped, 40 to 45 minutes. Transfer the tin to a wire rack and let the bread cool for 10 minutes. Using a knife, loosen the edges of the bread from the sides of the tin and turn the loaf out onto the wire rack to cool completely.

Soy and Linseed Bread

3⅓ cups (500 g) finely milled
   bread flour, plus extra for
   kneading
1 teaspoon salt
2 teaspoons caster sugar
2 teaspoons instant dry yeast
1½ cups (375 ml) warm water
2 x 400 g cans soybeans,
   drained (about 480 g)
2 tablespoons linseeds
2 teaspoons milk

Makes 1 loaf

Soybeans and linseeds are said to be great for women's health. Add them to your diet with this chewy loaf.

1 Sift 3 cups (450 g) of the flour into a bowl. Stir in the salt, sugar and yeast. Make a well in the centre, add the warm water and mix to form a soft dough. Turn the dough out onto a lightly floured surface and knead for 10 minutes, incorporating the remaining flour, until smooth and elastic.

2 Place the dough in a lightly oiled bowl and cover with lightly greased plastic wrap. Let the dough rise in a warm place until doubled in size, about 1 hour.

3 Preheat the oven to 190°C (Gas 5) and grease a large baking tray. Punch the dough down and turn it out onto a lightly floured surface. Add the soybeans and linseeds and knead into the dough until well combined. Shape the dough into a 15 x 25 cm oval, place on the baking tray and cut shallow slits across the top at 5 cm intervals. Brush with milk. Bake for 30 minutes, or until golden brown and hollow when tapped on top. Leave on the tray for 5 minutes, then transfer to a wire rack to cool.

Focaccia

7 g packet dry yeast
¼ teaspoon sugar
2 cups (500 ml) warm water
   (about 45°C)
4½–5½ cups (675–825 g) bread
   flour or plain flour
¼ cup (60 ml) olive oil, plus
   extra for drizzling
1 tablespoon salt
tiny sprigs fresh rosemary
sea salt

Makes 2 loaves

This chewy Italian bread can be topped with vegetables, grilled meats, cold cuts, cheese – or just olive oil.

1 In a small bowl, combine the yeast, sugar and water. Stir until the solids are dissolved. Let stand until the mixture is bubbly, about 10 minutes.

2 Pour 4½ cups (675 g) of the flour into a large bowl and make a well in the centre. Pour the yeast mixture, oil and salt into the well, then stir until well blended. Add additional flour as needed to reach the desired consistency.

3 Lightly flour a work surface; lightly coat a large bowl with olive oil. Turn the dough out onto the work surface and knead until smooth, about 10 minutes. Place the dough in the bowl, turning it to coat with the oil. Cover the bowl with lightly oiled plastic wrap and set in a warm place to rise for 1 hour.

4 Lightly grease two baking trays. Divide the dough in half and spread them on the trays. With your fingers, press down and outwards until each is a round loaf about 2 cm thick. Cover with lightly oiled plastic wrap and let rise for 10 to 20 minutes.

5 With your fingers, press the loaves down and out again. Cover again and let the loaves rise for 30 minutes.

6 Preheat the oven to 220°C (Gas 7). With your fingers, indent the loaves all over. Press a sprig of rosemary into each dent, drizzle the whole with oil, then sprinkle with salt. Bake until firm and golden, about 25 minutes. Serve warm.

Challah

two 7 g packets dry yeast

1 cup (250 ml) warm water
(about 45°C)

½ cup (125 ml) vegetable oil

⅓ cup (75 g) sugar

1 tablespoon salt

5 eggs

6–6½ cups (900–975 g) plain
flour

1 tablespoon sesame or poppy
seeds (optional)

Makes 2 loaves

The traditional bread of the Jewish Sabbath, this attractive loaf is braided and given a shiny coating of egg wash.

1 In a large bowl, combine the yeast and the warm water and stir until the yeast has dissolved. Add the oil, sugar, salt, 4 eggs and 4 cups (600 g) of the flour. Beat until all the ingredients are well blended and the consistency is smooth. Stir in enough of the remaining flour to form a firm dough.

2 Lightly flour a work surface. Turn the dough out onto the work surface and knead until firm and elastic, 6 to 8 minutes. Lightly grease a large bowl with butter or oil, place the dough in the bowl and turn it to coat the entire ball. Cover the bowl and let the dough rise in a warm place until doubled in size, about 1 hour.

3 Punch down the dough, turn it out onto another floured work surface, and divide in half. Divide each portion into thirds, then roll each piece into a rope about 45 cm long.

4 Lightly grease a baking tray. Place three dough ropes on the tray, pinching them together at one end. Braid the ropes together and pinch the opposite ends to seal them, then tuck the pinched ends under at both ends. Repeat with the remaining dough ropes to make a second loaf. Cover the loaves with a tea towel and let rise again until doubled in size, about 1 hour.

5 Preheat the oven to 180°C (Gas 4). In a small bowl, beat the remaining egg with 1 teaspoon cold water. Brush the egg mixture over the loaves. If desired, sprinkle the loaves with the sesame or poppy seeds. Bake until golden brown, 30 to 35 minutes. Transfer the loaves to wire racks and let them cool completely.

Take a mix-and-match approach to gift baskets

When pondering gift-giving with your own homemade items, take a tip from those high-end catalogues and pair natural partners in an attractive package – breads with jams, jellies or marmalades; pasta with homemade sauces; biscuits with cocoa, coffee or tea blends; muesli with fresh-baked muffins; canned fruit with a dessert sauce; soup with hearty rolls; pita breads with hummus. Whenever you browse through a garage sale, look for baskets, saucepans, ceramic or porcelain bowls and other fun packaging for your personalised gifts.

Brioche

2⅓ cups (350 g) plain flour
½ teaspoon salt
100 g butter, softened
1 teaspoon dry yeast
⅓ cup (80 ml) lukewarm milk
3 eggs
1½ tablespoons sugar
1 egg yolk, for brushing

Makes 20 brioche

Sweet and buttery, these French breakfast rolls are beautiful to look at and delicious to eat. Although they require a little bit of work, the result is spectacular.

1 If you have them, grease individual fluted brioche tins generously with butter. Otherwise, use two standard muffin tins.
2 Place the flour, salt and butter in a bowl. In a small bowl, sprinkle the yeast over the milk and stir until dissolved. Whisk in the eggs and sugar, then add to the flour mixture. Knead for 5 minutes using the dough hook of an electric mixer until the dough no longer sticks to the side of the bowl. (This dough is wet and sticky; an electric mixer makes the task of kneading much easier than if you try to work with your hands.)
3 Cover the dough and leave to rise in a cool place for 2 hours; it must not get too warm. Knead for 5 minutes, then cover and leave to rise again for 30 to 50 minutes, until doubled in size.
4 Turn the dough out onto a lightly floured work surface and shape into a cylinder. Slice into 25 pieces. Shape 20 pieces into balls and press them into the tins.
5 Using an index finger, make a deep hole in the centre of each of the 20 balls. Cut each remaining piece of dough into four, then shape into small balls. Pull a pointed cone of dough up from each one and push the point deep into the holes made in the large dough balls.
6 Beat the egg yolk with 2 tablespoons water and brush over the brioche. Cover with a tea towel and leave for 30 minutes, until doubled in size.
7 Preheat the oven to 220°C (Gas 7). Bake the brioche for 15 to 20 minutes, or until golden; they should slip out of the tins easily when they are done. Transfer to wire racks to cool.

Cinnamon–Raisin Swirl Bread

1 cup (250 ml) lukewarm milk
(about 45°C)

two 7 g packets dry yeast

1½ tablespoons sugar

2¼ cups (625 ml) lukewarm
water (about 45°C)

75 g butter or margarine,
melted

2 teaspoons salt

6–6½ cups (900–975 g) plain
flour

1 cup (125 g) seedless raisins,
soaked in hot water for
15–30 minutes, drained well

CINNAMON SWIRL FILLING

½ cup (110 g) sugar

1 tablespoon ground cinnamon

3 tablespoons butter or
margarine, melted

ICING

2 cups (250 g) sifted icing
sugar

2 tablespoons water

Makes 2 loaves

This beautiful bread – spiralled with cinnamon, thick with raisins and drizzled with icing – is a treat for all the senses, and will fill your house with a delicious aroma as it bakes.

1 In a large bowl, combine the milk, yeast and 1 teaspoon of the sugar. Stir until the solids are dissolved. Let stand until the mixture is bubbly, about 10 minutes. In a bowl, combine 1¼ cups (310 ml) of the warm water, 4 tablespoons of the butter, the salt and the remaining sugar. Stir the butter mixture into the yeast mixture.

2 Using a wooden spoon or an electric mixer with a dough hook attached, beat in the flour, 1 cup (150 g) at a time, until a soft dough forms. Continue to beat at medium speed until the dough is elastic, 7 to 8 minutes. If mixing by hand, knead on a floured work surface for 8 to 10 minutes.

3 Pour the remaining butter into a large bowl. Shape the dough into a ball and place in the bowl, turning it to completely coat it with butter. Cover the bowl with a tea towel and let the dough rise in a warm place until doubled in size, about 1 hour.

4 Lightly butter two 23 x 13 cm loaf tins. Lightly flour a work surface. Punch down the dough and turn it out onto the work surface. Knead the dough gently for 2 minutes. Divide the dough in half, cover and rest for 5 to 10 minutes. Working with one half at a time and using a rolling pin, roll each portion into a 15 x 40 cm rectangle. Sprinkle half the raisins over each portion of the dough and gently knead until evenly distributed. Cover the dough and rest for 10 minutes.

5 For the filling, combine the sugar, cinnamon and 2 tablespoons of the butter in a small bowl and stir until well blended. Using a rolling pin on a floured surface, again roll each dough half into a 15 x 40 cm rectangle. Spread each half with half the filling. Beginning on a short side, roll up the dough, in Swiss-roll fashion, to make a loaf; repeat with the remaining dough. Place the loaves, seam side down, in the loaf tins, cover with a tea towel and let rise for 1 hour.

6 Preheat the oven to 200°C (Gas 6). Brush the tops of the loaves with the remaining tablespoon of butter. Bake until the bread is brown and sounds hollow when tapped, 35 to 40 minutes. Transfer the tins to wire racks and let the bread cool for 10 minutes. Using a knife, loosen the edges of the bread from the sides of the tins, turn out the bread and leave on the wire racks to cool.

7 For the icing, combine the icing sugar and water in a small bowl and stir until smooth. Brush, pour or drizzle the icing over the cooled loaves.

Pita Bread

1½ cups (375 ml) warm water
  (about 45°C)
1 teaspoon dry yeast
1 teaspoon sugar
3 cups (450 g) bread flour
  or plain flour
1 heaped teaspoon salt
1½ teaspoons olive oil, plus
  extra for drizzling
3 tablespoons finely chopped
  fresh herbs, such as thyme,
  rosemary, coriander or
  parsley (optional)

Makes 4 pita breads

This popular staple of Middle Eastern and Mediterranean cuisine is a wonderfully versatile bread. You can stuff the pockets with almost anything you can think of to make a sandwich; slice the bread into triangles, toast it and serve with any dip; or even top it with tomato paste, marinated vegetables and mozzarella for a variation on pizza.

1 In a large bowl, combine the water and yeast; stir until the yeast has dissolved. Add the sugar and 1½ cups (225 g) of the flour. Using the paddle attachment of an electric mixer, stir until well blended. Cover the bowl with lightly oiled plastic wrap and let the dough rise in a warm place until doubled in size, about 2 hours.

2 Add the salt, olive oil and remaining flour. Again using the paddle attachment, beat the mixture until it is smooth and elastic, 5 to 10 minutes.

3 Lightly flour a work surface and lightly oil a large bowl. Turn the dough out onto the work surface and knead until smooth and elastic, 10 to 12 minutes. Place the dough in the bowl, turning it to completely coat it with the oil. Cover the bowl with lightly oiled plastic wrap and let the dough rise in a warm place for 1½ hours.

4 Preheat the oven to 240°C (Gas 8). Line a baking tray with baking paper or foil.

5 Lightly flour the work surface again and turn out the dough. Divide the dough into four balls. Using a rolling pin, roll each ball into a circle about 1 cm thick and 15 cm in diameter. Place on the baking tray, lightly brush each one with oil and, if desired, sprinkle with herbs. Bake until the pita breads are golden, about 8 minutes. Transfer to wire racks to cool.

Sourdough Bread

STARTER
2 cups (500 ml) lukewarm
   water (about 45°C)
7 g packet dry yeast
1½ cups (225 g) bread flour

DOUGH
1½ cups starter (see above)
2 tablespoons sugar
1 tablespoon salt
5–6 cups (750–900 g) bread
   flour
80 g butter, melted

Makes 2 loaves

The starter is essential to the chewy texture and signature flavour of sourdough bread. Once you have a starter, you use some for each loaf you bake, but continue to feed the starter to keep it going – an endless supply for a sensational bread.

1 Combine the starter ingredients in a glass or ceramic bowl and whisk until well blended. Cover the bowl loosely with waxed paper and set in a warm place for 12 hours or overnight.

2 To prepare the dough, combine the starter in a large bowl with the sugar, salt, 2½ cups (375 g) of the flour and 1 cup (250 ml) water. Using a wooden spoon or the paddle attachment of an electric mixer, beat the dough at medium speed until smooth, about 15 seconds.

3 If using an electric mixer, remove the paddle and attach a dough hook. Add ¼ cup (60 ml) of the melted butter and 2½ cups (375 g) of the remaining flour, ½ cup (75 g) at a time. Continue beating for about 10 minutes, adding an extra ½–1 cup (75–150 g) of flour, if necessary, to make a smooth and elastic dough. (If mixing by hand, you will probably have to knead in the last of the flour.)

4 Generously butter a large bowl. Using your hands, shape the dough into a ball and place in the bowl, turning it to completely coat it with the butter. Cover the bowl with a cloth and let the dough rise in a warm place until doubled in size, 1 to 1½ hours. Punch down the dough, cover again and allow to rise for 1½ hours longer.

5 Lightly flour a work surface and lightly grease two 20 cm round cake or spring-form tins. Punch down the dough again and turn out onto the work surface. Knead lightly until the dough is smooth, 2 to 3 minutes. Divide the dough in half and roll each half into a ball. Place one ball in each tin, cover both with a tea towel and let rise again until the dough is doubled in size, 45 minutes to 1 hour.

6 Preheat the oven to 180°C (Gas 4). Brush the loaves with the remaining melted butter. Using a sharp knife, cut a diagonal slash across the top of each loaf. Bake until the loaves are richly golden and sound hollow when tapped, 45 to 50 minutes. Transfer to a wire rack to cool.

Muffins

Apple and Raisin Muffins

2 cups (300 g) plain flour
3 teaspoons baking powder
1 teaspoon salt
½ teaspoon ground cinnamon
¼ teaspoon ground nutmeg
¾ cup (150 g) peeled, grated
   apple
⅓ cup (40 g) sultanas
⅔ cup (155 g) firmly packed
   soft brown sugar
¼ cup (30 g) chopped walnuts
   or pecans
2 eggs, well beaten
⅔ cup (170 ml) milk
¼ cup (60 ml) vegetable oil
1 cup (75 g) corn, bran or
   wheat flakes cereal

Makes 12 muffins

Grated apple is the sweetener in these muffins, which reduces the need for added sugar and lets the natural flavours stand out.

1 Preheat the oven to 200°C (Gas 6). Lightly grease a standard 12-hole muffin tin or line with paper cases.
2 In a large bowl, combine the flour, baking powder, salt, cinnamon and nutmeg. Add the apple, sultanas, sugar and nuts and stir until well blended. Make a well in the centre.
3 In a small bowl, combine the eggs, milk and oil. Mix well, then pour into the dry ingredients. Using a fork, stir just until the dry ingredients are moistened. Do not overmix; the batter should be lumpy. Fold in the cereal.
4 Spoon the batter into the holes or paper cases, filling them two-thirds full. Bake until the muffins are puffed and browned, 15 to 20 minutes. Transfer the tin to a wire rack and let the muffins cool for 5 minutes. Turn the muffins out (you may need to run a knife around the edges to loosen them). Serve warm.

Choc-chip Muffins

2 cups (300 g) plain flour
3 teaspoons baking powder
½ teaspoon bicarbonate of soda
½ cup (95 g) soft brown sugar
1 large egg
1 cup (250 ml) milk
¼ cup (60 g) unsalted butter,
   melted and cooled
⅔ cup (100 g) dark, milk or
   white chocolate chips

Makes 12 muffins

Melt-and-mix recipes such as these muffins are among the easiest baked goods you can make.

1 Preheat the oven to 200°C (Gas 6). Lightly grease a standard 12-hole muffin tin or line with paper cases.
2 Sift the dry ingredients into a large bowl and make a well in the centre.
3 Beat together the egg and milk and add to the dry ingredients with the melted butter. Lightly stir the mixture together with a fork, being careful not to overmix. Fold in the chocolate chips.
4 Fill the holes or paper cases three-quarters full, then bake for about 20 minutes, until the muffins are well risen, golden brown and cooked through. Transfer the tin to a wire rack and let the muffins cool for 5 minutes. Turn the muffins out (you may need to run a knife around the edges to loosen them). Serve warm or cool.

Blueberry Muffins

1½ cups (235 g) fresh
  blueberries, or thawed frozen
  blueberries
3 cups (450 g) plain flour
1 tablespoon baking powder
½ teaspoon bicarbonate of soda
1 teaspoon salt
¾ cup (165 g) sugar, plus
  extra for sprinkling
¼ cup (60 g) butter, melted
2 eggs, lightly beaten
1 cup (250 ml) buttermilk or
  natural yogurt
1½ teaspoons vanilla extract

Makes 12 muffins

You don't need to wait until blueberries are in season to make these muffins. Frozen berries work just as well, and are often more economical.

1 Preheat the oven to 200°C (Gas 6). Lightly grease a standard 12-hole muffin tin or line with paper cases.
2 In a bowl, toss the blueberries with 2 tablespoons of the flour until completely coated. Put the remaining flour in a large bowl with the baking powder, bicarbonate of soda, salt and sugar; stir to blend, then make a well in the centre.
3 In a small bowl, combine the butter, eggs, buttermilk or yogurt and vanilla. Mix well, then pour into the dry ingredients. Using a fork, stir just until the dry ingredients are moistened. Do not overmix; the batter should be lumpy. Fold in the blueberries.
4 Spoon the batter into the holes or paper cases, filling them two-thirds full; sprinkle the muffin tops with a little extra sugar. Bake until the muffins are golden, 20 to 25 minutes. Transfer the tin to a wire rack and let the muffins cool for 5 minutes. Turn the muffins out (you may need to run a knife around the edges to loosen them). Serve warm or cool.

Bran Muffins

1 cup (125 g) raisins
1¼ cups (185 g) plain flour
1 tablespoon baking powder
⅓ cup (75 g) sugar
1 teaspoon cinnamon
½ teaspoon salt
1 cup (70 g) bran cereal such
  as All-Bran (not flakes)
1 cup (250 ml) milk
1 egg
¼ cup (60 ml) vegetable oil

Makes 12 muffins

These low-fat, high-fibre muffins are excellent for a healthy breakfast.

1 Preheat the oven to 200°C (Gas 6). Lightly grease a standard 12-hole muffin tin or line with paper cases.
2 In a bowl, toss the raisins with 2 tablespoons of the flour until completely coated. Put the remaining flour in a bowl with the baking powder, sugar, cinnamon and salt. Stir until well blended.
3 In a large bowl, combine the bran cereal and milk; let the mixture stand for 2 minutes. Add the egg and oil and stir until well blended. Add the dry ingredients to the bran mixture and, using a fork, stir just until the dry ingredients are moistened; do not overmix. Fold in the raisins.
4 Spoon the batter into the holes or paper cases, filling them two-thirds full. Bake until the muffins are golden brown, 18 to 20 minutes. Transfer the tin to a wire rack and let the muffins cool for 5 minutes. Turn the muffins out (you may need to run a knife around the edges to loosen them). Serve warm or cool.

Herb and Bacon Muffins

1¾ cups (260 g) plain flour
2 teaspoons baking powder
½ teaspoon salt
3 tablespoons chopped fresh
  herbs
¼ cup (25 g) grated parmesan
1 tablespoon sugar
2 slices rindless bacon, cooked
  and cut into small bits
1 egg, beaten
1 cup (250 ml) milk
¼ cup (60 g) butter, melted

Makes 12 regular muffins or
24 mini muffins

You can add whatever herbs you fancy to this muffin recipe – fresh thyme, basil or marjoram would be superb.

1 Preheat the oven to 200°C (Gas 6). Lightly grease a standard 12-hole or 24-hole mini muffin tin or line with paper cases.
2 In a large bowl, sift together the flour, baking powder and salt. Add the herbs, cheese, sugar and bacon and stir until well blended, then make a well in the centre.
3 In a small bowl, combine the egg, milk and butter. Mix well, then pour into the dry ingredients. Using a fork, stir just until the dry ingredients are moistened. Do not overmix; the batter should be lumpy.
4 Spoon the batter into the holes or paper cases, filling them two-thirds full. Bake until the muffins are browned: 15 to 20 minutes for regular muffins, and 12 to 15 minutes for mini muffins. Transfer the tin to a wire rack and let the muffins cool for 5 minutes. Turn the muffins out (you may need to run a knife around the edges to loosen them). Serve warm.

Cheese and Cranberry Muffins

2 cups (300 g) plain flour
⅔ cup (155 g) firmly packed
  soft brown sugar
½ cup (60 g) finely grated
  cheddar
2½ teaspoons baking powder
½ teaspoon bicarbonate of soda
½ teaspoon salt
¼ teaspoon ground allspice
  or mixed spice
pinch of ground cayenne
  pepper
1¼ cups (310 ml) buttermilk
  or natural yogurt
¼ cup (60 g) butter, melted
1 egg, separated
1 cup (155 g) washed fresh or
  unthawed frozen cranberries

Makes 12 muffins

Savoury muffins make a substantial breakfast or snack on their own, or an unusual accompaniment to serve with soup or roast poultry.

1 Preheat the oven to 200°C (Gas 6). Lightly grease a standard 12-hole muffin tin or line with paper cases.
2 In a large bowl, combine the flour, sugar, cheese, baking powder, bicarbonate of soda, salt and spices. Stir until well blended, then make a well in the centre.
3 In a small bowl, whisk together the buttermilk or yogurt, butter and egg yolk. In another small bowl, beat the eggwhite until soft peaks form.
4 Pour the buttermilk mixture into the dry ingredients. Using a fork, stir just until the dry ingredients are moistened. Do not overmix; the batter should be lumpy. Fold in the eggwhite and cranberries.
5 Spoon the batter into the holes or paper cases, filling them three-quarters full. Bake until a skewer inserted in a muffin comes out clean, about 20 minutes. Transfer the tin to a wire rack and let the muffins cool for 5 minutes. Turn the muffins out (you may need to run a knife around the edges to loosen them). Serve warm or cool.

Rolls

Potato Dinner Rolls

2 tablespoons sugar
½ cup (125 ml) lukewarm
  water (about 45°C)
two 7 g packets dry yeast
1 cup (250 ml) milk
2 teaspoons salt
½ cup (125 g) butter, melted,
  plus 3 tablespoons extra
1 large all-purpose potato,
  peeled, diced and boiled,
  then pushed through a fine
  sieve or a potato ricer
6½–7 cups (approx 1 kg) plain
  flour
1 egg, lightly beaten

Makes 64 rolls

These classic homemade rolls will melt in your mouth.
The secret is the potato.

1 In a small bowl, combine the sugar, water and yeast and stir
  until the solids are dissolved. Let stand until the mixture is
  bubbly, about 10 minutes.

2 In a small saucepan over medium–high heat, bring the milk
  and 1 cup (250 ml) water to a boil. Pour into a large heatproof
  bowl, stir in the salt and ¼ cup (60 ml) of the melted butter
  and let cool for 10 minutes. Using a wooden spoon or electric
  mixer with a paddle attachment, add the potato, 2 cups
  (300 g) of the flour and the egg, beating at medium speed
  for 1 minute after each addition. Add the yeast mixture and
  beat for 1 minute longer.

3 If using the mixer, remove the paddle and attach a dough
  hook. Add another 4½ cups (675 g) flour and beat for
  3 to 5 minutes, until a soft, manageable dough forms, then
  continue adding the flour, ¼–½ cup (35–75 g) at a time,
  as needed to reach the desired consistency.

4 Generously butter a large bowl. Using your hands, shape
  the dough into a ball and place in the bowl, turning it to
  completely coat it with the butter. Cover the bowl with a
  tea towel and let the dough rise in a warm place until
  doubled in size, about 50 minutes.

5 Lightly flour a work surface; lightly grease six baking trays
  (or bake the rolls in batches). Punch down the dough and turn
  out onto the work surface. Divide the dough into four equal
  portions. Using a rolling pin, roll each dough portion one at
  a time into a 20 x 25 cm rectangle about 5 mm thick. Using
  a floured 7 cm pastry cutter, cut out 12 rounds. Gather the
  scraps together, and reroll; cut out four more rounds.

6 Brush each dough round with melted butter. Using
  the blunt side of a knife, crease each circle along
  the diameter and fold, stretching the top half so it
  covers the bottom half. Pinch the edges to seal.

7 Arrange the rolls on the baking trays and brush
  the tops with the remaining butter. Cover with
  a tea towel and let rise for 30 minutes.

8 Preheat the oven to 180°C (Gas 4). Bake the
  rolls until golden brown, about 30 minutes.
  Serve immediately, or cool on wire racks.

Bagels

1¾ cups (260 g) white bread
  flour
1¾ cups (175 g) rye flour
1½ teaspoons salt
7 g packet dry yeast
1 teaspoon caraway seeds
3 eggs
1 teaspoon treacle
2 teaspoons sunflower oil

Makes 12 bagels

These little bread rings, Jewish in origin, are delicious
teamed with savoury fillings such as smoked salmon
and a soft cheese, or egg and salad. The double cooking
method gives bagels their unique softness and slightly
chewy crust.

1 Place all the flour in a large mixing bowl and stir in the salt,
  yeast and caraway seeds. Make a well in the centre.
2 Lightly whisk 2 eggs with the treacle and oil, and pour into
  the well in the flour. Add 200 ml lukewarm water and mix
  to a soft dough.
3 Turn out onto a lightly floured surface and knead for 10 minutes,
  or until smooth and elastic. Place the dough in a large greased
  bowl, cover with a damp tea towel and leave to rise in a warm
  place until doubled in size, about 40 minutes.
4 Turn the dough out onto the floured work surface and knead
  lightly, then divide into 12 equal pieces. Form each into a
  sausage 20 cm long, then shape it into a ring. Dampen the
  ends with a little water, slightly overlap them, then gently
  pinch together to seal.
5 Arrange the bagels on a lightly oiled baking tray, cover
  with oiled plastic wrap and leave to rise in a warm place for
  20 minutes, or until slightly puffy.
6 Preheat the oven to 200°C (Gas 6). Bring a large saucepan of
  lightly salted water to the boil. Drop the bagels into the water,
  one at a time, and poach for 20 seconds. Lift them out with a
  large slotted spoon and return to the baking tray.
7 Lightly beat the remaining egg and brush it over the bagels.
  Bake for 14 to 15 minutes, or until well risen and golden brown.
  Transfer to a wire rack to cool. Store in an airtight container
  for up to 3 days.

Soda Bread Rolls

2 cups (300 g) plain flour
2 teaspoons bicarbonate
 of soda
1½ teaspoons salt
80 g solid vegetable shortening,
 such as Copha or Trex, or
 margarine
2 cups (300 g) wholemeal flour
1⅔ cups (420 ml) buttermilk
 or natural yogurt
fine oatmeal or caraway seeds,
 for sprinkling (optional)

Makes 8 rolls

You can sprinkle a little oatmeal or some caraway seeds over the tops of these rolls, if you like.

1 Preheat the oven to 200°C (Gas 6). Lightly grease a baking tray.
2 In a large bowl, sift together the plain flour, bicarbonate of soda and salt. Using a pastry blender or two knives, 'cut' in the shortening until the mixture resembles coarse crumbs. Stir in the wholemeal flour. Add the buttermilk or yogurt and stir to form a soft dough.
3 Lightly flour a work surface. Turn the dough out onto the work surface and knead until smooth, 4 to 5 minutes. Divide the dough into eight pieces and roll each into a ball. Place the dough balls on the baking tray, evenly spaced 5 to 7 cm apart. Using a sharp knife, cut a cross into the top of each ball.
4 Sprinkle with oatmeal or caraway seeds, if using. Bake until the rolls are crusty brown and sound hollow when tapped, about 20 minutes. Transfer the rolls to a wire rack to cool slightly. Serve warm.

Cinnamon Scrolls

7 g packet dry yeast

1 cup (250 ml) warm milk
(about 45°C)

½ cup (110 g) sugar

80 g butter, melted

2 eggs

1 teaspoon salt

4–4½ cups (600–675 g) plain
flour

CINNAMON FILLING

¾ cup (165 g) firmly packed
soft brown sugar

2 tablespoons ground cinnamon

¼ cup (60 g) butter, melted

CREAM CHEESE ICING

½ cup (125 g) butter, softened

1½ cups (185 g) icing sugar

¼ cup (60 g) cream cheese,
softened

½ teaspoon vanilla extract

pinch of salt

Makes 16 scrolls

Your whole house will be infused with the aroma of these sweet delicacies as they're baking. Cream cheese icing is the perfect finishing touch.

1 In a large bowl, combine the yeast and the milk; stir until the yeast has completely dissolved. Add the sugar, butter, eggs, salt and 2 cups (300 g) of the flour and beat until smooth. Stir in enough of the remaining flour to form a soft, sticky dough.

2 Lightly flour a work surface; lightly butter a large bowl. Turn the dough out onto the work surface and knead until smooth and elastic, 6 to 8 minutes. Place the dough in the bowl, turning it to completely coat it with butter. Cover the bowl with a tea towel and let the dough rise in a warm place until doubled in size, about 1 hour.

3 For the filling, mix the sugar and cinnamon in a small bowl until well blended. Lightly grease two 33 x 23 x 5 cm baking trays; re-flour the work surface.

4 Punch down the dough and turn out onto the work surface. Divide the dough in half. Using a rolling pin, roll each half into a 28 x 20 cm rectangle. Brush each rectangle with some of the melted butter. Sprinkle half the filling over each rectangle, leaving a 1–2 cm border around all the edges. Starting from a long side, roll up each rectangle in Swiss-roll fashion, then pinch the seams together to seal. Using a sharp knife, cut each roll into eight slices. Place the slices, cut side down, on the baking trays. Cover the trays and let the dough rise again until doubled in size, about 1 hour.

5 Preheat the oven to 180°C (Gas 4). Bake the rolls until golden brown, 20 to 25 minutes. Transfer the trays to wire racks and let the rolls cool for 5 to 10 minutes.

6 In a small bowl, beat all the icing ingredients together until smooth. Ice the warm scrolls and serve.

Hot Cross Buns

two 7 g packets dry yeast
2 cups (500 ml) warm milk
  (about 45°C)
80 g butter, softened
2 eggs, lightly beaten
¼ cup (55 g) sugar
1½ teaspoons salt
6–7 cups (900 g–1 kg) plain
  flour
½ cup (60 g) raisins
½ cup (75 g) dried currants
1 teaspoon ground cinnamon
¼ teaspoon ground allspice
  or mixed spice
1 egg yolk

ICING
2 cups (250 g) sifted icing
  sugar
2 tablespoons water

Makes 30 buns

This traditional Easter morning bun is just sweet enough and loaded with dried fruit.

1 In a large bowl, combine the yeast and milk and stir until the yeast has dissolved. Add the butter, eggs, sugar and salt, then stir until well blended.

2 In a bowl, combine 3 cups (450 g) of the flour, the raisins, currants, cinnamon and allspice. Add the flour mixture to the yeast mixture and stir until well blended. Add enough of the remaining flour to form a soft dough.

3 Lightly flour a work surface; generously butter a large bowl. Turn the dough out onto the work surface and knead until smooth and elastic, 6 to 8 minutes. Place the dough in the bowl, turning it to coat it completely with butter. Cover the bowl with a tea towel and let the dough rise in a warm place until doubled in size, about 1 hour.

4 Lightly grease three baking trays. Punch down the dough. Pinch off enough to form a ball about 4–5 cm in diameter. Repeat with the remaining dough, placing the dough balls 5 cm apart on the baking trays. Using a sharp knife, cut a cross on top of each dough ball. Cover with a tea towel and allow to rise again until doubled in size, about 30 minutes.

5 Preheat the oven to 180°C (Gas 4). Whisk the egg yolk with 2 tablespoons water, then brush over the risen buns. Bake the buns until golden brown, 15 to 20 minutes. Transfer the buns to wire racks to cool.

6 In a small bowl, combine the icing ingredients and stir until smooth. Place the icing in a piping bag, or place in a self-sealing plastic bag and snip off one corner. Pipe a cross in the cuts on top of each bun. Serve warm.

Sticky Buns

2 tablespoons sugar

½ cup (125 ml) lukewarm water (about 45°C)

two 7 g packets dry yeast

1 cup (250 ml) milk

2 teaspoons salt

½ cup (125 g) butter, melted, plus 3 tablespoons extra

1 large all-purpose potato, peeled, diced and boiled, then pushed through a fine sieve or a potato ricer

6½–7 cups (approx 1 kg) plain flour

1 egg, lightly beaten

FILLING

½ cup (115 g) firmly packed soft brown sugar

½ cup (125 ml) light corn syrup (optional)

2 teaspoons ground cinnamon

1 cup (250 g) softened butter, plus extra melted butter for brushing

2 cups (240 g) chopped pecans

Makes 30 buns

A nutty variation on the cinnamon roll, these gooey, sticky treats are sensational.

1 In a small bowl, combine the sugar, warm water and yeast; stir until the solids are completely dissolved. Let stand until the mixture is bubbly, about 10 minutes.

2 In a small saucepan over medium–high heat, bring the milk and 1 cup (250 ml) water to a boil. Pour into a large heatproof bowl, stir in the salt and ¼ cup (60 ml) of the melted butter and let cool for 10 minutes. Using a wooden spoon or electric mixer with a paddle attachment, add the potato, 2 cups (300 g) of the flour and the egg, beating at medium speed for 1 minute after each addition. Add the yeast mixture and beat for 1 minute longer.

3 If using the mixer, remove the paddle and attach a dough hook. Add 4½ cups (675 g) of the remaining flour and beat for 3 to 5 minutes, until a soft, manageable dough forms, then continue adding the flour, ¼–½ cup (35–75 g) at a time, as needed to reach the desired consistency.

4 Generously butter a large bowl. Using your hands, shape the dough into a ball and place in the bowl, turning it to completely coat it with the butter. Cover the bowl with a tea towel and let the dough rise in a warm place until doubled in size, about 50 minutes.

5 Lightly flour a work surface; lightly grease six baking trays (or bake the rolls in batches). Punch down the dough and turn out onto the work surface. Divide the dough in half. Using a rolling pin, roll each dough half into a 38 x 30 cm rectangle about 5 mm thick.

6 For the filling, combine the sugar, corn syrup (if using), cinnamon and butter in a small bowl and mix well. Spread half the filling over each rectangle, leaving a 2 cm border around all the edges. Sprinkle each rectangle with half the pecans. Lightly grease a 38 x 25 cm Swiss roll tin.

7 Starting from a long side, roll up each rectangle in Swiss-roll fashion, then pinch the seams together to seal; place seam side down. Using a sharp knife, cut each roll into fifteen 3 cm slices. Arrange the slices, not touching, in the Swiss roll tin. Cover with a tea towel and leave to rise for 20 minutes.

8 Preheat the oven to 180°C (Gas 4). Bake the buns until golden brown, about 40 minutes. Brush the buns with a little melted butter and bake for 5 minutes longer. Serve warm.

Cakes

Spice Cake

5 cups (950 g) Basic Cake Mix
   (page 61)
1¼ teaspoons ground nutmeg
1¼ teaspoons ground
   cinnamon
½ teaspoon ground cloves
¼ cup (60 g) butter
½ cup (125 g) sour cream
   or natural yogurt
2 eggs, lightly beaten

Makes 1 slab cake

Inviting on its own, this spice-filled cake is also wonderful with Chocolate Buttercream Icing (page 122). Much less expensive than a bakery cake, it is also tastier. This cake and the one that follows are outstanding examples of what you can do with the Basic Cake Mix from page 61.

1 Preheat the oven to 190°C (Gas 5). Generously grease a 33 x 23 x 5 cm slab tin or baking tray.
2 In a large heatproof bowl, combine the cake mix, nutmeg, cinnamon and cloves; stir to distribute the spices evenly.
3 In a small saucepan over medium–high heat, combine the butter and 1 cup (250 ml) water. Bring the mixture to a boil, then add to the cake mixture. Beat with a wooden spoon or electric beaters until well blended.
4 Stir in the sour cream and eggs; beat until they are well incorporated and no streaks of white remain.
5 Pour the batter into the slab tin. Bake until a skewer inserted into the centre of the cake comes out clean and the top of the cake springs back when lightly touched, about 40 minutes. Transfer the tin to a wire rack and let the cake cool completely before turning out.

Chocolate Cake

3½ cups (625 g) Basic Cake
    Mix (page 61)
½ cup (60 g) cocoa powder
1 cup (250 ml) milk
2 eggs, lightly beaten
3 tablespoons butter, melted

Makes 12 servings

If you like chocolate, this cake is guaranteed to please both your guests and your budget.

1. Preheat the oven to 190°C (Gas 5). Lightly grease and flour two 20 cm round cake tins.
2. In a large bowl, combine the cake mix and cocoa. Add half the milk, then beat for 2 minutes on medium speed, using electric beaters. Add the remaining milk, the eggs and butter, then beat for 2 minutes longer.
3. Divide the batter equally between the cake tins. Bake the cakes until a skewer inserted into the centre comes out clean and the top of the cake springs back when lightly touched, about 25 minutes.
4. Transfer the cake tins to wire racks and leave for 10 minutes to cool slightly. Run a knife around the edge of each cake to loosen it from the side of the tin, then carefully invert the tin and remove the cake. Set the cakes on the wire racks and let them cool completely. Fill and ice as desired.

Rich Dark Fruit Cake

2 cups (440 g) pitted prunes
⅓ cup (80 ml) brandy, sherry
    or orange juice
1 cup (230 g) firmly packed
    soft brown sugar
4 eggs
finely grated zest of 1 large
    lemon
finely grated zest of 1 large
    orange
3 cups (450 g) plain flour
2 teaspoons baking powder
1 teaspoon ground mixed spice
4 cups (750 g) top-quality
    mixed dried fruit
⅓ cup (80 ml) milk

Makes 32 slices

This moist, fruit-rich cake is so full of flavour that you won't notice that it is so much lower in fat than traditional recipes.

1. Preheat the oven to 180°C (Gas 4). Line a deep 23 cm round cake tin with baking paper.
2. In a food processor or using a hand-held mixer, purée the prunes and brandy to a smooth paste. Transfer the purée to a large bowl.
3. Add the sugar, eggs and lemon and orange zest, and whisk until the mixture is pale, thick and fluffy.
4. Sift the flour, baking powder and mixed spice onto the prune mixture, then fold in using a large metal spoon. Fold in the dried fruit and enough milk to make a soft dropping consistency.
5. Spoon the batter into the cake tin and smooth the top. Bake for 45 minutes, then reduce the oven temperature to 160°C (Gas 3). Continue baking for a further 1 hour 15 minutes, or until the cake is well risen, firm to the touch and a skewer inserted in the centre comes out clean. If, during baking, the top of the cake appears to be over-browning, cover loosely with a piece of foil.
6. Transfer the cake tin to a wire rack and let the cake cool for 10 to 15 minutes. Then remove the cake from the tin, peel off the paper and leave to cool completely on the rack. Store wrapped in foil, or in an airtight container.

Butter Cake

¾ cup (185 g) unsalted butter
1 cup (230 g) caster sugar
3 large eggs
2 cups (300 g) self-raising flour
¼ cup (60 ml) milk

Makes 8 servings

This is a dependable basic cake that will come in handy for all sorts of occasions.

1 Preheat the oven to 180°C (Gas 4). Grease a deep 20 cm round cake tin and line the base with baking paper.
2 Beat the butter until very soft, using electric beaters. Add the sugar and continue beating until the mixture is light, pale and fluffy.
3 Beat in the eggs gradually, adding a teaspoon of flour with each addition to prevent curdling. Fold in the rest of the flour alternately with milk, adding about a third at a time.
4 Pour the batter into the cake tin and bake for 50 to 60 minutes, or until a skewer inserted in the centre of the cake comes out clean.
5 Transfer the tin to a wire rack and let the cake cool for a few minutes, then turn out onto a wire rack to cool completely.

Angel Cake

1½ cups (375 ml) eggwhites (about 15 eggs)
1½ teaspoons cream of tartar
¼ teaspoon salt
1½ cups (330 g) sugar
1 cup (150 g) sifted plain flour or cake flour
2 teaspoons vanilla extract
¼ teaspoon almond extract

Makes 12 servings

Aptly named indeed, this cake is so light and airy that you'll swear it will float away if you don't eat it quickly. It's also free of any fat, and can be the base for many a light, luscious dessert. Suspending the cake upside down while it cools helps to create the cake's light texture.

1 Place the oven rack in the lowest possible position. Preheat the oven to 170°C (Gas 3); set out a 25 cm tube tin.
2 In a large bowl, combine the eggwhites, cream of tartar and salt. Beat until frothy, using electric beaters on medium speed. Gradually add the sugar, 2 tablespoons at a time, beating constantly. Increase the speed to high and continue beating until the mixture forms very soft peaks.
3 Fold the flour, ¼ cup (35 g) at a time, into the eggwhites, then fold in the vanilla and almond extracts.
4 Spoon the batter into the ungreased tube tin and gently smooth the top with a spatula. 'Cut' the spatula through the batter once to break and release any large air bubbles.
5 Bake until the top of the cake springs back when lightly touched, 50 to 60 minutes. Invert the tube tin with the central tube over the neck of a large bottle and let the cake cool completely. Using a knife, loosen the edges of the cake from the sides of the tin, then turn the cake out onto a cake plate.

Banana Cake

2 large, ripe bananas, about
    400 g in total
2 cups (300 g) self-raising
    flour
1 teaspoon baking powder
¼ cup (55 g) firmly packed
    soft brown sugar
⅓ cup (80 ml) sunflower oil
⅓ cup (80 ml) low-fat milk
2 eggs
1 cup (125 g) sultanas

Makes 8 servings

Quick and easy to prepare, this cake makes a healthy snack for hungry children or a handy addition to lunchboxes. And it's a great way to use up bananas that have been sitting in the fruit bowl for too long.

1. Preheat the oven to 180°C (Gas 4). Grease a deep 22 cm round cake tin and line the base with baking paper. Peel the bananas, then mash in a small bowl with a fork.
2. Sift the flour and baking powder into a large bowl and stir in the sugar. In a separate bowl, mix together the oil, milk and eggs, then add to the flour mixture. Stir in the sultanas and mashed bananas.
3. Pour the batter into the cake tin and bake for 50 to 55 minutes, until the cake is well risen and a skewer inserted in the centre comes out clean. Transfer the tin to a wire rack and let the cake cool for 15 minutes. Run a knife around the edge of the cake to loosen it, then turn it out onto a wire rack to cool completely. The cake can be kept in an airtight container for up to 4 days.

Orange Cake

3 eggs, separated, plus
    1 egg yolk
200 g butter, softened
1 cup (230 g) caster sugar
2 teaspoons grated orange zest
1½ cups (225 g) plain flour
3 teaspoons baking powder

GLAZE
125 ml (½ cup) orange juice
¼ cup (60 ml) orange liqueur
½ cup (110 g) sugar
1 teaspoon grated orange zest

Makes 8 servings

Store this cake in an airtight container and let it stand for a couple of days before eating it. You'll be rewarded with a full orange flavour.

1. Preheat the oven to 180°C (Gas 4). Grease a 24 cm spring-form tin and line it with baking paper.
2. Beat the eggwhites until stiff. Combine the 4 egg yolks, butter, sugar and orange zest in a bowl, then beat using electric beaters until the mixture is light and fluffy, about 5 minutes.
3. Sift the flour and baking powder, then stir into the butter mixture about a tablespoon at a time. Fold the eggwhite into the mixture with a metal spoon.
4. Pour the batter into the cake tin and and smooth the top. Bake for 35–40 minutes, or until golden brown. Remove the cake from the oven, but leave it in the tin.
5. Stir the glaze ingredients in a small saucepan over low heat until the sugar has dissolved. Prick the hot cake a few times with a fork and drizzle with the glaze. Transfer the tin to a wire rack and let the cake cool completely before removing the outer ring of the tin.

Cheesecake with Strawberry Glaze

CRUST
1¼ cups (155 g) crumbled
  shop-bought or homemade
  Anzac Biscuits (page 128) or
  Digestive Biscuits (page 130)
⅓ cup (90 g) butter or
  margarine, melted
¼ cup (55 g) sugar

FILLING
three 250 g packets cream
  cheese
1 cup (220 g) sugar
3 eggs
1 cup (250 g) sour cream

STRAWBERRY GLAZE
¼ cup (80 g) strawberry jam
1 tablespoon water
500 g fresh strawberries,
  hulled and thinly sliced

Makes 6 to 8 servings

Depending on availability, you can substitute raspberries, blackberries or blueberries in this recipe. Whatever you choose, you will have a dessert to rival an expensive bakery or deli cheesecake.

1 Preheat the oven to 170°C (Gas 3). Combine the crust ingredients in a bowl and toss using a fork until well blended. Press the crust mixture firmly over the base of a 23 cm spring-form tin.

2 For the filling, combine the cream cheese and sugar in a food processor or blender and pulse until well blended and smooth. With the motor running, add the eggs one at a time. Scrape down the sides of the bowl, add the sour cream and process until the mixture is smooth and well blended.

3 Pour the mixture into the cake tin and bake until the filling is only slightly wobbly in the middle, about 50 minutes (it will firm up as it cools). Transfer the tin to a wire rack and let the cheesecake cool to room temperature. Remove the sides of the tin before glazing the cheesecake.

4 For the glaze, combine the jam and water in a small saucepan and bring to a boil over medium–high heat. Remove from the heat and let the glaze cool slightly.

5 Brush the cheesecake with about one-third of the glaze. Beginning along an outside edge of the cake, arrange the strawberry slices in overlapping concentric circles over the cheesecake. Brush the remaining glaze lightly over the strawberries.

Cupcakes

225 g butter, softened
1 cup (230 g) caster sugar
1 teaspoon vanilla extract
4 large eggs
1⅔ cups (250 g) self-raising flour
1 tablespoon milk

ICING
½ cup (125 g) butter, softened
2 cups (250 g) icing sugar
2 tablespoons milk
food colouring (optional)

Makes 12

The icing on cupcakes isn't just to make them look pretty and add extra flavour; it also keeps them fresh.

1 Preheat the oven to 180°C (Gas 4). In a large bowl, cream the butter and sugar until pale and fluffy, using electric beaters.
2 Add the vanilla, then add the eggs one at a time, mixing well after each addition.
3 Sift the flour into the mixture. Using a plastic spatula or wooden spoon, fold in the flour and milk until combined.
4 Spoon the batter into 12 patty cases, filling them two-thirds full. Bake the cupcakes until golden, about 15 minutes. Turn the cupcakes out onto a wire rack to cool.
5 For the icing, beat the butter and icing sugar in a bowl using electric beaters until well creamed, about 2 minutes. Add the milk and food colouring, if using, mixing until combined.
6 Ice the cooled cupcakes and decorate as desired.

Vanilla Icing

⅓ cup (90 g) butter or margarine, softened
4 cups (500 g) icing sugar, sifted
¼ cup (60 ml) pouring cream
2 teaspoons vanilla extract
1–2 drops food colouring (optional)

Makes enough to fill and ice one 20–23 cm layer cake, 24 cupcakes or one 33 x 23 cm slab cake

This classic icing is easy and cheap to make, luscious to eat and versatile.

1 In a bowl, beat the butter until light and fluffy, using electric beaters on moderately high speed.
2 Reduce the speed to medium, and alternately add the sugar and the cream, a little at a time, beating constantly. Add the vanilla and beat until the icing is creamy. If desired, add food colouring to tint the icing.

VARIATION
Orange Buttercream Icing: Add ¼ cup (60 ml) orange juice and 1 tablespoon finely grated orange zest.

Chocolate Ganache Icing

¼ cup (55 g) caster sugar
50 g unsalted butter
2 cups (500 ml) pouring cream
2 tablespoons dark rum
500 g dark cooking chocolate, melted

Makes about 4 cups

Ganache is a decadent mixture of chocolate and cream that gives a rich and glossy icing – perfect for special-occasion cakes.

In a saucepan, combine the sugar, butter, cream and rum. Gently heat, stirring often, until the sugar has dissolved. Stir in the melted chocolate, then transfer to a bowl and chill the mixture for 30 minutes, or until set. Spread over the cooled cake.

Chocolate Buttercream Icing

⅓ cup (90 g) butter, softened
4 cups (500 g) icing sugar,
 sifted
¼ cup (60 ml) pouring cream
2 teaspoons vanilla extract
90 g dark chocolate, melted,
 or ½ cup (60 g) sifted cocoa
 powder

Makes enough to fill and ice
one 20–23 cm layer cake,
24 cupcakes or one 33 x 23 cm
slab cake

This is the icing that kids like to lick out of the bowl.
Inexpensive and easy to make, it is delicious.

1 In a bowl, beat the butter until light and fluffy, using electric
 beaters on moderately high speed.
2 Reduce the speed to medium, and alternately add the sugar
 and the cream, a little at a time, beating constantly. Add the
 vanilla and melted chocolate or cocoa powder and beat until
 the icing is creamy.

Simple Glaze Icing

¾ cup (90 g) icing sugar
1 tablespoon warm water,
 or as needed
food colouring (optional)

Makes enough to cover a
20 cm cake

This simplest of all icings is economical to make and
can be spread, drizzled or piped, depending on how
thick you make it.

Sift the icing sugar into a bowl and gradually mix in enough water
to make a smooth icing of the desired consistency. Add food
colouring, if using, a drop at a time, until the required depth of
colour is reached. Spread over the cooled cake.

Cream Cheese Icing

75 g cream cheese, softened
30 g butter, softened
1½ cups (185 g) icing sugar
finely grated zest of 1 lemon
1 tablespoon lemon juice

Makes enough to cover a
20 cm cake

This soft, rich, lemony icing is the classic topping for
carrot cake, but also goes well with other well-flavoured,
dense-textured cakes.

In a large bowl, combine all the ingredients. Beat with a wooden
spoon until smooth. Spread over the cooled cake.

Pies and Meringues

Basic Double Crust Pie Pastry

2¼ cups (335 g) flour
½ teaspoon salt
½ cup (125 g) cold butter,
    chopped
60 g vegetable shortening,
    such as Copha or Trex
5–6 tablespoons iced water

Makes enough for a 20–23 cm
double crust pie

Sweet and savoury pies are among the most popular items in the frozen food section of any supermarket, and sweet pies appear in every bakery section. (You'll find recipes for main-dish pies starting on page 176 and ones for sweet pies on page 125.) Don't waste your cash on ready-made piecrust. It's quick and easy, and if you know a few tricks, it will turn out light and flaky every time. Here is the basic recipe for a pie that has a top crust as well as a bottom one.

1 In a large bowl, sift together the flour and salt. Using a pastry blender or two knives, 'cut' in the butter and shortening until the mixture resembles coarse breadcrumbs.
2 Add the iced water, 1 tablespoon at a time, stirring the mixture with a fork to incorporate the water into the dough. Add water only until the dough begins to hold together. Handling the dough as little as possible, divide it in half, shape each half into a ball and wrap each ball in plastic wrap. Chill the dough balls for at least 1 hour before using.
3 For the bottom crust, place one ball of dough on a lightly floured board or pastry cloth. Flatten the ball slightly; then, using a lightly floured rolling pin, roll from the centre outwards in all directions. Make the dough circle large enough to cover the bottom and sides of a pie plate plus about 3 cm more.
4 For the top crust, place the remaining ball of dough on the lightly floured surface and flatten slightly. Roll the dough from the centre outwards in all directions until the circle is large enough to cover the pie plate plus about a 2 cm margin.

Basic Single Crust Pie Pastry

1½ cups (225 g) plain flour
¼ teaspoon salt
½ cup (125 g) cold butter,
  chopped
60 g vegetable shortening,
  such as Copha or Trex
3–4 tablespoons iced water

Makes enough for a 20–23 cm
single crust pie

Use this recipe when you are making an open-faced pie
or tart, such as one with a meringue or crumble topping.

1 In a large bowl, sift together the flour and salt. Using a pastry
   blender or two knives, 'cut' in the butter and shortening until
   the mixture resembles coarse breadcrumbs.
2 Add the iced water, 1 tablespoon at a time, stirring the mixture
   with a fork to incorporate the water into the dough. Add only
   enough water for the dough to hold together. Handling the
   dough as little as possible, shape it into a ball and wrap it in
   plastic wrap. Chill the dough ball for at least 1 hour before using.
3 Place the dough on a lightly floured board or pastry cloth.
   Flatten the ball slightly; then, using a lightly floured rolling pin,
   roll from the centre of the ball outward in all directions. Make
   the dough circle large enough to cover the bottom and sides
   of a pie plate plus about 3 cm more. Drape carefully over a pie
   plate, fold over the outer edge and trim or crimp it with your
   fingers to make a decorative edge. Fill and bake according to
   the pie recipe.
4 For a pre-baked pie shell, preheat the oven to 190°C (Gas 5).
   Place the pie shell on a baking tray and prick the bottom. Line
   the bottom with two layers of foil and add dried beans or pastry
   beads to weigh it down, otherwise the base will puff up during
   cooking. Bake 10 to 15 minutes, or until golden brown.

Puff Pastry

2½ cups (375 g) plain flour
⅔ cup (160 g) butter, chopped
¾ cup (185 ml) chilled water
125 g white vegetable
  shortening, such as Copha
  or Trex

Makes enough for a 20–23 cm
pie

This airy, crisp and flaky pastry can be used for the
top crust on pies, for sausage rolls, or to make delicate
pastries such as millefeuille.

1 Sift the flour into a bowl and rub in half the butter. Add the
   water and mix to a soft dough. On a lightly floured surface,
   roll the dough into a rectangle about 5 mm thick. Dot half the
   remaining butter over the top two-thirds of the rectangle, then
   fold the bottom third up and over the centre third. Then bring
   the top third down so that it covers the bottom third. Press
   edges together with the rolling pin.
2 Give the dough a quarter turn to the left so that the side joins
   are to the bottom and top. Roll out again into a rectangle
   5 mm thick. Dot vegetable fat over the top two-thirds of the
   pastry; fold and turn as before. Repeat, using the remaining
   butter. Wrap in plastic wrap and chill for 30 minutes.
3 Roll out and bake as directed in the recipe.

Shortcrust Pastry

¾ cup (185 g) unsalted butter,
   chilled and diced
1⅔ cups (250 g) plain flour
pinch of salt
3 tablespoons iced water

Makes enough to line a
22–26 cm loose-based flan tin

This is the classic crisp pastry for pies and tarts.
The trick is to handle it as little as possible (using a
food processor helps) and to chill it both before and
after rolling it out.

1 Place the butter, flour and salt in a bowl. Rub in the butter
   with your fingertips until the mixture resembles coarse
   breadcrumbs. Alternatively, combine in a food processor
   and pulse until the mixture resembles coarse breadcrumbs.
2 Add 2 tablespoons of the water and 'cut' in with two knives
   or a pastry blender, or pulse if using a food processor, just
   until the mixture comes together, adding a little more water
   as necessary. Do not overmix.
3 Turn the dough out onto a lightly floured work surface and
   knead just enough to bring it together into a ball. Shape the
   dough into a round. Flatten it a little, cover with plastic wrap
   and place in the refrigerator for at least 30 minutes, or
   preferably overnight.
4 Roll out the dough on a lightly floured work surface to about
   5 mm thick and use it to line an ungreased flan tin, pie dish
   or tartlet tins.
5 Prick the pastry several times with a fork. Chill for 30 minutes;
   this helps stop the pastry shrinking when it is baked.
6 Bake blind if instructed by the recipe.

Custard Pie

Basic Single Crust Pie Pastry
   (page 124)
4 eggs
2½ cups (625 ml) milk
½ cup (110 g) sugar
1 teaspoon vanilla extract
1 teaspoon almond extract
1 teaspoon salt
1 teaspoon ground nutmeg

Makes 6 to 8 servings

This creamy pie is never as good from a shop as it is
from your kitchen.

1 Preheat the oven to 200°C (Gas 6). Line a 23 cm pie dish with
   the piecrust; trim or turn under the edges of the dough and,
   if desired, form a decorative edge around the piecrust. Prick
   the bottom of the crust, line with foil or baking paper, fill with
   dried beans or pastry beads and bake it for 10 minutes.
2 Meanwhile, in a large bowl, beat the eggs. Add the remaining
   ingredients and stir to blend well. Pour the filling into the
   piecrust, then cover the edges of the crust with pieces of foil.
3 Bake until a knife inserted near the centre of the pie comes out
   clean, 20 to 25 minutes. Let the pie cool completely before
   serving; store in the refrigerator.

Perfect Apple Pie

Basic Double Crust Pie Pastry
  (page 123)
1 large egg, separated
4 tart apples, such as
  granny smith or jonathan
4 sweet apples, such as
  golden delicious
2 tablespoons lemon juice
½ cup (115 g) firmly packed
  soft brown sugar
½ cup (110 g) sugar
⅓ cup (50 g) sifted plain flour
¼ teaspoon ground cinnamon
⅛ teaspoon ground allspice
⅛ teaspoon grated nutmeg
2 tablespoons butter
1 tablespoon iced water

Makes 8 servings

Apple pie is a perennial favourite, and you will never enjoy a shop-bought example again after you have tasted the homemade type.

1 Preheat the oven to 220°C (Gas 7). Line a 23 cm pie dish with the bottom piecrust, letting the edges hang over about 3 cm. In a cup, whisk the eggwhite until frothy and brush over the bottom crust; reserve the egg yolk for the top crust glaze. Roll out the remaining piecrust. Cover the top crust with plastic wrap until ready to use.

2 Peel, core and slice all the apples about 5 mm thick, placing them in a large bowl. Sprinkle the apple slices with the lemon juice as you work to prevent browning. In a small bowl, combine the sugars, flour, cinnamon, allspice and nutmeg. Sprinkle the sugar mixture over the apple slices, tossing as you work to coat all the slices. Spoon the apple slices into the piecrust, mounding the slices higher in the centre. Cut the butter into small pieces and scatter among the apple slices.

3 Using a pastry brush, moisten the edges of the bottom piecrust with a little water. Carefully transfer the top crust to cover the pie filling. Fold the top edges of the pastry over and under the bottom crust edges; pinch the edges together to seal. Cut slits or make decorative vents; if desired, form a decorative edge around the piecrust. In a small bowl, whisk the reserved egg yolk and cold water together. Brush the glaze over the top of the pie, avoiding the slits or decorative vents.

4 Bake the pie for 15 minutes; reduce the temperature to 190°C (Gas 5) and bake until the filling is bubbly and the piecrust is golden brown, about 35 minutes more. If the crust edges are browning too quickly, cover them with pieces of foil. Place the pie on a rack to cool for at least 20 minutes before serving.

Meringue Shells

1 cup (250 ml) eggwhites
  (10 large eggs)
¾ cup (165 g) sugar
½ cup (60 g) sifted icing sugar

Makes 6 individual meringues
or 1 meringue pie shell

The finished appearance of the meringue shells should be dry and crisp, but not browned.

1 Preheat the oven to 130°C (Gas 1). Line a baking tray with baking paper.
2 In a large bowl with electric beaters on low, slowly beat the eggwhites until frothy. Still beating on low, gradually add ½ cup (110 g) of the sugar until the eggwhites look silvery. Increase the mixer speed to medium, and slowly add the remaining sugar, beating just until the eggwhites form stiff peaks. Using a spatula, fold in the icing sugar.
3 Fit a piping bag with a number 6 star tip, and fill the bag with the meringue. Pipe six coiled circles of meringue onto the baking tray. Pipe a second-tier ring of meringue along the outer edge of each of the first circles. (If you don't have a piping bag and nozzle, spoon six mounds of meringue onto the baking tray and, using the back of the spoon, press a hollow in the centre of each mound to make a shell.)
4 Bake the meringues for 1 hour; turn off the oven but do not open the oven door. Let the meringues stand in the warm oven for 1 hour longer. Transfer the meringues to wire racks to cool.

SERVING SUGGESTION
Meringue Shells with Raspberry Sauce: Sweetly tart raspberries are the perfect foil for crisp meringue shells. Make ¾ cup (185 ml) Raspberry Sauce (page 59). Place each meringue on a plate. Spoon raspberry sauce into each shell and serve immediately.

Pavlova

Meringue Shells (above)
2 cups (500 ml) whipping
  cream
2 tablespoons sugar
fresh fruit, such as 250 g
  strawberries, trimmed and
  sliced; or 4 kiwifruit, peeled
  and sliced, plus the pulp
  from 4 passionfruit

Makes 12 servings

Legend has it that this resplendent dessert was concocted in honour of the celebrated ballerina Anna Pavlova.

1 Preheat the oven to 130°C (Gas 1). Line a 35 cm baking tray with baking paper. Spoon the meringue onto the baking tray, forming a 30 cm round shape with slightly built-up edges. Bake for 1 hour; turn off the oven but do not open the oven door. Let the meringue stand in the warm oven for 1 hour longer. Transfer the meringue shell to a wire rack to cool.
2 In a large bowl, beat the whipping cream until it forms soft peaks, using electric beaters on moderately high. Gradually add the sugar, beating constantly until stiff peaks form.
3 Spoon the whipped cream into the meringue shell, mounding it decoratively. Arrange the fruit on top of the whipped cream and serve immediately.

Biscuits, Slices and Brownies

Chocolate Chip Cookies

1 cup (250 g) butter, softened
¾ cup (165 g) sugar
¾ cup (165 g) firmly packed
   soft brown sugar
2 eggs
1 teaspoon vanilla extract
2¼ cups (335 g) plain flour
1 teaspoon salt
1 teaspoon bicarbonate of soda
1 cup (170 g) dark chocolate
   chips
1 cup (125 g) chopped walnuts
   or pecans (optional)

Makes about 40 cookies

This American classic has been loved for generations. Although there are plenty of types to choose from in the shops, homemade are just better.

1 Preheat the oven to 180°C (Gas 4); lightly grease two or more baking trays.
2 In a bowl, beat the butter and sugar until well creamed, using electric beaters. Add the eggs one at a time, beating well after each addition. Add the vanilla and stir until well blended.
3 In a small bowl, combine the flour, salt and bicarbonate of soda. Add the flour mixture to the butter mixture, stirring until well blended. Add the chocolate chips and nuts, if using, and stir until they are evenly distributed.
4 Using a tablespoon, drop the dough onto the baking trays, spacing the mounds about 5 cm apart. Bake the cookies until golden brown, about 10 minutes. Transfer the cookies to wire racks to cool.

Anzac Biscuits

1 cup (150 g) plain flour
pinch of salt
1¼ cups (125 g) rolled oats
⅔ cup (145 g) caster sugar
¾ cup (65 g) desiccated coconut
½ cup (125 g) butter, chopped
2 tablespoons water
2 tablespoons golden syrup
1 teaspoon bicarbonate of soda

Makes about 30 biscuits

Also known as oatmeal biscuits, these economical, long-lasting, eggless biscuits were introduced during World War I when there were egg shortages.

1 Preheat the oven to 150°C (Gas 2). Lightly brush two baking trays with melted butter and line them with baking paper.
2 Sift the flour and salt into a bowl. Add the rolled oats, caster sugar and desiccated coconut and mix well.
3 In a small saucepan, combine the butter, water and golden syrup. Cook over medium heat until the butter melts and the mixture is well combined. Remove from the heat and stir in the bicarbonate of soda (the mixture will begin to froth). Working quickly, add the butter mixture to the dry ingredients and mix well to combine.
4 Roll the mixture into balls and place on the baking trays, allowing room for the biscuits to spread. Flatten each biscuit slightly with your fingertips. Bake for 8 minutes, then swap the trays around and bake for a further 7 to 8 minutes, or until the biscuits are golden around the edges. Allow to stand on the trays for 5 minutes before transferring the biscuits to a wire rack to cool completely. Repeat with the remaining biscuit mixture.

Peanut Butter Biscuits

½ cup (125 g) butter or
  margarine, softened
½ cup (110 g) sugar, plus
  extra for decorating
½ cup (115 g) firmly packed
  soft brown sugar
½ cup (125 g) Peanut Butter
  (page 33)
1 egg
½ teaspoon vanilla extract
1¼ cups (185 g) plain flour
½ teaspoon bicarbonate of soda
½ teaspoon baking powder

Makes 45 to 50 biscuits

Homemade biscuits are always so much better than
commercial types. These appeal to children and adults
alike, and are easy and delectable.

1 In a large bowl, beat the butter and sugars until well creamed,
  using electric beaters. Add the peanut butter, egg and vanilla
  and beat until smooth.
2 In a small bowl, combine the flour, bicarbonate of soda and
  baking powder. Add the flour mixture to the butter mixture
  and beat until well blended. Cover with plastic wrap and place
  in the refrigerator until the dough is chilled, about 1 hour.
3 Meanwhile, preheat the oven to 190°C (Gas 5). Set out two or
  more baking trays.
4 Pinch off a walnut-sized portion of the chilled dough. Using
  floured hands, roll the dough into a 3 cm diameter ball and
  place on one of the baking trays. Repeat with the remaining
  dough, spacing the balls about 5 cm apart. Using a fork
  dipped in sugar, flatten each dough ball by pressing the
  tines in a crisscross pattern on each biscuit.
5 Bake until the biscuits are set and lightly browned underneath,
  10 to 12 minutes. Transfer the biscuits to wire racks and leave
  to cool completely.

Coconut Macaroons

3 eggwhites
1 cup (220 g) sugar
2½ cups (225 g) desiccated
  coconut
1 cup (160 g) macadamia nuts
  or almonds, finely chopped

Makes about 35 macaroons

Desiccated coconut makes for a delectable macaroon,
which you can make better and more inexpensively
than any manufacturer.

1 Preheat the oven to 180°C (Gas 4); lightly grease two
  baking trays.
2 In a bowl, beat the eggwhites until soft peaks form, using
  electric beaters on high. Gradually add the sugar, beating
  after each addition, until stiff, glossy peaks form. Fold in the
  coconut and nuts until well blended.
3 Using a tablespoon, scoop out a portion of the dough.
  Using damp hands, roll the dough into a ball and place
  on the baking trays. Repeat with the remaining dough.
4 Bake the macaroons until lightly golden, 20 to 25 minutes.
  Transfer the macaroons to wire racks to cool completely.
  Store in an airtight container for 2 to 3 days.

Gingersnaps

185 g vegetable shortening, such as Copha or Trex

½ cup (110 g) sugar, plus extra for rolling

½ cup (115 g) firmly packed soft brown sugar

1 egg

¼ cup (90 g) molasses

2 cups (300 g) plain flour

2 teaspoons bicarbonate of soda

1½ teaspoons ground ginger

1 teaspoon ground cinnamon

½ teaspoon salt

Makes about 40 biscuits

The warm tang of ginger infuses each bite of these old-fashioned favourites. As they bake, the spicy aroma will warm the kitchen.

1 Preheat the oven to 180°C (Gas 4); lightly grease two or more baking trays.
2 In a large bowl, beat the shortening and sugars until well creamed, using electric beaters. Add the egg and molasses and beat until well blended.
3 In a small bowl, combine the flour, bicarbonate of soda, ginger, cinnamon and salt. Gradually add the flour mixture to the butter mixture, beating after each addition, until well blended.
4 Place some additional sugar in a small bowl. Pinch off a walnut-sized portion of the dough. Using your hands, roll the portion into a ball, then roll the ball in the sugar and place it on one of the baking trays. Repeat with the remaining dough, spacing the balls about 5 cm apart.
5 Bake the biscuits until lightly browned and crinkly, 12 to 15 minutes. Transfer the biscuits to a wire rack and leave to cool completely.

Digestive Biscuits

1 cup (150 g) wholemeal plain flour

1 teaspoon baking powder

½ teaspoon bicarbonate of soda

¼ cup (30 g) oatmeal

¼ cup (20 g) unprocessed bran

½ cup (115 g) firmly packed soft brown sugar

50 g butter or margarine

⅓ cup (80 ml) milk, or as needed

Makes 25 biscuits

These crunchy, golden biscuits are full of nutty, slightly sweet flavours. They are sliced from a long piece of dough, which you can make ahead and store in the refrigerator or freezer until needed.

1 Sift the flour, baking powder and bicarbonate of soda into a mixing bowl, tipping in any bran left in the sieve. Add the oatmeal, bran and sugar, and mix well to combine.
2 Rub in the butter with your fingertips until the mixture resembles breadcrumbs. Add 3 tablespoons of the milk and stir in well so the mixture forms a soft dough. If the mixture is a little dry, add the remaining milk.
3 Turn the dough out onto a sheet of plastic wrap and shape it into a log about 25 cm long. Wrap the plastic around the dough and roll it gently back and forwards to make a smooth shape. Twist the ends of the plastic together to seal. Chill the dough for about 30 minutes. (It can be kept for up to 4 days in the refrigerator.)
4 Preheat the oven to 190°C (Gas 5); line a baking tray with baking paper. Unwrap the dough and, using a very sharp knife, cut it into slices 1 cm thick. Place on the baking tray and bake until lightly browned, about 12 minutes.
5 Transfer the biscuits to a wire rack and leave to cool completely. Store in an airtight container for up to 5 days.

Shortbread

1 cup (250 g) butter, softened
⅔ cup (145 g) caster sugar,
  plus extra for sprinkling
2½ cups (375 g) plain flour

Makes 12 shortbreads

This crisp, rich, buttery treat, which originated in Scotland, will keep in an airtight container for about 4 weeks. It is pretty cut into shapes to serve or give as gifts at Christmas or other festive occasions.

1 Preheat the oven to 160°C (Gas 3). Grease a large baking tray and line with baking paper.
2 In a large bowl, cream the butter and sugar using electric beaters until pale and fluffy. Using a large metal spoon, fold in the flour in two to three batches and mix to a soft dough.
3 Turn the dough out onto a floured work surface and knead lightly and briefly until smooth. Flatten with floured hands into a 15 cm circle and place on the baking tray.
4 Using a rolling pin, roll the dough out into a neat 18 cm circle. With floured fingers, pinch the edges decoratively. Sprinkle with the extra sugar. With a sharp knife, mark the surface of the shortbread into 12 even wedges.
5 Bake until pale and firm, about 40 minutes. While still warm, cut the wedges along the score marks all the way through. Let the shortbreads cool completely on the baking tray.

Refrigerator Biscuits

1¾ cups (260 g) plain flour
½ teaspoon ground cinnamon
¼ teaspoon bicarbonate of soda
pinch of salt
¼ cup (60 g) butter, softened
⅔ cup (140 g) sugar
⅓ cup (80 g) firmly packed
  soft brown sugar
1 large egg
1 teaspoon vanilla extract
⅓ cup (90 g) light sour cream

Makes 72 biscuits

These are the ultimate standby; the dough is made ahead and kept in the freezer compartment of the refrigerator until you want to bake it.

1 In a bowl, sift together the flour, cinnamon, bicarbonate of soda and salt.
2 In a large bowl, cream the butter and sugars using electric beaters on high speed until pale and fluffy, about 4 minutes. Add the egg and vanilla and beat until well combined. Stir in the flour mixture with a wooden spoon, then stir in the sour cream.
3 Tear off a 50 cm sheet of plastic wrap and sprinkle lightly with flour. Transfer the dough to the plastic wrap and shape into a log 40 cm long. Roll the log tightly in the plastic wrap and refrigerate until firm, about 2 hours. (Alternatively, wrap the dough in heavy-duty foil and freeze for up to 1 month.)
4 Preheat the oven to 190°C (Gas 5). Slice the dough into rounds about 3 mm thick to make 72 biscuits. Place 1 cm apart on ungreased baking trays.
5 Bake the biscuits until crisp and golden brown around the edges, about 8 minutes, taking care not to overbake. (If you're using frozen dough, increase the baking time to 10 minutes.) Transfer the biscuits to wire racks to cool completely. Store in airtight containers.

Brownies

1 cup (150 g) chopped dark
  chocolate
1½ cups (225 g) plain flour
1 teaspoon baking powder
½ teaspoon salt
¾ cup (185 g) butter, softened
1½ cups (330 g) sugar
4 eggs
2 teaspoons vanilla extract
2 cups (250 g) chopped
  walnuts or pecans

Makes about 24 brownies

This recipe is studded with nuts, but you can substitute chocolate chips or just make a plain brownie. Bought ones are no match for warm brownies out of your oven, filling the air with the smell of chocolate and costing you much less.

1 Preheat the oven to 180°C (Gas 4). Line a 33 x 23 x 5 cm slab tin or baking tray with foil. Lightly grease and flour the foil.
2 In a small, heavy saucepan over the lowest heat, melt the chocolate, stirring occasionally. Remove from the heat and let the chocolate cool. Alternatively, melt the chocolate on low power in the microwave.
3 In a small bowl or on a sheet of wax paper, combine the flour, baking powder and salt.
4 In a large bowl, cream the butter for 2 minutes using electric beaters on medium speed. Add the sugar and beat for 2 minutes longer. Add the eggs, one at a time, beating well after each addition. Beat in the vanilla and cooled chocolate.
5 Using a wooden spoon, add the flour mixture to the chocolate mixture and stir until well blended. Stir in the nuts. Pour the batter into the slab tin.
6 Bake until a skewer inserted in the centre comes out clean, about 35 minutes. Transfer the tin to a wire rack and let the brownies cool before cutting.

If you run out of dark chocolate

If a recipe calls for 30 g dark chocolate and you don't have any, combine 3 tablespoons cocoa powder with 1 tablespoon softened butter, margarine or vegetable shortening (such as Copha or Trex). Add 1 tablespoon sugar, if you like, to make a sweeter mixture.

Chocolate Caramel Slice

1¼ cups (185 g) plain flour
½ cup (45 g) desiccated coconut
½ cup (125 g) unsalted butter
½ cup (95 g) lightly packed
   soft brown sugar

CARAMEL
400 g can sweetened
   condensed milk
3 tablespoons golden syrup
½ cup (115 g) caster sugar
¼ cup (60 g) unsalted butter

TOPPING
175 g dark cooking chocolate,
   chopped

Makes 12 slices

This rich, sticky and gooey treat is an all-time favourite.
It's a perfect crowd-pleaser for a fete, fair or party.

1 Preheat the oven to 180°C (Gas 4). Grease a shallow 20 cm
   square cake tin and line with baking paper.
2 Sift the flour into a bowl, then add the coconut. Combine
   the butter and sugar in a saucepan and stir over medium heat
   until the butter has melted and the sugar has dissolved.
3 Add the butter mixture to the flour mixture and stir until just
   combined. Press into the cake tin with the back of a metal
   spoon. Bake for 20 to 25 minutes, or until firm and golden.
   Transfer the tin to a wire rack and leave to cool.
4 For the caramel, put the condensed milk, golden syrup,
   sugar and butter in a heavy-based saucepan. Stir over low
   heat until the mixture boils. Pour over the cooked biscuit
   base and bake for 20 minutes. Transfer to a wire rack and
   leave to cool completely.
5 For the topping, melt the chocolate in a heatproof bowl
   set over a pan of barely simmering water. Spread over the
   cooled caramel with a palette knife and leave to set. When
   cool, cut into slices and serve.

Friands

6 eggwhites
¾ cup (185 g) butter, melted
1¼ cups (125 g) ground
   almonds
2 cups (250 g) icing sugar,
   plus extra for dusting
75 g (½ cup) plain flour
6 strawberries, halved

Makes 12 friands

The ground almonds make these pretty little cakes
very moist. Strawberries add to the soft texture and
complement the richness of the nuts.

1 Preheat the oven to 200°C (Gas 6). Grease a 12-hole standard
   muffin tin or friand tin and place on a baking tray.
2 Place the eggwhites in a bowl; whisk lightly with a fork until
   combined. Add the butter, ground almonds, sugar and flour
   and stir with a wooden spoon until just combined.
3 Spoon the batter into the prepared tin. Press a strawberry half
   lightly into each friand. Bake for about 25 minutes.
4 Transfer to a wire rack and leave to cool in the tin for 5 minutes,
   then turn out onto the wire rack to cool. Dust with icing sugar
   just before serving.

Fast Foods and Snacks

Potato Crisps ❖ Spicy Nut Mix ❖ Chips ❖ Oven-baked Chips ❖ Pizza ❖ Chicken Nuggets

Breakfast Treats

Traditional French Toast ❖ Baked French Toast ❖ Muesli Bar Slice ❖ Apricot Oat Flapjacks ❖ Scones ❖ Pancakes ❖ Waffles

Appetising Nibbles

Antipasto Platter ❖ Chicken Liver Pâté ❖ Ham, Pork and Veal Terrine ❖ Country Pork Sausages ❖ Devilled Eggs ❖ Globe Artichokes in Olive Oil ❖ Marinated Goat's Cheese ❖ Spinach and Feta Filo Triangles ❖ Quesadillas ❖ Curry Puffs

Dips

Baba Ghanoush ❖ Hummus ❖ Guacamole ❖ Beetroot Dip ❖ Taramasalata ❖ Tapenade ❖ Tzatziki

Cold Drinks

Classic Iced Tea ❖ Cranberry Iced Tea ❖ Iced Coffee ❖ Iced Coffee Slush ❖ Lemonade Syrup ❖ Ginger Beer ❖ Traditional Lemonade ❖ Lemon Squash ❖ Orange Blossom ❖ Non-alcoholic Punch ❖ Lemon Barley Water ❖ Bloody Mary Mix ❖ Bloody Mary ❖ Fruit Juice Spritzer ❖ Sangria

Hot Drinks

Caffe Latte ❖ Cappuccino Mix ❖ Cocoa ❖ Hot Chocolate Viennese ❖ Chai ❖ Hot Spiced Tea ❖ Hot Mulled Cider ❖ Hot Non-alcoholic Punch

Snacks, Nibbles and Drinks

When it comes to satisfying those afternoon
munchies, the recipes in this chapter provide
healthy alternatives to greasy fast food and bags
of salty snacks from the vending machine.

You'll find real honest-to-goodness homemade potato chips,
chicken nuggets and even pizza. And when you taste them,
you'll finally realise why these foods became so popular in
the first place. You may even spoil yourself and never be able
to settle for the commercial versions again. Your own pizza
dough, you'll discover, is yeasty and delicious, inviting new
and interesting toppings.

You'll also find recipes for those breakfast treats that we
often go out for – or buy frozen and pay far too much for. In
addition, there are recipes here that can be real money savers
when you entertain. You'll discover how easy it is to make your
own finger foods and dips, instead of hiring a caterer or buying
them from the local deli. The savoury treats in this chapter
include an antipasto platter, pâté and rich cheesy nibbles as
well as several delicious easy-to-make dips.

For an insatiable thirst or caffeine craving, the recipes here
provide not only some pleasing summer quenchers but also
some delightful and economical alternatives to the pricey
products at your local cafe.

Fast Foods and Snacks

Potato Crisps

vegetable oil for deep-frying
(about 8 cups/2 litres)
500 g roasting (floury)
potatoes, peeled
salt, to taste

Makes 4 servings

We are a nation of snackers, so we might as well make our own and ensure they are as healthy as they can be.

1 Pour the oil in a deep-fryer or large, heavy-based saucepan to a depth of about 8 cm. Insert a deep-fat thermometer and heat the oil to 190°C.
2 Meanwhile, slice the potatoes into rounds about 3 mm thick. As you work, drop the rounds into iced water. When ready to fry, lift the rounds from the water and pat dry on paper towels.
3 Place the potato slices in the fryer in small batches to avoid lowering the temperature of the oil; fry until crisp and golden, 3 to 5 minutes per batch. Using a slotted spoon or fryer basket, transfer the crisps to paper towels to drain. Let the oil reheat to the correct temperature before frying the next batch.
4 Lightly sprinkle the crisps with salt and serve.

Spicy Nut Mix

3 teaspoons vegetable oil
½ cup (80 g) almonds
½ cup (80 g) brazil nuts
½ cup (80 g) cashew nuts
½ cup (70 g) hazelnuts
½ cup (80 g) macadamia nuts
½ cup (80 g) peanuts
½ cup (50 g) pecans
½ cup (50 g) walnut halves
2 tablespoons sugar
½ teaspoon ground cayenne
pepper, or to taste
salt, to taste

Makes 4 cups (600 g)

This lightly spiced mixture of nuts is perfect for lunchbox snacks or party nibbles.

1 Heat the oil in a large, heavy-based, non-stick frying pan over medium heat. Add the nuts, tossing to coat.
2 Add the sugar, cayenne pepper and a pinch of salt and cook, stirring constantly, for 8 minutes, until the sugar has caramelised and the nuts are well coated. Serve the nuts hot or at room temperature.

Chips

vegetable oil for deep-frying
  (about 8 cups/2 litres)
500 g roasting (floury)
  potatoes, peeled
salt, to taste

Makes 4 servings

Who can resist these hot, crisp-on-the-outside, creamy-on-the-inside potato delights? The good news is that you can make them easily yourself, and because you control the frying and can do it right, very little fat will remain on the chips – making them a lot healthier than the fast-food variety.

1 Pour the oil in a deep-fryer or large, heavy-based saucepan to a depth of about 8 cm. Insert a deep-fat thermometer and heat the oil to 190°C.
2 Meanwhile, cut the potatoes into long strips about 5 mm square. As you work, drop the strips into a bowl of iced water. When ready to fry, lift the strips from the water and pat them completely dry on paper towels.
3 Place the potato strips in the fryer in small batches to avoid lowering the temperature of the oil; fry until brown and crisp, about 5 minutes per batch. Using a slotted spoon or fryer basket, transfer the chips to paper towels to drain. Keep warm on a hot tray or in a 100°C (Gas ½) oven. Let the oil reheat to the correct temperature before frying the next batch.
4 Sprinkle the chips with salt and serve hot.

Oven-baked Chips

2 tablespoons cornflour
2 tablespoons reduced-salt
  soy sauce
4 potatoes, peeled and cut
  into strips
1 tablespoon olive oil
¼ teaspoon salt

Makes 4 servings

A healthier alternative to the perennial favourite, these chips are loaded with flavour but are low in fat.

1 In a large bowl, combine the cornflour, soy sauce and 4 cups (1 litre) water, then whisk until well blended and smooth. Add the potatoes, toss gently, then cover and refrigerate for 1 hour.
2 Preheat the oven to 190°C (Gas 5). Drain the potatoes and place on paper towels to drain; pat dry. In a large bowl, toss the potatoes with the olive oil and sprinkle with the salt. Coat a baking tray with cooking spray. Arrange the potato strips in a single layer over the baking tray. Bake for 15 minutes, then turn the chips over and bake for 15 to 20 minutes longer, until tender and golden brown. Serve hot.

Pizza

¼ cup (60 ml) warm water
(about 45°C)
7 g packet dry yeast
1½ cups (225 g) unsifted
plain flour
¼ cup (60 ml) olive oil
½ teaspoon salt

TOPPING
polenta (cornmeal), for dusting
½ cup (125 ml) tomato sauce
or paste (or use a mixture
of each)
toppings as desired: grated
mozzarella, sliced pepperoni,
sliced mushrooms, capsicum
(pepper) strips, sautéed
Italian sausage, sliced olives,
thinly sliced onions, bacon,
pineapple, anchovies, etc

Makes a 30 cm pizza

Making your own pizza is not only thrifty but an easy way to please everyone – let each family member choose the topping for their part of the finished pizza. It will be easier if you have a baking stone or baking tiles for the bottom of the oven and a baker's paddle to transfer the pizza into and out of the oven. This recipe makes enough dough for single family-sized pizza, or you can divide it into four pieces to make individual pizzas so everyone can top their own.

1 In a small bowl, combine the warm water, yeast and ¼ cup (35 g) of the flour. Stir to combine, then cover and let rise for 30 minutes.

2 Stir down the yeast mixture; add ¼ cup (60 ml) room-temperature water, the remaining flour, the olive oil and salt. On a lightly floured surface, turn out the dough and knead for 10 minutes (or use the dough hook of an electric mixer and knead for 5 minutes).

3 For use within 1 day, wrap the dough tightly in plastic wrap and store in the refrigerator; let it sit at room temperature for 1 to 2 hours before using. (To freeze the dough for later use, wrap it tightly in plastic wrap, place in a self-sealing freezer-safe plastic bag, squeeze out all the air and seal. Freeze for up to 3 months. Thaw in the plastic wrap in the refrigerator for several hours, then bring the dough to room temperature before using.)

4 Remove the racks from your oven and place a baking stone on the bottom of the oven. Preheat the oven to 230°C (Gas 8) for about 20 minutes; it should be very hot. Dust a heavy upside-down baking tray or a wooden baker's paddle with polenta. On a lightly floured surface using a lightly floured rolling pin, roll the dough into a 30 cm circle. Flop the dough over the rolling pin and unroll onto the polenta-covered baking tray or paddle. (You can also sprinkle polenta on a regular baking tray and cook the pizza on an oven rack, but the crust may be soggier.)

5 Spread the tomato sauce or paste over the pizza dough, leaving a 2 cm margin. Scatter the toppings as desired.

6 Gently shake the pizza off the baking tray or paddle onto the baking stone. Bake until the crust is golden brown, about 20 minutes. Serve immediately.

Chicken Nuggets

750 g skinless chicken breasts
½ cup (75 g) Chicken
    Seasoning Mix (page 42)
2 cups (200 g) dry
    breadcrumbs
2 large eggs

Makes 6 servings

For many parents, these morsels are a life- and time-saver, but the cost of regularly buying them can really eat away at your budget.

1 Cut each chicken breast into 3 cm cubes. Place the seasoning mix in a self-sealing bag. Place the breadcrumbs in a large, shallow dish. In another shallow dish, whisk together the eggs and 2 tablespoons water until frothy.
2 Drop the chicken cubes, a few pieces at a time, into the bag of seasoning; seal and shake until they are well coated. Shake off any excess seasoning. Dip each cube into the beaten egg, then into the breadcrumbs, gently pressing the crumbs onto the chicken until they stick. Arrange on a large, non-stick baking tray and place in the refrigerator to chill for 30 minutes.
3 Preheat the oven to 200°C (Gas 6). Bake the chicken nuggets until they are golden brown and crisp, about 15 minutes, turning them once or twice during cooking. Serve hot or at room temperature.

Breakfast Treats

Traditional French Toast

4 eggs
1 cup (250 ml) milk
1 teaspoon vanilla extract
pinch of ground nutmeg
pinch of ground cinnamon
8 slices bread

Makes 4 servings

There are two methods for making French toast – this recipe is a quick fix in the morning; the recipe on the following page can be prepared the night before, then baked in the morning while the coffee brews.

1 In a bowl, lightly beat the eggs and the milk. Stir in the vanilla, nutmeg and cinnamon. Pour the mixture into a large, shallow dish with a flat base.
2 Coat a large frying pan with cooking spray. Heat the pan to hot but not smoking. Working one at a time, dip each piece of bread into the egg mixture, completely soaking it, then place the slice in the pan. Cook until the bread is brown on one side, flip it over, then cook the other side. Serve immediately, or keep warm briefly in a 100°C (Gas ½) oven while cooking the remaining toasts.

Baked French Toast

3 eggs
1½ cups (375 ml) milk
2 tablespoons unsalted butter
   or margarine, melted
3 tablespoons soft brown
   sugar
½ teaspoon finely grated
   lemon zest
pinch of ground nutmeg
pinch of ground cinnamon
14 slices French bread (about
   2 cm thick)
1 tablespoon icing sugar

Makes 4 servings

You can make this luscious toast the night before, then pop it into the oven in the morning.

1 In a bowl, beat the eggs, milk, butter, sugar, lemon zest, nutmeg and cinnamon. Pour half the mixture into a large greased baking dish or tray. Lay the bread slices on top in a single layer, pressing them as close together as possible. Pour the remaining mixture over the bread slices and cover the pan with foil. Refrigerate overnight, or for at least 2 hours.
2 Preheat the oven to 180°C (Gas 4). Bake, uncovered, until the toast is puffy and golden brown, 50 to 60 minutes. Sprinkle with the icing sugar. Serve hot with maple or blueberry syrup, honey, or fresh fruit, nuts and yogurt.

Muesli Bar Slice

½ cup (20 g) barley flakes
¼ cup (60 ml) cloudy apple
   juice, heated
⅓ cup (60 g) dried apricots
⅓ cup (40 g) sultanas
¼ cup (20 g) dried apples
¼ cup (30 g) sweetened dried
   cranberries
⅓ cup (60 g) dates
½ cup (50 g) toasted pecans
1 cup (100 g) rolled oats
¼ cup (35 g) wholemeal
   self-raising flour
2 tablespoons caster sugar
   (optional)
¼ cup (30 g) sunflower seeds
¼ cup (60 g) butter or
   margarine
¼ cup (90 g) honey
½ teaspoon vanilla extract
1 egg

Makes 20 slices

Try this muesli bar and you'll never have a packet one again. Full of nutritious foods, this is a great snack to take to work or pack in the lunchbox. Substitute your favourite mix of dried fruit or nuts.

1 Preheat the oven to 180°C (Gas 4) and grease a 30 x 20 cm cake tin. Line the base and two long sides with baking paper, extending the paper a few centimetres above the pan to help with removal later.
2 Place the barley flakes in a large heatproof bowl and pour the warm apple juice over them. Leave to stand while you chop up the dried fruit and pecans.
3 To the barley flakes, add the oats, flour, sugar (if using), dried fruit, pecans and sunflower seeds.
4 In a small saucepan, melt the butter with the honey over low heat. Cool a little, then add the vanilla extract and egg and stir to combine.
5 Pour the butter mixture over the oat mixture and mix thoroughly. Press the mixture into the cake tin and cook for 25 to 30 minutes, until lightly golden. Leave in the tin to cool, then cut into fingers or squares.

Apricot Oat Flapjacks

1⅓ cups (240 g) dried apricots,
  cut into quarters
1½ cups (375 ml) orange juice
grated zest of ½ orange
⅓ cup (75 g) crystallised
  ginger, roughly chopped
2 cups (200 g) rolled oats
2 tablespoons soft brown
  sugar
1 tablespoon sunflower seeds

Makes 8 flapjacks

These soft, chewy bars, packed with sweet fruit and
ginger, make an ideal mid-morning or afternoon snack.

1 Place the apricots in a saucepan with the orange juice and
  zest and bring to the boil. Reduce the heat and simmer,
  uncovered and stirring occasionally, for 25 to 30 minutes,
  until the liquid is absorbed. Purée in a food processor or
  using a hand-held mixer.
2 Meanwhile, heat the oven to 180°C (Gas 4). Line the base
  of a 22 cm round cake tin with non-stick baking paper.
3 Stir the ginger, rolled oats, sugar and sunflower seeds into
  the apricot purée and mix well, then tip into the tin and
  spread out evenly.
4 Bake for 30 to 35 minutes, until firm and golden brown.
  Cool slightly, cut into wedges, then leave to cool completely
  in the tin. Peel off the paper before serving.

Scones

3 cups (450 g) self-raising
  flour
1 teaspoon salt
2 teaspoons sugar
¼ cup (60 g) butter
1 cup (250 ml) milk

Makes about 12 scones

You can add all sorts of things to scones, including
currants, chopped dried apricots, or mini chocolate
chips – experiment with gusto!

1 Preheat the oven to 230°C (Gas 8). Line two baking trays
  with baking paper.
2 In a large bowl, stir together the flour, salt and sugar. Rub in
  the butter using your fingertips. Make a well in the centre of
  the flour and pour in the milk in a steady stream, stirring in
  the flour until a soft dough forms.
3 Turn the dough out onto a lightly floured surface and gently
  knead five to six times. Using a lightly floured rolling pin, roll
  out the dough to a 2 cm thickness and, using a floured 7 cm
  cutter, cut out scone rounds. Re-roll the scraps as necessary
  (do not knead again) and cut more scones.
4 Place the scones 5 cm apart on the baking trays and bake
  until golden brown, 10 to 15 minutes. Eat hot or just warm.

VARIATION
Scone Wedges: Follow steps 1–2 of the above recipe. Turn
the dough out onto a lightly greased baking tray and pat into
a large round. If desired, brush the top with milk and sprinkle
with sugar or a combination of sugar and cinnamon. Using a
floured knife, cut the dough round into 8 wedges, but don't
separate the pieces. Bake in the preheated oven for 12 minutes,
or until golden brown. Carefully separate the scone wedges
and serve immediately.

Pancakes

2 cups (300 g) Pancake and
  Waffle Mix (page 61)
2 large eggs, lightly beaten
1 cup (250 ml) milk

Makes 10 to 12 pancakes

Sliced bananas and strawberries, whole blueberries,
or even chocolate chips can be added to the pancake
batter for a luscious breakfast treat.

1 In a large bowl, combine all the ingredients and stir until just
   blended. Don't overmix – the batter should be slightly lumpy.
2 Coat a large frying pan with cooking spray. Heat the pan to hot
   but not smoking. Spoon the batter into the pan, using about
   ¼ cup (60 ml) per pancake, and cook over medium heat until
   bubbles form across the top, about 2 minutes. Flip the
   pancakes and cook the other side for about 2 minutes more.
   Serve immediately, or keep warm briefly in a 100°C (Gas ½)
   oven while cooking the remaining pancakes.

Waffles

2 large eggs, separated
1¾ cups (260 g) Pancake
  and Waffle Mix (page 61)
1 cup (250 ml) milk
3 tablespoons butter or
  margarine, melted
1 teaspoon vanilla extract
  (optional)

Makes about 5 waffles

A classic breakfast or brunch dish for special occasions,
waffles go perfectly with maple syrup, and also with
fresh fruit toppings.

1 Following the manufacturer's directions, preheat a waffle iron.
2 In a large bowl, lightly beat the egg yolks. Add the remaining
   ingredients and stir until the mixture is just moistened.
3 In a bowl, beat the eggwhites using electric beaters until soft
   peaks form. Using a rubber spatula, gently fold the eggwhites
   into the batter until no white streaks remain.
4 Cook the waffles following the manufacturer's directions.

The origin of waffles

Perhaps surprisingly, waffles
have been enjoyed for centuries.
From the time of the ancient
Greeks and throughout the
Middle Ages, flat cakes were
baked between two metal
plates, called wafer irons.
These were popular into the
13th century. At that time, an
enterprising craftsman forged
decorative plates to resemble
honeycombs. The name 'waffle'
is derived from the Dutch word
wafel, meaning 'wafer'. In the
20th century, an electric waffle
iron made these breakfast treats
even easier to make.

Appetising Nibbles

Antipasto Platter

500 g small new potatoes,
  quartered
¼ cup (60 ml) olive oil
1 teaspoon dried rosemary
1 teaspoon salt
1 large red capsicum (pepper),
  cut into 2 cm strips
1 large green capsicum
  (pepper), cut into 2 cm strips
2 zucchini (courgettes), cut
  into 2 cm slices
2 small red onions, cut into
  thin wedges
250 g button mushrooms
2 cloves garlic, crushed
250 g fresh mozzarella, sliced
250 g prosciutto, sliced
1 cup (185 g) oil-cured Greek
  black or green olives
sprigs of fresh rosemary
  or thyme

MARINADE
¼ cup (60 ml) balsamic
  vinegar
1 tablespoon extra virgin
  olive oil
1 tablespoon chopped fresh
  parsley
¼ teaspoon dried thyme
2 teaspoons dijon mustard
1 small clove garlic, finely
  chopped
1 teaspoon lemon zest
½ teaspoon salt
¼ teaspoon freshly ground
  black pepper

Makes 6 to 8 servings

The star of any buffet is an antipasto ('before the meal')
platter. This classic appetiser has colourful marinated
vegetables, cheese and cold meats in an eye-catching
arrangement. Accentuate the drama of the plate by
placing contrasting colours or shapes next to each other
– straight or diagonal patterns on a rectangular plate,
or concentric circles on a round or oval platter.

1 Preheat the oven to 230°C (Gas 8). In a large, shallow roasting
  tin, combine the potatoes, olive oil, rosemary and salt. Toss to
  coat the potatoes well, then bake, uncovered, for 15 minutes.
2 Add the capsicums, zucchini, onions and mushrooms to the
  roasting tin. Sprinkle the garlic over all the vegetables. Bake,
  uncovered, until the vegetables are lightly browned and
  tender, 35 to 45 minutes.
3 Meanwhile, combine the marinade ingredients in a small bowl.
  Whisk until well blended and smooth.
4 Pour the marinade over the cooked vegetables in the roasting
  tin, and stir gently until they are thoroughly coated. Let the
  vegetables cool to room temperature.
5 Arrange the marinated vegetables, mozzarella, prosciutto
  and olives in an attractive pattern on a large serving platter.
  Garnish with rosemary or thyme.

Chicken Liver Pâté

2 tablespoons butter

250 g chicken livers, cleaned,
    trimmed and halved

⅓ cup (90 g) cream cheese,
    at room temperature

1–2 tablespoons brandy

1 teaspoon salt

pinch of freshly ground black
    pepper

½ teaspoon dried thyme

pinch of ground nutmeg

Makes 4 servings

This smooth, rich paste is easy to make at home for your fanciest occasions. Serve it with toast wedges, water crackers or slices of baguette.

1 In a heavy-based frying pan, melt the butter over medium–high heat. Add the chicken livers and cook until lightly browned, 4 to 5 minutes.

2 Transfer the livers to a food processor or blender. Pour in the pan drippings, scraping up the browned bits in the pan and adding them also. Add the cream cheese, brandy, salt, pepper, thyme and nutmeg. Process until the mixture forms a smooth paste, 20 to 30 seconds. Taste and adjust the seasonings as desired.

3 Using a spatula, scrape the paste into a ramekin or serving bowl, smoothing the top. Cover and refrigerate overnight.

Ham, Pork and Veal Terrine

500 g diced cooked ham

500 g pork mince

500 g veal mince

1 clove garlic, crushed

1 teaspoon dried thyme

½ teaspoon dried marjoram

¼ teaspoon ground nutmeg
    or mace

1 teaspoon salt

pinch of freshly ground black
    pepper

½ cup (125 ml) dry white wine

4 small bay leaves

6–8 slices bacon

250 g chicken livers, cleaned,
    trimmed and halved

Makes about 10 servings

A simple, classic baked terrine is perfect for a picnic in summer or sampling by a roaring fire in winter with pumpernickel or crusty French bread.

1 Preheat the oven to 150°C (Gas 2). In a large glass or ceramic bowl, combine the ham, pork and veal. Add the garlic, thyme, marjoram, nutmeg or mace, salt and pepper. Using clean, damp hands, mix the ingredients until they are well blended. Mix in the wine, cover and refrigerate for 1 hour.

2 Arrange the bay leaves in the bottom of a 23 x 13 cm loaf tin. Line the sides of the tin crosswise with half the bacon slices, allowing the ends to hang over the edges of the tin. Pack half the meat mixture into the loaf tin. Arrange the chicken livers along the centre of the meat, then add the remaining meat mixture. Cover the terrine with the remaining bacon slices, tucking in the ends and folding the ends of the bottom slices over the top of the loaf.

3 Set the tin in a baking dish. Pour enough warm water into the baking dish to come halfway up the sides of the tin. Bake for 2 to 2½ hours, until the terrine pulls away from the sides of the tin and the juices run clear when it is pierced with a clean skewer or toothpick.

4 Set the tin on a wire rack and let the terrine cool. Pour off any liquid. When the terrine is completely cool, turn it out onto a plate, cover with plastic wrap and refrigerate overnight.

Country Pork Sausages

1 kg lean pork, trimmed
250 g uncooked pork fat
1½ teaspoons sea salt
1½ teaspoons dried sage, crumbled
½ teaspoon dried thyme, crumbled
¼ teaspoon crushed black peppercorns
1 small onion, finely chopped

Makes 10 to 12 sausages

Needing no casings, these hearty and delicious homemade sausages are ready to star at your next brunch. Because you make them, you know what's in them and you can adjust the seasonings to suit your own tastes.

1 Cut the pork and pork fat into 1 cm cubes. Place in a large bowl, cover and refrigerate until the meat is chilled.

2 In a small bowl, combine the salt, sage, thyme and the peppercorns. Sprinkle the seasoning mixture over the meat, add the onion, then mix all the ingredients together thoroughly using your hands.

3 Place half the sausage mixture in a food processor or blender and process to a medium-coarse consistency. Scrape the puréed mixture into another large bowl and repeat with the remaining sausage mixture. Cover and refrigerate for 12 hours or overnight, to let the texture firm up and allow the flavours to develop fully.

4 Using damp hands, divide the sausage mixture into 10 or 12 equal portions and roll each portion into a ball. Form each ball into a small sausage patty. Either cook immediately, or place the sausages on baking paper or freezer paper, with pieces of paper between any layers. Wrap the entire package of sausages in foil or a self-sealing plastic bag. Refrigerate the uncooked sausages for up to 2 days, or store in the freezer for up to 3 weeks.

5 To cook the sausages, heat a large, heavy-based frying pan over medium heat. Add the sausages and cook, turning them often, until browned on all sides and cooked through, 13 to 15 minutes. Drain off any fat as it accumulates, and transfer the cooked sausages to paper towels to drain completely before serving.

Devilled Eggs

12 eggs
½ cup (125 g) Classic
  Mayonnaise (page 29)
1 tablespoon mustard
1 tablespoon white wine
  vinegar
1 teaspoon salt
1 teaspoon sugar
1 teaspoon ground white
  pepper
½ cup (70 g) finely chopped
  celery
paprika (optional)

Makes 12 servings

Contrary to popular terminology, eggs should never actually be boiled or they will turn grey. You can cook the eggs up to 1 day ahead, but to avoid contamination they should not be stuffed until just before serving.

1 Place the eggs in a single layer in a large saucepan. Add enough cold water to cover the eggs by 2–3 cm. Set the saucepan over high heat and bring to a full boil; immediately remove the pan from the heat, cover and let stand for 15 minutes.

2 Drain the eggs and crack the wide end of each, then plunge into a large bowl of iced water. To peel, crack each shell all over by tapping it on a work surface. Hold each egg under cold running water while removing the shell. Set each shelled egg on a paper towel to drain as you peel them.

3 Using a small, sharp knife, cut each egg in half lengthwise. Using a small spoon, scoop out the yolks and put them in a sieve set over a bowl. Arrange the eggwhite halves on a plate and refrigerate. Using the back of a spoon, press the egg yolks through the sieve into the bowl.

4 Add the mayonnaise, mustard, vinegar, salt, sugar, pepper and celery to the sieved yolks. Using a fork, stir gently to combine all the ingredients well.

5 Using a small spoon or a piping bag fitted with a number 6 star tip, fill each eggwhite half with about 1 tablespoon of the egg-yolk mixture. If desired, sprinkle the eggs with a little paprika before serving.

VARIATIONS

Caper-Dill Eggs: To the mayonnaise, add 3 tablespoons drained and chopped capers, 3 tablespoons finely chopped fresh dill and ½ teaspoon ground white pepper.

Chilli Eggs: To the mayonnaise, add ½ teaspoon chilli powder, or to taste, and 1 teaspoon ground cumin.

Curried Eggs: To the mayonnaise, add 1 tablespoon curry powder, or to taste, and 3 tablespoons chopped tomato chutney.

Spicy Eggs: To the mayonnaise, add 3 tablespoons bottled horseradish, or to taste, and 2 tablespoons finely chopped fresh parsley.

Globe Artichokes in Olive Oil

1 kg (about 6 small) fresh
  young globe artichokes
1 large lemon, halved
4 cups (1 litre) white wine
  vinegar
1 tablespoon sea salt
1 tablespoon dill seeds
1 tablespoon black
  peppercorns
2 bay leaves
2 sprigs fresh herbs such as
  rosemary, dill or marjoram
2 cloves garlic, sliced
2 small fresh red chillies
3–4 cups (750 ml–1 litre) extra
  virgin olive oil

Makes 6 servings

The end of winter is the time to find small, tender baby artichokes at the markets. Use these seasoned artichokes in salads or as part of an antipasto platter, serve them with strong-flavoured cheeses or just enjoy them on their own.

1 Using scissors, cut off the outer, tough leaves of each artichoke; trim off the pointed tip of each remaining leaf. Using a sharp knife, cut each artichoke in half lengthwise and rub the cut halves with the lemon halves to prevent browning. Fill a bowl with cold water and place the artichoke halves in the bowl with any remaining juice in the lemons. Let stand for 1 hour.
2 In a large, non-aluminium saucepan, combine the vinegar, salt, dill seeds, peppercorns and bay leaves. Bring the mixture to a boil over medium–high heat.
3 Drain the artichokes and add them to the saucepan; reduce the heat to medium–low and simmer for 10 minutes.
4 Drain the artichokes again and let them dry; discard the cooking liquid. Transfer the artichokes to two large, warmed, sterilised, wide-mouthed jars, dividing them equally (see Safe Bottling and Preserving, page 72). Add 1 herb sprig, half the garlic slices and 1 chilli to each jar. Pour the olive oil over the artichokes, leaving a 5 mm space between the top of the oil and the rim of the jar. Wipe the rims, cover and store in the refrigerator for up to 1 month. The artichokes will be ready for eating in a few days.

Marinated Goat's Cheese

1 goat's cheese (100–125 g)
¼ teaspoon mixed peppercorns
  (black, white, green)
⅛ teaspoon coriander seeds,
  crushed
fresh thyme sprigs
fresh rosemary sprigs
fresh fennel sprigs
1 bay leaf
1 small red chilli
1 clove garlic
½ cup (125 ml) olive oil

Makes 1 round

How do you make a good thing even better? In the case of goat's cheese, you marinate it yourself in herb-infused olive oil. You can buy marinated goat's cheese, but this is easy and made to your own taste.

1 Centre the goat's cheese in a warmed, sterilised, wide-mouthed jar. Tuck the peppercorns, coriander seeds, herb sprigs, bay leaf, chilli and garlic around the cheese.
2 Pour in the olive oil until the top of the oil is 5 mm from the rim of the jar. Wipe the rim, cover the jar, then label and date it. Store in the refrigerator for up to 1 month; the cheese will be ready for eating in 1 week.

Spinach and Feta Filo Triangles

80 g butter or margarine, plus
an extra 2 teaspoons, melted
1 small onion, finely chopped
300 g frozen chopped spinach,
thawed and squeezed dry
1 tablespoon finely chopped
fresh dill or ¼ teaspoon
dried dill, crumbled
½ cup (75 g) crumbled feta
1 egg, lightly beaten
6 sheets frozen filo pastry,
thawed

Makes 12 triangles

It's true that filo, the multilayered Greek dough, is difficult and time-consuming to make. Purchased filo dough, however, is a wonderful base for appetisers, desserts or other dishes that can be expensive to buy finished. Follow the packet directions to thaw the frozen dough; once opened, the dough will keep in the refrigerator for about 1 week.

1 Preheat the oven to 180°C (Gas 4). Melt the butter in a large frying pan over medium heat. Add the onion and sauté until translucent, 3 to 5 minutes. Add the spinach and cook for 2 minutes longer. Stir in the dill, then transfer to a large bowl. Add the feta and egg and stir until the mixture is well blended.

2 Lay one sheet of the filo pastry on a work surface and brush lightly with 1 teaspoon of the melted butter. Top the pastry with a second sheet of filo, brush with butter, and repeat with a third sheet of filo.

3 Using a sharp knife or pizza cutter, and a ruler if you like, cut the stack of buttered filo sheets lengthwise into six strips about 5 cm wide. Cut the strips in half to make 12 in total. Place 1 tablespoon of the spinach–feta mixture at the end of each strip. Fold the end of each strip diagonally over the filling to form a triangle. Continue folding diagonally along the entire strip, alternating directions and ending with a triangular package. When each triangle is complete, brush the top with some of the butter. Repeat to make 12 triangles in total.

4 Line a baking tray with baking paper. Arrange the filo triangles on the tray and bake until golden brown, about 25 minutes.

Quesadillas

four 20 cm flour tortillas
1 cup (125 g) grated cheddar
   or other tasty cheese
1 large red capsicum (pepper),
   cut into 5 mm slices
¼ cup (50 g) cooked fresh or
   thawed frozen corn kernels
3 spring onions with tops,
   thinly sliced
3 tablespoons chopped fresh
   coriander
¼ cup (60 g) homemade or
   shop-bought salsa
Guacamole (page 51) sour
   cream or natural yogurt
   (optional)

Makes 4 servings

You can serve a quesadilla as a lunch dish or use a pizza cutter to cut it into small triangles and arrange on a plate with sour cream and guacamole as an appetiser.

1 Preheat the oven to 220°C (Gas 7). Place each tortilla on a 30 cm square of foil. Sprinkle each tortilla with the cheese, capsicum, corn, spring onion, coriander and salsa, dividing the toppings equally. Moisten the edges of one tortilla and fold in half, encasing the toppings; press the edges together. Repeat with the remaining tortillas.
2 Move a folded tortilla so it is centred on the top half of the foil square. Fold each side edge of the foil over the quesadilla. Fold the bottom half of the foil up and over the quesadilla until the top and bottom foil edges are even; fold the edges over twice to make a packet. Repeat with the remaining quesadillas and arrange on a baking tray.
3 Bake the quesadillas until the cheese melts, about 7 minutes. Remove the baking tray from the oven, unwrap the quesadillas and arrange them on a plate or serving platter. If desired, serve with a dollop of guacamole, sour cream or yogurt.

Curry Puffs

800 g potatoes, peeled
   and diced
1¼ cups (160 g) frozen
   baby peas
1½ tablespoons curry powder
½ teaspoon salt
6 sheets frozen butter puff
   pastry, just thawed
1 egg, beaten

Makes 24

These traditional Malaysian snacks are usually deep-fried, but using puff pastry and baking them in the oven gives a much lighter, puffier result.

1 Preheat the oven to 200°C (Gas 6). Put the potatoes in a saucepan of cold water, bring to the boil and cook, covered, until they are just tender. Add the peas and cook for a further 2 minutes. Remove from the heat and drain well. Add the curry powder and salt, then roughly mash.
2 Using a 10 cm pastry cutter, cut four circles from each sheet of pastry. Put 1 tablespoon of the potato mixture on each pastry circle. Fold in half and press the edges together. Starting at one end, fold a little of the pinched edge back over itself and continue to the other end, forming a neatly braided edge.
3 Arrange the curry puffs on baking trays, brush with beaten egg and bake for 20 to 25 minutes, until puffed and golden.

Dips

Baba Ghanoush

1 large eggplant (aubergine),
  about 1.2 kg
¼ cup (60 ml) lemon juice
1 tablespoon extra virgin
  olive oil
2 cloves garlic, quartered
¼ cup (65 g) tahini (sesame
  paste)
salt and freshly ground black
  pepper, to taste

Makes about 2 cups (440 g)

Much loved in the Middle East, this smoky favourite,
available in supermarkets and delis, gets its flavour
from charring the eggplant first. You can make this
delicious dip yourself and serve it with pita triangles.

1 Preheat the grill. Using a sharp fork or skewer, prick the
  eggplant all over. Place the eggplant on the grill tray 15 cm
  from the heat source. Grill, turning every 5 minutes, until the
  skin is blackened and the eggplant is soft, about 20 minutes.
  Remove the eggplant and leave until cool to the touch.
2 Using a sharp knife, peel the eggplant. Roughly chop the
  flesh and place in a food processor or blender. Add the lemon
  juice, olive oil, garlic and tahini. Pulse until the mixture is well
  blended and of a spreadable consistency. Taste and season
  as desired with salt and pepper.
3 Scrape the dip into a bowl, then cover and refrigerate for at
  least 2 hours before serving to let the flavours develop.

Hummus

2 cups (480 g) cooked or
  drained, rinsed, canned
  chickpeas
1 tablespoon extra virgin
  olive oil
2 cloves garlic, quartered
½ teaspoon ground cumin
¼ cup (65 g) tahini
  (sesame paste)
¼–½ cup (60–125 ml) lemon
  juice
salt and freshly ground
  pepper, to taste
finely chopped fresh parsley
  or paprika, for sprinkling

Makes 1½ cups (330 g)

Another staple of Middle Eastern cooking, hummus
is excellent with pita triangles, crudités or bagel chips,
but it can be used as a spread in sandwiches too.

1 In a food processor or blender, combine the chickpeas,
  olive oil, garlic, cumin and tahini. Process until the mixture
  is of a rough consistency.
2 With the motor running, slowly pour in the lemon juice a little
  at a time until the desired consistency is reached. Taste the
  hummus and season with salt and pepper. Before serving,
  sprinkle with parsley or paprika.

Guacamole

2 ripe avocados, halved
1 tomato, cored, seeded and
  finely chopped
½ cup (80 g) finely chopped
  red onion
4 tablespoons chopped fresh
  coriander
2 tablespoons lime juice
¾ teaspoon salt
¾ teaspoon ground cumin
  (optional)
hot pepper sauce (optional)

Makes 2½ cups (550 g)

This creamy blend of avocados, tomato, red onion and coriander is a divine dip for chips, crudités, pretzels and more. It can also be a memorable addition to taco salads, grilled poultry or fish, and is a must for wraps.

1 Using a spoon, scoop out the avocado flesh into a glass or ceramic bowl. Using a fork, mash the avocado, but not until completely smooth – there should be small chunks of flesh.
2 Add the tomato, onion, coriander and lime juice, and stir with the fork until the ingredients are well blended but the consistency is still slightly rough. If desired, stir in the cumin and hot pepper sauce to add more heat to the guacamole.
3 Spoon dip into a serving bowl. Serve immediately, or cover and refrigerate until ready to serve.

Beetroot Dip

5 red beetroot (about 1 kg)
1¼ cups (310 g) natural low-fat
  yogurt
2 cloves garlic, crushed
¼ cup (60 ml) lemon juice
2 tablespoons extra virgin
  olive oil
½ teaspoon ground cumin
½ teaspoon ground coriander
½ teaspoon ground cinnamon
½ teaspoon paprika
freshly ground black pepper,
  to taste

Makes 4 servings

Serve this beautifully vibrant dip with chargrilled pita toasts for a casual start to a barbecue, or use it as a scrumptious sandwich filler.

1 Cut off the beetroot stems 1 cm from the roots (no closer). Scrub the roots very gently but thoroughly, being careful not to nick the skin.
2 Cook the beetroot in a large pot of simmering, salted water for 40 to 60 minutes, until tender. Drain and allow to cool slightly. When cool enough to handle, rub off the skins. It is a good idea to wear rubber gloves when doing this so your hands don't become stained.
3 Finely chop, grate or process the beetroot in a food processor, then transfer to a serving bowl.
4 Add the yogurt, garlic, lemon juice, oil, cumin, coriander, cinnamon and paprika and mix well. Season to taste with pepper, cover and refrigerate until required. Serve with warm crusty bread.

Taramasalata

200 g smoked cod's roe
40 g (1 thick slice) stale white
  bread, crusts removed
2 tablespoons milk
⅓ cup (80 ml) vegetable oil
¼ cup (60 ml) olive oil
¼ cup (60 ml) lemon juice
1 clove garlic, crushed
freshly ground black pepper,
  to taste
wedge of lemon
sprigs of fresh flat-leaf parsley

Makes 4 servings

Quick and easy to make, this classic smoked cod's roe dip can be served as a snack with drinks or as a more formal starter with strips of pita bread.

1 Soak the cod's roe in a bowl of cold water for about 1 hour to remove some of the saltiness.
2 When you're ready to prepare the dip, soak the bread in the milk for 5 minutes. Rinse and drain the roe thoroughly, cut in half lengthwise, then, with the skin side down on a board, scrape the roe off the skin with a knife. Put the roe in a blender or food processor.
3 Squeeze the bread dry and add it to the roe. Blend together, trickling in first the vegetable oil, then the olive oil, while the motor is running.
4 Now add the lemon juice, a little at a time, adding a little extra, if desired, for a sharper taste. If the mixture is slightly thick, you can loosen it with a little boiling water, rather than adding more oil or lemon juice. Add the garlic and season to taste with pepper.
5 Spoon the taramasalata into a bowl, cover and refrigerate until ready to serve. Garnish with a lemon wedge and parsley sprigs.

Dips are not just for dipping

So much more than something to plunge crackers, chips (crisps) or crudités into, dips are a versatile culinary performer. Many can be used as condiments, toppings for various dishes, fillings for omelettes or spreads for sandwiches. Experiment!

Tapenade

1 cup (185 g) oil-cured
  Mediterranean or Greek
  black olives, pitted
6–8 anchovy fillets
¼ cup (40 g) capers, rinsed
  and squeezed dry
2 cloves garlic, halved
2 teaspoons lemon juice
3–4 tablespoons extra virgin
  olive oil
freshly ground black pepper,
  to taste

Makes about 1 cup (250 g)

Not for the timid palate, this rich spread combines the heady taste of olives, anchovies, capers and garlic. When bought from a deli, it's a pricey treat. Make your own and enjoy it on toasted slices of Italian bread, drizzled with extra virgin olive oil.

1 In a food processor or blender, purée the olives, anchovy fillets, capers, garlic and lemon juice until the mixture is finely chopped.
2 Add 3 tablespoons of the olive oil, pulsing on and off, until the mixture is a spreadable, grainy paste; add more olive oil as needed to reach the desired consistency. Taste the tapenade and season with pepper.

Tzatziki

1 cucumber, peeled, sliced
  lengthwise and seeded
2 cups (500 g) natural yogurt
1 clove garlic, crushed
1 tablespoon finely chopped
  fresh mint
2 tablespoons olive oil, plus
  extra for drizzling
sea salt and freshly ground
  black pepper, to taste

Makes about 2½ cups (625 g)

A creamy cucumber concoction to cool the fires of the spiciest dish, this quintessential Greek dip is a logical choice in summer, when cucumbers are plentiful. You can buy it in supermarkets, but it is easy to make your own. Serve it with crudités, chips or pita triangles, as a dressing for Greek salad, or as an accompaniment for grilled kebabs or fish.

1 Cut the cucumber into small dice and spread between layers of paper towel to dry well.
2 In a bowl, combine the yogurt, cucumber, garlic, mint and olive oil and stir until well blended. Taste the tzatziki and season with salt and pepper.
3 Spoon into a serving bowl, cover and refrigerate until required. Serve drizzled with olive oil.

Cold Drinks

Classic Iced Tea

2 tablespoons tea leaves,
   or 6 tea bags
Sugar Syrup (opposite),
   to taste
ice cubes
lemon wedges or small fresh
   mint sprigs (optional)

Makes 4 servings

Always best when it is freshly made, iced tea is an economical thirst quencher.

1 In a kettle, bring 2 cups (500 ml) cold water to a full, rolling boil.
2 Rinse a teapot with boiling water and discard the water. Place the tea in the pot and slowly pour the boiling water over the tea. Cover the teapot and let the tea steep for 3 to 5 minutes.
3 Stir the tea once. Strain the tea into a large jug, add the another 2 cups (500 ml) cold water and sweeten to taste with sugar syrup.
4 To serve, fill glasses with ice cubes and pour the cold tea over the ice; if desired, garnish each serving with a lemon wedge or mint sprig.

Cranberry Iced Tea

4 tablespoons tea leaves,
   or 6 tea bags
2 cups (500 ml) cranberry
   juice
Sugar Syrup (opposite),
   to taste
ice cubes
fresh or frozen whole
   cranberries or lime slices
   (optional)

Makes 4 servings

This fruity red tea is perfect for a special occasion.

1 In a kettle, bring 2 cups (500 ml) cold water to a full, rolling boil.
2 Rinse a teapot with boiling water and discard the water. Place the tea in the pot and slowly pour the boiling water over the tea. Cover the teapot and let the tea steep for 3 to 5 minutes.
3 Stir the tea once. Strain the tea into a large jug, add the cranberry juice and sweeten to taste with sugar syrup.
4 To serve, fill glasses with ice cubes and pour the cold tea over the ice; if desired, garnish each serving with a few whole cranberries or a lime wedge.

Sugar syrup: the perfect sweetener

Keep a jar of this sugar syrup in your refrigerator to sweeten iced teas and coffees. Because the sugar is already dissolved, you'll get the ideal sweetness without any graininess added. Here's how to make it:

In a small saucepan, combine 2 cups (440 g) sugar and 2½ cups (625 ml) water over medium heat. Cook, stirring frequently, until the mixture boils and the sugar has dissolved completely. Remove the saucepan from the heat, cover and let stand for 1 to 2 minutes to allow the steam to dissolve any unmelted crystals on the side of the saucepan. Pour the cooled syrup into a 750 ml bottle, seal tightly and store in the refrigerator. Makes 3 cups (750 ml)

Iced Coffee

2 cups (500 ml) milk
3 tablespoons Caramel Sauce (page 60), plus 2 teaspoons extra (optional)
2 teaspoons instant espresso coffee granules
8–10 ice cubes
4 tablespoons whipped cream

Makes 2 servings

Whip up this gourmet-style coffee concoction for almost nothing, without leaving home or standing in line.

1 In a food processor or blender, combine the milk, 3 tablespoons of the caramel sauce, if using, the coffee granules and ice cubes. Process until the mixture is smooth.
2 Pour the mixture into two chilled glasses. Top with whipped cream and drizzle with the remaining caramel sauce if desired. Serve immediately.

Iced Coffee Slush

3 cups (750 ml) hot strong brewed coffee
½–1 cup (110–220 g) sugar
6 cups (1.5 litres) milk
1½ teaspoons vanilla extract

Makes 12 servings

This chilly delight will take the heat out of summer without making a hole in your purse or requiring a trip to a coffee shop.

1 In a freezer-safe bowl, combine the coffee and the amount of sugar desired. Stir until the sugar has completely dissolved, then cover and refrigerate until thoroughly chilled. Stir in the milk and vanilla. Re-cover the bowl and place in the freezer until the mixture is solid.
2 Several hours before serving, transfer the bowl to the refrigerator. Using a mallet, break up the coffee mixture, then place in a food processor or blender and process until slushy. Serve immediately.

Lemonade Syrup

3 cups (660 g) sugar
3 cups (750 ml) lemon juice
(about 16 lemons)
2 tablespoons grated lemon
zest

Makes about 5½ cups
(1.4 litres) syrup

Whip up a batch of this syrup whenever you see lemons on sale, then keep it on hand to make the best homemade lemonade you've ever tasted – in a flash! This makes a much less expensive and better-tasting lemonade than anything you can buy.

1 Place the sugar in a 6 cup (1.5 litre) heatproof container. Add 1 cup (250 ml) boiling water, stirring constantly until the sugar has completely dissolved. Leave to cool.
2 Stir in the lemon juice and zest until well blended. Cover and store in the refrigerator for up to 1 week.

VARIATION
Limeade Syrup: Substitute 3 cups (750 ml) fresh lime juice and 2 tablespoons grated lime zest and proceed as above.

Ginger Beer

GINGER BEER 'MOTHER'
½ teaspoon dried yeast
2 tablespoons sugar
2 tablespoons ground ginger

SUGAR SYRUP
4 cups (900 g) sugar
½ cup (125 ml) strained lemon
juice

Makes 6 litres

This fizzy and refreshing treat is made by fermenting sugar syrup with a yeast mixture called the 'ginger beer mother' or 'ginger beer plant'.

1 For the ginger beer 'mother', place the yeast and ½ teaspoon of the sugar in a large jar. Add 1 cup (250 ml) warm water and ½ teaspoon of the ginger. Mix well, cover the jar with a cloth and leave at room temperature for 8 days, mixing in ½ teaspoon each of the remaining sugar and ginger every day.
2 For the sugar syrup, put the sugar in a large saucepan with 6 cups (1.5 litres) cold water. Heat, stirring, just until the sugar has dissolved. Remove from the heat and add 4.5 litres warm water and the lemon juice. Stand, if necessary, until lukewarm.
3 Strain the yeast mixture into the syrup, through a sieve lined with a double thickness of muslin (cheesecloth), and stir well. Keep the sediment on the muslin for making further batches of ginger beer. Stir the syrup mixture well and pour into clean, sturdy bottles, preferably fitted with clip-on seals, or else with screw-tops. Fill the bottles only to the base of the necks, and seal. Leave in a cool place for about 5 days – in hot weather, the ginger beer will be ready in 3–4 days.
4 To make further batches of ginger beer, return half the ginger beer 'mother' left on the muslin to the jar (discard the rest), and add 1 teaspoon each of ground ginger and sugar and 1 cup (250 ml) water (no more yeast is needed).
5 Repeat the process as before, feeding the 'mother' with ½ teaspoon each of ginger and sugar daily. After 8 days, mix with the sugar syrup and bottle as before.

Traditional Lemonade

¼–⅓ cup (60–80 ml) Lemonade
   Syrup (opposite)
ice cubes
lemon wedge or fresh mint
   sprig (optional)

Makes 1 serving

Tart, sweet and very refreshing, this old-fashioned syrup-based lemonade is quick, delicious and cheap.

In a tall glass, combine the desired amount of syrup with ¾ cup (185 ml) water and stir until well blended. Add some ice cubes and, if desired, garnish with a lemon wedge or mint sprig.

Lemon Squash

4 strips (about 8 cm each)
   lemon zest, cut into thin
   slices
1 cup (250 ml) Lemonade
   Syrup (opposite)
3 cups (750 ml) chilled soda
   water or sparkling mineral
   water
ice cubes
lemon slices or small fresh
   mint sprigs (optional)

Makes 4 servings

This is the fizzy version of economical lemonade, loaded with bright lemon taste and bubbles.

1 In a 2 litre jug, combine the lemon zest and syrup to taste. Stir until well blended.
2 Just before serving, pour in the soda water or sparkling mineral water; stir gently to blend the ingredients. Fill glasses with ice cubes, pour the lemon squash over the ice, and if desired, garnish with a lemon wedge or small mint sprig.

VARIATION
Lime Squash: Prepare as directed, substituting lime zest and Limeade Syrup (opposite) for the lemon zest and Lemonade Syrup or to taste. Garnish with lime wedges or strawberries.

Orange Blossom

1 large strip orange zest
1 teaspoon caster sugar, plus
   a saucer of extra sugar for
   dipping
¼ cup (60 ml) gin
30 ml orange juice
1 slice orange

Makes 1 serving

For a non-alcoholic version of this festive drink, you can substitute sparkling water for the gin and add it after shaking the orange juice and sugar. This is a popular cocktail that is easy and inexpensive to make at home.

1 Rub the orange zest around the rim of a chilled martini glass. Dip the rim into the saucer of sugar.
2 In a cocktail shaker, combine the 1 teaspoon of sugar, gin and orange juice. Cover and shake until well blended. Place a strainer over the glass and pour the mixture through. Garnish with the orange slice.

Non-alcoholic Punch

300 g frozen raspberries
300 g frozen strawberries
1½ cups (330 g) sugar
10 whole cloves
½ teaspoon ground cardamom
6 strips (about 8 x 1 cm each)
   orange zest
1 vanilla bean, split
2 cups (500 ml) orange juice
2 cups (500 ml) soda water or
   sparkling mineral water
ice cubes

Makes 10 servings

Beautifully coloured, and with the tang of raspberries, strawberries and oranges, this is a spicy, fizzy fruit punch for parties.

1 In a large, non-aluminium saucepan, combine the berries, sugar, cloves, cardamom, orange zest, vanilla bean and 6 cups (1.5 litres) water. Bring to a boil over medium–high heat. Reduce the heat to medium–low and simmer, uncovered, for about 10 minutes, stirring occasionally.
2 Place a large sieve over a large jug. Pour the berry mixture through, straining out the solids; do not press the solids. Let cool to room temperature, then stir in the orange juice.
3 Just before serving, stir in the soda water or sparkling mineral water. Serve the punch over ice.

Lemon Barley Water

⅔ cup (140 g) pearl barley
60 g sugar cubes
2 lemons, washed
ice cubes and lemon slices,
   to serve

Makes 4 servings

Less sweet and heavy than most bought varieties, homemade lemon barley water is free from artificial colourings and flavourings.

1 Rinse the barley in a sieve under cold running water and drain well. Place in a saucepan, cover with cold water and bring to the boil, then reduce the heat and cook gently for 5 minutes. Pour the barley back into the sieve and rinse again.
2 Put the barley in a large jug or bowl. Rub each sugar cube over the skins of the lemons to extract the oils, then add the cubes to the jug or bowl.
3 Pour in 6 cups (1.5 litres) boiling water and stir until the sugar has dissolved. Cover the jug or bowl with a clean tea towel and leave to infuse for 3 hours, or until cold.
4 Squeeze the juice from both lemons and add it to the barley water. Strain through a nylon sieve into a serving jug. Cover and chill for 1 hour. Put several ice cubes and a few lemon slices in each of four tall glasses, pour in the lemon barley water and serve.

Bloody Mary Mix

2¼ cups (560 ml) tomato juice
¼ cup (60 ml) lemon juice
½ teaspoon black pepper
½ teaspoon salt
½ teaspoon celery seeds
1 teaspoon worcestershire
  sauce
½ teaspoon hot chilli sauce,
  such as Tabasco

Makes 2½ cups (625 ml)

Keep this mix ready to go in the refrigerator and you can whip up fantastic Bloody Marys in a flash – or just serve it over ice as a spicy tomato juice treat. You can buy Bloody Mary mixes, but the homemade version is livelier and much, much cheaper.

Combine all the ingredients in a 1 litre jar with a tight-fitting lid. Seal tightly and shake to blend well. Refrigerate for up to 1 week; shake well before using.

Bloody Mary

½ cup cracked ice
⅓ cup (80 ml) vodka
150 ml Bloody Mary Mix
  (above)
1 celery stalk

Makes 1 serving

This spicy drink stands up to even the most flavourful foods. Homemade with your own mix, it's a treat without being a threat to your budget.

Place the cracked ice in a tall glass. Pour the vodka and Bloody Mary mix over the ice. Garnish with the celery stalk.

Fruit Juice Spritzer

3 cups (750 ml) chilled dry
  white wine or fruit juice
  of choice
1½ cups (375 ml) chilled fruit
  juice of choice, or a
  complementary juice
1½ cups (375 ml) chilled
  carbonated beverage
  (soda water, lemonade
  or ginger ale)
ice cubes
fresh mint leaves or citrus
  wedges (optional)

Makes 8 servings

Here is a lovely, light, fizzy cooler that you can customise to suit your taste and your menu – try cranberry–raspberry juice, pineapple juice, grape juice, pink grapefruit juice, tangerine juice or anything else that takes your fancy. If you don't use wine, you can blend 2 juices instead. A wonderful start to a summer party that won't break the bank.

1 Combine all the liquids in a 2 litre jug.
2 Serve straight or over ice cubes. If desired, garnish individual glasses with mint leaves or citrus wedges.

Sangria

2 oranges, sliced
2 lemons, sliced
2 cinnamon sticks
¾ cup (185 ml) brandy
1 bottle (750 ml) red wine
1 bottle (750 ml) sparkling
   cider, chilled
ice cubes

Makes about 7 cups (1.75 litres)

The colour of garnets, full of fruit and always welcome whatever the season, sangria is an easy-to-make, delightful wine punch from Spain. Homemade is fresher tasting and a lot less pricey.

1 In a large punch bowl or glass jug, combine the oranges, lemons, cinnamon and brandy.
2 Pour the wine and cider over the fruit mixture, gently stirring until the punch is well blended. Just before serving, add ice cubes as desired.

Hot Drinks

Caffe Latte

1½ cups (375 ml) milk
⅔ cup (170 ml) freshly brewed
   espresso
sweetened cocoa powder
   (optional)

Makes 2 servings

Why buy a cup of special coffee when you can so easily make it yourself, at a fraction of the price and without having to leave home?

1 In a small saucepan over low heat, cook the milk just until tiny bubbles begin to form around the edges of the saucepan, 10 to 15 minutes; do not let the milk come to a boil. If a skin forms on the milk's surface, remove it with a spoon.
2 Divide the espresso between two 250 ml cups or mugs. Add ⅓ cup (80 ml) of the hot milk to each cup.
3 Using an electric mixer or wire whisk, beat the remaining hot milk until it is frothy. Spoon the milk froth into the cups, dividing it equally. If desired, sprinkle a little sweetened cocoa powder over the foam before serving.

VARIATIONS
Chocolate Mint Latte: Prepare as directed above, adding a finely chopped 15 g chocolate-covered peppermint patty to each cup along with the espresso.
Caffe Latte à l'Orange: Prepare as directed above, adding 1 tablespoon Grand Marnier or other orange-flavoured liqueur to each cup along with the espresso.

Cappuccino Mix

1 cup (100 g) skim milk
  powder
1 cup (100 g) instant chocolate
  milk powder
⅔ cup (30 g) instant coffee
  granules or espresso powder
½ cup (110 g) sugar
½ teaspoon ground cinnamon
¼ teaspoon ground nutmeg

Makes about 3 cups (350 g)
dry mix

Love the convenience of instant special coffees to keep
at the office or to brew a fast cup for an afternoon
pick-me-up? Make your own and you'll save a bundle.

Combine the ingredients in an airtight container. Cover
and shake until well blended. For 1 cup (250 ml) of instant
cappuccino, place 3 tablespoons in a mug or coffee cup.
Add ¾ cup (185 ml) boiling water and stir until the mix has
completely dissolved.

Cocoa

2 tablespoons sugar
1 tablespoon cocoa powder
¾ cup (185 ml) milk
miniature marshmallows
  (optional)
1 stick cinnamon (optional)

Makes 1 serving

On a cold, blustery day, there's nothing quite like hot
cocoa made the good old-fashioned way.

1 In a small saucepan, combine the sugar, cocoa and ¼ cup
  (60 ml) water. Over medium heat, bring the mixture to a boil,
  stirring constantly until the sugar has dissolved. Lower the
  heat and simmer for 2 minutes, whisking constantly.
2 Stir in the milk. Increase the heat to medium and cook until
  the cocoa is heated through; do not allow the mixture to boil.
3 To serve, pour the cocoa into a mug or cup. If desired, top with
  several marshmallows and use the cinnamon stick as a stirrer.

Hot Chocolate Viennese

⅓ cup (40 g) cocoa powder
⅓ cup (75 g) sugar
2½ cups (625 ml) milk
1½ cups (375 ml) freshly
  brewed strong coffee
  or espresso

Makes 4 servings

Chocolate, coffee and hot milk – triple yum! This is a
cafe treat that you can enjoy much more cheaply at home.

1 In a saucepan, combine the cocoa powder and sugar, pressing
  out any lumps. Stirring constantly, pour in enough of the milk
  to moisten the dry mixture, about ½ cup (125 ml); whisk in the
  coffee and the remaining 2 cups (500 ml) milk.
2 Cook over medium–low heat, stirring occasionally, until the
  mixture steams but does not boil, 8 to 10 minutes. Pour the
  hot chocolate into mugs or coffee cups and serve.

Chai

2 tea bags
1 stick cinnamon
6 cardamom pods, crushed
1 whole clove
¼ teaspoon ground ginger
2½ cups (625 ml) milk
⅓ cup (75 g) sugar
cinnamon sticks (optional)

Makes 4 servings

The spicy, creamy tea drink that is ever-more popular, chai is a lovely afternoon soother or stimulator. It is convenient and economical to make your own.

1 In a small saucepan, combine the tea bags, cinnamon stick, cardamom, clove, ginger and 2 cups (500 ml) water; bring the mixture to a boil over medium–high heat. Reduce the heat, cover and simmer for 5 minutes.
2 Stir in the milk. Increase the heat, return the mixture to a boil, then boil for 1 minute. Remove the saucepan from the heat, place a sieve over a warmed teapot and pour the mixture through; discard the solids. Add the sugar and stir until it has dissolved.
3 Divide among four mugs or cups and, if desired, serve with a cinnamon stick as a stirrer.

Hot Spiced Tea

2 sticks cinnamon
6–12 whole allspice
1 teaspoon whole cloves
12 tea bags
1 cup (230 g) firmly packed
  soft brown sugar
1 cup (250 ml) cranberry juice
½ cup (125 ml) orange juice
¼ cup (60 ml) lemon juice

Makes 3 litres

Give extra zest to hot tea with this inviting spice mixture – it will make your kitchen smell fabulous while it warms you to your toes. No mix can match this hot spiced tea at any price. It's the perfect drink for a winter afternoon.

1 Cut a 10 cm square of double-thickness muslin (cheesecloth). Put the cinnamon sticks, allspice and cloves in the centre. Bring together the corners of the fabric to form a bag; secure with a piece of kitchen string.
2 Place the spice bag in a large, non-aluminium saucepan and add 12 cups (3 litres) water. Bring to a boil over high heat, then remove from the heat and add the tea bags. Cover the pan and let the tea steep for 5 minutes. Remove and discard the tea bags and spice bag.
3 Stir in the sugar until dissolved. Add the juices, stirring until the ingredients are well blended. Return the saucepan to low heat, and gently heat the spiced tea through before serving.

Hot Mulled Cider

4 cups (1 litre) apple cider
10 whole cloves
10 black peppercorns
4 strips (about 8 x 1 cm each)
 orange zest
1 stick cinnamon, cracked
1 vanilla bean, split

Makes 4 servings

One of the best warm-me-ups, this cider has some surprises in its spice. You don't have to go to a ski lodge to enjoy it.

1 In a saucepan, combine all the ingredients and bring to a boil over medium heat. Remove the saucepan from the heat and let the mixture steep for 30 minutes. Remove and discard the spices.
2 Return the saucepan to low heat and slowly cook until the cider begins to steam. Ladle the cider into warm mugs, wait 3 to 5 minutes and serve.

Hot Non-alcoholic Punch

4 cups (1 litre) hot brewed tea
1 cup (220 g) sugar
4 cups (1 litre) cranberry juice
4 cups (1 litre) apple juice
2 cups (500 ml) orange juice
¾ cup (185 ml) lemon juice
24 whole cloves
2 sticks cinnamon
1 orange, sliced

Makes 12 to 16 servings

A traditional holiday punch served warm or cool, this recipe is festive for parties and quite economical when you make it up fresh.

1 In a large, non-aluminium saucepan over medium–high heat, combine the hot tea and sugar, stirring until the sugar has dissolved. Add the juices, 12 cloves and the cinnamon sticks. Bring the mixture to a boil and boil for 2 minutes.
2 Remove the saucepan from the heat. Pour the mixture into a heatproof punch bowl. Insert the remaining cloves into the orange slices and float them on the punch as garnish. Serve the punch warm or cooled to room temperature.

Deli-style Dishes

Brilliant Basic Mince ❖ Chilli Con Carne ❖ Tomato Herb Tarts ❖ Barbecue Sauce ❖ Barbecued Spareribs ❖ Baked Beans ❖ Stir-fried Vegetables ❖ Chinese Crispy Beef Stir-fry ❖ Refried Beans ❖ Curry with Rice ❖ Pork Korma with Potatoes and Spinach ❖ Thai Green Chicken Curry ❖ Pad Thai Noodles with Prawns ❖ Singapore Noodles ❖ Chinese Fried Rice ❖ Basic Rice Pilaf ❖ Tandoori Chicken

Main-dish Pies

Classic Chicken Pie ❖ Shepherd's Pie ❖ Spicy Beef Pie ❖ Quiche Lorraine

Pasta Dishes

Spaghetti Bolognese ❖ Spaghetti with Speedy Tomato Sauce ❖ Pasta with Fresh Tomato Sauce ❖ Pasta Puttanesca ❖ Fettuccine Alfredo ❖ Penne with Four-cheese Sauce ❖ Spaghetti Marinara ❖ Penne All'amatriciana ❖ Pasta with Classic Basil Pesto ❖ Pasta with Mushroom Pesto ❖ Pasta with Sun-dried Tomato Pesto ❖ Ravioli ❖ Lasagne

Soups

Beef Barley Soup ❖ Black Bean Soup ❖ Chicken Noodle Soup ❖ Clam Chowder ❖ Cream of Tomato Soup ❖ Quick Prawn Laksa ❖ Pumpkin Soup ❖ Lentil Soup ❖ Minestrone ❖ French Onion Soup ❖ Vegetable Soup ❖ Pea and Ham Soup ❖ Gazpacho

Salads

Classic Coleslaw ❖ Greek Salad ❖ Potato Salad ❖ Thai Beef Salad ❖ Egg Salad ❖ Pasta Salad ❖ Caesar Salad ❖ Creamy Chicken Salad ❖ Curried Chicken Salad ❖ Turkey Salad ❖ Tuna Salad ❖ Crab Salad ❖ Prawn Salad ❖ Tuscan-style Three-bean Salad ❖ Salade Niçoise

Take-away Food and Ready Meals

Have you noticed how the prepared-food aisles are taking up more and more space in your supermarket? We are increasingly reliant on ready-made meals, and supermarkets are simply responding to this demand.

The only problem is that these eat-as-they-are or pop-in-the-microwave dishes carry an enormous price premium for the little extra convenience that they provide.

This chapter is devoted to the true convenience foods you can make fresh in your own kitchen. Most make minimal demands on your time. And many are foods that you can make ahead – or leave simmering in a slow cooker – for a meal later.

On the following pages, you'll find tasty meat and bean dishes, and satisfying savoury pies similar to those that you might find at the deli counter or in the supermarket freezer section. You'll also find a tempting selection of delicious, easy-to-make pasta dishes. (For a special treat, try them with the fresh pastas from Chapter 1.) There are hearty soups that will fill your kitchen with wonderful aromas, delight your family, and use up leftovers – and unlike the canned versions, homemade soups can provide more flavour with a lot less salt. You'll also find a wide selection of deli-style salads that you can make with minimal fuss, ranging from versatile sides such as Coleslaw to main dishes like Caesar Salad and Creamy Chicken Salad – and unlike some deli salads, they will never have too much mayonnaise!

Deli-style Dishes

Brilliant Basic Mince

2 tablespoons olive or
canola oil
2 onions, chopped
2 cloves garlic, finely chopped
1 celery stalk, chopped
2 carrots, chopped
1 kg lean beef or pork mince
2 teaspoons dried basil
1 teaspoon dried oregano
1 teaspoon salt
½ teaspoon freshly ground
black pepper
large pinch of sugar
1 tablespoon worcestershire
sauce
410 g can chopped tomatoes

Makes about 6 cups (1.5 kg)

This versatile base recipe can be made with either beef or pork. You can use it in the following recipe and in the Spaghetti Bolognese on page 179.

1 In a large heavy-based saucepan, heat the oil over medium heat. Add the onions, garlic, celery and carrots and sauté until softened, about 5 minutes, stirring occasionally. Crumble the mince into the pan, breaking it up with a large spoon; cook, stirring occasionally, until the meat is no longer pink. Drain off as much fat as possible.

2 Add the remaining ingredients and stir until well mixed. Reduce the heat, cover and simmer for 20 to 25 minutes.

3 Remove from the heat and allow to cool completely. Spoon off any visible fat, then divide the mixture among three or four 2 cup (500 ml) self-sealing, freezer-safe plastic bags. Seal, label, date and freeze. The mixture will keep for up to 3 months in the freezer.

Chilli Con Carne

2 cups (350 g) Brilliant Basic
Mince (above), thawed
1 tablespoon chilli powder,
or to taste
1 teaspoon ground cumin
2 x 420 g cans red kidney
beans, drained and rinsed
hot chilli sauce, to taste
hot cooked rice, tortilla chips,
grated cheddar, sour cream
or natural yogurt (optional)

Makes 6 servings

This will be the fastest chilli you've ever put together using fresh meat.

1 In a saucepan, combine the mince mixture, chilli powder, cumin and kidney beans. Mix well, then cover and cook over medium–high heat until heated through, about 10 minutes. Add some hot chilli sauce to your desired level of spiciness.

2 Serve over rice or with tortilla chips, if desired. Sprinkle a little cheese over each serving or top with a dollop of sour cream or yogurt, if desired.

Tomato Herb Tarts

1 sheet frozen puff pastry
½ cup (60 g) finely grated
    cheddar
2 tablespoons grated parmesan
450 g ripe tomatoes, peeled
    and sliced
2 tablespoons finely chopped
    fresh parsley
2 tablespoons finely chopped
    fresh basil
2 tablespoons finely chopped
    fresh thyme
1 tablespoon virgin olive oil
freshly ground black pepper,
    to taste

Makes 4 to 6 tarts

Using frozen puff pastry means you can rustle up these individual tarts in a jiffy.

1 Preheat the oven to 200°C (Gas 6).
2 Place the puff pastry on a work surface. Using a large, round cutter, cut out 4 to 6 circles and place on a baking tray. Bake until puffed and golden brown, 10 to 12 minutes.
3 Remove from the oven and sprinkle some of the cheddar and parmesan over each pastry circle, leaving a small border around the edges. Layer the tomato slices over the cheese, then sprinkle with the herbs. Drizzle with the olive oil and sprinkle with pepper.
4 Return to the oven and bake until the cheese is completely melted, about 5 minutes. Turn the oven off and let the tarts stand for a few minutes before removing them from the oven. Serve immediately, or at room temperature.

Barbecue Sauce

1½ cups (375 ml) tomato sauce
1 cup (250 ml) cider vinegar
⅔ cup (170 ml) peanut or
    safflower oil
⅓ cup (80 ml) worcestershire
    sauce
½ cup (115 g) firmly packed
    soft brown sugar
3 tablespoons mild yellow
    mustard
½ teaspoon freshly ground
    black pepper
juice of 1 large lemon
1–2 fresh red chillies, finely
    chopped (optional)

Makes about 3 cups (750 ml)

Meant for spareribs (see Barbecued Spareribs, page 168), this tangy homemade sauce also goes well with chicken. As well as saving you money, it's a satisfying condiment to make as you can adjust the ingredients to suit your own tastes.

Put all the ingredients in a saucepan and mix to combine. Bring to a boil over medium heat; immediately reduce the heat to low, then cover and simmer until the sugar has completely dissolved and the sauce has thickened slightly, about 20 minutes.

If you run out of brown sugar

If a recipe calls for ½ cup (115 g) firmly packed brown sugar and you don't have any on hand, stir 1 tablespoon molasses into ½ cup (110 g) regular granulated sugar.

Barbecued Spareribs

2.25 kg pork spareribs,
in 6–8 rib portions
3 cups (750 ml) Barbecue
Sauce (page 167)

Makes 6 servings

You get the most succulent results when you prepare your own ribs at home; a side benefit is that it's also very economical.

1 Place the ribs in a large self-sealing bag, glass baking dish or non-metallic bowl. Pour 2 cups (500 ml) of the barbecue sauce over the ribs and toss to coat. Cover and refrigerate overnight.
2 On a covered kettle-style barbecue, follow the manufacturer's directions to prepare the coals for the indirect method of cooking. Add the ribs and cook for 1 to 1½ hours, basting frequently with the marinating sauce.
3 In a small saucepan, warm the remaining barbecue sauce over low heat and serve on the side with the ribs.

Baked Beans

450 g dried beans, picked
through and rinsed
⅓ cup (115 g) maple syrup
1 teaspoon mustard powder
1 teaspoon salt
½ teaspoon freshly ground
black pepper
125 g salt pork
1 onion, peeled

Makes 6 servings

Why buy a can when you can make your own baked beans? Use borlotti, cannellini or haricot (navy) beans, or use a mixture of all three. The beans can be baked slowly one day, then reheated or served cold for breakfast or lunch the next.

1 Place the beans in a large saucepan and add enough water to cover by 5 cm. Bring to a boil and boil for 2 minutes. Remove the saucepan from the heat, cover and leave to soak for 1 hour.
2 Add more water to cover the beans and return the pan to the heat. Bring to a boil, reduce the heat and simmer until the beans are tender, about 1 hour, adding more water as necessary to keep the beans covered. Drain the beans, reserving the cooking liquid.

3 Preheat the oven to 130°C (Gas 1). Transfer the beans to a casserole dish. In a bowl, combine the maple syrup, mustard, salt and pepper and pour the mixture over the beans. Cut the pork into 1 cm slices, up to but not through the rind. Add the pork and onion to the bean mixture, pressing them down to immerse them. If needed, add the reserved cooking liquid until the beans are completely covered.
4 Cover and bake for 4 hours, adding more reserved cooking liquid or water as needed so the beans don't dry out. Remove the lid and bake for 1 hour more, or until the beans are tender.

Stir-fried Vegetables

1½ tablespoons soy sauce
1½ tablespoons mirin or dry
  sherry
1 tablespoon honey
2 tablespoons Vegetable Stock
  (page 51)
2 tablespoons vegetable oil
750 g mixed fresh vegetables,
  prepared and cut into even-
  sized pieces
1 clove garlic, crushed
2–3 cm piece fresh ginger,
  peeled and grated
2 teaspoons sesame oil

Makes 4 servings

Stir-frying really makes the most of vegetables, retaining their colour, crunch, flavour and texture.

1 In a small jug, combine the soy sauce, mirin or sherry, honey and stock. Mix well, then set aside.
2 In a wok or large deep frying pan, heat the oil. Add any of the tougher, slower-cooking vegetables (such as carrots, broccoli, celery, green beans and baby corn) and stir-fry over high heat for 30 seconds. Pour in 1–1½ tablespoons of water, cover with a lid and cook over high heat for 2 minutes.
3 Next add the more tender, quicker-cooking vegetables (such as capsicums/peppers, snow peas/mangetout, bean sprouts and spring onions), along with the garlic and ginger. Stir-fry until they are almost tender, about 2 minutes.
4 Finally, stir in any delicate leafy vegetables (such as shredded greens or bok choy) and cook for 1 more minute, until all are cooked but still retain some bite and their bright colour.
5 Pour in the reserved sauce and stir-fry for 1 minute, until all the vegetables are coated in the sauce. Transfer to a serving platter, drizzle with the sesame oil and serve.

Chinese Crispy Beef Stir-fry

200 g lean beef steak
2 teaspoons cornflour
1 teaspoon five-spice
1 carrot, peeled
1 small leek, white part only,
  trimmed
6 spring onions, sliced
  diagonally
½ red capsicum (pepper), cut
  into strips
100 g dried rice noodles
1½ tablespoons soy sauce
1½ tablespoons rice wine
1½ tablespoons vegetable oil
1 large clove garlic, finely
  chopped
2–3 cm piece fresh ginger,
  peeled and finely chopped
1 red chilli, seeded and finely
  chopped
soy sauce, for drizzling

Makes 2 servings

Make the most of prime lean beef by stir-frying it with healthy vegetables, wholesome noodles and aromatic Asian-style flavourings.

1 Cut the meat across the grain into 5 cm wide pieces, then cut each piece into very thin strips. Place in a small bowl with the cornflour and five-spice and mix together until meat is coated.
2 Cut the carrot and leek into 5 cm lengths, then cut each piece into thin matchsticks. Combine in a bowl with the spring onions and capsicum.
3 Put the noodles in a heatproof bowl, pour some lightly salted boiling water over them and soak for 3 minutes. Drain and refresh in cold water, then drain again. Mix the soy sauce, rice wine and 1½ tablespoons of water in a small jug or bowl.
4 Place a wok or a large frying pan over high heat. When hot, add 1 tablespoon of the oil. When the oil begins to smoke, toss in the meat and stir-fry until cooked through, 2 to 3 minutes; remove with a slotted spoon. Add the remaining oil with the garlic, ginger and chilli. Stir-fry for 30 seconds, then add the vegetables and toss for another 30 seconds.
5 Stir in the soy sauce mixture. As soon as the liquid is bubbling, mix in the drained noodles, then the meat. Serve immediately, with soy sauce to drizzle over the top.

Refried Beans

2 tablespoons vegetable oil
1 large onion, chopped
2 x 420 g cans pinto, black or
   red kidney beans, drained
   and rinsed
1 teaspoon ground cumin
salt, to taste
chilli powder, to taste
   (optional)

Makes 4 to 6 servings

Craving homemade refried beans but crunched for time? That's not a problem with this recipe.

1 In a large heavy-based saucepan, heat the oil over medium heat. Add the onion and sauté until just softened. Add the beans, cumin, salt and chilli powder, if using. Cook, stirring, until heated through, 5 to 10 minutes. Remove the pan from the heat.
2 Using a potato masher, mash the bean mixture to the desired consistency. Place back over medium heat and cook until the mixture is thick and creamy in texture, about 15 minutes.

Curry with Rice

¼ cup (35 g) plain flour
½ teaspoon salt
¼ teaspoon freshly ground
   black pepper
650 g boneless, skinless
   chicken or turkey breasts
   or thighs (or lamb), cut into
   2–3 cm cubes
¼ cup (60 ml) vegetable oil
1 large brown onion, chopped
2 cloves garlic, finely chopped
2 small celery stalks, chopped
1–2 tablespoons Curry Powder
   (page 45)
1¾ cups (440 ml) Chicken
   Stock (page 50)
4 carrots, cut crosswise into
   1 cm slices
½ cauliflower, cut into florets
1¼ cups (250 g) basmati rice

Makes 4 servings

Flavourful, economical and easy to prepare, curry is deliciously adaptable, and a tasty way to use up leftovers. Meat, poultry, seafood, vegetables – just about anything goes when it comes to making a curry.

1 In a large, self-sealing bag, combine the flour, salt and pepper. Working in small batches, add the meat to the bag, seal well, then shake to coat the meat with the flour mixture.
2 In a large heavy-based saucepan with a tight-fitting lid, heat the oil over medium–high heat. Add half the meat to the pan and sauté until lightly brown, about 5 minutes. Remove and drain on paper towels. Repeat with the remaining meat.
3 In the oil and juices left in the pan, sauté the onion, garlic and celery until soft, about 5 minutes. Add the curry powder, stock, carrots, cauliflower and reserved meat. Reduce the heat to low, then cover and simmer until the cauliflower is just tender, 20 to 30 minutes.
4 Meanwhile, in a large saucepan, cook the rice according to the packet directions. Transfer to a large warm serving bowl, spoon the curry over the rice and serve immediately.

Pork Korma with Potatoes and Spinach

1 tablespoon vegetable oil

2 large onions, sliced

500 g lean pork mince

2 cloves garlic, crushed

8 green cardamom pods, crushed and pods discarded

1 tablespoon cumin seeds

600 ml Chicken Stock (page 50), hot

750 g small new potatoes, scrubbed and halved

2 teaspoons cornflour

1 cup (250 g) natural yogurt

salt and freshly ground black pepper, to taste

¾ cup (80 g) ground almonds

250 g baby English spinach leaves

¼ cup (25 g) flaked almonds, lightly toasted

Makes 4 servings

Thickened with ground almonds and yogurt, this dish is rich and creamy, yet not as indulgent as traditional kormas. Serve with warm chappati or naan breads.

1 In a large, heavy-based saucepan or flameproof casserole dish, heat the oil. Add the onions and cook over medium heat for 10 minutes. Transfer to a bowl.

2 Add the mince, garlic, cardamom and cumin seeds to the pan or dish. Cook, stirring often and breaking up the meat with a large spoon, until the meat has changed colour, about 5 minutes. Return about half the onions to the pan, pour in the stock and bring back to a boil. Reduce the heat, cover and simmer for 15 minutes.

3 Stir in the potatoes and bring back to simmering point, then cover and cook until the potatoes are tender, about 20 minutes.

4 Meanwhile, blend the cornflour with about ½ cup (125 g) of the yogurt and the ground almonds to make a paste. Stir this mixture into the curry and bring just to a boil, stirring. Reduce the heat and simmer until slightly thickened, about 1 minute. Season to taste with salt and pepper.

5 Reserve a few small spinach leaves for garnishing, then fold the rest through the korma until they are just wilted and bright green. Mix the flaked almonds with the remaining onions.

6 Serve the curry drizzled with the remaining yogurt and topped with the almond and onion mixture and spinach leaves.

Thai Green Chicken Curry

4 boneless, skinless chicken breasts (about 600 g in total)

350 g new potatoes, scrubbed

6 spring onions

8 grape or cherry tomatoes

400 ml can light coconut milk

600 ml Chicken Stock (page 50), hot

2 tablespoons Green Curry Paste (page 46)

2 tablespoons lime juice

¾ cup (115 g) shelled fresh or thawed frozen peas

4 tablespoons chopped fresh coriander

salt and freshly ground black pepper, to taste

Makes 4 servings

Keep the fat content low in a tangy Thai curry by not pre-frying the ingredients; simply simmer them in light coconut milk and stock with potatoes, peas and tomatoes.

1 Cut the chicken breasts into thin strips across the grain and cut the potatoes into chunks. Slice the spring onions diagonally and halve the cherry or grape tomatoes.

2 Pour the coconut milk and stock into a wok or large frying pan. Stir in the curry paste and heat until boiling. Stir in the chicken strips and potatoes, then bring back to a boil.

3 Reduce the heat and simmer, uncovered, until the chicken and potatoes are just tender, about 15 minutes.

4 Stir in the spring onions, lime juice, peas and tomatoes and simmer for a further 3 to 4 minutes. Stir in the coriander and season to taste with salt and pepper.

Pad Thai Noodles with Prawns

1 tablespoon lime juice

2 tablespoons salt-reduced
   soy sauce

1 tablespoon fish sauce

24 small peeled raw prawns,
   about 250 g in total

250 g packet dried rice noodles
   (medium thickness)

¼ cup (60 ml) vegetable oil

1 teaspoon sesame oil

2 small red chillies, deseeded
   and finely chopped

150 g fresh baby corn, halved
   lengthwise

2¼ cups (200 g) bean sprouts

200 g bok choy, finely shredded

220 g can water chestnuts,
   drained and sliced

1 cup (250 ml) canned
   reduced-fat coconut milk

1 lime, cut into wedges

Makes 4 servings

Typical Thai flavours, including chilli, lime and coconut, combine in this aromatic stir-fry of prawns, noodles and Asian vegetables.

1 In a bowl, mix together the lime juice, soy sauce and fish sauce. Add the prawns and toss together, then set aside to marinate for a few minutes.

2 Meanwhile, put the noodles in a large heatproof bowl. Pour boiling water over to cover, add 1 teaspoon of the vegetable oil and stir gently. Soak for 4 minutes, then drain thoroughly.

3 Lift the prawns out of the marinade and pat dry with a paper towel. Heat a wok or heavy-based frying pan until very hot, then add 1 teaspoon of the vegetable oil and all of the sesame oil and swirl to coat the wok. Add the prawns and chillies and stir-fry until the prawns turn pink, about 2 minutes. Remove with a slotted spoon, leaving any remaining oil in the wok.

4 Add the rest of the oil to the pan. Toss in the corn and stir-fry for 30 seconds. Add the bean sprouts and bok choy and stir-fry for 1 minute, then add the reserved marinade. Cook for a few seconds, stirring all the time, then add the water chestnuts and drained noodles. Stir-fry for a further 1 minute.

5 Return the prawns to the wok and pour in the coconut milk. Toss everything together over high heat until bubbling. Serve immediately, with lime wedges to squeeze over.

Singapore Noodles

170 g dried rice vermicelli
  noodles
2 tablespoons peanut oil
200 g peeled small raw prawns
200 g boneless, skinless
  chicken breasts, thinly sliced
6 spring onions, thinly sliced
  diagonally
3 teaspoons grated fresh
  ginger
1 small red capsicum (pepper),
  thinly sliced
2 teaspoons curry powder
1 teaspoon ground turmeric
3 teaspoons Chinese rice wine
2 tablespoons light soy sauce
2 tablespoons Chicken Stock
  (page 50)
¾ cup (115 g) frozen peas,
  thawed
3 eggs, beaten
fresh coriander sprigs,
  to garnish
lime quarters, to serve

Makes 4 servings

A perennial favourite at Singaporean food stalls and a popular take-away dish all over the world, this tasty, home-cooked version will feed the family for much less than purchased noodles – and they'll taste much fresher and less oily, too.

1 Soak the noodles according to the packet directions, then drain and set aside.
2 In a wok, heat 1 tablespoon of the oil. Fry the prawns and chicken, in batches, until just cooked, then remove to a plate.
3 Heat the remaining oil and stir-fry the spring onions, ginger and capsicum until just beginning to soften, then stir in the curry powder and turmeric and cook for 1 minute.
4 Stir in the rice wine, soy sauce and stock until combined, then add the peas and drained noodles and toss until the peas are tender.
5 Push the noodles to one side of the wok and pour in the beaten eggs. Cook stirring, for 1 minute, then mix the egg through the noodles.
6 Return the prawns and chicken to the wok and toss until warmed through and well combined.
7 Serve the noodles in bowls, garnished with coriander sprigs and a wedge of lime.

Chinese Fried Rice

1½ cups (300 g) long-grain
  white rice
2 tablespoons vegetable oil
2 eggs, lightly beaten
2 cloves garlic, chopped
1 red capsicum (pepper), diced
1 carrot, diced
3 Chinese sausages, sliced,
  or 100 g diced ham
½ cup (80 g) frozen peas,
  thawed and drained
2 spring onions, sliced
2 tablespoons soy sauce
2 teaspoons sugar
2 teaspoons shrimp paste
  (optional)

Makes 4 servings

Once you have made fried rice the first time, you'll realise how versatile it is. Use whatever leftover or seasonal vegetables you like. Fried rice is so easy to make at home that you'll never need to go out and buy it again! The secret is to cook the rice the night before to obtain the right texture – or use up any leftover rice that happens to be in the fridge.

1 Wash the rice under cold running water until the water almost runs clear. Drain, then place in a saucepan with 2¼ cups (560 ml) cold water. Cover with a tight-fitting lid and place over medium heat until the water comes to a boil, then reduce the heat to a simmer and cook until the rice has absorbed all the liquid, about 15 minutes. Remove from the heat and stand, covered, for 10 minutes.
2 Spread the rice out on a tray, allow to cool, then cover lightly with plastic wrap. Refrigerate overnight.
3 In a wok or large frying pan, heat 1 tablespoon of the oil over medium heat. Add the eggs and cook for 1 minute, stirring until lightly scrambled, then remove from the wok. Add the remaining oil to the wok and briefly cook the garlic until fragrant, then add the capsicum and carrot and toss until softened, 1 to 2 minutes.
4 Add the Chinese sausage or ham, toss for another minute, then add the cooked rice. Keep tossing until the rice is reheated, breaking up any large clumps as you go. At the last minute, add the peas, spring onions, soy sauce, sugar, egg and shrimp paste, if using. Mix together well and serve.

Basic Rice Pilaf

1 tablespoon olive oil
or vegetable oil
1 cup (200 g) long-grain white
rice
2 cups (500 ml) Chicken Stock
(page 50)

Makes 4 to 6 servings

Once you know how to make pilaf (seasoned rice or other grains), you have the base for an almost infinite variety of dishes. Try using brown rice, wild rice, burghul (bulgur) or barley instead of white rice; stir in cooked meats, seafood or vegetables, add a handful of toasted pine nuts, pistachios or pecans – and suddenly you have a gourmet meal in minutes.

1 In a heavy-based saucepan, heat the oil over medium–high heat until very hot. Add the rice and stir constantly until the oil is absorbed and the rice is translucent, about 5 minutes.
2 Add the stock, increase the heat to high and bring the mixture to a boil. Stir once, lower the heat and cover the pan tightly. Simmer until the liquid is absorbed and the rice is tender, 15 to 20 minutes.

Tandoori Chicken

3 cloves garlic, crushed
1 teaspoon paprika
¾ teaspoon ground cumin
¾ teaspoon ground coriander
½ teaspoon cinnamon
½ teaspoon chilli powder
½ teaspoon freshly ground
black pepper
2 cups (500 g) natural yogurt
4 skinless, bone-in chicken
breast halves (about 1 kg
in total)
1 small red onion, finely
chopped
1 cucumber, seeded and diced
½ cup (25 g) chopped fresh
coriander

Makes 4 servings

A favourite at many Indian restaurants around the world, Tandoori Chicken isn't difficult to make at home. Marinating the chicken overnight in the yogurt ensures a great result as the enzymes in the yogurt tenderise the flesh and make it creamy and moist.

1 In a shallow glass or ceramic baking dish, combine the garlic, spices and a dash of salt. Stir in 1 cup (250 g) of the yogurt until well blended. Make several slashes in the flesh of the chicken with a sharp knife, cutting almost to the bone. Place the chicken, cut side down, in the yogurt mixture. Cover and refrigerate for at least 2 hours or overnight, turning the chicken several times.
2 Preheat the oven to its highest setting. Lift the chicken from its marinade and place in a shallow baking dish; discard any leftover marinade. Bake the chicken for 20 minutes, then reduce the oven temperature to 120°C (Gas ½) and bake for a few more minutes, until cooked through but still juicy.
3 Meanwhile, combine the onion, cucumber, coriander and the remaining yogurt in a bowl and mix well. Serve the chicken with the yogurt mixture on the side.

Main-dish Pies

Classic Chicken Pie

1 large potato, peeled and
  chopped
1 carrot, sliced
½ cup (125 g) butter
1 small chopped brown onion
½ cup (75 g) plain flour
¾ teaspoon salt
½ teaspoon dried thyme,
  crumbled
½ teaspoon freshly ground
  black pepper
1½ cups (375 ml) Chicken
  Stock (page 50)
¾ cup (185 ml) milk
2 cups (300 g) chopped cooked
  chicken
½ cup (80 g) frozen peas
½ cup (75 g) frozen corn
Basic Double Crust Pie Pastry
  (page 123)

Makes 6 servings

Frozen chicken pies are no match for this lovely dish, which cleverly uses up the leftovers from a roast chicken. The pie can be made ahead and frozen, tightly covered with freezer-safe foil, for up to 3 months.

1 Put the potato and carrot in a large saucepan and cover with water. Bring to a boil, then reduce the heat, cover and simmer until just tender, 8 to 10 minutes. Drain the vegetables and set aside.
2 Melt the butter in a large heavy-based saucepan over medium heat. Add the onion and sauté until tender. Stir in the flour, salt, thyme and pepper until well blended, then gradually add the stock and milk, stirring constantly. Bring the mixture to a boil; cook, stirring constantly, until it has thickened. Stir in the chicken, peas, corn, potato and carrot. Remove the mixture from the heat.
3 Preheat the oven to 220°C (Gas 7). Roll out the pastry to line a 23 cm pie dish. Ease the pastry into the dish, then trim the edge. Spoon the chicken mixture into the pastry case. Roll out the remaining pastry to make a lid, then cut some slits or decorative vents in the pastry. Carefully place the pastry lid over the filling; fold the top edge over and under the bottom crust edges, then pinch the edges together to seal. If desired, you can form a decorative edge around the rim using a fork or with your fingers.
4 Bake the pie until the crust is golden brown, 35 to 40 minutes. Remove from the oven and allow the pie to stand for 15 minutes before serving. To bake a frozen pie, cover the edge with pieces of foil, place on a baking tray and bake in a 220°C (Gas 7) oven for 30 minutes. Reduce the oven temperature to 180°C (Gas 4) and bake for an additional 70 to 80 minutes, or until the crust is golden brown.

Shepherd's Pie

5 boiling (waxy) potatoes
⅔ cup (170 ml) pouring cream
  or creamy milk
3 tablespoons butter
salt and freshly ground black
  pepper, to taste
freshly grated nutmeg
2 tablespoons vegetable oil
1 onion, chopped
1 clove garlic, crushed
2 teaspoons worcestershire
  sauce
2 tablespoons tomato sauce
2 tablespoons chopped fresh
  mixed herbs (such as parsley,
  thyme, marjoram or mint)
500 g cooked lamb, trimmed
  of fat, then minced
⅔ cup (170 ml) lamb gravy
  or Beef Stock (page 49)

Makes 4 servings

This is a favourite way to transform leftovers from the weekend roast into a satisfying meal for all the family.

1 Preheat the oven to 180°C (Gas 4). Peel and quarter the potatoes. Boil or steam until the potatoes tender, then drain and mash well. Heat the cream or milk and half the butter in a saucepan and beat into the mashed potatoes. Season well with salt, pepper and a little nutmeg. Cover and keep warm.

2 In a saucepan, heat the oil over medium heat. Add the onion and garlic and sauté until soft and golden, about 5 minutes. Stir in the worcestershire sauce, tomato sauce and herbs. Stir in the lamb and gravy or stock. Transfer to a baking dish and spoon the mashed potatoes over the top. Smooth the potato topping, then score the surface decoratively.

3 Dot the remaining butter over the mashed potato and bake for 45 minutes, or until the pie is golden brown and thoroughly heated through.

Spicy Beef Pie

2 potatoes
450 g lean beef mince
2–3 spring onions, sliced
1 large carrot, finely chopped
1 clove garlic, finely chopped
½ teaspoon dried thyme
½ teaspoon dried sage
½ teaspoon salt
½ teaspoon freshly cracked
  black pepper
¼ teaspoon celery salt
pinch of ground cinnamon
3 tablespoons finely chopped
  fresh parsley
¼ cup (60 ml) chilli sauce
Basic Double Crust Pie Pastry
  (page 123)
1 tablespoon dijon mustard
1 tablespoon milk

Makes 6 servings

Transform the humble meat pie into a special dish.

1 Peel and quarter the potatoes. Cook in a large saucepan of boiling water until tender. Drain, mash and set aside.

2 Meanwhile, brown the beef in a large heavy-based saucepan over medium heat until no pink remains. Drain the liquid from the pan and return to the heat. Stir in the spring onions, carrot, garlic, thyme, sage, salt, pepper, celery salt and cinnamon and sauté for 4 to 5 minutes. Add the mashed potatoes, parsley and chilli sauce. Stir to combine, then remove from the heat.

3 Preheat the oven to 230°C (Gas 8). Roll out the pastry to line a 23 cm pie dish. Ease the pastry into the dish, then trim the edge. Brush the mustard over the inside of the pastry case, then spoon the beef mixture into the pastry case. Roll out the remaining pastry to make a lid, then cut some slits or decorative vents in the pastry. Carefully place the pastry over the filling; fold the top edge over and under the bottom crust edges, then pinch the edges together to seal. If desired, form a decorative edge around the rim using a fork or with your fingers. Brush the top of the pastry with the milk.

4 Bake for 10 minutes, reduce the temperature to 180°C (Gas 4) and bake until the crust is golden brown, about 25 minutes.

Quiche Lorraine

Basic Single Crust Pie Pastry
(page 124)
6 slices good-quality bacon,
diced and lightly fried
1½ cups (185 g) grated gruyère
1½ cups (375 ml) pouring
cream
4 eggs
½ teaspoon salt
small pinch of ground cayenne
pepper
small pinch of ground nutmeg

Makes 6 main course or
12 appetiser servings

Deliciously creamy, this much-loved quiche takes its
name from the Lorraine region in France. The filling
was originally made with just eggs, cream and bacon,
but now includes cheese – a good gruyère or other Swiss
cheese. A shop-bought quiche, while convenient, will
never taste as good as your own, fresh from the oven.

1 Preheat the oven to 200°C (Gas 6). Line a 23 cm pie dish
with the pastry and flute the edges. Place in the refrigerator
and rest for 15 to 20 minutes.
2 Fill the pastry case with baking beads or dried beans and
bake for 10 minutes. Remove from the oven and remove the
baking beads or beans.
3 Sprinkle the cooked bacon around the pastry case, then
sprinkle with the cheese. In a large bowl, beat the cream,
eggs, salt, cayenne pepper and nutmeg until well blended.
Carefully pour the cream mixture into the pastry case.
4 Bake for 15 minutes, then reduce the oven temperature to
180°C (Gas 4). Bake for another 15 to 20 minutes, or until
the filling is set in the centre. Remove from the oven and
allow the quiche to stand for 10 minutes before serving to
allow the custard to set.

If you run out of cream

Thick cream: If a recipe calls for
1 cup (250 ml) thick cream (not for
whipping) and you don't have any on
hand, whisk together ¾ cup (185 ml)
milk with ⅓ cup (80 ml) melted butter
until well blended.

Light cream: If a recipe calls for 1 cup
(250 ml) light cream and you don't have
any on hand, whisk together ¾ cup
(185 ml) milk with ¼ cup (60 ml) melted
butter until well blended.

Pasta Dishes

Spaghetti Bolognese

2 cups (350 g) Brilliant Basic
　Mince (page 166), thawed
410 g can chopped tomatoes
¾ cup (185 g) tomato paste
½ cup (125 ml) dry red wine
2 teaspoons dried basil,
　crumbled
1 teaspoon dried oregano,
　crumbled
500 g spaghetti
grated parmesan, for
　sprinkling

Makes 6 to 8 servings

Please a hungry crowd in just 30 minutes with this classic spaghetti recipe.

1　In a large heavy-based saucepan over medium heat, combine the mince mixture, tomatoes, tomato paste, wine, basil and oregano. Stir until well combined. Bring to a boil over high heat, then reduce the heat to low and simmer, stirring occasionally, for about 30 minutes.
2　Meanwhile, cook the spaghetti according to the packet directions, then drain.
3　Serve the spaghetti topped with the meat sauce and sprinkled with parmesan.

Spaghetti with Speedy Tomato Sauce

410 g can roma tomatoes
¾ cup (185 g) tomato paste
1 teaspoon dried oregano,
　crumbled
1 teaspoon dried basil,
　crumbled
1 teaspoon sugar
½ teaspoon salt
¼ teaspoon freshly ground
　black pepper
500 g spaghetti
grated parmesan, for
　sprinkling

Makes about 6 servings

You'll never need to buy bottled sauce again with this super recipe. Using the most basic pantry ingredients, this entire meal is ready in no time at all. In summer, when fresh tomatoes are plentiful and cheap, substitute fresh, chopped tomatoes for the canned variety.

1　In a large saucepan over medium heat, combine the tomatoes, tomato paste, oregano, basil, sugar, salt and pepper. Bring to a boil, then reduce the heat and simmer for 15 to 20 minutes.
2　Meanwhile, cook the spaghetti according to the packet directions, then drain.
3　Serve the sauce over the spaghetti and sprinkle with parmesan.

Pasta with Fresh Tomato Sauce

1.25 kg ripe fresh tomatoes,
   or an 800 g can roma
   tomatoes, chopped
2 tablespoons olive oil
3 cloves garlic
2 tablespoons tomato paste
2–3 tablespoons chopped fresh
   basil leaves, or 2 teaspoons
   dried basil, crumbled
1 teaspoon sugar
1 teaspoon salt
¼ teaspoon freshly ground
   black pepper
500 g pasta, such as spaghetti,
   vermicelli or linguine,
   cooked and drained
grated parmesan, for
   sprinkling

Makes about 6 servings or
3 cups (750 ml) sauce

Bursting with rich, juicy, vine-ripened tomatoes, this classic sauce forms the base for many other pasta sauces. This is a great way to use up over-ripe tomatoes as they impart an especially intense flavour. If tomatoes are not in season, you can use canned, but the flavour won't be nearly as good.

1 If using fresh tomatoes, score a cross in the base of each tomato and place in a heatproof bowl. Cover with boiling water, leave for 30 seconds, then plunge in cold water and peel the skin away from the cross. Cut the tomatoes in half and scoop out the seeds, then chop the flesh.
2 In a large, heavy-based saucepan, heat the olive oil over medium heat. Add the garlic and cook for 1 minute. Add the tomatoes, tomato paste, basil and sugar and bring to a boil, stirring constantly. Reduce the heat to low and simmer until the sauce thickens, 12 to 15 minutes.
3 Stir in the salt and pepper. Serve over hot cooked pasta, sprinkled with a little parmesan.

Pasta Puttanesca

2 tablespoons olive oil
2 cloves garlic, finely chopped
1 cup (135 g) halved, pitted,
   large black Greek olives
¼ cup (35 g) drained capers
8 chopped anchovies
3 cups (750 ml) Fresh Tomato
   Sauce (above)
¼ teaspoon dried red chilli
   flakes, or to taste
500 g pasta, cooked and
   drained

Makes 6 servings

For a true taste of the Mediterranean without leaving home, try this rich tomato sauce – salty, piquant and just a little spicy!

1 In a large heavy-based saucepan, heat the olive oil over medium–low heat. Add the garlic and sauté until soft, about 2 minutes. Add the olives, capers, anchovies, tomato sauce and chilli flakes to taste.
2 Increase the heat to medium–high. Simmer the sauce for 15 minutes, stirring often. Serve over hot cooked pasta.

If you run out of tomato sauce

If a recipe calls for 2 cups (500 ml) tomato sauce and you don't have any on hand, combine ¾ cup (185 g) tomato paste and 1 cup (250 ml) water and whisk until well blended.

Fettuccine Alfredo

3 tablespoons butter
4 tablespoons finely chopped
   French shallots
300 ml thick cream
1 cup (250 ml) pouring cream
½ teaspoon salt
pinch of ground nutmeg
¾ cup (75 g) grated parmesan
500 g fettuccine, cooked and
   drained

Makes 4 servings

The king of cream sauces, Alfredo has a rich flavour that is entirely dependent on the quality of the cheese, so indulge in the best. You will still pay less than restaurant prices – and you'll find that shop-bought Alfredo sauces just don't compare.

1 In a saucepan over medium heat, melt the butter. Add the shallots and sauté until they are soft, 3 to 4 minutes. Stir in all the cream, with the salt and nutmeg. Increase the heat to high and bring the mixture to a boil, stirring constantly. Reduce the heat to low and simmer until the sauce thickens, 4 to 5 minutes. Stir in the parmesan.
2 Place the hot cooked fettuccine in a large, warm serving bowl. Pour the sauce over, toss well and serve.

Penne with Four-cheese Sauce

3 tablespoons butter
2 cloves garlic, finely chopped
2 tablespoons plain flour
1 cup (250 ml) pouring cream
1 cup (250 ml) milk
1 cup (125 g) grated fontina
   cheese
1 cup (150 g) grated provolone
   cheese
½ cup (75 g) grated mozzarella
½ cup (50 g) grated parmesan
½ teaspoon salt
¼ teaspoon ground white
   pepper
500 g penne or other pasta,
   such as farfalle or rotini,
   cooked and drained

Makes 4 servings

If you love cheese, this dish is for you – not one, but four intriguing cheeses combine to make a superb pasta sauce. It's so simple to make, and much, much better than anything you'll find in a bottle!

1 In a large, non-stick saucepan over medium heat, melt the butter. Add the garlic and sauté until soft, about 2 minutes. Stir in the flour and cook until bubbly, about 1 minute. Remove the pan from the heat and gradually whisk in the cream and milk. Place back over medium heat and cook, stirring often, until the sauce just boils and thickens, 3 to 5 minutes.
2 Add the cheeses, salt and pepper and cook, stirring constantly, until the cheeses melt and the sauce is smooth, 1 to 2 minutes.
3 Place the hot cooked pasta in a warm serving bowl. Pour the sauce over, toss well and serve.

Spaghetti Marinara

2 tablespoons extra virgin olive oil
1 onion, chopped
2–3 cloves garlic, chopped
2 tablespoons chopped fresh parsley
1 cup (250 ml) dry white wine
410 g can chopped tomatoes
pinch of dried red chilli flakes
¼ teaspoon sugar
pinch of saffron threads
freshly ground black pepper, to taste
8 mussels, scrubbed and beards removed
2 cleaned squid, tentacles cut into bite-sized pieces and the bodies cut into rings
300 g raw tiger or king prawns, peeled and deveined
400 g spaghetti
fresh oregano or marjoram sprigs, to garnish

Makes 4 servings

Turn your kitchen into a cheery Italian trattoria with this delightful old classic. You could pay a small fortune for this dish in a restaurant – or make it at home and have it just the way you like it.

1 In a large saucepan, heat the olive oil. Add the onion and sauté until softened but not browned, 5 to 7 minutes. Add the garlic and parsley and cook for 1 minute more.
2 Pour in the wine and bring to a boil. Adjust the heat so that the wine boils steadily, and cook until the wine has almost all evaporated, about 15 minutes.
3 Stir in the tomatoes, chilli flakes, sugar and saffron. Reduce the heat and cook gently for 15 minutes. Season to taste with pepper.
4 Add the mussels. Cover and cook over medium heat until the mussels start to open, about 5 minutes. Add the squid and prawns and cook until the prawns turn pink, a further 3 to 4 minutes. Remove the pan from the heat. Discard any mussels that have not opened, then cover the pan to retain the heat.
5 Meanwhile, cook the spaghetti according to the packet directions, then drain. Return the pasta to the empty pan, add some of the tomato sauce and toss until the pasta is coated.
6 Serve the pasta with the remaining tomato sauce and seafood piled on top, garnished with small herb sprigs.

Penne All'amatriciana

⅓ cup (80 ml) olive oil, plus extra, for drizzling
1 onion, finely chopped
2 cloves garlic, crushed
200 g bacon slices or pancetta, chopped
2 x 410 g cans chopped tomatoes
½ teaspoon dried red chilli flakes, or to taste
salt and freshly ground black pepper, to taste
400 g penne
⅓ cup (35 g) grated parmesan, plus extra, to serve
2 tablespoons finely chopped fresh parsley

Makes 4 servings

This is a great stand-by for a super-quick pasta dish as all the ingredients are usually in the fridge or pantry. Vary the chilli to suit your family's tastes.

1 In a heavy-based saucepan, heat the olive oil over medium heat. Add the onion and garlic and sauté until soft but not brown, about 5 minutes. Add the bacon and fry lightly. Stir in the tomatoes and chilli flakes and cook, stirring from time to time, for about 20 minutes. Season to taste with salt and pepper.
2 Meanwhile, cook the penne according to the packet directions, then drain.
3 Transfer the tomato sauce mixture to a large serving bowl. Add the hot pasta and parmesan and toss until well combined. Sprinkle with chopped parsley and serve immediately, with a little extra olive oil for drizzling and grated cheese.

Pasta with Classic Basil Pesto

250 g (about 2 bunches) fresh
   basil, leaves picked
2 cloves garlic
¼ cup (60 ml) extra virgin
   olive oil
2 tablespoons butter, softened
½ cup (50 g) grated parmesan
¾ cup (115 g) pine nuts
½ teaspoon grated lemon zest
1 teaspoon salt
¼ teaspoon freshly ground
   black pepper
500 g pasta, cooked and
   drained

Makes 1½ cups (375 g) or
4 servings

It pays to use extra virgin olive oil when making pesto, because the sauce is not cooked and the flavour of the oil shines through, marrying beautifully with the basil, garlic and parmesan. Homemade pesto tastes so much fresher than any bottled pesto sauce – and is almost as quick and simple as opening a jar.

1 Pack the basil leaves and garlic cloves into a food processor or blender. Process at high speed until all the leaves are puréed, about 2 minutes, scraping down the side of the bowl as needed. With the motor still running, pour in the olive oil in a slow, steady stream.

2 Add the butter, parmesan, pine nuts, lemon zest, salt and pepper. Scraping down the sides of the bowl several times, purée until the mixture forms a paste, about 3 minutes. Add 1 to 2 tablespoons of water if the mixture seems too stiff.

3 While the pasta is still very hot, add the pesto, about ½ cup (125 g) at a time, tossing thoroughly after each addition to evenly distribute it through the pasta; if the pesto is too sticky, add 1 tablespoon hot water to thin it slightly. Serve hot.

Pesto: more than green basil sauce

In Italian, 'pestare' means 'to pound' – and that is the technique used to make the simple, classic sauce known as pesto. Most people are familiar with the green sauce made from pulverised basil leaves, but not all pestos are made from basil – they're not even all green. The technique used is what makes a sauce a pesto.

Pasta with Mushroom Pesto

2 tablespoons butter
1 clove garlic, finely chopped
300 g fresh mushrooms, thinly
  sliced
2 tablespoons butter, softened
2 tablespoons snipped fresh
  chives or spring onion tops
½ cup (50 g) grated parmesan
¾ teaspoon salt
¼ teaspoon freshly ground
  black pepper
500 g pasta, cooked and
  drained

Makes about ¾ cup (185 g) or
4 servings

When mushrooms are on special, try this delightfully earthy variation on the pesto theme. Experiment with the different-flavoured varieties, or even use a mixture.

1 In a large frying pan over medium–high heat, melt the butter. Add the garlic and mushrooms and sauté until golden, 2 to 3 minutes.
2 Transfer the mushroom mixture to a food processor or blender. Add the softened butter, chives, parmesan, salt and pepper and process to a smooth purée.
3 While the pasta is still very hot, add the mushroom pesto, a few good dollops at a time, tossing thoroughly after each addition to evenly distribute it through the pasta; if the pesto is too sticky, add 1 tablespoon hot water to thin it slightly. Serve hot.

Pasta with Sun-dried Tomato Pesto

1 cup (50 g) tightly packed
  fresh basil leaves
½ cup (75 g) sun-dried
  tomatoes in oil, undrained
¼ cup (30 g) chopped walnuts,
  raw or lightly toasted
1 small red chilli, seeded and
  chopped (optional)
½ cup (125 ml) extra virgin
  olive oil
⅓ cup (35 g) grated parmesan
500 g pasta, cooked and
  drained

Makes about 1 cup (250 g) or
4 servings

Intense tomato flavours are enhanced by walnuts in yet another version of pesto – and again, you'll find it always tastes far better when it is freshly made.

1 Put the basil in a food processor or blender. Process at high speed until all the leaves are puréed, about 2 minutes, scraping down the side of the bowl as needed. Add the tomatoes with their liquid, walnuts and chilli, if using, and process to a purée. With the motor still running, pour in the olive oil in a slow, steady stream.
2 Scrape the pesto mixture into a large bowl. Fold in the parmesan until it is incorporated.
3 While the pasta is still very hot, add the pesto, a few good dollops at a time, tossing thoroughly after each addition to evenly distribute it through the pasta; if the pesto is too sticky, add 1 tablespoon hot water to thin it slightly. Serve hot.

Ravioli

1 batch Simple Fresh Pasta
(page 62)

**PROSCIUTTO–RICOTTA
FILLING**
2 teaspoons olive oil
30 g prosciutto, roughly
chopped
3 cloves garlic, finely chopped
1 cup (250 g) ricotta
½ cup (50 g) grated parmesan
1 egg yolk
½ cup (30 g) finely chopped
fresh basil
½ teaspoon salt
¼ teaspoon freshly ground
black pepper

TOMATO SAUCE
2 teaspoons olive oil
1 small brown onion, chopped
2 cloves garlic, finely chopped
800 g can chopped roma
tomatoes
½ teaspoon salt
grated or shaved parmesan,
for sprinkling

Makes 12 ravioli, about
4 servings

You can fill these mouthwatering morsels with just about anything you like – plus a soft cheese of some kind, such as the ricotta used below.

1 Prepare the pasta dough. Cover dough and let sit for 1 hour.
2 Meanwhile, prepare the prosciutto–ricotta filling. In a large non-stick frying pan, heat the olive oil over medium heat. Add the prosciutto and garlic and cook until the garlic is soft, about 2 minutes. Transfer the mixture to a bowl and allow to cool to room temperature. Add the ricotta, parmesan, egg yolk, basil, salt and pepper and stir gently to blend; set aside.
3 Divide the dough into two equal portions. Cover one portion. On a lightly floured surface, roll out the second portion into a 23 x 30 cm rectangle, about 2 mm thick. Using a sharp knife or pastry wheel, cut the rectangle into four strips about 8 cm wide and 23 cm long.
4 On two of the dough strips, drop three equal mounds of the filling, spacing the mounds about 3 cm apart and leaving a 1 cm margin all around the edges. Using a pastry brush, brush the dough margins with water. Carefully place the remaining dough strips on top; firmly press along the edges and around each mound to seal the dough strips together firmly. Cut each strip crosswise into three ravioli. Repeat with the remaining dough portion to make 12 ravioli.
5 Prepare the tomato sauce. In a heavy-based saucepan, heat the olive oil over medium heat. Add the onion and sauté until soft, about 5 minutes. Add the garlic and cook for 2 minutes more. Add the tomatoes and salt and bring to a boil over medium heat; reduce the heat to a bubbling simmer and cook, stirring often, until the sauce thickens slightly, about 10 minutes.
6 Meanwhile, in a large pot of boiling water, cook the ravioli until firm–tender, about 6 minutes. Drain well, divide among warm serving plates and top with some of the tomato sauce. Serve with parmesan for sprinkling over.

Lasagne

2 tablespoons butter or
  olive oil
300 g mushrooms, roughly
  chopped
1 quantity Spaghetti Bolognese
  sauce (page 179)
1 batch Simple Fresh Pasta
  (page 62), cooked until
  almost tender and drained,
  or 500 g instant lasagne
  sheets
½ cup (50 g) grated parmesan
1 cup (150 g) grated
  mozzarella

TOMATO SAUCE
2 x 800 g cans chopped roma
  tomatoes
1 brown onion, finely chopped
4 cloves garlic, finely chopped
3 tablespoons chopped fresh
  basil
½ teaspoon dried thyme,
  crumbled
½ teaspoon salt
½ teaspoon freshly ground
  black pepper
2 tablespoons plain flour,
  mixed with ¼ cup (60 ml)
  cold water

Makes 6 servings

Homemade lasagne is a wonderfully welcoming dish.
When you make it yourself you know exactly what's in
it – and you can use the ingredients that you happen to
like best. A winner all round.

1 Prepare the tomato sauce. In a large heavy-based saucepan,
  combine the tomatoes, onion, garlic, basil, thyme, salt and
  pepper. Mix well and bring to a boil over medium–high heat.
  Reduce the heat to medium–low and simmer for 15 minutes,
  stirring occasionally to break up the tomatoes. Slowly whisk in
  the flour paste and simmer, stirring constantly, until the sauce
  thickens, about 2 minutes.
2 In a large frying pan, melt the butter or heat the olive oil
  over high heat. Add the mushrooms and cook until light
  brown, about 5 minutes. Transfer to a large bowl and add
  the bolognese sauce and 4 cups (1 litre) of the tomato
  sauce. Mix well.
3 Spread the remaining tomato sauce over the bottom of an
  ungreased 23 x 33 cm baking dish. Top with a single layer
  of slightly overlapping lasagne sheets, half the bolognese
  sauce and half the parmesan. Repeat the layers, beginning
  with the lasagne sheets. Scatter the mozzarella over the top
  of the lasagne.
4 Cover the dish with foil and bake until the sauce is bubbly,
  45 to 55 minutes. Remove from the oven and stand for
  10 minutes before serving.

Soups

Beef Barley Soup

1 tablespoon butter
1 carrot, chopped
1 celery stalk, chopped
1 onion, chopped
4 cups (1 litre) Beef Stock
  (page 49)
2 cups (350 g) chopped cooked
  roast beef
410 g can chopped tomatoes
1 cup (220 g) quick-cooking
  barley
1½ teaspoons salt
½ teaspoon dried basil,
  crumbled
½ teaspoon dried oregano,
  crumbled
½ teaspoon freshly ground
  black pepper
½ cup (80 g) frozen peas

Makes 8 servings

The culinary use of barley can be traced back to the Stone Age. Pearl barley is the type most often used for soups – it is polished and the bran has been removed. Homemade beef barley soup is filling and delicious, a bargain all around.

1 In a large heavy-based saucepan, melt the butter over medium heat. Add the carrot, celery and onion and sauté until the vegetables are tender, about 5 minutes.
2 Pour in the stock and 4 cups (1 litre) water. Add the roast beef, tomatoes, barley, salt, basil, oregano and pepper and bring to a boil. Reduce the heat, cover and simmer for 20 minutes, stirring occasionally.
3 Remove the lid and stir in the peas. Simmer, uncovered, for 5 minutes longer. Ladle into bowls and serve.

Make the most of soup

One of the all-time, soul-satisfying comfort foods, homemade soup is simple to prepare, highly nutritious and usually extremely economical. It is a wonderful way to use up all kinds of leftovers, from vegetable peelings to pot roast. Best of all, it is a filling meal you can make in a single pot. Add a tossed green salad and crusty bread or rolls and you've got all the bases covered.

Black Bean Soup

2 cups (440 g) dried black
  beans, sorted and rinsed
8 thick slices bacon, rind
  removed, cut crosswise into
  1 cm strips
2 large brown onions, chopped
2 celery stalks, chopped
2 carrots, chopped
2 cloves garlic, finely chopped
2 bay leaves
1 teaspoon dried thyme,
  crumbled
½ teaspoon hot red pepper
  sauce
3 tablespoons chopped fresh
  coriander
2 tablespoons lemon juice
sour cream or natural yogurt
  (optional)
8 fresh coriander sprigs
  (optional)

Makes 8 servings

From the southwest of the United States of America
comes this stick-to-your-ribs favourite. Black beans are
loaded with fibre, are a good source of iron and contain
plenty of B vitamins. Homemade black bean soup can
feed a crowd for practically nothing. You just can't buy
anything this good in a can!

1 Place the beans in a large heavy-based saucepan and add
  enough cold water to cover. Over high heat, bring the mixture
  to a boil, then cook for 2 minutes. Remove the saucepan from
  the heat, cover and let the beans stand for 1 hour. Drain the
  beans and discard the cooking liquid; set the beans aside.

2 Return the saucepan to medium–high heat and add the bacon
  strips. Sauté until the bacon is crisp, 5 to 8 minutes. Using a
  slotted spoon, transfer the bacon to paper towels to drain.

3 In the bacon drippings in the saucepan, sauté the onions,
  celery, carrots, garlic, bay leaves and thyme over medium heat
  until the vegetables are tender, 8 to 10 minutes.

4 Add 8 cups (2 litres) water and the reserved beans and return
  to a boil. Reduce the heat to medium–low, cover and simmer
  for 45 minutes. Remove and discard the bay leaves.

5 Place 1 cup (250 ml) of the bean mixture in a food processor
  or blender. Process to a smooth purée, then pour back into
  the saucepan. Add the reserved bacon, hot pepper sauce,
  coriander and lemon juice and stir until well combined.

6 Ladle into soup bowls. Serve garnished with a dollop of sour
  cream or yogurt and a coriander sprig, if desired.

Chicken Noodle Soup

1 teaspoon butter
1 carrot, chopped
1 celery stalk, chopped
1 onion, chopped
6 cups (1.5 litres) Chicken
  Stock (page 50)
1½ cups (225 g) chopped
  cooked chicken
1 teaspoon salt
½ teaspoon dried marjoram
½ teaspoon dried thyme
pinch of freshly ground pepper
200 g packet egg noodles
1 tablespoon finely chopped
  fresh parsley

Makes 6 servings

There is nothing quite as comforting as a steaming bowl of homemade chicken noodle soup. Our version is so quick and easy that you may never bother with commercially produced varieties again. This soup is also very versatile. For a more exotic version, borrow from the kitchens of South East Asia: leave out the marjoram, thyme and parsley and instead flavour the soup with herbs and spices such as fresh ginger, chilli and coriander – you could also add some sliced shiitake mushrooms and bean sprouts at the end for some slippery, crunchy texture.

1 In a large saucepan, melt the butter over medium heat. Add the carrot, celery and onion and sauté until the vegetables are tender, 8 to 10 minutes.
2 Add the stock, chicken, salt, marjoram, thyme and pepper. Bring to a boil, then reduce the heat and stir in the noodles. Cook until the noodles are tender, about 10 minutes. Stir in the parsley, ladle into bowls and serve.

Clam Chowder

1 kg (about 24) clams in
  shells, scrubbed
4 slices bacon, rind removed,
  chopped
1 large onion, chopped
2 tablespoons plain flour
500 g all-purpose potatoes,
  peeled and cubed
2 cups (500 ml) milk
2 teaspoons fresh thyme
  leaves
1 bay leaf
pinch of ground cayenne
  pepper
3 tablespoons chopped fresh
  flat-leaf parsley

Makes 4 servings

This creamy, rich version originated in the New England region of the United States. If clams aren't available, substitute vongole (baby clams), mussels or pipis, or a 200 g can of clams.

1 In a large saucepan over high heat, bring the clams and 2 cups (500 ml) water to a boil. Reduce the heat, cover and simmer for 5 minutes, then remove the lid. Using tongs or a slotted spoon, transfer the clams to a large bowl as they open. Strain the clam broth, then add enough water to make up 375 ml (1½ cups); set aside.
2 Wipe out the saucepan and place over medium heat. Sauté the bacon and onion until the onion is golden, about 7 minutes. Sprinkle with the flour and cook, stirring constantly, just until bubbling but not browned, about 1 minute.
3 Add the potatoes, milk, reserved clam broth, thyme, bay leaf and cayenne pepper. Bring to a simmer over medium heat. Simmer, stirring occasionally, until the potatoes are tender, about 10 minutes.
4 Meanwhile, remove the clams from their shells and cut into bite-sized pieces if necessary. Stir the clams into the chowder and cook until heated through, about 2 minutes. Discard the bay leaf. Ladle the chowder into individual bowls and serve sprinkled with parsley.

Cream of Tomato Soup

2½ cups (500 g) chopped
  peeled tomatoes, fresh or
  canned
1 small celery stalk, diced
1 small onion, diced
1 tablespoon vegetable oil
2 tablespoons plain flour
1 cup (250 ml) pouring cream
1 teaspoon salt (optional)
pinch of freshly ground black
  pepper
3 tablespoons sour cream
  (optional)
3 teaspoons finely chopped
  fresh parsley (optional)

Makes 3 servings

Pair this with a grilled cheese sandwich and you've got the ultimate comfort meal. If you have eaten canned tomato soup all your life, you're in for a big treat!

1 In a saucepan over medium–high heat, combine the tomatoes, celery and onion. Bring to a boil, reduce the heat to low, cover and simmer for 15 minutes, stirring often. Remove from the heat and let the mixture cool for 10 minutes.

2 Transfer the tomato mixture to a food processor or blender. Process to a smooth purée.

3 Heat the oil in a large saucepan over medium heat. Add the flour and stir until the mixture is smooth. Gradually add the cream, stirring constantly. Bring to a boil and cook for 2 minutes.

4 Gradually add the tomato mixture, stirring constantly. Add the salt, if using, and the pepper. Continue to cook until the soup is heated through.

5 Ladle into bowls and garnish each with a dollop of the sour cream and a sprinkle of the parsley, if desired.

Quick Prawn Laksa

250 g packet rice vermicelli
1 tablespoon peanut oil
3 tablespoons Laksa Paste
  (page 44)
3 cups (750 ml) Fish, Chicken
  or Vegetable Stock (pages 50
  and 51)
400 ml can coconut milk
1 kg raw prawns, peeled and
  deveined, tails left on
1 teaspoon salt
1 heaped cup (100 g) bean
  sprouts
3 tablespoons roughly chopped
  fresh Vietnamese mint
⅔ cup (20 g) fresh coriander
  leaves
1 small red chilli, seeded
  and sliced
lime wedges, to serve

Makes 4 servings

Vary the ingredients in this traditional South East Asian noodle soup to suit the ingredients you have on hand. You can use cooked chicken, tofu, mixed seafood or a combination of all three, if you desire.

1 Put the noodles in a heatproof bowl and pour in boiling water to cover. Leave to soak for 10 minutes, then drain and set aside.

2 In a wok, heat the oil over medium heat. Add the laksa paste and fry until fragrant, about 1 minute. Stir in the stock and bring to a boil. Add the coconut milk and simmer for 2 to 3 minutes. Add the prawns and cook until they turn pink, about 4 minutes. Stir in the salt.

3 Divide the noodles among four bowls and top each with some bean sprouts and fresh herbs. Pour the soup over the noodles, dividing the prawns evenly. Serve garnished with chilli slices and lime wedges on the side.

Pumpkin Soup

1.5 kg pumpkin
2 tablespoons olive oil
2 large onions, chopped
2 carrots, chopped
4 tomatoes, peeled and
  chopped
8 cups (2 litres) Chicken Stock
  (page 50) or Vegetable Stock
  (page 51)
juice of 1 lemon
¼ teaspoon freshly grated
  nutmeg
⅔ cup (160 g) red lentils,
  rinsed
1 teaspoon salt
freshly ground black pepper,
  to taste
1 cup (250 ml) milk
fresh crusty bread, to serve

Makes 12 servings

Colourful pumpkin soup has been a beloved winter warmer for generations. When pumpkins are plentiful and cheap, make up a double quantity of soup and freeze in usable portions for up to 3 months.

1 Using a large sharp knife, cut the pumpkin into large bits. Remove and discard the seeds, cut away the skin, then roughly chop the flesh.
2 In a large saucepan, heat the olive oil. Add the onions and carrots and sauté over low heat until the onions are softened but not browned, about 5 minutes.
3 Add the chopped pumpkin, tomatoes, stock, lemon juice, nutmeg, lentils, salt and pepper to taste. Bring to a boil, then reduce the heat, cover and simmer for 35 minutes, or until the vegetables and lentils are tender.
4 Remove the saucepan from the heat and allow the soup to cool slightly. Working in batches, purée the soup in a food processor or blender. Return the soup to the saucepan, stir in the milk and season to taste. Reheat the soup for 5 to 10 minutes, then pour into heated mugs or bowls and serve with fresh crusty bread.

Lentil Soup

1 cup (185) dried brown or
  green lentils, sorted and
  rinsed
6 cups (1.5 litres) Chicken
  Stock (page 50)
1 tablespoon vegetable oil
1 large onion, chopped
1 clove garlic, finely chopped
2½ cups (500 ml) chopped
  fresh tomatoes
2 small carrots, sliced
½ teaspoon dried thyme
¼ teaspoon dried marjoram

Makes 8 servings

Long a staple of Indian and Middle Eastern cooking, lentils are an excellent source of fibre, protein, folate and iron, which makes this soup very good for you – the perfect low-cost, one-dish dinner.

1 In a large saucepan over medium–high heat, combine the lentils and the stock. Bring to a boil, reduce the heat to low and simmer for 30 minutes.
2 Meanwhile, heat the oil in a large frying pan over medium–high heat. Add the onion and garlic and sauté until tender, about 5 minutes.
3 Add the onion mixture to the lentils. Stir in the tomatoes, carrots, thyme and marjoram and cook until the lentils and vegetables are tender, about 30 minutes.

Minestrone

1 tablespoon olive oil

1 large brown onion, chopped

2 cloves garlic, finely chopped

3½ cups (875 ml) Beef Stock (page 49)

420 g can white beans, drained

410 g can chopped roma tomatoes

2 cups (150 g) roughly shredded cabbage

2 large carrots, thinly sliced

1 teaspoon dried oregano

1 teaspoon dried basil

½ teaspoon salt

½ teaspoon freshly ground black pepper

50 g pasta shells

1 small zucchini (courgette), sliced

grated parmesan, for sprinkling

Makes 8 servings

Italian cooks have no definite rules for what goes into minestrone – so long as there's a hearty mix of vegetables, white beans and pasta or rice. Humble and inexpensive, a homemade minestrone trumps the canned variety every time. To make it vegetarian, use vegetable stock instead of beef stock.

1 In a large, non-stick saucepan, heat the olive oil over medium–high heat. Add the onion and garlic and sauté until the onion is soft, about 5 minutes. Stir in the stock, beans, tomatoes, cabbage, carrots, oregano, basil, salt and pepper.

2 Bring to a boil and stir in the pasta. Reduce the heat, cover and simmer for 15 minutes, or until the vegetables and pasta are tender. Stir in the zucchini and cook, uncovered, for 3 minutes.

3 Ladle into bowls and serve sprinkled with parmesan.

French Onion Soup

2 tablespoons butter
5 brown onions, thinly sliced
2 tablespoons sugar
3½ cups (875 ml) Beef Stock (page 49)
¼ cup (60 ml) brandy (optional)
½ teaspoon salt
½ teaspoon freshly ground black pepper
4 baguette slices, about 1 cm thick, toasted
4 tablespoons grated gruyère

Makes 4 servings

Easier to make than you may think, this classic of French cooking is mostly a matter of slicing onions! Nothing in a can or a packet compares.

1 Preheat the oven to 200°C (Gas 6). In a large heavy-based saucepan, melt the butter over medium–high heat. Add the onions and sugar, increase the heat to high and sauté until the onions are lightly golden, about 10 minutes. Reduce the heat to medium–low and sauté for 10 minutes longer, stirring occasionally.
2 Add the stock and 5 cups (1.25 litres) water. Increase the heat to high and bring to a boil, then reduce the heat to medium–low and simmer for 20 minutes. Add the brandy, if using, and the salt and pepper. Increase the heat to high and return to a boil.
3 Place four 1 cup (250 ml) ramekins or soup bowls on a sturdy baking tray. Ladle soup into the bowls. Place a baguette slice on top of each soup and sprinkle each slice with 1 tablespoon of the cheese.
4 Bake until the cheese has melted, about 5 minutes. Serve hot.

Vegetable Soup

3 tablespoons olive oil
1 large red onion, diced
5 cloves garlic, finely chopped
2 large carrots, thinly sliced
4 yellow summer squashes, diced
2 zucchini (courgettes), diced
250 g green beans, sliced
1 kg tomatoes, peeled and chopped
500 g new potatoes, diced
5 cups (1.25 litres) Vegetable Stock (page 51)
¾ teaspoon salt
¾ teaspoon dried marjoram
½ teaspoon freshly ground black pepper

Makes 4 servings

The best vegetable soup is made with the freshest produce and it doesn't come from a can. You make it yourself from what's ripe in the garden or what's in season at the local farmers' market.

1 In a large saucepan, heat the olive oil over medium heat. Add the onion and garlic and cook until soft, about 5 minutes. Add the carrots and cook, stirring frequently, until the carrots are soft, about 5 minutes.
2 Add the squashes, zucchini, green beans, tomatoes, potatoes, stock, salt, marjoram and pepper. Increase the heat to high and bring to a boil, then reduce the heat to medium–low. Cover and simmer until the vegetables are tender, 40 to 50 minutes.

Pea and Ham Soup

500 g packet dried green
   split peas
1 ham bone
1 large onion, chopped
1 teaspoon salt
½ teaspoon freshly ground
   black pepper
½ teaspoon dried thyme,
   crumbled
1 bay leaf
1 large carrot, diced
1 celery stalk, diced

Makes 10 servings

This is a great soup to make when you have a ham bone in the house. It's hearty, filling, supremely economical and will feed a whole family with plenty to spare.

1 Put the split peas in a large heavy-based saucepan and pour in enough water to cover them by 5 cm. Bring to a boil over high heat, then boil for 2 minutes. Remove from the heat, cover and let stand for 1 hour. Drain and rinse the peas, discarding the soaking liquid. Return the peas to the saucepan.
2 Add 10 cups (2.5 litres) water, the ham bone, onion, salt, pepper, thyme and bay leaf. Bring the mixture to a boil over high heat, then reduce the heat to low. Cover and simmer for 1½ hours, stirring occasionally.
3 Transfer the ham bone to a cutting board and leave until cool enough to handle. Remove the meat from the bone; discard the bone. Dice the meat and return to the saucepan.
4 Add the carrots and celery and simmer over medium–low heat until the soup reaches the desired consistency and the vegetables are tender, 45 to 60 minutes. Remove and discard the bay leaf before serving.

Gazpacho

3 cups (600 g) chopped
   tomatoes
2 celery stalks, chopped
1 green capsicum (pepper),
   chopped
1 cucumber, chopped
3 tablespoons fresh parsley,
   finely chopped
1 tablespoon fresh chives,
   finely chopped
1 spring onion, thinly sliced
1 clove garlic, finely chopped
5 cups (1.25 litres) tomato
   juice
⅓ cup (80 ml) red wine vinegar
¼ cup (60 ml) olive oil
1 teaspoon salt
½ teaspoon worcestershire
   sauce
½ teaspoon freshly ground
   black pepper

Makes 10 servings

One of the great joys of summer is fresh tomatoes – and this chilled soup is the most refreshing way to use that bounty. Whip up a batch and keep it in the refrigerator for a quick, refreshing snack, lunch, or start to a barbecued dinner. It's a treat you can make better than supermarkets or delis because you can adapt it to your individual taste.

In a large, non-metallic bowl, combine all the ingredients. Stir until well blended, then cover and refrigerate for several hours, or overnight.

Salads

Classic Coleslaw

1 small green cabbage,
    shredded and immersed
    in iced water for 1 hour
3 carrots, grated
1 cup (250 g) Classic
    Mayonnaise (page 29)
⅓ cup (75 g) sugar
¼ cup (60 ml) cider vinegar

Makes 10 to 12 servings

The quintessential side salad for a perfect picnic, tangy slaw offers crunchy texture and good nutrition. No deli slaw – at any price – can compare with your own.

1 Drain the cabbage and transfer to paper towels. Blot with additional towels until it is completely dry. Place in a large bowl, add the carrots and toss until thoroughly mixed.
2 In a small bowl, combine the mayonnaise, sugar and vinegar. Stir until well blended and smooth.
3 Pour the dressing over the cabbage mixture and toss until well coated.

Greek Salad

3 ripe tomatoes
3 small Lebanese (short)
    cucumbers
2 large red onions
2 green capsicums (peppers)
⅔ cup (115 g) black olives
100 g pickled mild or hot
    chillies
⅓ cup (80 ml) olive oil
2 tablespoons red wine
    vinegar
salt and freshly ground black
    pepper, to taste
300 g fetta
1 teaspoon dried oregano, or
    2 teaspoons fresh oregano
    leaves

Makes 4 servings

This popular salad has many variations and can even include rice-stuffed vine leaves and anchovies. Interestingly, it does not traditionally include lettuce.

1 Cut the tomatoes into wedges. Thickly slice the cucumbers in rounds. Slice the onions, but not too thinly. Cut the capsicums into strips.
2 Place all the vegetables in a salad bowl. Top with the olives and pickled chillies.
3 To make the vinaigrette, whisk 3 tablespoons of the olive oil and all the vinegar until combined; add salt and pepper to taste. Drizzle over the salad.
4 Cut the fetta into thick cubes or crumble coarsely, then add to the salad. Sprinkle with the oregano, drizzle with the remaining olive oil and serve.

Potato Salad

1 kg potatoes, skin left on,
   cut into same-sized chunks
1 tablespoon cider vinegar
1 teaspoon sugar
1 small celery stalk, chopped
1 small red onion, chopped
¼ cup (45 g) chopped stuffed
   olives
½ teaspoon salt
½ teaspoon celery seeds
¾ cup (185 g) Classic
   Mayonnaise (page 29)
   or salad dressing
2 hard-boiled eggs, peeled
   and chopped

Makes 4 servings

What would a picnic or barbecue be without this stalwart standby adding its creamy goodness? Shun the gluggy deli version and make your own. Boiling or 'waxy' potatoes, such as new potatoes, are ideal for potato salads as they hold their texture when cooked.

1 Put the potatoes in a large saucepan with enough water to cover. Bring to a boil over high heat and boil until the potatoes are tender, 20 to 30 minutes. Drain the potatoes and remove the peels. When the potatoes are cool enough to handle, cut into large dice and place in a bowl.
2 Drizzle the vinegar over the potatoes, then sprinkle with the sugar. Add the celery, onion, olives, salt and celery seed. Add the mayonnaise and eggs and fold gently until well combined. Cover and refrigerate for at least 1 hour before serving.

Thai Beef Salad

500 g rump steak
½ cup (125 ml) salt-reduced
   soy sauce
2 cloves garlic, crushed
100 ml lime juice
500 g broccoli florets
4 tablespoons fresh mint
   leaves
4 tablespoons fresh basil
   leaves
3 tablespoons fresh coriander
   leaves
1 small cucumber, halved
   lengthwise and sliced
2 red chillies, thinly sliced
2 teaspoons soft brown sugar

Makes 4 servings

A salad with substance that even the men enjoy! Drenched with flavour, beautiful beef makes a meal of this fresh and zingy salad. Adjust the chilli heat to suit your taste.

1 In a large non-metallic bowl, combine the steak, ¼ cup (60 ml) of the soy sauce, the garlic and 2 tablespoons of the lime juice. Toss to coat, then leave to marinate for 10 minutes.
2 Preheat the grill to high. Cook the steak for 2 minutes on each side, then set aside to rest.
3 Steam or microwave the broccoli until tender–crisp. Leave to cool for 10 minutes, then place in a large bowl with the mint, basil and coriander. Add the cucumber slices.
4 Slice the steak and add to the salad. Mix together the chillies, sugar, remaining soy sauce and remaining lime juice. Stir gently through the salad and serve.

Egg Salad

4 hard-boiled eggs, peeled
  and chopped
¼ cup (55 g) chopped green
  olives
¼ cup (60 g) Classic
  Mayonnaise (page 29)
  or salad dressing

Makes 4 servings

Dark pumpernickel or a flavourful rye bread sets off
the creamy texture and taste of this old favourite –
always infinitely better when you make it yourself
with the ingredients you like best.

In a bowl, combine all the ingredients; gently fold until they are
all well blended.

Pasta Salad

250 g pasta, such as fusilli,
  farfalle or penne
1 red capsicum (pepper), cut
  into thin strips
1 yellow capsicum (pepper),
  cut into thin strips
2 tablespoons olive oil
2 tablespoons red wine
  vinegar
½ teaspoon salt
¼ teaspoon freshly ground
  black pepper
2 tablespoons finely chopped
  fresh parsley
2 tablespoons finely chopped
  fresh basil
2 tablespoons drained capers
2 cloves garlic, finely chopped
1 small red onion, diced
1 cup (200 g) peeled, seeded
  and chopped tomatoes

Makes 4 servings

This salad uses capsicums (peppers) for a splash
of colour, but this basic pasta salad is also a good place
to use whatever vegetables are in season – just blanch
or sauté them before tossing them through the pasta.
Again, fresh is definitely best!

1 Cook the pasta according to the packet directions. Drain
  and place in a large serving bowl.
2 Add the remaining ingredients and toss until well combined.
3 Cover and leave to stand at room temperature for 30 minutes
  for the flavours to develop. Toss gently again before serving.

Caesar Salad

2 small cos (romaine) lettuces
4 large iceberg lettuce leaves
50 g block of parmesan
2 slices sourdough bread,
    crusts removed
2 tablespoons olive oil

ANCHOVY DRESSING
4 anchovy fillets
1 clove garlic, roughly chopped
100 ml olive oil
1 very fresh large egg yolk
2 tablespoons lemon juice
2 tablespoons dijon mustard
1 tablespoon worcestershire
    sauce
salt and freshly ground black
    pepper, to taste

Makes 4 servings

In 1924 in Tijuana, Mexico, Caesar Cardini first mixed cos lettuce, parmesan and croutons, and dressed it with a mixture of garlic, lemon juice, egg, olive oil and worcestershire sauce. People have been enjoying it ever since. You can pay good money for a rather ordinary caesar salad in a cafe or restaurant; naturally, it will never be as good as the one you make at home!

1 Cut the cos and iceberg lettuce leaves into bite-sized pieces. Using a vegetable peeler or cheese grater, shave the parmesan into thin slivers.
2 To make the anchovy dressing, place the anchovy fillets and garlic in a bowl and mash to a paste. Whisk in the olive oil, egg yolk, lemon juice, mustard and worcestershire sauce. Season with salt and pepper.
3 To make the croutons, cut the bread into small cubes. In a large non-stick frying pan, heat the olive oil over medium heat. Add the bread cubes and cook until golden brown on all sides, taking care they do not burn. Set aside and keep warm.
4 Arrange the lettuce leaves and shaved parmesan on individual serving plates. Drizzle the dressing over the salad, sprinkle with the croutons and serve.

Creamy Chicken Salad

2 cups (500 g) Classic
    Mayonnaise (page 29)
2 celery stalks, chopped
1 tablespoon mustard
1¼ teaspoons poppy seeds
½ teaspoon salt
4 cooked skinless, boneless
    chicken breasts, cubed
chopped pecans, to serve

Makes about 10 servings

Serve this old favourite on a bed of lettuce, with fruit, or as a filling for sandwiches. It's especially exquisite if you use homemade mayonnaise.

1 In a large bowl, combine the mayonnaise, celery, mustard, poppy seeds and salt. Stir until well blended.
2 Add the cooked chicken and gently fold to coat. Cover and place in the refrigerator for 3 to 4 hours, until the salad is chilled. Sprinkle with pecans before serving.

Curried Chicken Salad

½ cup (125 g) Classic
   Mayonnaise (page 29)
½ cup (140 g) chutney
1–3 tablespoons curry powder,
   to taste
2 cooked skinless, boneless
   chicken breasts, cubed

Makes about 6 servings

A piquant filling for pita bread, this salad is also
sensational served with tropical fruit or cooked rice.

1. In a large bowl, combine the mayonnaise, chutney and curry
powder. Stir until well blended.
2. Add the cooked chicken and gently fold to coat. Cover and
place in the refrigerator for 3 to 4 hours, until the salad is
chilled and the flavours have developed.

Turkey Salad

1 cup (150 g) chopped cooked
   turkey
¼ cup (60 g) Classic
   Mayonnaise (page 29)
1 small celery stalk, finely
   chopped
1 tablespoon chilli sauce

Makes 4 servings

A great way to use up leftover Christmas turkey, this
recipe gives you wonderful sandwiches for next to
nothing. Serve the salad on wholemeal rolls with lettuce
or salad leaves.

In a bowl, combine all the ingredients; gently fold until they are
all well blended.

Tuna Salad

¼ cup (60 g) plus 1 tablespoon
   Classic Mayonnaise
   (page 29)
3 tablespoons finely chopped
   red onion
3 tablespoons sweet pickle
   relish
2 tablespoons chopped celery
2 tablespoons lemon juice
1 tablespoon drained capers
1 tablespoon finely chopped
   fresh dill
¼ teaspoon salt
2 x 185 g cans tuna, drained

Makes 4 servings

Not your average tuna salad, this version is made
special with capers, red onion and dill. It's much better
than any you'll find at the deli.

1. In a bowl, combine the mayonnaise, onion, relish, celery,
lemon juice, capers, dill and salt. Stir until the dressing is
well blended and smooth.
2. Add the tuna and gently fold until well combined.

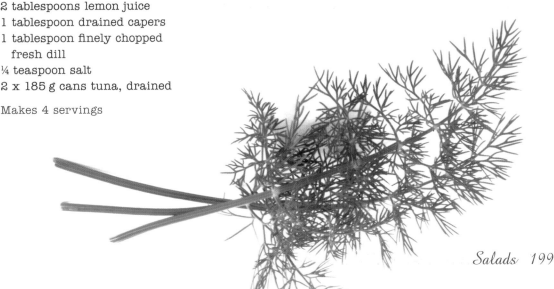

Crab Salad

¼ cup (60 g) Classic
　Mayonnaise (page 29)
3 tablespoons finely chopped
　celery
3 tablespoons finely chopped
　fresh parsley
2 tablespoons lemon juice
¼ teaspoon salt
pinch of ground cayenne
　pepper
500 g cooked fresh crabmeat,
　chopped
3 tablespoons diced red
　capsicum (pepper)

Makes 4 servings

Though this salad is fabulous in a sandwich or served
on wholegrain crackers, for an eye-catching buffet-table
dish, mound it in wedges of fresh papaya and sprinkle
with a little chopped fresh parsley. If using canned or
frozen crabmeat, thaw and drain first. Crab salad is a
special treat, so buy better quality crab and make your
own. You'll appreciate the difference.

1　In a large bowl, combine the mayonnaise, celery, parsley,
　　lemon juice, salt and cayenne pepper. Stir until well blended
　　and smooth.
2　Add the crabmeat and capsicum and gently fold until they
　　are well combined.

Prawn Salad

¼ cup (60 g) Classic
　Mayonnaise (page 29)
¼ cup finely chopped celery
2 tablespoons lemon juice
2 tablespoons finely chopped
　fresh tarragon
¼ teaspoon salt
pinch of ground cayenne
　pepper
500 g peeled cooked prawns

Makes 4 servings

This luscious salad is lovely served on a bed of mixed
greens, as a filling for soft rolls, or with flatbreads.
Buy the freshest prawns, use your own mayonnaise
and you'll have restaurant quality in your own kitchen
for a fraction of the price.

1　In a bowl, combine the mayonnaise, celery, lemon juice,
　　tarragon, salt and cayenne pepper. Stir until well blended
　　and smooth.
2　Add the prawns and gently fold until well combined.

Tuscan-style Three-bean Salad

300 g green beans, trimmed
   and halved
400 g can red kidney beans,
   rinsed and drained
400 g can cannellini or
   butterbeans, rinsed and
   drained
1 small red onion, finely
   chopped
2 large tomatoes, seeded and
   chopped
3 tablespoons chopped fresh
   flat-leaf parsley
3 tablespoons olive oil
2 tablespoons lemon juice
1 clove garlic, crushed
salt and freshly ground black
   pepper

Makes 4 servings

This classic salad uses cannellini beans, red kidney beans and fresh green beans, but depending on what you have in your pantry, combinations of different beans can be used. Another great stand-by for when the cupboards run bare.

1 Half-fill a saucepan with water and bring to a boil. Add the green beans and cook until just tender, 5 to 7 minutes. Drain, rinse with cold water and drain again. Place in a serving bowl.
2 Add the canned beans, onion, tomatoes and parsley.
3 Mix together the olive oil, lemon juice and garlic, season with salt and pepper, then mix through the salad.
4 Serve immediately, or cover and refrigerate until required.

Salade Niçoise

2 carrots, peeled
500 g green beans, trimmed
500 g small red new potatoes
1 large French shallot, finely
   chopped
1 tablespoon dijon mustard
1 tablespoon drained capers
1 tablespoon red wine vinegar
¼ cup (60 ml) olive oil
1 cos (romaine) lettuce,
   washed and cut 5 cm thick
2 hard-boiled eggs, peeled and
   halved lengthwise
½ cup drained, Roasted Red
   Capsicums in Oil (page 73)
   or bottled red capsicum
   (pepper), cut into long strips
3 roma tomatoes, cut
   lengthwise into 8 wedges
24 niçoise olives
185 g can oil-packed tuna,
   drained

Makes 4 servings

A gorgeous and appetising array of tuna, eggs and vegetables, this great classic from the South of France is a picture-perfect composed salad. Delight your family and friends with your own version – fresh and custom-made. No restaurant can match that or your costs.

1 Parboil the carrots and slice thinly. Blanch the beans and cut in half, crosswise. Boil the new potatoes and slice thinly.
2 In a large bowl, combine the shallot, mustard, capers, vinegar and oil. Whisk until well blended, then pour half the dressing into a small bowl and set aside.
3 Add the lettuce to the large bowl and toss to coat with the dressing. Divide the lettuce among four serving plates.
4 Arrange the egg halves, capsicum strips, tomatoes, carrots, beans, potatoes, olives and tuna over the lettuce on each plate. Drizzle some of the reserved dressing over each salad, or serve it on the side.

Confectionery

Gumdrops ❖ Butterscotch ❖ Lollipops ❖ Caramels ❖ Fudge ❖ Pastel Peppermints ❖ Pralines ❖ Peanut Brittle ❖ Toffee Bars ❖ Rocky Road ❖ Fruit and Nut Truffles ❖ Marshmallows ❖ Candied Citrus Peels

Custards, Mousses and Puddings

Chocolate Pudding ❖ Panna Cotta ❖ Rice Pudding ❖ Bread and Butter Pudding ❖ Crème Brûlée ❖ Crème Caramel ❖ Chocolate Mousse ❖ Mango Mousse

Fruit Desserts

Brandied Peaches ❖ Dried Fruit Compote ❖ Wine-poached Pears with Strawberries ❖ Fruit Salad ❖ Chocolate-dipped Strawberries

Ice Cream

French Vanilla Ice Cream ❖ Blueberry Ice Cream ❖ Peach Ice Cream ❖ Mango Ice Cream ❖ Strawberry Ice Cream ❖ Honey Banana Ice Cream ❖ Coconut-pineapple Ice Cream ❖ Rocky Road Ice Cream ❖ Rich Chocolate Ice Cream ❖ Chocolate Chocolate-chip Ice Cream ❖ Mint Chocolate-chip Ice Cream ❖ Peppermint Ice Cream ❖ Butter Pecan Ice Cream ❖ Ice Cream Cake

Frozen Yogurt

Lemon Frozen Yogurt ❖ Strawberry Frozen Yogurt ❖ Passionfruit Frozen Yogurt

Ices, Granitas, Sherbets and Sorbets

Orange Ice ❖ Blood-orange Champagne Granita ❖ Cappuccino Granita ❖ Kiwi Granita ❖ Peach Granita ❖ Lime Sherbet ❖ Strawberry Milk Sherbet ❖ Cassis Sorbet ❖ Citrus Sorbet ❖ Honeydew Sorbet ❖ Lemon Sorbet ❖ Raspberry Sorbet ❖ Strawberry Sorbet

Frozen Iceblocks

Frozen Fruit Ice ❖ Frozen Jelly Yogurts ❖ Chocolate Pops ❖ Strawberry Pops ❖ Tropical Pops ❖ Chocolate-nut Frozen Bananas

Easy-to-make Sweet Treats

Sometimes we all crave a little sweetness, so this chapter provides a collection of recipes for an array of sweet treats – confectionery, custards, fruity delights, irresistible ice creams, frozen yogurts and sorbets – that will more than satisfy that yearning.

What all these recipes have in common is that they are made with all-natural ingredients, with none of the fillers, stabilisers or artificial sweeteners that often give shop-bought sweets that slightly artificial taste. Treats such as these are so astonishingly good when you make them yourself that you may never bother buying a packet of confectionery or a supermarket sweet again. As an added bonus, treats you make at home won't cost nearly as much as shop-bought alternatives.

Some people might be daunted by the idea of making their own confectionery, but our grandparents thought nothing of it, and it's really no more difficult than making biscuits – sometimes even easier. And whether you're making marshmallows, lollipops or peanut brittle, they really do taste so much better than the wrapped products that now abound on supermarket shelves.

On the following pages you'll find hot and cold fruit desserts, along with custards and puddings. And when summer comes, you'll have a full assortment of ice creams, frozen yogurts, ices, granitas, sorbets and sherbets that you can try – topped perhaps with one of the dessert sauces from Chapter 1.

Confectionery

Gumdrops

three 7 g sachets powdered
   gelatine
1½ cups (330 g) sugar, plus
   extra, for coating
¼–½ teaspoon flavouring
   extract of your choice
two food colourings of your
   choice

Makes about 450 g

Also known as jubes, these chewy goodies can be tailored to the occasion: for Christmas, use red and green food colouring and peppermint extract; for spring, try yellow and orange colouring and lemon or orange extract. Children will want to help make them.

1 Sprinkle the gelatine over ½ cup (125 ml) water and leave to stand for 5 minutes.
2 In a small saucepan, combine the sugar and ¾ cup (185 ml) water over medium heat. Bring the mixture to a boil, stirring constantly. Add the gelatine mixture, reduce the heat and simmer, stirring constantly, for 5 minutes. Remove from the heat and stir in the flavouring extract.
3 Divide the mixture between two small bowls. Add 2 to 4 drops of the desired colour into each bowl and stir until the colour is even.
4 Lightly grease two 20 x 10 x 5 cm loaf (bar) tins. Pour one coloured gumdrop mixture into one loaf tin and the other mixture into the other tin. Chill until firm, about 3 hours.
5 Lightly coat a work surface with extra sugar and fill a small saucer with some more sugar. Cover a baking tray with baking paper. Using a sharp knife, loosen the edges of the gumdrop mixture from the side of the tins, then turn out onto the sugared surface. Cut each portion into 1 cm cubes, then roll each cube in the sugar in the saucer until completely coated.
6 Place the gumdrops on the baking tray and leave at room temperature, uncovered, until they are dry on all sides, 3 to 4 hours; turn the gumdrops every hour to allow each side to dry. Cover with plastic wrap and store in the refrigerator.

Checking the sugar thermometer

The one crucial item you need for making confectionery is a good-quality sugar thermometer, which you should test before each use. To do this, in a saucepan bring some water to a boil and dip the thermometer in: it should read 100°C. Adjust your recipe temperature up or down based on your test.

Butterscotch

melted butter, for brushing
2½ cups (575 g) firmly packed
    soft brown sugar
½ cup (110 g) light corn syrup
    or glucose syrup (optional)
¼ cup (90 g) honey
½ teaspoon salt
250 g butter, cut into cubes
½ teaspoon rum extract

Makes about 650 g

Butterscotch is very inexpensive to make. Rich and deliciously buttery, this recipe calls for a little rum extract to create its distinctive flavour.

1 Brush a 38 x 25 x 3 cm baking tin with the melted butter.
2 In a heavy-based saucepan, combine the sugar, syrup (if using) and ¾ cup (185 ml) water over medium heat. Cover and bring to a boil, without stirring. Remove the lid and continue to cook until a sugar thermometer reads 130°C ('soft crack' stage).
3 Add the honey, salt and butter cubes. Cook, stirring constantly, until the mixture reaches 150°C ('hard crack' stage). Remove from the heat and stir in the rum extract.
4 Pour the butterscotch into the baking tray without scraping it; do not spread. Allow to cool until almost set, 1 to 2 minutes. Using a sharp knife, score the butterscotch into 2–3 cm squares and leave to cool completely.
5 Break the butterscotch squares along the scored lines. Store in an airtight container.

Lollipops

12 lollipop sticks
1 cup (220 g) sugar
2 tablespoons light corn syrup
    or glucose syrup
4–8 drops food colouring
    of your choice
2–3 drops flavouring oil
    of your choice

Makes 12 lollipops

Few goodies are as evocative of childhood as these brightly coloured sweets on a stick. Flavouring oils can be purchased at health-food shops – the flavour is more intense than flavour extracts, and as they are not alcohol-based, the flavour won't evaporate either.

1 Line a large baking tray with foil. Arrange the lollipop sticks on the tray, spacing them 10 cm apart.
2 In a heavy-based saucepan, combine the sugar, syrup and ½ cup (125 ml) water over medium heat. Cook, stirring, until the sugar has dissolved. Cover the saucepan, increase the heat to high and boil the mixture for 1 minute to wash down any sugar crystals. Remove the lid and boil the syrup until it registers 155°C on a sugar thermometer. Immediately remove the saucepan from the heat and set it on a wire rack.
3 Let the syrup cool for 5 minutes, then add the food colouring and flavouring oil, stirring until the colour is even.
4 Spoon the coloured syrup over the top end of each lollipop stick, making a puddle about 5 to 8 cm in diameter. Leave the lollipops until they are completely cool and hardened. Wrap each lollipop in plastic wrap or cellophane and secure the wrapping.

Caramels

melted butter, for brushing
1 cup (220 g) sugar
1 cup (220 g) dark corn syrup
   or glucose syrup (optional)
1 cup (250 g) butter
400 ml can sweetened
   condensed milk
1 teaspoon vanilla extract

Makes 64 pieces

Chewy, gooey and irresistible, homemade caramels make wonderful treats for Christmas stockings or as little gifts.

1. Line a 20 cm square baking tin with foil. Grease the foil with butter.
2. In a heavy-based saucepan, combine the sugar, syrup (if using) and butter over medium heat. Bring to a boil, stirring constantly, then reduce the heat slightly and boil slowly for 4 minutes without stirring.
3. Remove from the heat and stir in the condensed milk. Place back over medium–low heat and cook until a sugar thermometer reads 115°C ('soft ball' stage), stirring constantly. Remove from the heat and stir in the vanilla.
4. Pour the mixture into the baking tin and leave until cool. Remove from the tin and cut into 2–3 cm squares. Wrap each caramel individually in baking paper, cellophane or plastic wrap, twisting the ends to seal.

Fudge

3⅓ cups (750 g) sugar
1 cup (185 g) soft brown sugar
1 cup (250 g) butter
400 ml can evaporated milk
2 cups (350 g) semi-sweet
   chocolate chips
two 200 g milk chocolate bars,
   broken into pieces
⅓ cup (50 g) chopped semi-
   sweet cooking chocolate
1 teaspoon vanilla extract
2 cups (240 g) chopped pecans

Makes about 2 kg

With not one but three kinds of chocolate, makes this a deep, rich, chocolatey dream of a fudge.

1. Grease a 38 x 25 x 3 cm baking tin.
2. In a large saucepan, combine the sugars, the butter and evaporated milk over medium heat. Cook, stirring, until the sugar has completely dissolved. Increase the heat to high and bring to a boil, then boil for 5 minutes, stirring constantly.
3. Remove from the heat. Add all the chocolate, place back over low heat and stir until melted. Fold in the vanilla and pecans until well blended.
4. Pour the mixture into the baking tin, spreading it evenly, then refrigerate until firm. Using a sharp knife, cut the cooled fudge into squares.

Pastel Peppermints

3 tablespoons butter, softened

⅓ cup (75 g) light corn syrup or glucose syrup (optional)

½–1 teaspoon peppermint extract

4 cups (500 g) icing sugar

two food colourings of your choice

1 cup (220 g) sugar, approximately

Makes about 7½ dozen

Pretty confections perfect for a wedding or baby shower.

1 In a small bowl, combine the butter and syrup (if using). Add the peppermint extract and half the icing sugar and beat until well blended. Add another 1 cup (125 g) icing sugar and beat well.

2 Lightly coat a work surface with the remaining icing sugar. Turn the mixture out onto the surface and knead until the icing sugar is completely absorbed and the mixture is smooth.

3 Divide the mixture into three portions. Set aside one portion to remain white; tint the remaining portions by adding 1 to 2 drops of food colouring and kneading until each portion is the desired colour.

4 Line a baking tray with baking paper. Place the sugar in a shallow bowl or saucer. Pinch off a walnut-sized piece of the peppermint mixture. Using your hands, roll it into a ball, then roll it in the sugar. Place on the baking tray and flatten into a round, using a fork. Repeat with the remaining peppermint mixture. Leave to stand, uncovered, at room temperature for 1 day, then store in an airtight container.

Pralines

melted butter, for brushing

1 cup (220 g) sugar

1 cup (230 g) firmly packed soft brown sugar

1 cup (250 ml) milk

8 large Marshmallows (page 210)

2 cups (240 g) roughly chopped pecans

2 tablespoons butter

½ teaspoon vanilla extract

pinch of ground cinnamon

Makes about 2 dozen

For the best-tasting pralines, select the freshest and finest-quality pecans you can find. Homemade pralines are an easy, inexpensive treat to share with friends.

1 Lightly brush two baking trays with melted butter.

2 In a heavy-based saucepan, combine the sugars, the milk and marshmallows over low heat. Cook, stirring constantly, until the marshmallows are completely melted. Increase the heat to medium and cook, stirring occasionally, until a sugar thermometer reads 112°C to 115°C ('soft ball' stage). Without stirring or scraping, pour the hot mixture into a second heavy-based saucepan. Add the pecans, butter, vanilla and cinnamon. Stir rapidly until the mixture is thickened and creamy, about 3 minutes.

3 Using a tablespoon, drop the mixture onto the baking trays, placing the pralines about 2–3 cm apart. Flatten them slightly and leave until set. Store in an airtight container.

Peanut Brittle

2¾ cups (600 g) sugar
3 tablespoons unsalted butter
1½ cups (250 g) lightly salted
  peanuts

Makes about 45 pieces

Crunchy with peanuts, melt-in-your-mouth delicious, this is a classic sweet that the whole family can help to make and package as gifts. It's not nearly as much fun to buy it.

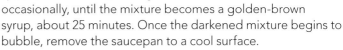

1. Grease a 23 x 33 cm baking tray and line with foil.
2. In a large, heavy-based saucepan, combine the sugar, butter and ⅔ cup (170 ml) water over medium heat. Mix with a wooden spoon, then simmer, stirring occasionally, until the mixture becomes a golden-brown syrup, about 25 minutes. Once the darkened mixture begins to bubble, remove the saucepan to a cool surface.
3. Add the peanuts to the syrup and stir until evenly distributed. Pour the mixture into the baking tray, spreading it evenly and ensuring that the peanuts are distributed equally.
4. Leave to cool and set completely, about 30 minutes.
5. Using a knife handle, break the peanut brittle into bite-sized pieces. Store in an airtight container in a cool, dry place for up to 1 month.

Toffee Bars

melted butter, for brushing
435 g butter, softened
2 cups (440 g) sugar
1 tablespoon light corn syrup
  or glucose syrup (optional)
1 cup (120 g) chopped pecans
¼ teaspoon salt
450 g milk chocolate

Makes about 1 kg

A crunchy confection that's sure to delight.

1. Brush a 38 x 25 x 3 cm baking tin with some melted butter.
2. In a heavy-based saucepan, melt the softened butter over medium heat. Add the sugar and syrup (if using) and stir until a sugar thermometer reads 145°C ('soft crack' stage). Remove from the heat, then stir in the pecans and salt.
3. Quickly pour the toffee mixture into the baking tin. Leave to stand for 5 minutes. Using a sharp knife, score the top of the toffee into bars, then leave at room temperature until cool. Break or cut the toffee into bars along the score lines.
4. Line one or two baking trays with baking paper. In a heavy-based saucepan over low heat, melt the milk chocolate, stirring often.
5. Dip each toffee bar into the chocolate until it is completely coated, then place on the baking trays. Leave to stand at room temperature until the chocolate has set.

Rocky Road

400 g chocolate chips or
    chocolate block
2 cups (320 g) dry-roasted
    peanuts, or 250 g broken
    sweet biscuits
250 g packet of marshmallows,
    roughly chopped
100 g packet of glace cherries,
    chopped

Makes 40 squares

Chocolate and cherries and light-as-air marshmallows molten together appeal to the inner child in us all.

1 Grease a 23 x 33 cm baking tray or slice tin and line it with baking paper.
2 In the top of a double boiler, melt the chocolate over low heat, stirring occasionally until smooth. Transfer to a large bowl and stir in the remaining ingredients, combining well and breaking up any big bits of biscuit, if using.
3 Pour into the baking tray and chill until firm. Cut into squares and store in an airtight container.

Fruit and Nut Truffles

250 g bittersweet chocolate,
    chopped
2 tablespoons thick cream
2 tablespoons Cognac or rum
1¼ cups (225 g) finely chopped
    apricots
½ cup (60 g) finely chopped
    hazelnuts, plus 30 hazelnut
    halves
2 tablespoons crystallised
    ginger, finely chopped
2 tablespoons icing sugar,
    sifted

Makes 30 truffles

Serve these sumptuous sweets with an after-dinner espresso, or as part of an indulgent afternoon tea.

1 Line a large baking tray with baking paper or foil. Lay a large sheet of baking paper on a work surface.
2 Melt half the chocolate in the top of a double boiler over low heat, stirring occasionally until smooth. Remove the top saucepan from heat and add the cream and Cognac, beating until well blended. Add the apricots, hazelnuts, ginger and sugar and combine well. Put the saucepan in the refrigerator and chill the mixture until it is firm enough to handle.
3 Using a spoon, scoop up a walnut-sized portion of the mixture. Using your hands, roll the portion into a 2–3 cm-diameter ball and place on the prepared work surface. Repeat with the remaining mixture.
4 In the top of the double boiler, melt the remaining chocolate over low heat, stirring occasionally until smooth. Remove the double boiler from the heat.
5 Using a fork, spear one fruit ball and dip into the melted chocolate until completely coated; allow any excess chocolate to run back into the saucepan. Place on the baking tray and top with a hazelnut half. Repeat with the remaining ingredients.
6 Refrigerate on the baking tray until the truffles are chilled and the chocolate has set. Refrigerate in an airtight container for up to 1 month.

Marshmallows

¼ cup (30 g) icing sugar
¼ cup (30 g) cornflour
1½ tablespoons powdered
  gelatine
½ cup (110 g) sugar
⅔ cup (150 g) light corn syrup
  or glucose syrup (optional)

Makes about 36 marshmallows

An electric stand mixer makes these marshmallows quick and easy to whip up. They cost less than the commercial ones and children will love the process.

1 Line a 33 x 23 x 5 cm baking tin with baking paper. In a small sieve, combine 1 tablespoon of the icing sugar and 1 tablespoon of the cornflour and sift the mixture over the baking tin.
2 Pour ⅓ cup (80 ml) water into a heatproof bowl. Sprinkle the gelatine over and leave to stand for 5 minutes.
3 Place the bowl in a large saucepan of simmering water and stir until the gelatine has dissolved. Add the sugar and stir until the sugar has dissolved. Remove the bowl from the water and add the syrup (if using). Using an electric mixer, beat until the mixture is creamy and thick, 10 to 15 minutes. Leave to cool.
4 Using a wet spatula, spread the mixture into the baking tin, smoothing the top. Leave to cool and set, about 20 minutes.
5 Carefully lift the marshmallow mixture onto a cutting board. Put another 1 tablespoon of the remaining icing sugar and cornflour in the sieve and lightly dust over the top. Using a sharp knife, cut the marshmallow into small squares.
6 Combine the remaining icing sugar and cornflour in a cup. Dip each marshmallow square into the mixture until completely coated. Store in an airtight container in a cool, dry place for 1 to 2 weeks.

If you run out of corn syrup

If a recipe calls for 1 cup (220 g) light corn syrup and you don't have any on hand, you can use glucose syrup. Alternatively, combine 1 cup (220 g) sugar and an additional ¼ cup (60 ml) of the liquid used in the recipe and stir until blended.

Candied Citrus Peels

3 firm ripe lemons or oranges
¼ cup (55 g) sugar

Makes about 1 cup

Dip these zesty citrus strips in chocolate for an easy confection, or use them as exquisite decorations on cakes, ice cream and other desserts.

1 Using a swivel-bladed vegetable peeler, remove the peel from the citrus fruit, avoiding the bitter white pith. Using a sharp knife, cut the peel into strips. For decorations, cut it into matchstick-thin strips; for dipping in chocolate, cut it into larger strips.
2 Put the citrus strips in a small saucepan and add enough cold water to cover. Bring to a boil over high heat, then immediately drain the strips and rinse under cold running water.
3 Return the strips to the saucepan. Add the sugar and ½ cup (125 ml) water. Over medium heat, cook the mixture until the liquid has evaporated and the strips are bright and shiny.
4 Spread a sheet of foil over a work surface. Transfer the candied peel to the foil to cool, keeping the strips separate. Refrigerate in an airtight container for up to 6 months.

Custards, Mousses and Puddings

Chocolate Pudding

¾ cup (165 g) sugar
1½ tablespoons cornflour
pinch of salt
2 cups (500 ml) milk
⅓ cup (50 g) chopped
   semi-sweet chocolate
1 egg
2 tablespoons butter
1 teaspoon vanilla extract

Makes 4 to 6 servings

Like a grilled cheese sandwich, chocolate pudding is pure comfort food. You can make it from a packet or take a few more minutes and make a much better one from scratch.

1 In a saucepan, combine the sugar, cornflour and salt. Add the milk and stir until smooth. Add the chocolate and stir constantly over medium heat until the mixture boils and thickens. Reduce the heat and simmer, stirring constantly, for 2 minutes. Remove the saucepan from the heat.
2 Beat the egg in a bowl until foamy, using electric beaters. Gradually stir in about ½ cup (125 ml) of the hot milk mixture, then pour the egg mixture into the remaining hot milk mixture. Cook over low heat, stirring constantly, for 2 minutes longer.
3 Remove the saucepan from the heat and stir in the butter and vanilla. Immediately pour the pudding into a bowl or individual dessert dishes. Leave to cool to room temperature, then refrigerate.

Panna Cotta

2 cups (500 ml) milk
1 tablespoon powdered gelatine
⅓ cup (80 g) caster sugar
100 ml whipping cream
1 strip orange zest
1 vanilla bean, split

RHUBARB AND STRAWBERRY
   COMPOTE
400 g rhubarb, trimmed and
   cut into 5 cm lengths
juice of 1 orange
2 tablespoons caster sugar
450 g ripe strawberries, hulled
   and sliced

Makes 4 servings

The traditional recipe for this 'cooked cream', from the Piedmont region of Italy, is made with rich double cream. This lighter version, served with a pretty rhubarb and strawberry compote, is delightfully smooth and creamy yet much lower in fat. Prepare it the day before serving, if possible.

1 Pour 150 ml of the milk into a saucepan. Sprinkle the gelatine over and leave to stand for 5 minutes.

2 Stir in the sugar, then set the pan over low heat. Warm gently, without boiling, until the sugar and gelatine have completely dissolved, stirring frequently.

3 Remove the pan from the heat and add the remaining milk, the cream and orange zest. Scrape the seeds from the vanilla bean into the milk. Add the vanilla bean to the milk and leave to infuse for 10 minutes while preparing the compote.

4 In a saucepan, combine the rhubarb, orange juice and sugar. Bring just to a simmer, then cook gently until the rhubarb is tender but still holding its shape, 3 to 4 minutes. Spoon the rhubarb into a serving dish using a slotted spoon. Boil the juice remaining in the pan to reduce it slightly until syrupy. Pour the juice over the rhubarb and gently stir in the sliced strawberries. Leave to cool.

5 Strain the milk mixture through a fine sieve into a jug, then pour into four ⅔ cup (170 ml) moulds, cups or ramekins. Allow to cool, then cover and chill for at least 3 hours, until set.

6 To serve, run the tip of a knife around the edge of each ramekin. Place an inverted serving plate over the top of each ramekin and turn them upside down, holding the two firmly together. Lift off the ramekin. Spoon some of the compote around the panna cotta and serve the remaining compote separately.

Rice Pudding

melted butter, for brushing
3½ cups (875 ml) milk
½ cup (100 g) long-grain
 white rice
⅓ cup (75 g) sugar
½ teaspoon salt (optional)
½ cup (60 g) raisins
1 teaspoon vanilla extract
ground cinnamon, for
 sprinkling (optional)

Makes about 6 servings

You can buy commercially made rice pudding, but it just isn't as beautifully textured and creamy as homemade. Rice pudding thickens on cooling, so if serving cold, stir in a little extra milk, or serve with summer berries.

1. Preheat the oven to 170°C (Gas 3). Brush a 6 cup (1.5 litre) baking dish with melted butter.
2. In a saucepan, combine the milk, rice, sugar and salt, if using. Bring to a boil over medium heat, stirring constantly. Pour into the baking dish, then cover and bake for 45 minutes, stirring every 15 minutes.
3. Stir in the raisins and the vanilla. Cover again and bake for 15 minutes longer. Remove from the oven and sprinkle with cinnamon, if desired. Serve warm or chilled.

Bread and Butter Pudding

2 cups (500 ml) milk
1¼ cups (310 ml) thick cream
1 vanilla bean, split
 lengthwise
1 day-old light fruit loaf,
 cut into slices 1 cm thick
⅓ cup (90 g) unsalted butter,
 softened
⅓ cup (40 g) sultanas
6 egg yolks
½ cup (115 g) caster sugar
1 tablespoon freshly grated
 nutmeg
⅓ cup (75 g) raw sugar or
 soft brown sugar

FOR THE SAUCE
1 cup (230 g) caster sugar
6 egg yolks
1¼ cups (310 ml) dry cider

Makes 6 servings

The homely appeal of bread baked in custard is timeless. In this version, fruit loaf is used for extra flavour and a frothy cider sauce adds its own tang.

1. In a saucepan, gently heat the milk and cream with the vanilla bean until almost boiling. Remove from the heat, cover and leave to infuse for 30 minutes.
2. Meanwhile, spread each slice of bread liberally with butter and cut them in half diagonally. Overlap the slices attractively in a buttered, shallow, ovenproof dish, scattering sultanas over the pieces as you go.
3. In a large bowl, whisk the egg yolks and caster sugar until pale and creamy. Strain the infused milk and cream onto the egg mixture and whisk well. Pour evenly over the buttered fruit bread and leave to soak for 20 minutes.
4. Meanwhile, preheat the oven to 180°C (Gas 4). Sprinkle the nutmeg and raw sugar evenly over the pudding and set the dish in a roasting tin. Pour in enough boiling water to come halfway up the side of the baking dish. Bake until the custard is just set and the top is golden and crisp, about 45 minutes.
5. About 15 minutes before the pudding is due to come out of the oven, start making the sauce. Put the sugar and egg yolks in a heatproof bowl and place snugly over a pan of barely simmering water, making sure that the bottom of the bowl does not touch the water. Whisk until the mixture is pale and creamy and the sugar has dissolved. Still whisking, slowly pour in the cider and continue to whisk for 5 minutes, or until the mixture froths up to a creamy mousse. Whisk for another 5–10 minutes, or until the sauce is light and foamy.
6. Pour the sauce into a jug and serve with the hot pudding.

Crème Brûlée

3 cups (750 ml) milk
¾ cup (165 g) sugar
1 vanilla bean, split
  lengthwise
4 strips (each 1 x 7.5 cm)
  orange zest
3 strips (each 1 x 5 cm)
  lemon zest
3 strips (each 1 x 5 cm)
  lime zest
¼ teaspoon salt
3 eggs, plus 3 egg yolks
¾ cup (165 g) firmly packed
  soft brown sugar

Makes 8 servings

Who can resist a smooth, rich and elegantly turned-out custard when it's hiding under a fine layer of brittle but gooey sweet caramel? You don't need to splash out on fancy restaurants to enjoy this creamy classic when it's simple enough to make at home.

1 Set eight ungreased ¾ cup (185 ml) ramekins on a folded tea towel in a large baking tin, spacing the ramekins well apart.
2 In a saucepan, combine the milk with ¼ cup (55 g) of the sugar, the vanilla bean, citrus zest strips and salt. Bring to a simmer over medium heat, then remove from the heat, cover and leave to infuse for 30 minutes.
3 Preheat the oven to 170°C (Gas 3). In a large bowl, whisk the eggs, egg yolks and remaining sugar until just blended. Set a large sieve over the bowl and pour the milk mixture through into the egg mixture. Whisk until the ingredients are blended.
4 Spoon the custard into the ramekins. Pour enough water into the baking tin to come halfway up the side of the ramekins. Bake, uncovered, until a knife inserted into the centre of a custard comes out clean, about 45 minutes. Remove the ramekins from the baking tin to wire racks.
5 Preheat the grill to high. Sprinkle 1½ teaspoons of the brown sugar over the top of each custard. Set the ramekins 15 to 20 cm from the grill heat source and grill until the sugar melts, about 45 seconds.
6 Remove the ramekins to wire racks and allow to cool to room temperature. Serve at room temperature or slightly chilled, but do not refrigerate too long or the crust will begin to soften.

Crème Caramel

CARAMEL

½ cup (110 g) sugar

½ cup (125 ml) water

CUSTARD

3 cups (750 ml) milk

¾ cup (165 g) sugar

1 vanilla bean, split lengthwise

4 strips (each 1 x 7.5 cm) orange zest

3 strips (each 1 x 5 cm) lemon zest

3 strips (each 1 x 5 cm) lime zest

¼ teaspoon salt

3 eggs, plus 3 egg yolks

Makes 8 servings

A close relative of the revered Crème Brûlée (opposite), the sauce of a creme caramel dribbles deliciously down the sides of the custard when the whole creation is inverted onto the plate. To make a lower-fat version, substitute 3 cups (750 ml) evaporated skim milk for the whole milk, 1½ cups (350 g) egg substitute (available from health food shops) for the whole eggs and yolks, and reduce the sugar in the custard to ⅔ cup (140 g).

1 To prepare the caramel, combine the sugar and water in a small saucepan over medium–high heat. Bring to a boil and continue to boil until the sugar turns amber in colour, about 5 minutes.

2 Pour the caramel into eight ungreased ¾ cup (185 ml) ramekins. Tilt each ramekin so the caramel coats the bottom and about 2.5 cm of the sides. Place the ramekins on a folded tea towel in a baking tin that is large enough to hold them all without touching.

3 To make the custard, combine the milk in a saucepan with ¼ cup (55 g) of the sugar, the vanilla bean, citrus zest strips and salt. Bring to a simmer over medium heat, then remove from the heat, cover and leave to infuse for 30 minutes.

4 Preheat the oven to 170°C (Gas 3). In a large bowl, whisk the eggs, egg yolks and remaining sugar until just blended. Set a large sieve over the bowl and pour the milk mixture through into the egg mixture. Whisk until the ingredients are blended.

5 Spoon the custard into the caramel-coated ramekins. Pour enough water into the baking tin to come halfway up the side of the ramekins. Bake, uncovered, until a knife inserted into the centre of a custard comes out clean, about 45 minutes.

6 Remove the ramekins to wire racks and allow the custards to cool to room temperature; refrigerate until ready to serve.

7 To serve, run a knife around the edge of the custards to loosen them, then invert the ramekins onto rimmed dessert plates or shallow dessert bowls. Allow the caramel to run down the custards and form a pool around them.

Tips for making custard

Although it is easy to make, custard requires a bit of cooking know-how. The main rule is don't overmix the eggs. More egg yolks make for a smoother texture, which in turn requires a slower cooking time; the container used for baking will determine the cooking time, so it's safest to stick to the one specified in the recipe. If you remember these simple principles you'll get great custard every time.

Chocolate Mousse

1½ cups (225 g) chopped
  semi-sweet chocolate
3 eggs, separated
¾ cup (185 ml) thick cream
½ cup (110 g) sugar
1 teaspoon vanilla extract

Makes 8 servings

The ultimate mousse experience – and the finer the quality of chocolate you use, the more outstanding the final result. Expensive at a gourmet shop or restaurant, chocolate mousse can be made at home for much less and tastes even better.

1 In the top of a double boiler, melt the chocolate over low heat, stirring occasionally until smooth.

2 Meanwhile, beat the egg yolks in a bowl until thick, using electric beaters. Pour a little of the melted chocolate into the egg yolks, whisking constantly, then whisk all the egg yolk mixture back into the double boiler.

3 Add ¼ cup (60 ml) of the cream and whisk until well blended. Cook, stirring constantly, until the mixture thickens and reaches 70°C on a sugar thermometer, about 4 minutes. Remove the top of the double boiler and allow the mixture to cool to room temperature, whisking often.

4 In a small saucepan, combine the sugar and ¼ cup (60 ml) water. Bring to a boil over medium heat. Using a pastry brush dipped in water, brush down the sides of the saucepan, then cook the syrup without stirring until it reaches 115°C on a sugar thermometer, about 5 minutes.

5 In a heatproof bowl, beat the eggwhites until frothy, using electric beaters on medium speed. Place the bowl in a larger saucepan of boiling water (double-boiler style). With the beaters on low speed, gradually whisk the boiling sugar syrup into the eggwhites until the meringue peaks stiffly and a sugar thermometer inserted at the centre reaches 70°C. Whisk a few tablespoons of the hot meringue into the chocolate mixture, then fold in the remaining meringue.

6 In a small bowl, beat the remaining cream until it forms soft peaks, using electric beaters on high speed. Beat in the vanilla. Fold the whipped cream into the chocolate mixture until no white streaks remain.

7 Spoon into individual serving dishes or glasses, then cover and refrigerate for at least 1 hour, or until serving.

Mango Mousse

3 mangoes (about 1 kg in
    total), peeled, stoned and
    sliced
¼ cup (60 ml) lime juice
½ teaspoon ground ginger
3 teaspoons powdered gelatine
2 tablespoons sugar
½ cup (125 g) light sour cream

Makes 6 servings

Nothing signals the arrival of summer more than the presence of juicy mangoes. Prepare this light mousse for friends and bask in the warmth of their admiration.

1 Reserve 12 small mango slices. In a food processor, purée the remaining mango with the lime juice and ginger. Leave in the food processor and set aside.
2 Sprinkle the gelatine over ½ cup (125 ml) water and leave to stand for 5 minutes.
3 In a small saucepan, combine the sugar and ½ cup (125 ml) water and bring to a boil. Add the gelatine mixture and stir until well dissolved.
4 Add the syrup mixture to the mango purée and process until well combined. Add the sour cream and process again briefly just to blend.
5 Spoon into dessert bowls or glasses and top with the reserved mango slices. Cover and refrigerate for 2 hours, or until the mousse has chilled and set.

Fruit Desserts

Brandied Peaches

2 cups (440 g) sugar
½ cup (125 ml) brandy
1 tablespoon whole cloves
2 cinnamon sticks
zest of 1 lemon, slivered
zest of 1 orange, slivered
4 peaches, peeled, stoned
    and halved

Makes 4 servings

You can buy brandied peaches in jars at gourmet shops, but you can just as easily – and much more cheaply – delight your loved ones by making your own.

1 Pour 3 cups (750 ml) water into a large, heavy-based saucepan. Add the sugar, brandy, cloves, cinnamon sticks and citrus zest and bring to a strong boil over high heat.
2 Reduce the heat to medium. Prick the peach halves several times with a fork and add them to the saucepan. Cover and reduce the heat to the lowest simmer. Gently poach until the peaches are just cooked but still firm, about 20 minutes.
3 Serve the brandied peaches hot, warm or chilled.

Dried Fruit Compote

1¼ cups (275 g) pitted prunes
⅔ cup (85 g) sultanas
½ cup (80 g) dried figs
½ cup (90 g) dried apricots
1½ cups (375 ml) orange juice
⅓ cup (80 ml) water
¼ cup (55 g) sugar
1 cinnamon stick, broken
¼ teaspoon ground ginger
pinch of ground cloves
pinch of freshly ground
   black pepper
¾ teaspoon vanilla extract
   (optional)

Makes 6 servings

For a fast and fantastic dessert, keep these dried fruits on hand in your pantry, then simply poach them as required. They're soft and enticingly spicy.

1 In a saucepan, combine all the ingredients except the vanilla. Bring to a boil over high heat, then reduce the heat to low. Cover and simmer until the fruit is tender, 25 to 30 minutes.
2 Remove the saucepan from the heat. Remove and discard the cinnamon sticks. Allow the mixture to cool to room temperature, then stir in the vanilla, if using.
3 Serve at room temperature or chilled. The compote can be refrigerated in an airtight container for up to 3 days.

Wine-poached Pears with Strawberries

4 cups (1 litre) red wine
1 cup (220 g) sugar
3 tablespoons thinly sliced
   fresh ginger
2 cinnamon sticks
zest of 1 lemon, slivered
zest of 1 orange, slivered
4 firm ripe pears, such as
   bosc or bartlett, peeled and
   cored with stems intact
300 g strawberries, hulled

Makes 4 servings

This is a restaurant dessert you can make at home for a modest sum and enjoy extravagantly. Serve them with a drizzle of homemade Custard (page 59).

1 In a large, heavy-based saucepan, combine the wine, sugar, ginger, cinnamon sticks and citrus zest slivers. Bring to a strong boil over high heat.
2 Reduce the heat to medium and add the pears. Cover and reduce the heat to the lowest simmer. Gently poach until the pears are just cooked but still firm, about 15 minutes.
3 Remove from the heat and allow to cool for 5 minutes, then stir in the strawberries. Using a slotted spoon, remove the pears and strawberries to a serving platter or individual bowls.
4 Return the saucepan to high heat and bring the poaching liquid to a boil; boil until the liquid is reduced to about 1½ cups (375 ml). Pour the hot poaching liquid over the pears and strawberries and serve.

Fruit Salad

1 large mango, peeled,
  stoned and sliced
250 g cherries, pitted
⅔ cup (120 g) seedless green
  grapes
250 g strawberries, hulled
  and cut in half
3 large apricots, halved,
  stoned and sliced
¾ cup (65 g) desiccated coconut
2 teaspoons caster sugar
generous pinch of ground
  cayenne pepper
generous pinch of mustard
  powder
pinch of salt

Makes 6 servings

This recipe is easily adapted to showcase other summer
fruits and berries. Mustard and cayenne pepper add a
subtle spicy heat.

1 Place all the fruit in a large serving bowl.
2 Finely grind the desiccated coconut in a spice mill or using a
  pestle and mortar. Add the sugar, spices and salt and mix well.
3 Add the coconut mixture to the fruit and stir well to combine.
4 Cover and refrigerate for at least 2 hours, preferably overnight,
  to allow the flavours to blend and develop. Serve cold.

Chocolate-dipped Strawberries

1 cup (150 g) chopped
  good-quality dark chocolate
12 large strawberries, hulls
  left on
finely chopped nuts or
  sprinkles (optional)

Makes 12

These are so simple to make and cost a mere fraction
of the bought ones. You can substitute white chocolate
if you prefer, or make a mixture of white and dark.

1 Line a baking tray with baking paper.
2 In the top of a double boiler, melt the chocolate over low heat,
  stirring occasionally until smooth.
3 Holding the strawberries by their leaves, dip them one at a
  time into the melted chocolate, allowing the excess chocolate
  to run back into the pan. Dip into some finely chopped nuts
  or sprinkles, if desired.
4 Place on the baking tray and stand in a cool place until set.

Ice cream

French Vanilla Ice Cream

1¾ cups (440 ml) milk
2½ cups (625 ml) thick cream
1 cup (220 g) sugar
1 vanilla bean, split
  lengthwise
¼ teaspoon salt
6 egg yolks

Makes 1 litre

This is the real thing – rich, creamy and full of the strong, wonderful scent of vanilla.

1 In a large saucepan, combine the milk, cream, ½ cup (110 g) of the sugar, the vanilla bean and salt. Scald the mixture over medium heat just until small bubbles appear.

2 In a bowl, whisk the egg yolks and remaining sugar until well blended. Gradually whisk a little milk mixture into the egg mixture, then pour both mixtures into the saucepan. Cook over low heat, whisking constantly, until the custard coats the back of a spoon, about 15 minutes.

3 Remove from the heat and allow to cool to room temperature. Remove the vanilla bean and scrape the seeds into the custard; discard the pod. Cover the saucepan and refrigerate until the custard is cold, 1 to 2 hours.

4 Transfer the custard to an ice-cream maker and freeze according to the manufacturer's instructions.

Churn it yourself: ice-cream makers

Few pleasures in life compare with homemade ice cream – or frozen yogurt. But to make it, you need an ice-cream maker. As a general rule, homemade ice cream costs much less than commercial varieties. An ice-cream maker will pay for itself in no time. Keep an eye out at discount sales.

❖ **Hand crank churns** These old-fashioned machines use a combination of rock salt and ice packed around the churn to freeze the cream mixture. As the handle is cranked, the interior paddles stir the cream mixture while it is freezing. Naturally, the harder the ice cream gets, the harder it is to turn the handle, so you get a good workout before the delicious reward. This machine works well for family gatherings or parties, where people can trade off on the cranking but everyone enjoys the results.

❖ **Electric ice-cream makers** These handy machines are more costly up front but much easier on you, so you are likely to end up using them more frequently than a hand-churned model. Larger electric makers do both the freezing and the churning for you. A less costly version requires a freezer for the insert to be frozen ahead of time, but still does the arm-tiring churning for you.

Blueberry Ice Cream

300 g blueberries, washed
  and stemmed if necessary
1⅓ cups (300 g) sugar
4 strips (each 1 x 5 cm)
  lemon zest
½ teaspoon ground white
  pepper
½ teaspoon ground ginger
1¾ cups (440 ml) milk
2½ cups (625 ml) thick cream
1 vanilla bean, split
  lengthwise
¼ teaspoon salt
6 egg yolks

Makes 1 litre

When blueberries come into season, towards the end
of summer, indulge in this glorious concoction served
in glass bowls so everyone can admire the colour as
well as the taste.

1 In a saucepan, combine the blueberries, ⅓ cup (75 g) of
   the sugar and the lemon zest. Cook over medium heat,
   stirring very frequently, until the blueberries are very soft,
   4 to 5 minutes.
2 Place a fine sieve over a bowl. Pour the blueberry mixture
   through the sieve, pressing with the back of a wooden spoon
   to extract all the juice; discard the solids. Stir in the pepper
   and ginger and set aside.
3 In a large saucepan over medium heat, combine the milk,
   cream, ½ cup (110 g) of the sugar, the vanilla bean and salt.
   Scald the mixture just until small bubbles appear.
4 In a bowl, whisk the egg yolks and remaining sugar until well
   blended. Gradually whisk a little milk mixture into the egg
   mixture, then pour both mixtures into the saucepan. Cook
   over low heat, whisking constantly, until the custard coats
   the back of a spoon, about 15 minutes.
5 Remove from the heat and allow to cool to room temperature.
   Remove the vanilla bean and scrape the seeds into the custard;
   discard the pod. Cover the saucepan and refrigerate until the
   custard is cold, 1 to 2 hours.
6 Pour the reserved blueberry mixture into the custard and stir
   until well blended. Transfer to an ice-cream maker and freeze
   according to the manufacturer's instructions.

Peach Ice Cream

2 large, ripe peaches
⅓ cup (55 g) firmly packed
   soft brown sugar
1 tablespoon lemon juice
¼ teaspoon ground ginger
1¾ cups (440 ml) milk
2½ cups (625 ml) thick cream
1 cup (220 g) sugar
1 vanilla bean, split
   lengthwise
¼ teaspoon salt
6 egg yolks

Makes 1 litre

Ripe, juicy peaches are a true taste of summer, so how could they be any better? In a luscious ice cream that you've made yourself!

1 Blanch, peel and stone the peaches, then finely chop them. Place in a bowl with the brown sugar, lemon juice and ginger and toss until well blended. Set aside.
2 In a large saucepan, combine the milk, cream, ½ cup (110 g) of the sugar, the vanilla bean and salt. Scald the mixture over medium heat just until small bubbles appear.
3 In a bowl, whisk the egg yolks and remaining sugar until well blended. Gradually whisk a little milk mixture into the egg mixture, then pour both mixtures into the saucepan. Cook over low heat, whisking constantly, until the custard coats the back of a spoon, about 15 minutes.
4 Remove from the heat and allow to cool to room temperature. Remove the vanilla bean and scrape the seeds into the custard; discard the pod. Cover the saucepan and refrigerate until the custard is cold, 1 to 2 hours.
5 Pour the reserved peach mixture into the custard and stir until well blended. Transfer to an ice-cream maker and freeze according to the manufacturer's instructions.

Mango Ice Cream

2 large ripe mangoes, peeled,
   stoned and chopped
¾ cup (170 g) caster sugar
⅔ cup (170 ml) milk
⅔ cup (170 ml) orange juice
⅔ cup (170 ml) thick cream

Makes 1 litre

When mangoes are cheap and plentiful, make this ice cream for a luxurious treat. At other times, you could use frozen mango cheeks.

1 In a food processor, purée the mango flesh with the sugar, milk and orange juice until smooth.
2 Transfer the mango mixture to an ice-cream maker and churn according to the manufacturer's instructions.

Lowering the fat in homemade ice cream

We love the richness and texture of full-fat ice cream, but our bellies and thighs are not always so appreciative. Fortunately, it is not hard to lower the fat in homemade ice cream – and since it is home-churned as well, you should still have satisfyingly creamy results. The trick is to substitute an equal amount of evaporated skim milk for the whole milk, and ¾ cup (180 g) egg substitute (available from health food shops) for the egg yolks when making a 1 litre batch.

Strawberry Ice Cream

1¾ cups (440 ml) milk
2½ cups (625 ml) thick cream
1⅓ cups (300 g) sugar
1 vanilla bean, split
   lengthwise
¼ teaspoon salt
6 egg yolks
4 strips (each 1 x 7.5 cm)
   orange zest
300 g strawberries

Makes 1 litre

Celebrate the start of summer with homemade ice cream studded with sweet fresh strawberries.

1 In a large saucepan, combine the milk, cream, ½ cup (110 g) of the sugar, the vanilla bean and salt. Scald the mixture over medium heat just until small bubbles appear.
2 In a bowl, whisk the egg yolks and another ½ cup (110 g) sugar until well blended. Gradually whisk a little milk mixture into the egg mixture, then pour both mixtures into the saucepan. Add the orange zest strips and cook over low heat, whisking constantly, until the custard coats the back of a spoon, about 15 minutes.
3 Remove from the heat and allow to cool to room temperature. Remove the vanilla bean and scrape the seeds into the custard; discard the pod. Remove and discard the orange zest strips. Cover the saucepan and refrigerate until the custard is cold, 1 to 2 hours.
4 Rinse and hull the strawberries. Place the strawberries in a food processor or blender with the remaining sugar and purée to the desired consistency.
5 Stir the strawberries into the custard and stir until well blended. Transfer to an ice-cream maker and freeze according to the manufacturer's instructions.

Honey Banana Ice Cream

6 egg yolks
2 cups (500 ml) milk
½ cup (175 g) honey
2 teaspoons vanilla extract
2 cups (500 ml) thick cream
3 ripe bananas, mashed

Makes about 1.25 litres

Gingersnaps (page 130) make a perfect partner for this smooth number.

1 In the top of a double boiler set over simmering water, combine the egg yolks and milk. Whisk until well blended, then stir in the honey and vanilla. Cook over medium heat, whisking constantly, until the mixture coats the back of a spoon and registers 75°C on a sugar thermometer.
2 Pour into a large bowl, then cover and refrigerate until the mixture is chilled, about 1 hour.
3 Add the cream and mashed bananas to the mixture and stir until well blended. Transfer to an ice-cream maker and freeze according to the manufacturer's instructions.

Coconut-pineapple Ice Cream

1⅓ cups (330 ml) milk
3 eggs
1 cup (220 g) sugar
½ cup (30 g) flaked coconut
2 teaspoons vanilla extract
450 g can crushed pineapple, drained
1⅓ cups (330 ml) thick cream

Makes about 1 litre

A taste of the tropics in every bite, this coconut-pineapple ice cream is rich and cooling – a piña colada in a bowl!

1 In a small, heavy-based saucepan, scald the milk over medium–high heat just until tiny bubbles appear.
2 In a heavy-based saucepan, combine the eggs and sugar over low heat. Pour the scalded milk into the egg mixture, whisking constantly. Cook, whisking constantly, until the mixture coats the back of a spoon and registers 75°C on a sugar thermometer.
3 Set a fine sieve over a large bowl. Pour the custard through the sieve; discard the solids. Whisk in the coconut and vanilla until well blended, then stir in the pineapple and cream. Cover and refrigerate until the custard is cold, 1 to 2 hours.
4 Transfer the custard to an ice-cream maker and freeze according to the manufacturer's instructions.

Rocky Road Ice Cream

5⅔ cups (1.4 litres) milk
⅓ cup (90 g) butter, melted
275 g semi-sweet chocolate
2¾ cups (600 g) sugar
¾ teaspoon salt
6 cups (1.5 litres) thick cream
3 cups (150 g) miniature marshmallows
2¼ cups (375 g) mini chocolate chips
1½ cups (180 g) chopped pecans
1½ tablespoons vanilla extract

Makes about 4.5 litres

Chocolate chips, marshmallows and pecans come together in this popular ice cream creation. Once you've made your own, you'll wonder how you could have spent so much money on commercially prepared ice cream.

1 In a large, heavy-based saucepan, combine the milk and butter over medium–high heat. Cook, stirring constantly, until the mixture registers 80°C on a sugar thermometer. Add the chocolate, sugar and salt and stir until the chocolate has melted and the sugar has dissolved completely.
2 Remove the saucepan from the heat and place it in a large bowl of ice water to cool the mixture quickly; stir and chill for 2 minutes. Remove the saucepan and allow to cool completely.
3 Pour the mixture into a large bowl. Then add the cream, marshmallows, chocolate chips, pecans and vanilla and stir until well blended. Cover and refrigerate until the mixture is cold, 30 minutes.
4 Working in batches, transfer the mixture to an ice-cream maker and freeze according to the manufacturer's instructions. Keep the remaining mixture refrigerated until ready to freeze; stir well before adding to the ice-cream maker.
5 Leave in the ice-cream maker or place in the freezer to firm for 2 to 4 hours before serving.

Rich Chocolate Ice Cream

1¼ cups (310 ml) milk
3 eggs
¾ cup (165 g) sugar
⅓ cup (50 g) finely chopped
  unsweetened chocolate
2 teaspoons vanilla extract
¼ teaspoon salt
2 cups (500 ml) thick cream

Makes about 1 litre

A rich, thick chocolate custard is the base for this decadent delight.

1 In a small, heavy-based saucepan, scald the milk over medium–high heat just until tiny bubbles appear.
2 In a heavy-based saucepan, combine the eggs and sugar over low heat. Whisking constantly, pour the scalded milk into the egg mixture. Cook, whisking constantly, until the mixture coats the back of a spoon and registers 75°C on a sugar thermometer.
3 Set a fine sieve over a large bowl. Pour the custard through the sieve; discard the solids. Whisk in the chocolate, vanilla and salt until well blended. Stir in the cream. Cover and refrigerate until the custard is cold, 1 to 2 hours.
4 Transfer the custard to an ice-cream maker and freeze according to the manufacturer's instructions.

Chocolate Chocolate-chip Ice Cream

1¾ cups (440 ml) milk
2½ cups (625 ml) thick cream
1 cup (230 g) firmly packed
  soft brown sugar
¼ teaspoon salt
6 egg yolks
¼ cup (30 g) cocoa powder
1 teaspoon vanilla extract
½ cup (85 g) mini chocolate
  chips

Makes 1 litre

What could be better than chocolate? More chocolate! Remember, however, that just because homemade ice cream is cheaper, it doesn't have fewer kilojoules!

1 In a large saucepan, combine the milk, cream, ½ cup (110 g) of the sugar and the salt. Scald the mixture over medium heat just until small bubbles appear.
2 In a bowl, whisk the egg yolks and remaining sugar until well blended. Whisk in the cocoa until well combined. Gradually whisk a little milk mixture into the egg mixture, then pour both into the saucepan. Cook over low heat, whisking constantly, until the custard coats the back of a spoon, about 15 minutes.
3 Remove from the heat and allow to cool to room temperature. Whisk in the vanilla. Cover the saucepan and refrigerate until the custard is cold, 1 to 2 hours.
4 Add the chocolate chips and stir until evenly distributed. Transfer the custard to an ice-cream maker and freeze according to the manufacturer's instructions.

Mint Chocolate-chip Ice Cream

1¾ cups (440 ml) milk
2½ cups (625 ml) thick cream
80 g (1 bunch) fresh mint,
  leaves rinsed, picked off and
  puréed (this should yield
  enough to fill a 250 ml cup)
1 cup (220 g) sugar
¼ teaspoon salt
6 egg yolks
1 teaspoon vanilla extract
½ cup (85 g) mini chocolate
  chips

Makes 1 litre

Mint and chocolate are a natural combination and this is a popular flavour for ice cream, made using fresh mint. You won't find ice cream this lovely in a tub!

1 In a large saucepan, combine the milk, cream, puréed mint, ½ cup (110 g) of the sugar and the salt. Scald the mixture over medium heat just until small bubbles appear.
2 In a bowl, whisk the egg yolks and remaining sugar until well blended. Gradually whisk a little milk mixture into the egg mixture, then pour both mixtures into the saucepan. Cook over low heat, whisking constantly, until the custard coats the back of a spoon, about 15 minutes.
3 Remove from the heat and allow to cool to room temperature. Whisk in the vanilla. Cover the saucepan and refrigerate until the custard is cold, 1 to 2 hours.
4 Add the mini chocolate chips and stir until evenly distributed. Transfer to an ice-cream maker and freeze according to the manufacturer's instructions.

Peppermint Ice Cream

4 egg yolks
1⅓ cups (330 ml) milk
45 g butter, melted
¾ cup (165 g) sugar
¼ teaspoon salt
2 cups (500 ml) thick cream
1–1½ tablespoons vanilla
  extract
1¼ cups (200 g) crushed
  peppermint-flavoured boiled
  lollies (sweets)

Makes 1 litre

Here's a cute concoction that you won't come across in the shops every day!

1 In a large, heavy-based saucepan, combine the egg yolks, milk, melted butter, sugar and salt over low heat. Cook, stirring constantly, until the mixture coats the back of a spoon and registers 70°C on a sugar thermometer.
2 Remove the saucepan from the heat and place it in a large bowl of ice water to cool the mixture quickly; stir and chill for 2 minutes. Stir in the cream and vanilla. Remove from the heat and let the mixture cool completely.
3 Cover the saucepan with plastic wrap and refrigerate for several hours or overnight, until the mixture is very cold.
4 Stir in the crushed peppermint lollies until evenly distributed. Transfer to an ice-cream maker and freeze according to the manufacturer's instructions.
5 Leave in the ice-cream maker or place in the freezer to firm for 2 to 4 hours before serving.

Butter Pecan Ice Cream

¾ cup (90 g) chopped pecans
3 tablespoons butter, melted
pinch of salt
¼ cup (55 g) plus 1 tablespoon
    sugar
½ cup (115 g) firmly packed
    soft brown sugar
2 tablespoons cornflour
2 eggs, beaten
⅓ cup (80 ml) maple syrup
2½ cups (625 ml) milk
1 cup (250 ml) thick cream
2 teaspoons vanilla extract

Makes about 2 litres

Toasting the pecans really brings out their flavour.
Maple syrup adds extra goodness!

1 Preheat the oven to 180°C (Gas 4). Spread the pecans in a
   single layer in a baking tin. Drizzle with the melted butter,
   sprinkle with the salt and 1 tablespoon of the sugar and toss
   to coat. Toast in the oven for 15 minutes, then stir and toast
   for 15 minutes longer. Remove from the oven and allow to
   cool completely.
2 In the top of a double boiler set over simmering water, combine
   the remaining sugar, brown sugar, cornflour, eggs and maple
   syrup. Stir until well blended, then gradually stir in the milk.
   Increase the heat to high and cook, stirring constantly, until
   the mixture thickens and coats the back of a spoon.
3 Remove from the heat and let the custard cool to room
   temperature. Cover the saucepan and refrigerate until the
   custard is cold, for several hours or overnight.
4 Add the toasted pecans, cream and vanilla and stir until
   evenly distributed. Transfer to an ice-cream maker and freeze
   according to the manufacturer's instructions.
5 Leave in the ice-cream maker or place in the freezer to firm
   for 2 to 4 hours before serving.

Ice Cream Cake

1½ cups (185 g) crumbled
    chocolate sandwich biscuits
    or Oreo biscuits
2 tablespoons butter, melted
3 cups (750 ml) ice cream
    flavour of your choice,
    softened
¾ cup (185 ml) Chocolate Sauce
    (page 60)
3 cups (750 ml) another ice
    cream flavour of your choice,
    softened
½ cup (60 g) grated chocolate
    or toasted slivered almonds

Makes 8 to 10 servings

This frozen cake is perfect for a summer birthday – or
any time you need an easy but sensational dessert. Use
whatever ice cream combination takes your fancy.

1 In a small bowl, combine the biscuit crumbs and melted butter
   and toss until well blended. Press the mixture over the bottom
   and halfway up the side of a 20 cm spring-form tin. Place the
   tin in the freezer for 30 minutes.
2 Spoon your first ice cream variety into the spring-form tin,
   spreading it in an even layer over the crust. Freeze again until
   the ice cream is firm, about 30 minutes.
3 Pour the chocolate sauce into the tin, spreading it evenly over
   the ice cream layer. Freeze until firm, about 15 minutes.
4 Spoon the second ice cream variety into the tin, spreading
   it evenly over the hardened chocolate sauce. Using a knife or
   spatula dipped in hot water, smooth the top of the cake, then
   sprinkle with either the grated chocolate or almonds. Cover
   with plastic wrap and freeze for at least 1 hour.
5 To serve, wipe the bottom of the tin with a hot, damp cloth,
   then carefully release and remove the sides. Cut the cake
   using a sharp knife dipped in hot water.

Frozen Yogurt

Lemon Frozen Yogurt

4 cups (1 kg) low-fat natural
   yogurt
1⅔ cups (360 g) sugar
⅓ cup (80 ml) lemon juice
1 tablespoon grated lemon zest
4 drops yellow food colouring
   (optional)

Makes 1.25 litres

Light and refreshing, the tang of lemon really comes
through in this homemade frozen yogurt. Try a scoop
with fresh berries.

1 In a bowl, combine the yogurt, sugar, lemon juice and
   lemon zest; stir until well blended. If a brighter yellow colour
   is desired, stir in the food colouring.
2 Transfer the mixture to an ice-cream maker and freeze
   according to the manufacturer's instructions.
3 Leave in the ice-cream maker or place in the freezer to firm
   for 2 to 4 hours before serving.

Strawberry Frozen Yogurt

2 cups (500 g) low-fat natural
   yogurt
2 cups (500 ml) puréed fresh
   strawberries
400 ml can sweetened
   condensed milk
1 cup (250 ml) milk
3 teaspoons vanilla extract

Makes 1.5 litres

Fresh strawberries add just the right touch of sweetness
to this simple, speedy frozen yogurt.

1 In a large bowl, combine all the ingredients and stir until
   well blended.
2 Working in batches if needed, pour the mixture into an
   ice-cream maker, filling it two-thirds full; store the remaining
   yogurt in the refrigerator until ready to freeze. Following
   the manufacturer's instructions, freeze the yogurt. Leave in
   the ice-cream maker or place in the freezer to firm for 2 to
   4 hours before serving.
3 Remove from the freezer 30 to 45 minutes before serving
   to soften slightly.

Passionfruit Frozen Yogurt

½ cup (125 ml) milk
1 teaspoon powdered gelatine
5 passionfruit
¾ cup (165 g) sugar
1 teaspoon lemon juice
1½ cups (375 g) Greek-style
   yogurt
1 eggwhite
⅓ cup (35 g) full-cream
   milk powder

Makes about 1 litre

Fresh passionfruit adds a deliciously tangy note to
frozen yogurt. Use full-cream milk and yogurt here
for best results.

1 Pour the milk into a small saucepan and stir in the gelatine.
Leave to stand for 1 minute, then stir over low heat until the
gelatine has dissolved. Set aside.

2 Cut each passionfruit in half. Scoop the pulp and seeds into
a bowl, discarding the shells. Stir in the sugar, lemon juice and
dissolved gelatine until combined, then stir in the yogurt.

3 In another bowl, beat the eggwhite, milk powder and ⅓ cup
(80 ml) water until stiff but not dry, using electric beaters. Fold
gently into the yogurt mixture and transfer to an ice-cream
maker. Following the manufacturer's instructions, churn until
frozen. Serve immediately or transfer to the freezer.

Frozen yogurt: an alternative to ice cream

Once only the province of health food
aficionados, frozen yogurt has grown
wildly in popularity. Generally lower in
fat and kilojoules (though not always)
than ice cream, frozen yogurt combines

the slight tanginess associated with yogurt
with the cool creaminess of ice cream. For
the most healthy results, use non-fat or
reduced-fat yogurt when making it. You'll
need an ice-cream maker to prepare it.

Ices, Granitas, Sherbets and Sorbets

Orange Ice

1 cup (220 g) sugar
350 g frozen orange juice
  concentrate, thawed
2 tablespoons lemon juice
115 ml milk
1 tablespoon melted butter

Makes 10 to 12 servings

This lovely treat requires only five ingredients and
no ice-cream maker!

1 In a saucepan, combine the sugar and 1 cup (250 ml) water
over high heat. Boil, stirring frequently, until the sugar has
completely dissolved, about 1 minute.
2 Remove from the heat and stir in the orange juice concentrate,
lemon juice and 2 cups (500 ml) water. Stir until well blended.
Pour into a large bowl, cover and freeze until firm.
3 Remove the bowl from the freezer and beat the mixture until
smooth, using electric beaters. Add the milk and melted
butter and beat again until well blended. Cover and return
to the freezer.
4 Leave to stand at room temperature for 20 minutes to soften
before serving.

Blood-orange Champagne Granita

1½ cups (330 g) sugar
2 cups (500 ml) blood orange
  juice
2 cups (500 ml) Champagne
  or sparkling wine
pinch of salt

Makes 12 servings

If blood oranges are unavailable, substitute ruby red
or pink grapefruit.

1 In a saucepan, combine the sugar and 1 cup (250 ml) water
over medium heat, stirring constantly until the sugar has
dissolved. Bring to a boil, reduce the heat and simmer for
3 minutes. Remove from the heat and leave until the syrup
is cool, about 1 hour.
2 Pour the syrup into a large bowl. Stir in the orange juice,
Champagne and salt until well blended.
3 Pour the mixture into a large, shallow tin. Cover with plastic
wrap and place in the freezer. As the granita freezes, stir it with
a fork every 45 minutes, two or three times, to break up the ice
and create an icy, flaky texture. Cover with plastic wrap and
freeze for 8 hours, or overnight.
4 When ready to serve, soften the granita in the refrigerator for
15 minutes. Then, using an ice-cream scoop or large spoon,
scrape across the top to bring up the granita in thin shavings.
Serve in chilled glasses or bowls.

Cappuccino Granita

1¼ cups (310 ml) brewed
   strong black coffee or
   espresso
¼ cup (55 g) sugar
100 ml Kahlúa or other
   coffee-flavoured liqueur
1 cup (250 ml) thick cream
1 tablespoon icing sugar
cocoa powder, for dusting

Makes 6 to 8 servings

An Italian specialty, this granita goes well with a few chocolate-covered coffee beans.

1 In a small bowl, combine the coffee, sugar and ¼ cup (60 ml) of the Kahlúa.
2 Pour the mixture into a large, shallow tin. Cover with plastic wrap and place in the freezer. As the granita freezes, stir it with a fork every 45 minutes, two or three times, to break up the ice and create an icy, flaky texture. Cover with plastic wrap and freeze for 8 hours, or overnight.
3 In a bowl, beat the cream, icing sugar and remaining Kahlúa until soft peaks form, using electric beaters.
4 To serve, use an ice-cream scoop or large spoon to scrape across the top of the granita to bring up thin shavings. Place the granita in individual chilled serving bowls and top each with a dollop of the Kahlúa cream. Sprinkle with a dusting of cocoa powder and serve.

Kiwi Granita

2 cups (440 g) sugar
juice of 2 lemons
6 large, ripe kiwi fruit,
   peeled and chopped

Makes about 1 litre

A lovely green with a lively, tart taste, this granita would be a fitting finale to a rich meal.

1 In a saucepan, combine the sugar, half the lemon juice and 1 cup (250 ml) water over medium heat, stirring constantly until the sugar has dissolved. Bring to a boil, reduce the heat and simmer for 3 minutes. Remove from the heat and leave until the syrup is just warm.
2 Purée the kiwi fruit in a food processor or blender. Add the remaining lemon juice and blend. Pour the kiwi fruit purée into the sugar syrup and mix well.
3 Pour the mixture into a large, shallow tin. Cover with plastic wrap and place in the freezer. As the granita freezes, stir it with a fork every 45 minutes, two or three times, to break up the ice and create an icy, flaky texture. Cover with plastic wrap and freeze 6 hours, or until solid.
4 When ready to serve, soften the granita in the refrigerator for 15 minutes. Then, using an ice-cream scoop or large spoon, scrape across the top to bring up the granita in thin shavings. Serve in chilled glasses or bowls.

Peach Granita

½ cup (110 g) sugar
4 ripe peaches, peeled, stoned
  and chopped
1 tablespoon peach schnapps
  or other fruit liqueur

Makes about 1 litre

An out-of-this-world cooler for a hot summer's day,
this granita is an easy home project.

1 In a saucepan, combine the sugar and 1 cup (250 ml) water
   over medium heat, stirring constantly until the sugar has
   dissolved. Bring to a boil, reduce the heat and simmer for
   3 minutes. Remove from the heat and leave until the syrup
   is cool, about 1 hour.
2 In a food processor or blender, purée the peach pieces.
   Add the syrup and schnapps and blend.
3 Pour the mixture into a large, shallow tin. Cover with plastic
   wrap and place in the freezer. As the granita freezes, stir it with
   a fork every 45 minutes, two or three times, to break up the ice
   and create an icy, flaky texture. Cover with plastic wrap and
   freeze for 6 hours, or until solid.
4 When ready to serve, soften the granita in the refrigerator for
   15 minutes. Then, using an ice-cream scoop or large spoon,
   scrape across the top to bring up the granita in thin shavings.
   Serve in chilled glasses or bowls.

Lime Sherbet

4¼ cups (950 g) sugar
2 tablespoons grated lime zest
1½ cups (375 ml) lime juice
3 tablespoons lemon juice
7½ cups (1.9 litres) milk
½ cup (125 ml) buttermilk
1 drop green food colouring
  (optional)

Makes about 2.5 litres

Refreshingly tart, this homemade sherbet is better than
any you can buy and costs much less.

1 In a large bowl, combine the sugar, lime zest, lime juice and
   lemon juice and stir until the sugar has dissolved. Gradually stir
   in the milk and buttermilk. If a brighter green colour is desired,
   stir in the food colouring.
2 Working in batches if needed, pour the mixture into an
   ice-cream maker, filling it two-thirds full; store the remaining
   mixture in the refrigerator until ready to freeze. Following
   the manufacturer's instructions, freeze the sherbet. Leave in
   the ice-cream maker or place in the freezer to firm for 2 to
   4 hours before serving.
3 Remove the sherbet from the freezer 10 minutes before
   serving to soften slightly.

Strawberry Milk Sherbet

300 g strawberries, rinsed
  and hulled
1 cup (250 ml) milk
1 cup (220 g) sugar

Makes about 2 cups

Smooth as ice cream but made with milk for a lighter treat, this sherbet is easy to make at home and an inexpensive treat whenever you want it.

1 In a food processor or blender, purée the strawberries until just smooth.
2 In a saucepan, combine the milk and sugar over high heat and bring to a boil. Remove from the heat and leave until the milk mixture is just warm.
3 Pour the milk mixture into a bowl. Add the strawberry purée and whisk until well blended.
4 Pour the mixture into an ice-cream maker and freeze according to the manufacturer's instructions.

Cassis Sorbet

½ cup (110 g) sugar
1 cup (250 ml) cassis
  (blackcurrant liqueur)

Makes about 2 cups

A blackcurrant liqueur, cassis has a smooth, strong flavour that makes this sorbet particularly delicious as a formal dinner dessert – one that makes both your guests and your hip pocket happy.

1 In a saucepan, combine the sugar and 1½ cups (375 ml) water over high heat. Bring to a boil, stirring constantly until the sugar has dissolved. Remove from the heat and leave until the syrup is just warm.
2 Pour the syrup into a bowl. Add the cassis and stir until the mixture is well blended.
3 Pour the mixture into an ice-cream maker and freeze according to the manufacturer's instructions.

Citrus Sorbet

½ cup (110 g) sugar
1¼ cups (310 ml) orange juice
¼ cup (60 ml) lemon juice
¼ cup (60 ml) lime juice

Makes about 2 cups

Oranges, lemons and limes all lend their distinctive notes to this refreshing sorbet. This is one you're not likely to find in a shop!

1 In a saucepan, combine the sugar and 1 cup (250 ml) water over high heat. Bring to a boil, stirring constantly until the sugar has dissolved. Remove from the heat and leave until the syrup is just warm.
2 Pour the syrup into a bowl. Add all the citrus juice and stir until well blended.
3 Pour the mixture into an ice-cream maker and freeze according to the manufacturer's instructions.

Honeydew Sorbet

6 cups (1 kg) honeydew melon
  cubes
¾ cup (165 g) sugar
¼ cup (60 ml) Midori or other
  melon-flavoured liqueur

Makes about 2 cups

Serve a scoop of this delicate sorbet in a wedge of fresh
honeydew. Or try substituting your favourite melon in
this recipe.

1 Place all the ingredients in a food processor or blender and
   purée until blended to a smooth consistency. Refrigerate until
   completely chilled.
2 Pour the mixture into an ice-cream maker and freeze according
   to the manufacturer's instructions.

Lemon Sorbet

1½ cups (330 g) sugar
1 tablespoon grated lemon zest
1½ cups (375 ml) lemon juice

Makes about 1 litre

Wonderfully tart, this classic sorbet works either
as a dessert or as a palate cleanser between courses.
As a variation, add ½ cup (10 g) fresh mint leaves to
the syrup before it cools, then strain before freezing.

1 In a saucepan, combine the sugar and 3 cups (750 ml) water
   over high heat. Bring to a boil, stirring constantly until the
   sugar has dissolved. Remove from the heat and leave until
   the syrup is just warm.
2 Pour the syrup into a bowl. Add the lemon zest and lemon
   juice and stir until well blended.
3 Pour the mixture into an ice-cream maker and freeze according
   to the manufacturer's instructions. Leave the sorbet in the
   ice-cream maker or place in the freezer to firm for 2 to 4 hours
   before serving.
4 Remove the sorbet from the freezer 10 minutes before serving
   to soften slightly.

Raspberry Sorbet

300 g packet frozen
  raspberries, thawed
1 cup (220 g) sugar
1 tablespoon lemon juice

Makes about 2 cups

Since it uses frozen raspberries, you can make this
sorbet any time of the year. Try drizzling with a little
Chocolate Sauce (page 60) before serving.

1 In a food processor or blender, purée the raspberries
   until smooth.
2 In a saucepan, combine the sugar and 1 cup (250 ml) water
   over high heat. Bring to a boil, stirring constantly until the
   sugar has dissolved. Remove from the heat and leave until
   the syrup is just warm.
3 Pour the syrup into a bowl. Add the raspberry purée and
   lemon juice and stir until well blended.
4 Pour the mixture into an ice-cream maker and freeze
   according to the manufacturer's instructions.

Strawberry Sorbet

1 kg strawberries, rinsed
   and hulled
1¾ cups (300 g) sugar
2 cups (500 ml) orange juice,
   strained
2 tablespoons Grand Marnier
   or other orange-flavoured
   liqueur

Makes about 3 cups

Look for really ripe, firm red strawberries for their extraordinary flavour and ravishing colour. This sorbet is another treat you can make much better and more frugally at home.

1 Cut the strawberries in half and place in a small bowl with the sugar and orange juice. Mix gently and leave to stand for 1 hour.
2 In a food processor or blender, purée the strawberry mixture until smooth. Add the liqueur and pulse until well blended.
3 Pour the mixture into a large, shallow tin and freeze until just firm but not hard, 1 to 2 hours.
4 Spoon the mixture back into the food processor and pulse until the mixture becomes slushy. Refreeze, then repeat. Return the mixture to the tin and freeze until solid.
5 Before serving, place the tin in the refrigerator and let the sorbet soften slightly for about 15 minutes.

Frozen Iceblocks

Frozen Fruit Ice

85 g packet fruit-flavoured
   jelly crystals
10–12 plastic iceblock moulds
   or 100 ml paper cups
10–12 plastic iceblock sticks
   or spoons

Makes 10 to 12 ices

Whether you call them iceblocks, lollipops or popsicles, these treats are delicious on a hot summer's day.

1 In a bowl, combine the jelly crystals and 1 cup (250 ml) boiling water, stirring until completely dissolved. Stir in 200 ml cold water.
2 Pour the jelly mixture into the moulds or paper cups and freeze until the iceblocks are almost firm, about 2 hours.
3 Insert an iceblock stick or spoon into the centre of each iceblock. Freeze until firm, 4 to 8 hours.
4 To serve, unmould or tear the paper cup from the iceblock.

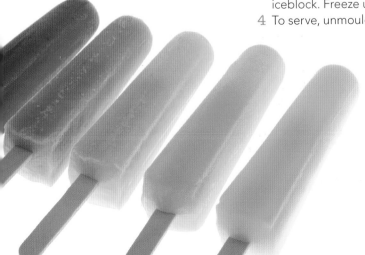

Frozen Jelly Yogurts

85 g packet fruit-flavoured
   jelly crystals
1½ cups (375 g) vanilla or
   natural yogurt
300 g chopped fruit, such
   as mango, strawberries
   or raspberries
10–12 plastic iceblock moulds
   or 100 ml paper cups
10–12 plastic iceblock sticks
   or spoons

Makes 10 to 12 jelly yogurts

Whip up these creamy, fruit-flavoured frozen yogurts at home – they go down very nicely on a hot day.

1 In a bowl, combine the jelly crystals and 1 cup (250 ml) boiling water, stirring until completely dissolved. Stir in 200 ml cold water. Cool the jelly to room temperature.
2 Whisk in the yogurt, then stir in the fruit.
3 Spoon the mixture into the moulds or paper cups and freeze until almost firm, about 2 hours.
4 Insert an iceblock stick or spoon into the centre of each yogurt. Freeze until the yogurts are firm, 2 to 4 hours.
5 To serve, unmould or tear away the paper cup from the pop.

Chocolate Pops

100 g packet instant chocolate
   pudding mix
3 cups (750 ml) milk
¼ cup (55 g) sugar
½ cup (125 ml) whipping
   cream
12–13 plastic iceblock moulds
   or 100 ml paper cups
12–13 plastic iceblock sticks
   or spoons

Makes 12 to 13 pops

A great way to enjoy chocolate when the going gets hot!

1 In a saucepan, combine the pudding mix, milk and sugar over medium heat. Bring to a boil and cook, stirring constantly, for 2 minutes. Remove from the heat and leave to stand for 30 minutes, stirring several times, until the mixture is cool.
2 In a small bowl, whip the cream until soft peaks form, using electric beaters. Fold the whipped cream into the milk mixture until well blended and no streaks of white remain.
3 Pour the mixture into the moulds or paper cups and freeze until firm, almost firm, about 2 hours.
4 Insert an iceblock stick or spoon into the centre of each pop. Freeze until the pops are firm, 2 to 4 hours.
5 To serve, unmould or tear away the paper cup from the pop.

Strawberry Pops

600 g strawberries, rinsed
   and hulled
½ cup (125 ml) apple juice
   concentrate
8 plastic iceblock moulds
   or 100 ml paper cups
8 plastic iceblock sticks
   or spoons

Makes 8 pops

Fresh strawberries make these pops extra special – much lovelier than any sold in the shops.

1 In a large bowl, mash the strawberries roughly, leaving some chunks of strawberry intact. Add the apple juice concentrate and stir until well blended.
2 Spoon or pour the mixture into the moulds or paper cups and freeze until the pops are almost firm, about 2 hours.
3 Insert an iceblock stick or spoon into the centre of each pop. Freeze until the pops are firm, 4 to 8 hours.
4 To serve, unmould or tear away the paper cup from the pop.

Tropical Pops

6 cups (1 kg) chopped fresh
  tropical fruit, such as
  pineapples, papayas and/or
  mangoes, peeled and cored
  as needed, cut into bite-sized
  pieces, reserving any juices
24 small plastic iceblock
  moulds, or ½ cup (125 ml)
  paper cups
3 cups (750 ml) mixed tropical
  fruit punch, or orange or
  pineapple juice
24 plastic iceblock sticks
  or spoons

Makes 24 pops

If you can't be sipping tropical drinks, you can at least keep your cool with these inexpensive tropical ices. This recipe makes 24 little pops, but you could make them in larger moulds or paper cups.

1 In a large bowl, combine the fresh fruit with any juices collected during their preparation. Stir well to distribute the fruits equally.
2 Spoon the fruit mixture into the moulds or paper cups, filling them three-quarters full.
3 Pour some of the fruit punch or juice into each mould or cup, leaving room at the top for the liquid to expand. Freeze until the pops are almost firm, about 2 hours.
4 Insert an iceblock stick or spoon into the centre of each pop. Freeze until the pops are firm, 4 to 8 hours.
5 To serve, unmould or tear away the paper cup from the pop.

Chocolate-nut Frozen Bananas

8 wooden skewers, with
  the sharp ends cut off
8 small bananas, peeled
225 g dark chocolate
3 tablespoons margarine
1 cup (125 g) chopped walnuts,
  toasted
1 cup (125 g) chopped
  macadamia nuts, toasted

Makes 8 servings

Bananas are one of those versatile fruits that can be frozen and eaten out of hand. But for a special treat, try dipping them in chocolate and nuts!

1 Line a baking tray with plastic wrap.
2 Insert one skewer into each banana, about halfway down the length of the fruit. Place the bananas on the baking tray, cover with plastic wrap and freeze until frozen solid, about 8 hours.
3 Place a small heatproof bowl over a saucepan of simmering water, ensuring the base of the bowl does not touch the water. Add the chocolate and margarine and melt, stirring occasionally. Remove the bowl from the heat.
4 On a shallow plate, combine the walnuts and macadamia nuts and toss to mix well.
5 Remove the bananas from the freezer. Holding one banana by the skewer over the bowl of chocolate, spoon the chocolate over the banana, coating it completely. Then hold the banana over the nuts and sprinkle them over the banana to coat the chocolate. Return the banana to the baking tray. Repeat to coat all the bananas.
6 Return the baking tray to the freezer until the chocolate hardens. Wrap each banana separately in plastic wrap, then place in a large, self-sealing freezer-safe plastic bag and store in the freezer.

Part 2

Health and Beauty Care

  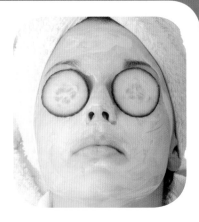

Face Care

Anti-wrinkle Eye Cream ❖ Tired Eye Remedy ❖ Simple Eye Makeup Remover ❖ Rich Neck Moisturiser ❖ Artichoke Facial ❖ Basic Skin Toner ❖ Peachy Complexion Cream ❖ Cucumber Astringent ❖ Eggwhite Toner ❖ Lemon Skin Toner ❖ Facial Cleansing Mask ❖ Green Clay Purifying Face Mask ❖ Deep-cleansing Facial ❖ Almond Mayonnaise Scrub ❖ Honey Mask ❖ Banana, Sour Cream and Honey Face Mask ❖ Youthful Skin Face Mask ❖ Oatmeal Exfoliant ❖ Mask for Oily Skin ❖ Galen's Cold Cream ❖ Strawberry Yogurt Mask

Care for Lips and Mouth

Honey Lip Balm ❖ Cocoa Lip Balm ❖ Chocolate Chip Lip Balm ❖ Refreshing Mouthwash ❖ Spicy, Minty Mouthwash ❖ Bacteria-fighting Citrus Mouthwash ❖ Toothpaste

Shampoos, Conditioners and Rinses

Beer Shampoo ❖ Dandruff Treatment ❖ Highlighting Rinse ❖ Chamomile Shampoo ❖ Instant Dry Shampoo ❖ Thick Hair Conditioner for Everyone ❖ Nourishing Conditioner ❖ Natural Head Lice Treatment

Body Care Treatments

Warm Herbal Body Treatment ❖ Citrus Moisturising Treatment ❖ Green Aloe Moisturising Lotion ❖ Shaving Gel for Women ❖ Summer Body Splash ❖ Simple Fragrant Body Splash ❖ Citrus Cologne Splash ❖ Cellulite Massage Oil ❖ Almond Exfoliating Body Scrub ❖ Simple Sugar Scrub for Dry Skin ❖ Cranberry Sugar Scrub ❖ Body Powder ❖ Body Spray ❖ Deodorant

Bath Products

Bubble Bath for Kids ❖ Conditioning Bubble Bath ❖ Bath Gel ❖ Liquid or Gel Soap ❖ Almond Rose Soap ❖ Cinnamon Soap ❖ Strawberries and Cream Bath Bags ❖ Herbal Bath Bag ❖ Cinnamon Oatmeal Milk Bath ❖ Gentle Milk Bath ❖ Zingy Citrus Bath Salts ❖ Bath Cookies ❖ Basic Bath Powder ❖ Easy Bath Powder ❖ Delicately Scented Bath Powder

Nail, Hand and Foot Care

Gardener's Hand Cream ❖ Cuticle Cream ❖ Warm Oil Hand Treatment ❖ Polenta Hand Scrub ❖ Love Your Feet Cream ❖ Soothing Footbath ❖ Eucalyptus Foot Lotion ❖ Strawberry Foot Scrub ❖ Refreshing Foot Spray ❖ Leg Massage Cream

Just for Men

Rosemary Shaving Soap ❖ Lightly Scented Aftershave ❖ Shaving-cut Lotion ❖ Aloe Aftershave Gel ❖ Muscle Rub

Your Own Beauty Products

Some of the most seductive ads on television and in magazines are for beauty products – scents and skin care products in beautiful packages.

They are all very intriguing and inviting until you read the small print and realise that you don't know what all those ingredients are or what they are designed to do. And, although you may feel that the price doesn't matter, you just might want to know what is going onto your skin.

Making your own beauty products is neither difficult nor mystifying. With just a little time and effort, you can even give yourself spa treatments that will benefit your spirits as well as your skin – with face masks, exfoliants and wrinkle fighters. Your wallet will be spared. You might even want to involve friends in the making and using of these recipes for special spa treatment sessions.

For everyday use, you can make cleansers, moisturisers and toners; toothpaste and gargles; shampoos and hair rinses; shaving gels and refreshing splashes – with or without scent. For your bath, you can prepare lovely bath gels from soap slivers; almond, rose or cinnamon soap; and several bath scrubs and milk baths. For hands and feet, there are special creams and soaks. There is also a selection of recipes for homemade men's toiletries: shaving soap, aftershaves, a shaving-cut lotion and a muscle rub.

Face Care

Anti-wrinkle Eye Cream

30 ml elder flower water
¼ cup (60 ml) avocado oil
30 ml almond oil
20 ml wheatgerm oil
30 ml lanolin
30 ml glycerine
2 drops geranium essential oil
1 vitamin E capsule, 500 IU

Apply this cream with a gentle touch around the eye, using light, circular strokes. It is especially geared for the soft tissue under and around the eyes.

1 Warm the elder flower water in a non-reactive saucepan over low heat.
2 In the top of a double boiler, set over simmering water, warm the avocado, almond and wheatgerm oils. Stir in the lanolin until melted. Remove from heat.
3 Gradually beat in the warmed elder flower water. Stir in the glycerine and geranium essential oil. Pierce the vitamin E capsule with a needle, squeeze out the contents, and stir in.
4 Pour the mixture into a clean wide-mouthed 170 g glass jar with a tight-fitting lid. Store in a cool, dark place.

Tired Eye Remedy

1 cup (250 ml) boiling water
2–3 rose petals

Here's a simple soak you can apply to soothe irritated or inflamed eyes. The price is just a few rose petals from your garden.

1 Pour the boiling water over the rose petals into a bowl. Steep for about 10 minutes. Cool and strain the petals out.
2 Soak 2 large cotton balls in the rose tea and apply over closed eyelids. Rest and relax.

Simple Eye Makeup Remover

1 teaspoon glycerine
3 teaspoons distilled water
20 ml olive, jojoba or baby oil

Why should you spend good money on eye makeup remover when you can make a pure and gentle but very effective solution in your own kitchen?

1 Shake all the ingredients in a small glass bottle.
2 Apply a little solution to makeup remover pads or a cottonwool ball, press against the eyelid for a minute to loosen makeup, then gently wipe the makeup away.

Fast relief with witch hazel eye compresses

We give our eyes a constant workout while reading, watching TV and staring at the computer screen. Here's a basic eye care remedy that costs very little and provides a very valuable service. Just keep a small jar of witch hazel in the refrigerator. Soak 2 cotton pads in the chilled liquid, lie down, cover both eyelids, and relax for 5 minutes.

Rich Neck Moisturiser

1 teaspoon dried chamomile
1¼ cups (310 ml) boiling water
45 ml avocado oil
45 ml almond oil
2 teaspoons jojoba oil
30 g shaved or grated
  cosmetic-grade beeswax
2 teaspoons glycerine
20 drops lemon essential oil

In your beauty regimen, don't forget the neck, which can show the first signs of ageing. Products like this often sell at beauty counters for a considerable amount of money, but you can make it quite inexpensively with natural ingredients. This recipe uses oils to keep the skin supple. Use a small amount and massage from the neckline all the way to the chin.

1 Place the chamomile in a large cup and add the boiling water. Cover and allow to steep for 15 minutes. Strain the liquid into another cup.
2 In the top of a double boiler, set over simmering water, warm the avocado, almond and jojoba oils. Add the beeswax. Stir until melted. Remove from heat and beat in 30 ml of the warmed chamomile infusion, drop by drop until the mixture thickens and cools. Thoroughly mix in the glycerine and lemon essential oil.
3 Spoon into a sterilised, wide-mouthed, 170 g glass or ceramic jar with a tight-fitting lid. Store in a cool, dark place.

Know your skin type

To pick the best products for your skin, you need to know your skin type. Most people have a combination of skin types – particularly on the face – where oily areas around the chin, nose and forehead are different from the normal or dry skin around the eyes and on the cheeks. There are four basic skin types:

❖ **Normal skin** is clear, supple, and soft. It is neither too dry nor too oily, and it is not overly sensitive to sun, humidity or the environment.
❖ **Dry skin** looks dull, feels tight after washing, and needs sun protection and frequent moisturising to prevent flaking.
❖ **Oily skin** feels soft and supple, but it looks shiny and needs cleaning several times a day. Oily skin tends to support large pores and is more prone to pimples and blackheads than dry or normal skin.
❖ **Sensitive skin** is easily burned by the sun and irritated by chemicals found in many commercial skin products that may cause rashes or blotching.

Artichoke Facial

1 fresh artichoke heart, well cooked, or canned hearts in water, not oil
2 teaspoons light oil (avocado, olive or canola)
1 teaspoon vinegar or fresh lemon juice

Artichoke conditions dry or damaged skin. It reduces flaking and restores suppleness. Enjoy making this recipe in your kitchen laboratory.

1 Mash the artichoke heart in a ceramic bowl. Mix in the oil and vinegar or lemon juice. Stir well until a smooth paste is formed.
2 Massage on your face and neck. Let sit for 10 to 15 minutes. Rinse off with warm water and pat dry.

Basic Skin Toner

1 teaspoon dried chamomile
⅓ cup (80 ml) boiling water
2 drops essential oil

A gentle cleanser or first step in your daily ritual. You can custom-design this basic skin toner to suit your skin type. See the box on page 259 to choose the essential oils that are right for you.

1 Place the chamomile and boiling water in a cup. Cover and allow to steep for 15 minutes. Strain the liquid through a fine sieve into a sterile ½ cup (125 ml) glass bottle that has a tight-fitting lid. When cool, add the essential oil and shake well to mix. Allow to stand for 48 hours, shaking periodically.
2 Pour the liquid through a paper coffee filter into a sterile glass bottle. Cap the bottle and store in a cool, dark place.
3 Apply daily with a cotton ball.

Peachy Complexion Cream

1 ripe peach
thick (double) cream

This wonderful rich combination is easily made. You'll find it helps give your complexion that fabled glow. And you can't find anything like it in the shops.

1 Mash the peach by hand or purée it in a food processor.
2 Add enough cream to the pulp to give you a soft, creamy mixture. Spoon into a clean glass jar with a tight-fitting lid and store in the refrigerator.
3 Once a day, apply the mixture to your face and massage in.

Fixed oil vs. essential oil

Olive oil, almond oil and vegetable oils are all derived primarily from seeds. They are 'fixed oils' that are non-volatile. Essential oils, distilled from leaves or flowers, are volatile and flammable. They evaporate even at low temperatures, and they are potentially toxic if they are inhaled or used incorrectly.

Most essential oils must be diluted in a fixed, or 'carrier', oil before they are applied to the skin. The exceptions are lavender and tea-tree essential oils, but even they should be used sparingly.

Cucumber Astringent

1 cucumber

Straight from your garden or the greengrocer, you can make this skin bracer in a jiffy. In summer, this is a refreshing and light treat for your skin. But any time of year, a simple cucumber astringent will perk you up.

1 Peel the cucumber and purée it in a food processor. Apply the purée to your skin using a cotton pad, gently swathing your face. Rinse off with cool water.
2 Refrigerate any leftovers in a clean, covered container. The mixture should keep for 1 to 2 days.

Eggwhite Toner

1 eggwhite

For the price of an egg, you can make this one-ingredient toner that leaves your skin feeling tight and silky smooth.

1 Clean your face thoroughly using any natural cleanser.
2 Whisk the eggwhite just before applying it to your face. Leave it on for about 15 minutes.
3 Wash off with tepid water and pat skin dry.

Lemon Skin Toner

¼ cup (60 ml) lemon juice
½ cup (125 ml) distilled water
⅓ cup (80 ml) witch hazel

You can toss this toner together in just a few seconds from items you have in your pantry. Total cost to you: small change.

1 Combine all the ingredients. Pour into a clean bottle or decorative cosmetics container. Shake well before using. Apply with a clean cotton ball.
2 Keep in the refrigerator indefinitely.

Facial Cleansing Mask

7 g packet dry yeast
3 drops lemon juice
2 teaspoons water

This simple recipe is aimed at deep cleansing and is especially suited for young faces and the treatment of oily skin.

1 In a small bowl, mix the yeast, lemon juice and water vigorously until a thick paste forms. If necessary, add more water to achieve the correct consistency for applying to the face.
2 Pat the mixture on the face, avoiding the eyes. Allow to sit for 10 to 15 minutes. Rinse off with warm water. Pat skin dry.

Green Clay Purifying Face Mask

1 teaspoon apricot kernel oil
2 drops palmarosa
3 teaspoons green (bentonite) clay powder
warm water

Green clay – also known as bentonite – is the most commonly used clay in face masks. It can absorb large quantities of water. In this mask, it is used to draw out excess sebum and dirt from deep down, making the mask suited to oily complexions. Green clay powder can be purchased online or in health-food shops, and is a much cheaper option than commercially prepared masks. Palmarosa is an essential oil available at health-food or 'new age' shops.

1 Clean your face thoroughly using any natural cleanser. In a small dish, mix the apricot oil and the palmarosa together. Put the green clay in a small bowl and stir in the apricot oil mixture. Add just enough warm water to make a spreadable paste. With your fingers, work the mixture thoroughly to incorporate all the ingredients.
2 Apply the mask immediately, avoiding the eyes. Let it sit for 10 to 15 minutes. As the moisture evaporates, you will feel the mask tighten.
3 Rinse the mask off with warm water, pat skin dry and follow with an application of toner and then moisturiser.

Instant grape cleanser for your face

Here's a sweet way to clean and refresh your skin. Split 3 or 4 large green or red grapes, remove any seeds, and rub the fleshy interior on your face and neck. The grapes condition your skin and reduce dryness, restoring suppleness. Rinse with cool water and gently pat skin dry.

Deep-cleansing Facial

3 teaspoons yogurt (any kind)
3 teaspoons finely ground
  oatmeal
½ teaspoon honey

Imagine! You can mix up this deep-cleansing face mask for less than the cost of a morning newspaper.

1. Before starting, clean your face thoroughly with any natural cleanser so that you can immediately apply the deep-cleansing facial mixture when it has been stirred together.
2. In a clean bowl, combine the yogurt and oatmeal and mix to a spreadable consistency. In a small glass bowl sitting in a larger bowl of hot water, warm the honey and pour it into the yogurt and oatmeal mixture. Using a spoon, blend.
3. Immediately apply the mask to your face, avoiding the eyes, and let it stay on for 10 to 15 minutes. Wash it off with warm water. Pat skin dry and apply a toner and moisturiser.

Almond Mayonnaise Scrub

¼ cup (40 g) whole, natural
  almonds
⅛ teaspoon mayonnaise
1 teaspoon red wine or cider
  vinegar
½ cup (125 ml) water

Don't be afraid of this one, but keep in mind that it is for very dry skin. Mayonnaise will nourish the face. Almonds will provide a mild exfoliation.

1. Clean your face thoroughly with any natural cleanser. Grind the almonds in a blender or food processor until they form a meal. Whirl in the mayonnaise. Set aside.
2. In a small bowl, combine the vinegar and water. Rinse your face with this mixture.
3. Now gently and thoroughly massage your face with the almond-mayonnaise scrub. Leave it on your skin for 10 minutes. Rinse off with warm water and pat skin dry.

Honey Mask

⅔ cup (85 g) quick-cook oats
½ cup (125 ml) hot water
½ apple, cored but with peel on
40 g plain yogurt
30 ml honey
1 eggwhite

The mask's ingredients would make up a solid breakfast, but they're nourishing for your skin, too. For the cost of a bowl of cereal, it's a good deal for a meal or a mask.

1. Clean your face thoroughly with any natural cleanser. In a small bowl, stir the oats into the hot water until you have a smooth mixture. Let stand for about 5 minutes or until the mixture thickens to a paste.
2. Put the apple, yogurt, honey, and eggwhite in a blender or food processor and pulse for 45 seconds just to mix. Now add the oat mixture and pulse for 20 seconds more.
3. Apply this mask evenly to the face, avoiding the eyes, and let sit for 15 minutes or until skin feels tight. Rinse thoroughly with warm water and pat skin dry.

Banana, Sour Cream and Honey Face Mask

½ banana
3 teaspoons honey
30 ml sour cream

Although this recipe sounds somewhat like dessert, it's actually an enriching mask for your face. The banana is an astringent, the honey conditions and the sour cream binds them together in a mask. You could travel to a fancy spa for a treatment like this, but making it at home will cost you next to nothing. Enjoy!

1 Clean your face thoroughly with any natural cleanser. In a small bowl, mash the half-banana. Stir in the honey and sour cream.

2 Apply to your face, avoiding the eyes, and let set for 10 minutes. Gently wipe off with a damp washcloth. Rinse clean with warm water. Pat your skin dry.

Youthful Skin Face Mask

¼ cup (60 ml) thick (double) cream
1 medium banana
1 vitamin E capsule, 500 IU

In this variation of the banana facial mask, banana is again the astringent. It induces a tightening or tingling sensation and thereby gives the effect of decreasing the appearance of wrinkles.

1 Clean your face thoroughly with any natural cleanser. In a small bowl, mash together the cream and banana. Pierce the vitamin E capsule with a needle, squeeze out the contents, and stir in.

2 Smooth onto your face and neck. Leave on for 10 to 15 minutes. Remove with damp cloth. Rinse clean with warm water. Pat your skin dry.

When Vitamin E is called for

Several of the recipes in this part of the book call for using vitamin E. You can buy vitamin E oil as a liquid at most pharmacies, but when you only need a small amount, it's sometimes more practical to use a 500 IU vitamin E capsule. Just pierce the capsule with a needle and squeeze out the contents.

A quick banana wrinkle fighter

Peel away the years with this easy facial treatment. Banana is an astringent that induces a tightening or tingling sensation on the skin, which helps decrease the appearance of wrinkles. When bananas are at their best and cheapest, this is a very reasonable facial treatment. Clean your face thoroughly with any natural cleanser. Mash ¼ of a ripe banana until very creamy and spread it all over your face, avoiding the eyes. Leave on for 15 to 20 minutes. Rinse with warm water and then splash cold water on your face. Gently pat your skin dry.

Oatmeal Exfoliant

2 heaped teaspoons fine
   oatmeal
1 teaspoon bicarbonate of soda
lukewarm water

Here's a treat for your face that might be part of a spa regimen. You can mix this up in a jiffy to use as a cleanser anytime you're in the mood. Cost to you: almost negligible.

1 Clean your face thoroughly with any natural cleanser.
2 In a small bowl, stir together the oatmeal and bicarbonate of soda. (The oatmeal needs to be fine; if necessary, first pulse it in a food processor or blender.) Add enough lukewarm water to make a paste. Apply to face and rub gently. Rinse and gently pat the skin dry.

Mask for Oily Skin

1 teaspoon brewer's yeast
⅓ cup (90 g) yogurt, or as
   needed

The combination of brewer's yeast and yogurt deep-cleanses oily skin without over-drying. This inexpensive homemade mask leaves skin feeling fresh and revitalised.

1 Clean your face thoroughly with any natural cleanser. In a small bowl, mix the brewer's yeast with the yogurt to make a thin paste. Pat this mixture onto the oily areas of your face. Allow the mask to dry for 15 to 20 minutes.
2 Rinse with warm water. Splash with cool water. Gently pat dry.

Galen's Cold Cream

30 g cosmetic-grade beeswax, grated or shaved

⅓ cup (80 ml) light olive oil

30 ml distilled water or rose water

3 drops geranium essential oil

This recipe for cold cream is believed to have been devised by the Greek philosopher and doctor, Galen, in the 2nd century AD. It is still every bit as effective today and will cost you very little compared to the name brands at cosmetics counters.

1 In the top of a double boiler, over simmering water, melt the beeswax gently.

2 In a small saucepan over low heat, heat the oil slightly and then pour it into the melted wax. Using a fork, beat this mixture until combined.

3 Now heat the water or rose water in the saucepan and then stir it into the oil and wax mixture, one drop at a time. Remove from heat and stir until the mixture is cooled and thick. Stir in the essential oil.

4 Using a wooden spoon, put the mixture into a clean 150 g wide-mouthed jar with a tight-fitting lid. Store in a cool, dark place for several months.

How to apply a face mask

Women have used face masks for centuries to clean and tone the skin, and give it a glowing vitality. Face masks give their best results if used regularly – once a week is not too often.

1 To make the process easier, sit or stand before a mirror. Cover your shoulders with a clean towel and have a damp washcloth or hand towel ready for wiping up any drips.

2 Apply the mask with a clean cotton ball or with your fingers. The mask should cover your face from the hairline to the chin, missing only the area around the eyes.

3 Leave the mask on for 15 minutes the first few times you use it. Later, if your skin is not irritated and you like the mask's effects, you can slowly increase the time to 30 minutes. To best enjoy the facial mask, lie down, shut your eyes, and relax while the mask is working.

4 When the time is up, remove the mask with your fingers over a basin. If the mask has dried, splash warm water on your face and try again to remove the mask with your fingers. Then use a wet washcloth to remove the last residue of the mask. Finally, splash your face with cool water, pat the skin dry, and apply a toner and moisturiser.

Strawberry Yogurt Mask

1 handful ripe strawberries
3 teaspoons ground almonds
30 g yogurt

If you grow strawberries in your garden, pluck a few to use in this treatment. Your face will thank you for this gentle, delicious treat that leaves the skin smooth and refreshed.

1 Clean your face thoroughly with any natural cleanser. In a small bowl, mash the strawberries and almonds until completely blended together. Stir in the yogurt to make a spreadable paste.
2 Apply immediately or refrigerate and use within 1 day on a clean face.

Care for Lips and Mouth

Honey Lip Balm

90 g cosmetic-grade beeswax, grated or shaved
½ cup (125 ml) extra virgin olive oil
30 g honey
½ capsule vitamin E, 500 IU

You'll get a kick out of making lip balm at home. You'll feel a little bit like a mad scientist, and a little bit like a truly creative cook. The following three formulations are inexpensive to make and provide a lot of lip gloss or balm for the buck. Consider dividing the lip balm mixture into several small containers, so that you can carry some with you.

1 In a microwave or the top of a double boiler, melt the beeswax and oil together. Do not boil. If the mixture starts to boil, remove from heat and allow it to cool. Once the beeswax and oil are blended, stir in the honey. Then pierce the vitamin E capsule with a needle, squeeze out half the contents, and stir in. Pour the resulting mixture into clean containers with tops.
2 Let the lip balm sit at room temperature for 48 hours until it arrives at the proper consistency for spreading. You can carry a small container of lip balm around with you during the day, but you may find it keeps better in the refrigerator overnight.

Cocoa Lip Balm

90 g cosmetic-grade beeswax,
  grated or shaved
½ cup (125 ml) extra virgin
  olive oil
½ teaspoon cocoa powder
½ capsule vitamin E, 500 IU

Remember, although this concoction smells sweet, it is not a food product. If you plan to give the balm to a child, label it accordingly and explain how to use it.

1   In a microwave or the top of a double boiler, melt the beeswax and oil together. Do not boil. If the mixture starts to boil, remove from the heat and allow it to cool. Once the beeswax and oil are blended, stir in the cocoa powder. Pierce the vitamin E capsule with a needle, squeeze out half the contents, and stir it in. Pour the resulting mixture into clean containers with tops.

2   Let the lip balm sit for 48 hours at room temperature until it arrives at the proper consistency for spreading. You can carry a small container of lip balm around with you during the day, but you may find it keeps better in the refrigerator overnight.

Chocolate Chip Lip Balm

90 g cosmetic-grade beeswax,
  grated or shaved
½ cup (125 ml) extra virgin
  olive oil
½ capsule vitamin E, 500 IU
3–6 chocolate chips

When you cook up this little treat in your kitchen, you may be tempted to eat it, but this yummy-smelling lip balm is not a food. Be sure to label it as lip balm and to supervise its use on children.

1   In a microwave or the top of a double boiler, melt the beeswax and oil together. Do not boil. If the mixture starts to boil, remove from the heat and allow it to cool. Once the beeswax and oil are blended, pierce the vitamin E capsule with a needle, squeeze out half the contents, and stir in. Stir in the chocolate chips and pour the resulting mixture into clean containers with tops.

2   Let the lip balm sit for 48 hours at room temperature until it arrives at the proper consistency for spreading. You can carry a small container of lip balm around with you during the day, but you may find it keeps better in the refrigerator overnight.

A fast, hard-working mouthwash

For fighting bacteria and removing food particles caught in your teeth, this inexpensive recipe is about as effective a mouthwash as you can get. It uses the standard 3 per cent hydrogen peroxide sold in pharmacies. Hydrogen peroxide, however, may irritate sensitive teeth or delicate tissue in the mouth, so this rinse should not be used any more than 3 times a week. In a cup, mix 30 ml hydrogen peroxide solution with 30 ml water. Swish the mixture in your mouth for 30 seconds, then spit it out – don't swallow it.

Refreshing Mouthwash

1 cup (250 ml) water
15 g angelica seeds
dash of peppermint oil
   or lemon verbena

For just a few cents or pence, you can cook up a potful of this rinse that tastes good and can be safely used as often as you like. Unlike more expensive commercial mouthwashes, it has no alcohol.

1 In a small saucepan over medium heat, bring the water to a boil. Remove from the heat. Stir in the angelica seeds and peppermint oil or lemon verbena. Let the mixture sit for 10 minutes. Strain off and discard the solids.
2 Store the liquid in a clean, covered container in the refrigerator and use every day. It should keep indefinitely.

Spicy, Minty Mouthwash

1 cup (250 ml) water
1 teaspoon whole cloves
1 teaspoon ground cinnamon
1 teaspoon peppermint extract
2 teaspoons finely chopped
   fresh parsley

This simple recipe offers a kick that will make your mouth feel wonderful for hours. Use it as often as you like – it's inexpensive and doesn't burn like some commercial mouthwashes with alcohol in them.

1 In a small saucepan, bring the water to a boil over medium heat. Remove the pan from the stove and stir in the cloves, cinnamon, peppermint extract and parsley. Let the mixture sit for 10 minutes. Strain off the solids.
2 Pour the liquid into a clean, tightly covered container and store in the refrigerator, where it will keep indefinitely. Use as a gargle and mouthwash.

Bacteria-fighting Citrus Mouthwash

¾ cup (185 ml) vodka
30 drops lemon essential oil
25 drops bergamot essential oil
1¼ cups (310 ml) distilled
   water

Fight the damaging bacteria that dwell in your mouth with this lemon-tasting mouthwash with an alcohol base that acts as a disinfectant. Rinse and swish or gargle, but don't swallow the liquid.

1 Place the vodka and the lemon and bergamot essential oils in a sterilised 500 ml glass bottle with a tight-fitting lid. Shake the mixture vigorously to combine.
2 Add the distilled water and shake until well blended. Leave in the refrigerator for 1 week to mature, shaking the bottle from time to time.
3 To use, shake the bottle and mix 1 part of the mixture with 3 parts lukewarm distilled water in a small drinking glass. Rinse, but do not swallow the mouthwash.

Toothpaste

½ cup (140 g) bicarbonate
  of soda
2 teaspoons salt
3 teaspoons glycerine
10 or more drops peppermint
  or wintergreen flavouring
1 drop green or blue food
  colouring (optional)
warm water

Once you perfect your own homemade toothpaste recipe by adjusting the ingredients to your liking, you should be able to keep a family of four in toothpaste for a whole year for less than the cost of one commercial tube!

1 In a small bowl, mix the bicarbonate of soda and salt. Add the glycerine, flavouring and, if desired, 1 drop food colouring. Add warm water, a drop at a time, until the texture and consistency seem right. Spoon the mixture into a clean squeeze bottle or any convenient, clean container with a tight lid.
2 You may have to adjust the amount of glycerine to arrive at a consistency that suits you. This toothpaste will keep indefinitely in a covered container.

Shampoos, Conditioners and Rinses

Beer Shampoo

¾ cup (185 ml) beer
1 cup (250 ml) shampoo
  (any kind)

This concoction will leave your hair with wonderful body. The proteins from the malt and hops in the beer coat the hair and build it up, helping to repair damage.

1 In a non-reactive pan, boil the beer until it reduces to ¼ cup (60 ml). Cool the beer and add it to the 1 cup of shampoo in a clean bottle with a tight cap.
2 Wash your hair as usual. Rinse thoroughly.

Dandruff Treatment

2 teaspoons dried rosemary
2 teaspoons dried thyme
⅔ cup (170 ml) boiling water
⅔ cup (170 ml) cider vinegar

Over-the-counter dandruff treatments can be costly. You can create this herbal remedy for considerably less than you'll pay for a commercial treatment.

1 Place the herbs in a heatproof ceramic bowl. Pour in the boiling water. Cover and allow to steep for 15 to 20 minutes.
2 Strain the liquid into a clean, 300 ml bottle with a tight-fitting lid. Add the vinegar and shake. Store in a cool, dark place.
3 After shampooing, rinse hair thoroughly and then massage a small amount of the herbal treatment into the scalp. Between shampoos, massage a small amount into the scalp before going to bed.

A quick, sweet-smelling vinegar hair rinse

Pick up a bottle of raspberry or plum vinegar at your next shop. It's inexpensive in the supermarket and can do double duty in the kitchen. Use a few spoonfuls for this recipe and the rest for salad dressings.

Rather than prepare this rinse ahead of time, simply bring a clean 1 or 2 cup (250–500 ml) measuring cup containing 30–45 ml scented vinegar into the shower. After shampooing, add water and rinse your hair with the solution. You can use this every time you shampoo, if you like.

Vinegar restores the proper acidic pH balance to hair. This rinse will remove remnants of shampoo and give your hair more shine.

Highlighting Rinse

juice of 1 lemon
2 teaspoons chamomile tea

This is a rich hair dressing that provides sheen and elegance to tired hair. People with light-coloured hair will find that it helps them get clean, honest-looking highlights. It can also be used as a pressing solution for hair straightening.

1 In a small bowl, mix the lemon juice and tea. To achieve blonde highlights, use an inexpensive straw hat with lots of holes in it. Pull strands of hair you would like to lighten through the holes with a crochet hook or pencil.
2 Douse the strands with the rinse. Sit in the sun for 1½ hours, protecting your body from the sun's rays, of course.

What herbs in hair rinses do

❖ **Chamomile** Keeps scalp and hair follicles healthy
❖ **Comfrey** Soothes scalp irritations
❖ **Elder berries** Traditionally used to add colour to grey hair
❖ **Lemongrass** Tones scalp
❖ **Nettle** An astringent that helps relieve skin irritations and itching
❖ **Parsley** Helps to relieve skin irritations

❖ **Rosemary** Believed to enhance colour of dark hair and help control dandruff
❖ **Sage** An astringent for oily hair and a benefit for damaged or fragile hair
❖ **Thyme** Has antiseptic, tonic and astringent properties
❖ **Yarrow** Acts as a tonic for the hair

Chamomile Shampoo

1 handful fresh or dried
  chamomile flowers
1¼ cups (310 ml) boiling water
15 g pure soap flakes or
  leftover slivers of soap
3 teaspoons glycerine
5 drops yellow food colouring

This mild shampoo leaves your hair clean and healthy. The recipe gives you a chance to use those leftover slivers of soap that you wonder why you save. Forget those well-advertised, costly shampoos – you need only 3 teaspoons of this inexpensive shampoo per washing.

1 Place the flowers in a heatproof bowl and add the boiling water. Let stand for 15 minutes, then strain into another heatproof bowl.
2 Clean out the first bowl. Combine in it the soap flakes and the chamomile mixture and let them stand until the soap softens – a few minutes. Beat in the glycerine and food colouring until well blended.
3 Pour the mixture into a clean 450 ml bottle with a tight-fitting lid. Keep in a cool, dark place.

Instant Dry Shampoo

3 teaspoons cornflour or finely
  ground oatmeal

This home-style, penny-pinching recipe is tailor-made for that moment when you need a quick pick-me-up or you haven't got time to wash your hair.

1 Sprinkle small amounts of cornflour or oatmeal onto the hair, lifting it up in sections to let the powder get to the scalp. Rub the dry shampoo through the hair to absorb excess oil.
2 Comb the hair to remove tangles, then spend 5 to 10 minutes brushing (depending on the length and thickness of the hair) to remove all traces of the powder and prevent the suggestion of dandruff. Shake and blow on your hairbrush to clean it while you brush your hair.

Thick Hair Conditioner for Everyone

½ ripe avocado
¼ cup (60 ml) coconut milk,
  or as needed

This two-ingredient conditioner offers a protein boost for your hair that in turn will make it feel thicker and more luxuriant. You don't need to go to an expensive hair salon to revitalise your hair.

1 In a small bowl, mash the avocado with a spoon. Mix in the coconut milk to form a thick gel-like substance.
2 Apply entire recipe to clean hair and comb through. Leave the conditioner on the hair for 10 to 15 minutes. Rinse thoroughly.

Nourishing Conditioner

30 ml olive oil
3 teaspoons lemon juice
½ teaspoon apple cider vinegar
1 egg

Use this to leave your hair feeling cleansed and enriched at a fraction of the cost of salon treatments.

1 In a blender, combine the ingredients and whirl until blended. Alternatively, whisk vigorously until combined.
2 Use entire recipe to condition hair after a regular shampoo. Leave on the hair for 10 to 15 minutes. Rinse clean.

Natural Head Lice Treatment

¼ cup (60 ml) olive oil
20 drops tea-tree oil
15 drops rosemary essential oil
15 drops lemon essential oil
15 drops thyme essential oil
small amount of regular
   shampoo (any kind)

Try this herbal remedy for an effective, gentler alternative to those harsh commercial treatments.

1 Combine the olive oil and essential oils in a small bowl, add a small amount of shampoo and mix well.
2 Massage into dry hair, making sure it is thoroughly covered.
3 Cover the hair with a towel, plastic wrap or a shower cap and leave for 1 hour.
4 Shampoo the mixture out of the hair, then comb the hair carefully with a nit comb to remove any dead lice and nits.

Body Care Treatments

Warm Herbal Body Treatment

8 cups (2 litres) water
4 chamomile tea bags or other
   gentle herbal tea
3 peppermint tea bags
sprigs of fresh rosemary or
   sage (optional)

This warm, scented spa-style treatment will relax and rejuvenate you – for the cost of a few tea bags!

1 In a large saucepan, bring the water to a boil. Remove from heat and add the tea bags and herbs. Cover pan and steep for 10 to 15 minutes. Once the tea has cooled to a comfortably warm temperature, remove the tea bags and herbs.
2 Drop several clean but dispensable hand towels into the tea until saturated, then wring them out. Wrap your upper arms and legs with the tea-soaked towels. You may also place a soaked towel on your torso, but don't put one on your face.
3 Lie down on a protected bed, couch or pad and rest for 10 to 15 minutes. Remove the towels and relax while cooling off for another 10 to 15 minutes. Shower off the residue.

Caution: Heat treatments such as this are not recommended for people with high blood pressure or heart problems.

Citrus Moisturising Treatment

1 egg yolk
30 ml lemon juice
1 cup (250 ml) olive oil

This creamy moisturiser will leave your skin soft and silky, while barely leaving a mark on your grocery bill.

1 In a medium bowl, whisk the egg yolk, lemon juice and olive oil together until the mixture reaches a creamy consistency. Thin with more lemon juice as desired.
2 Massage into your skin as an intense moisturising treatment before a shower or bath. Apply a light coating on your hands, arms, legs and face. Gently massage into nails and cuticles. Apply about 1 tablespoon to each foot. Gently massage your toes, one by one, and then the arch of your foot, moving to the heel. Relax and allow the moisturiser to soak in for 10 to 15 minutes. Wipe away the excess and then step into the shower or tub to complete the treatment.
3 Store any leftovers in the refrigerator for a day or two.

Green Aloe Moisturising Lotion

1 cup (250 ml) aloe vera gel
1 teaspoon vitamin E oil (if necessary, break several 500 IU capsules)
5–10 drops essential oil of your choosing
25 g cosmetic-grade beeswax, grated or shaved
½ cup (125 ml) vegetable oil

It takes no time and very little money to cook up this delightful body lotion that has aloe vera, an antioxidant, as its primary ingredient. You scoop the gel out of aloe vera leaves or you can buy it at a health-food shop.

1 In a medium bowl, stir together the aloe vera gel, vitamin E and essential oil. Set aside.
2 In the top of a double boiler over simmering water, melt together the beeswax and vegetable oil. Stir until smooth and well blended. Remove from heat.
3 Slowly and continuously pour the melted mixture into the bowl with the aloe vera mixture, using a handheld electric mixer at slow speed to combine. Run a clean rubber spatula around the rim of the bowl to incorporate all the ingredients. Continue mixing until all the ingredients are blended.
4 Pour the final mixture into one sterilised 350 g jar or two sterilised 170 g jars with tight-fitting lids. You can use sterilised jam jars, if you have them. Keep the lotion in the refrigerator for up to 6 weeks.

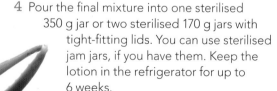

The best body oil for your skin type

To make body oil, put 20 ml almond oil in a small sterile glass jar with a tight-fitting lid. Add the appropriate drops of essential oils listed below for your skin type, shake and pour a little into your palm, so that you can apply it to the rest of your body. Each blend will give you four body rubs.

Normal skin
8 drops lavender
6 drops geranium
2 drops chamomile

Dry skin
8 drops patchouli
4 drops geranium
2 drops carrot

Oily skin
10 drops lemon
6 drops geranium
4 drops sandalwood

Sensitive skin
3 drops geranium
2 drops patchouli

Shaving Gel for Women

30 ml conditioner
30 ml shampoo (preferably the same brand as the conditioner used)
½–1 teaspoon baby oil
1 teaspoon hand cream

Using just four ingredients you probably already have at home, you can make your very own gel for shaving legs and underarms. It's a good recipe to make in a pinch, but it will also help you cut one more expense from your weekly shopping bill.

1 Start with a clean bottle with a secure cap. Pour the conditioner into the bottle, then add the shampoo. Mix together. Add the baby oil and then the hand cream. Secure top and shake until all the ingredients are well blended. Let mixture sit for about 1 hour before using.
2 Lather legs or underarms with the gel, shave and rinse skin thoroughly. The shaving gel should keep for about 1 month in the bathroom. If the mixture separates, just shake it up before you use it.

Summer Body Splash

⅓ cup (80 ml) vodka
10 drops lavender essential oil
5 drops lime essential oil
5 drops lemon essential oil
5 drops lemongrass essential oil
2 cups (500 ml) distilled or boiled water

Refresh yourself with a splash of this delicate mixture of fruit and flower scents just perfect for hot summer days and nights.

1 Pour the vodka and essential oils into a sterilised 600 ml bottle with a tight-fitting stopper. Stopper the bottle and shake for several minutes. Add the distilled or boiled water and shake for several minutes more. Set aside for at least 48 hours or up to 3 weeks.
2 Place a paper coffee filter in a sieve and drip the liquid through the filter into a ceramic or glass bowl. Pour the liquid back into the large bottle or into a few smaller sterilised bottles. Keep one bottle in the refrigerator and store the others in a cool, dark place until needed.

What is a cool, dark place?

When you make home remedies and beauty products, you are usually told to store them in a cool, dark, dry place. Where is that?

If you seal things in amber or opaque containers, that takes care of dark (most homemade preparations are weakened by exposure to sunlight). A cool, dry place could be the linen cupboard or a shelf in a wardrobe that is not near any hot pipes, or a garage cupboard if the garage is dry. A safe last resort is the refrigerator.

Simple Fragrant Body Splash

1 cup (250 ml) water
drops perfume oil

If you have a favourite perfume oil that you'd like to wear in a lighter concentration, you'll love this easy recipe. Keep this spritzer in your purse for a pick-me-up on a warm day.

1 Have on hand a clean 250 ml spray bottle. Pour the water into the bottle and drip the perfume oil drops into the water. Cover the top with your thumb and shake well.
2 Screw the top on and your body splash is ready.

Citrus Cologne Splash

1 lime
½ cup (125 ml) methylated spirits
3 teaspoons lemon extract or orange extract

Make this cooling scent at home for spare change.

1 Juice the lime and strain out the pulp. Combine the methylated spirits, lime juice and lemon or orange extract in a clean bottle with a tight-fitting lid. Shake well.
2 Dab on pulse points. You may also transfer the splash to a spray bottle. Store the splash in the refrigerator.

Cellulite Massage Oil

30 ml almond oil
½ teaspoon jojoba oil
½ teaspoon carrot oil
14 drops geranium essential oil
6 drops lemongrass essential oil
4 drops cypress essential oil

Include this massage oil – along with regular exercise and a healthy diet – in your tool kit to help lessen cellulite. A regular massage with this oil may help increase circulation and break down fatty deposits.

1 Combine all the ingredients in a 45–60 ml sterilised glass jar with a tight-fitting lid. Shake vigorously.
2 After a bath or shower, pat your skin dry and massage a small amount of the oil on cellulite-affected areas, using circular movements. Use ¼ to ½ teaspoon, depending on the size of the area you are treating. Apply only once a day.

Almond Exfoliating Body Scrub

¼ cup (60 g) coarse sea salt
¼ cup (60 ml) baby oil
½ teaspoon almond extract,
vanilla extract, or lightly
scented perfume oil

Scented, gritty body scrubs are all the rage. Here's a recipe you can make at home for next to nothing.

1 In a small bowl, stir the salt and baby oil together until the oil is thoroughly incorporated into the salt. Add the extract and stir until it, too, is incorporated.
2 Use in the shower, after you are thoroughly wet. Apply with your hands, a washcloth or a body puff scrubber. Massage in and rinse off.

Simple Sugar Scrub for Dry Skin

1 cup (220 g) sugar
½ cup (125 ml) olive,
grapeseed or other oil
2 drops vanilla or almond
extract (optional)

Here's another yummy body scrub that costs less than a cup of coffee for three or four uses.

1 In a medium bowl, combine the sugar and oil. Mix with a wooden spoon until you achieve a pastelike blend. Add extract if desired and stir until incorporated.
2 Transfer to a clean, airtight glass container to slow breakdown of the oil.
3 In the shower, massage this mixture gently over damp skin. It will exfoliate and moisturise at the same time. Do not use on broken, irritated or scarred skin. Avoid the eyes. This is an especially oily mixture, so it is really best for dry skin.
4 Store the mixture in the refrigerator for 6 months to 1 year.

Cranberry Sugar Scrub

½ cup (80 g) frozen
cranberries
1 teaspoon glycerine
¼ cup (60 ml) sweet almond oil
¼ cup (55 g) sugar
2 drops orange essential oil
15 g oat powder (grind oatmeal
in blender if needed)

The beauty of sugar scrub recipes is the way they offer up scent while managing to exfoliate, nourish, and polish the skin. Here is another spa-quality product you can make in your own kitchen.

1 In the container of a food processor, combine cranberries, glycerine and almond oil and process for 30 seconds – just enough to blend the ingredients without turning the berries to pulp. You want to keep the mixture thick.
2 Transfer the mixture to a bowl and stir in the sugar. Stir in the essential oil. Add just enough of the oat powder to create a cohesive mixture that you can apply to your skin.
3 In the shower, rub the mixture on your skin. Massage in and remove with warm water.

Body Powder

½ cup (75 g) arrowroot
20 g white cosmetic clay powder
7 drops lavender essential oil
5 drops clary sage essential oil
2 drops patchouli essential oil

This fresh-smelling and silky after-shower powder can be used every day. For a more feminine product, use just lavender and rose essential oils.

1 In a medium bowl, mix the arrowroot with the white cosmetic clay. Add the essential oils and mix well with your fingers.
2 Store in a tightly covered container for a couple of days to allow the powder to absorb the oils, then use all over your body as desired.

Body Spray

3 teaspoons finely chopped orange peel
3 teaspoons finely chopped lemon peel
45 ml vodka
3 teaspoons witch hazel
1 cup (250 ml) water
5 drops lemon verbena essential oil
10 drops bergamot essential oil
10 drops orange essential oil

This citrusy mixture smells good, tones the skin, and feels delightfully cool.

1 In a small jar with a tight top, add orange and lemon peels to the vodka. Cover and leave for 1 week in a cool, dark place.
2 Strain the liquid into a clean spray bottle. Add the witch hazel, water and the essential oils. Shake well and use as needed. Store in the refrigerator for up to 2 weeks.

Deodorant

¼ cup (60 ml) distilled witch
  hazel
30 ml sage alcohol-based
  herbal extract
10 drops grapefruit-seed
  extract
10 drops clary sage essential oil
5 drops patchouli essential oil

Here's a serious homemade underarm deodorant that won't stain your clothes or strain your wallet.

1 In a small spray bottle, combine all the ingredients.
2 Shake well and spray under arms as needed.

Bath Products

Bubble Bath for Kids

½ cup (125 ml) shampoo
¾ cup (185 ml) water
¼ teaspoon table salt

This simple recipe provides a scented, bubbly bathful of suds that you know are safe for your child and, as a bonus, helps you recycle extra shampoo. As always, parents should supervise children's use of such products. Beware of slippery tubs. Bubble baths are fun, but children shouldn't use them daily. Too much of a good thing could irritate sensitive skin.

1 In a medium bowl, mix the shampoo and water. Gently stir until blended. Add the salt. Stir until the mixture thickens.
2 Pour through a funnel into a clean bottle with a tight cap. This bubble bath will keep safely for months in the bathroom.

Conditioning Bubble Bath

¼ cup (60 ml) gentle
  dishwashing liquid
5–6 cups (1.25–1.5 litres)
  water
30 ml glycerine

For an inexpensive, fun and squeaky-clean bubble bath, this recipe gives you lots of bubbles and cleans up the tub as well. To be extra safe, test the solution on your child's inner arm to make sure he or she is not allergic to the solution. As always, parents should handle bubble bath products. Keep out of children's reach.

1 In a small bucket, swish all the ingredients together, altering the balance as you see fit. Pour into a bathtub of warm water for long-lasting bubbles. You may want to bring a bubble wand to the tub.
2 Keep an eye on children in the tub, which may be extra slippery with the bubble bath. Infants and very young children should not take bubble baths.

Bath Gel

½ cup (125 ml) distilled or
   bottled water (not tap water)
one 10 g sachet unflavoured
   gelatine
½ cup (125 ml) baby shampoo

This recipe is especially suited for children or adults with sensitive skin. It's easy to make and costs very little for a 250 ml jar. Wrap a grosgrain ribbon around the jar and you've got a delightful homemade gift.

1 In a small saucepan, bring the water to a boil. Add the gelatine and stir until it is dissolved. Remove the mixture from heat. Slowly stir in the baby shampoo. Let this mixture cool until it's tepid enough to put in a clean, decorative wide-mouthed jar with a tight-fitting lid.
2 Place the jar in the refrigerator to set the gel.
3 Use a few teaspoons of gel per bath. Bath gel should keep for up to 1 month in the refrigerator.

Liquid or Gel Soap

2 cups (200 g) pure soap
   flakes or grated bar soap
8 cups (2 litres) water
30 ml glycerine

This bath or hand soap is easy to cook up and is a good way to use up old slivers of bar soap. Transfer the liquid soap to an empty pump container and you can supply your bathroom for just a portion of the price you'd pay at the shops.

1 In a large pot or Dutch oven, combine all the ingredients. Cook over low heat, stirring occasionally, until the soap flakes have dissolved.
2 Transfer the mixture to a clean 2 litre container and cover tightly. For a thinner gel soap, increase the water to 4 litres.

Almond Rose Soap

5 g dried red rose petals
2½ cups (250 g) pure soap
   flakes
⅔ cup (170 ml) boiling water
½ cup (125 ml) rose water
20 g ground almonds
9 drops geranium essential oil

Here's a simple method of soap-making that uses just a few basic tools. You'll create a fragrant soap that gently cleans and exfoliates.

1 Pound the rose petals with a mortar and pestle. In a large bowl, combine the ground petals, soap and water and stir until smooth. If the soap starts to solidify, place the bowl over near-boiling water.
2 Stir in the rose water and ground almonds. Allow to cool. Stir in the essential oil.
3 Shape the mixture into 6 balls and flatten them slightly. Allow the soap to harden between sheets of wax paper. Keep any unused soap in a cool, dark place until needed.

Cinnamon Soap

1 kg leftover soap (or buy bulk
  bars)
3 teaspoons spring water
1 teaspoon glycerine
½ teaspoon cinnamon
  essential oil
3 teaspoons sweet orange
  essential oil
10 drops clove bud essential
  oil (optional)

You'll enjoy making this rich, spicy soap, which gives
you another opportunity to use up leftover soap scraps.

1 Coarsely grate the scraps of soap into a large mixing bowl.
   Add the spring water, glycerine and essential oils. Mix well.
2 Cover the bowl with a clean cloth and allow it to stand for
   about 15 minutes, until the soap is slightly soft and pliable.
   (If your soap scraps are fairly new, they may be soft and not
   need much softening time.)
3 Scoop the mixture up by the handful and press or roll it into
   small balls. Compress it tightly. Place on wax paper. Allow the
   soap balls to dry and harden for 1 to 2 days.

Strawberries and Cream Bath Bags

½ cup (60 g) oats (regular
  or quick-cook)
½ cup (50 g) milk powder
40 g almond meal (if
  necessary, grind almonds
  in blender, coffee grinder
  or food processor)
16 drops strawberry essential
  oil

Here's a charming idea you can make that provides a
relaxing and soothing bath. The oatmeal mixture may
help relieve dry or itching skin. For extra-sensitive skin,
reduce or eliminate the essential oil. Dress up this bath
product by scooping it into attractive cloth bags bought
at a crafts store to create your own inexpensive version
of exclusive bath goodies.

1 In a small bowl, combine the oatmeal, milk powder and almond
   meal, stirring to mix well. Stir in the essential oil until blended.
   Divide the mixture among 3 pretty cloth bags, and tie them
   at the top. Tie a generous loop of string or ribbon to the top
   of each bag.
2 When ready to use, hang the bag from the bath tap by its loop.
   When you fill the bath, the water will run over the mixture
   inside the bag, dispersing it into the bath.
3 Keep the bath bags in a cool, dark place until ready to use.

Herbal Bath Bag

1 large handful mixed herbs
  (rosemary, lovage, lavender,
  lemongrass, sage, parsley
  or peppermint)
muslin (cheesecloth)

This is a simple luxury for your bath. It makes you smell
good afterwards, but it is also delightful while you soak.

1 Place herbs of your choice in a doubled square of muslin
   (cheesecloth). Gather up the corners and tie securely.
2 Toss the herb bag into a hot bath to soften and scent the
   water. Once you're in the bath, rub it all over your skin, paying
   particular attention to areas where odour is a problem.

Cinnamon Oatmeal Milk Bath

1 cup (100 g) milk powder
½ cup (140 g) bicarbonate
   of soda
½ cup (60 g) finely ground
   oatmeal
2 teaspoons cornflour
1 teaspoon cream of tartar
1 teaspoon cinnamon

Mixing up this pleasantly scented bath will give you a double benefit. You'll gain as much pleasure making the concoction as you will from soaking in it. The combination of milk powder, oatmeal and cornflour will leave you feeling silky and soft. The cinnamon will gently warm you and offer up a soothing aroma.

1 Place all the ingredients in a food processor and whirl to combine. Transfer into a clean, tightly covered, moisture-proof container, where it will keep indefinitely.
2 Add about ½ cup (75 g) of the milk bath to a full tub of warm water and enjoy the soak.

Gentle Milk Bath

⅓ cup (35 g) milk powder
¼ cup (30 g) cornflour
drops essential oil of your
   choice

You can shake up a soothing milk bath anytime you want to escape into a warm tub. Milk will leave your skin smooth and silky.

1 Pour the milk powder and cornflour into a clean jar with a tight top. Shake well. Add the essential oil and shake to incorporate thoroughly. If the mixture starts to clump, use your fingers to dissolve the lumps.
2 For a bath, put the mixture under the running water. Splash around with your hand to disperse it in the tub.

Note: You may double or triple this recipe and store it indefinitely by omitting the oil. Store the combined milk powder and cornflour in an airtight container; use ½ cup (50 g) for each bath. Add the essential oil to the tub separately after swishing in the combined powders.

Zingy Citrus Bath Salts

2 cups (500 g) Epsom salts
½ cup (160 g) sea salt
1 teaspoon glycerine
12 drops mandarin orange
    essential oil (or more if you
    like a stronger fragrance)
12 or more drops orange food
    colour

Mix up a large batch of colourful, soothing bath salts. They're every bit as good as any you'd find in boutiques or on pharmacy shelves, selling for a whole lot more than you'll pay here.

1 Gently stir all the ingredients in a large bowl until they are well combined and the colour is evenly distributed. You might want to add more colour for a stronger shade, but do it 1 drop at a time.
2 Transfer the salts to a tight-lidded pretty jar and label.
3 Use up to ½ cup (160 g) of bath salts per bath, adding it while the water runs.

Bath Cookies

2 cups (500 g) fine sea salt
½ cup (60 g) cornflour, plus
    more for rolling dough
½ cup (140 g) bicarbonate
    of soda
3 teaspoons dried, chopped
    lavender or sage (optional)
2 eggs
30 ml vegetable oil
1 teaspoon vitamin E oil
    (if necessary, break open
    several 500 IU capsules)
8 drops essential oil or
    perfume oil of your choosing

If you like experimenting with recipes in the kitchen, you'll get a real kick out of making these 'cookies' for the tub. Bakers will recognise the steps in dough-making, rolling and baking, but there's a twist! Make one batch for yourself and another for friends.

1 Preheat the oven to 180°C (Gas 4). In a large bowl, combine the salt, cornflour and bicarbonate of soda. Stir in the chopped herbs, if using. Stir in the eggs, vegetable oil, vitamin E oil and essential oil and keep stirring until you form a dough.
2 Rub cornflour on a rolling pin and spread some on a work surface. Roll the dough out to about 2 cm. Cut into shapes with cookie cutters or a scone cutter. Place your 'cookies' on an ungreased biscuit sheet about 2–3 cm apart. Bake for 10 to 12 minutes. Cool and store in a tight-topped biscuit tin in a cool, dry place.
3 When ready to use, place 1 or 2 of your bath cookies into the tub as the water runs.

Basic Bath Powder

½ cup (140 g) bicarbonate
    of soda
½ cup (60 g) cornflour

For an after-bath or after-shower touch, this fragrance-free homemade powder is so natural, it's a safe bet that your great-grandmother used it. Keep a container of this mixture in your bathroom. Apply with a powder puff or sprinkle it on from a shaker-top jar.

In a small bowl, stir the ingredients to combine. Store the bath powder in a wide-mouthed glass jar or plastic container or keep in a shaker-top jar. The powder should keep indefinitely.

Easy Bath Powder

1 cup (150 g) powdered
    arrowroot
1 cup (125 g) cornflour
¼ cup (70 g) bicarbonate
    of soda

This simple combination creates a refreshing finish to the shower or bath and costs very little to make.

In a medium bowl, stir together all the ingredients. Store in an airtight container. The powder should keep indefinitely.

Delicately Scented Bath Powder

30 g crumbled dried chamomile
    flowers
¼ cup (30 g) cornflour
3 teaspoons ground orris root
½ teaspoon alum

This variation provides a lightly scented powder suitable for adults. While alum is used as an antiperspirant and deodorant for adults, it is best to use a simple sprinkle of cornflour on children or babies.

1 Combine all the ingredients in a bowl and mix well. Let stand for a few days.
2 Sift mixture through a flour sifter. Pour into a powder shaker or other container. The powder should keep indefinitely.

Nail, Hand and Foot Care

Gardener's Hand Cream

30 g cosmetic-grade beeswax,
    grated or shaved
½ cup (125 ml) sesame oil
3 teaspoons coconut oil
1 teaspoon honey
30 ml calendula tea
3 drops lavender essential oil
½ teaspoon bicarbonate of soda

This hand cream is especially good for hard-working hands. It costs very little to make the entire recipe, but because you are using unpreserved vegetable oils, if you don't have a cool, dark place to store the hand cream or a friend to share with, consider halving the recipe. To make calendula tea, pour a cup of boiling water over half a teaspoon of dried calendula flower petals and let it steep until cool.

1 In a small microwave-safe bowl, mix all the ingredients. Set the microwave to a medium heat and cook for 30 seconds or until the beeswax is melted. Remove from the oven with a pot holder and allow to cool.
2 Pour the mixture into a wide-mouthed, sterilised jar with a tight top. Store in cool, dark place until ready to use.

Cuticle Cream

30 g paraffin wax
½ cup (125 ml) mineral oil
  (or baby oil)
3 teaspoons coconut oil
3 teaspoons glycerine

Here's a spa treatment that you can make in the comfort of your own kitchen.

1 In the top of a double boiler over simmering water, combine the paraffin with the oils. Stir until the paraffin is melted and the mixture is blended. Stir in the glycerine and remove the pan from the heat. Let the mixture cool.
2 Apply the cooled cream to cuticle area. Rub in and allow to rest for 10 minutes or so.
3 Trim cuticles with a cuticle tool. Massage away the cream by applying a gentle body or hand lotion and rubbing lightly, then rinsing with warm water.

Warm Oil Hand Treatment

3 teaspoons olive or other
  cooking oil
1 teaspoon almond extract or
  1 drop lavender essential oil
  (optional)
2 small plastic bags that will
  fit over your hands

Manicurists can charge a great deal for hot oil hand treatments. Here is a delightfully simple and effective recipe you can create from ingredients in the pantry.

1 Place the oil in a microwave-safe dish and heat it on medium–high for a few seconds until it is warmed, but not hot. Add the almond extract or lavender oil, if desired. Stir.
2 Rub the oil on your hands, massaging your fingers and palms. Cover your hands with the plastic bags and wrap a clean hand towel over the bags. Sit comfortably for about 5 minutes.
3 Remove the bags and rinse your hands with warm water, massaging away the oil. Gently pat dry with the towel and apply a light hand lotion.

Polenta Hand Scrub

¼ cup (35 g) polenta
  (cornmeal)
45 ml milk
1 drop almond oil (or almond
  extract)

This gentle massage scrub costs small change to make and leaves your hands smooth and soft.

1 In a small saucepan, mix the polenta with the milk. Heat the mixture over a low heat until it forms a paste. Remove from heat and stir in the almond oil. Allow to cool.
2 Spread the mixture on your hands and allow to sit for 10 minutes. Gently scrub your hands with the mixture and then rinse off with warm water.

Love Your Feet Cream

30 g cosmetic-grade beeswax, grated or shaved
¾ cup (185 ml) almond oil

Our feet take a lot of abuse. Here's a special treatment to apply to dry, cracked feet that will leave them soft and pretty and costs much less than a visit to the salon for a pedicure.

1 Place the beeswax and almond oil in the top of a double boiler over simmering water. Stir together until they are blended and the wax has melted. Remove from heat and pour into two 125 g sterilised containers with tight tops.
2 Allow mixture to cool before applying to feet. Spread on feet at night before bedtime. Wear a pair of clean cotton socks over the cream. In the morning, your feet will be much softer.

Soothing Footbath

3 teaspoons sea salt
2 drops lavender essential oil
1 drop rosemary essential oil
1 drop bay essential oil
1 drop geranium essential oil
rose petals (optional)

Gently soothe tired, sore feet by soaking them in this deliciously scented footbath. Relax in the knowledge you'll be saving a pretty penny by making it yourself. Use a large plastic washing up bowl or baby bath if you don't have a special foot tub.

1 Fill a soaking pan or small tub with enough warm water to cover the feet.
2 Stir in the sea salt until it dissolves. Use your toes to stir, if you wish. Add the essential oils, mixing them well. Float the rose petals on the surface, if desired.
3 Soak your feet in the tub for 10 minutes, or until the water has cooled off. Pat your feet dry with a towel.

Eucalyptus Foot Lotion

3 teaspoons almond oil
1 teaspoon avocado oil
1 teaspoon wheatgerm oil
10 drops eucalyptus
essential oil

Use this rich and refreshing foot lotion to follow the Soothing Footbath (opposite) or simply to salve sore feet.

1 Put all the ingredients in a small, sterilised glass bottle with a tight-fitting stopper. Shake the liquid vigorously until it is completely combined.
2 Store the bottle in a cool, dark place. Shake well before using.

Strawberry Foot Scrub

2 teaspoons coarse salt
30 ml olive oil
8 fresh strawberries

Can't get to the spa for a luxury treatment for those tired feet? Work this simple and sweetly scented natural scrub into your feet and feel like a queen.

1 Pour salt into a mixing bowl. Add the oil and stir to combine. Hull the strawberries and slice or chop them. Add strawberries to the salt and oil mixture and mash with a potato masher or fork. The resulting mixture should be chunky but well blended.
2 Rub this mixture onto your feet, massaging the balls of the feet and the heels. If desired, use a body puff or foot brush. Rinse off and coat feet with a gentle lotion.

Refreshing Foot Spray

45 ml witch hazel
3 teaspoons rose flower water, orange blossom water or distilled water
⅛ teaspoon glycerine
10–15 drops of essential oil of your choice

This clean, fresh blend is great for hot summer days. Carry a little spray bottle of it with you and spritz it on tired feet.

Pour all the ingredients into a clean spray bottle and shake. The spray will keep for 2 months in a plastic container.

Leg Massage Cream

45 ml anhydrous (water-free) lanolin
45 ml olive oil
30 ml apricot oil

Treat yourself to a massage from your knees to your toes with this easy-to-make cream designed especially for the legs.

1 Put all the ingredients together in the non-reactive top of a double boiler over simmering water. Heat and stir with a wooden spoon until the lanolin has liquefied.
2 Pour the mixture into a sterilised 125 g jar with a tight-fitting lid and allow to cool. Keep in a cool, dark place.

Just for Men

Rosemary Shaving Soap

⅔ cup (170 ml) rose water
1¼ cups (125 g) pure soap
   flakes
4 drops rosemary essential oil
3 drops lemon essential oil
2 drops bay essential oil
1 drop sage essential oil

Rinse your face with fresh water, then lather up your beard with this fragrant soap before shaving. Be sure to rinse off the lather thoroughly.

1 Warm the rose water in a non-reactive saucepan over low heat. Place the soap flakes in the top of a double boiler over simmering water. Stir the warmed rose water into the flakes to moisten. Keep stirring the mixture until the soap has melted to a smooth gel (if necessary use a potato masher to dissolve the soap). Remove from the heat and cool to lukewarm.

2 Stir in the essential oils and spoon the soap into a sterilised shallow 200 ml glass jar with a tight-fitting lid. Set aside to harden for 3 to 5 days. Keep handy in a cool, dark place.

Lightly Scented Aftershave

½ cup (125 ml) witch hazel
½ cup (125 ml) rose water

Aftershave splashes serve two purposes: to soothe the just-shaved beard area and to offer a pleasant scent. Instead of purchasing costly scented aftershaves, make this at home for a fraction of the price.

1 Combine the witch hazel and rose water in a sterilised jar. Splash on the face directly after shaving. Keep tightly covered. The aftershave should keep indefinitely on the bathroom shelf.

Shaving-cut Lotion

20 ml witch hazel lotion
13 drops lavender essential oil
7 drops geranium essential oil

Apply a drop of this simple, inexpensive and effective lotion to stop bleeding and help prevent infection in the event of a razor nick.

Put all the ingredients in a sterilised 30 ml glass bottle with a tight-fitting lid. Shake well to combine. Keep in a cool, dark place. Shake before using.

Aloe Aftershave Gel

½ cup (125 ml) aloe vera gel
25 ml distilled water
3 teaspoons witch hazel
10 drops essential or
  fragrance oils of your choice

This alcohol-free gel is suitable for men or women because it refreshes and is safe for sensitive skin. See if you don't love it as much as anything you can buy. Aloe vera gel is available in health-food shops – or you can scoop it out of the leaves of a plant.

1 Combine all the ingredients in the container you're going to store the gel in. Stir until well mixed. Cover the container with a tight-fitting lid.
2 Keep in a cool, dark place. The gel should keep indefinitely.

Muscle Rub

1 teaspoon lanolin
45 ml extra virgin olive oil
7 g cosmetic-grade beeswax,
  shaved or grated
2–3 drops arnica essential oil
6 drops ginger essential oil
drops lemon essential oil

This salve really does wonders for hard-working muscles. Massage into stressed, stiff and aching shoulders, neck, back or feet. (While suitable for both men and women, this is not recommended for pregnant women.)

1 In a heatproof glass measuring cup with a pour spout, combine the lanolin, olive oil and beeswax. Place the cup in a hot-water bath until the wax is nearly melted. At this point, remove the cup from the water bath and stir the mixture with a clean utensil to evenly mix the ingredients.
2 Allow the mixture to cool. When the mixture begins to harden around the edges of the cup, add the essential oils and stir to incorporate them.
3 Pour into a sterile wide-mouthed jar and allow to cool before capping. Store in a cool, dark place for several months.

Digestive Distress

Soothing Tea for Heartburn ❖ Stomach-calming Tea ❖ Settler for Motion Sickness ❖ Hiccup Reliever ❖ Anti-diarrhoea Tea ❖ Electrolyte Drink ❖ Laxative ❖ Herbal Tea for Flatulence ❖ Haemorrhoid Pads

Colds, Congestion and Fever

Chest Rub ❖ Chest Compress ❖ Mustard Seed Plaster ❖ Mustard Powder Plaster ❖ Cough Suppressant Tea ❖ Cough Suppressant ❖ Steam Cough Relief ❖ Cough Drops ❖ Gargle Solution ❖ Slippery Elm Tea ❖ Steam Treatment ❖ Sore-throat Lozenges ❖ Decongestant Salve ❖ Herbal Inhalant ❖ Humidifier Booster ❖ Saline Spray for Sinuses ❖ Drops for Earache ❖ Fever Tea ❖ Spray for Fever

Bug Bites, Hives and Itching

Insect Repellent ❖ Soothing Gel for Insect Bites ❖ Essential Oil Itch Soother ❖ Sandfly Bite Lotion ❖ Skin Rash Drying Paste ❖ Healing Oil Bath ❖ Healing Calendula Lotion ❖ Salve for Eczema or Dermatitis ❖ Honey Ointment ❖ Anti-itching Solution for Hives ❖ Oatmeal Bath for Hives ❖ Anti-itch Wrap

Skin Outbreaks

Acne Facial Scrub ❖ Cleansing Liquid for Acne ❖ Acne Cleansing Pads ❖ Overnight Acne Cream ❖ Hot Compress for Boils ❖ Antibacterial Drawing Paste ❖ Antibacterial Oil ❖ Ringworm Paste ❖ Dandelion Wart Treatment ❖ Herbal Wart Treatment

Cuts, Bruises and Burns

First-aid Antiseptic ❖ Calendula Ointment ❖ Healing Ointment ❖ Cleansing Soap ❖ Compress for Bruises ❖ Anti-bruising Oil ❖ Oil Rub for Burned Skin ❖ Soothing Oil for Mild Burns ❖ Burn Spray ❖ Antiseptic Lotion for Burns ❖ Sunburn Cooler

Foot Care Products

Antifungal Foot Powder ❖ Antifungal Foot Ointment ❖ Antifungal Solution ❖ Corn Plaster ❖ Salicylic Acid Corn Remover

Lips and Mouth

Balm for Chapped Lips ❖ Cold Sore Ointment ❖ Mouthwash for Mouth Ulcers ❖ Cold Sore Paste

Dental Care

Mouthwash ❖ Mints ❖ Toothpaste ❖ Gum Tonic ❖ Antibacterial Mouthwash ❖ Super Dental Floss ❖ Toothache-relieving Rinse ❖ Toothache-relieving Dental Paste

Joints and Muscles

Hot Pepper Rub ❖ Massage Cream ❖ Quick-and-dirty Muscle Rub ❖ Muscle Soak ❖ Liniment ❖ Cold Pack for Strains and Sprains ❖ Castor Oil Rub for Back Pain

Women's Problems

Muscle Relaxant for Cramps ❖ Hot Compress for Cramps ❖ Anti-cramp Tea ❖ Ginger Tea for Morning Sickness ❖ PMS Tea ❖ Yeast Infection Cream

Headaches

Headache Compresses ❖ Chamomile Tea ❖ Lemon Balm Tea ❖ Migraine Tea ❖ Headache Massage Oil ❖ Headache Oil with Vitamin E

Anxiety and Fatigue

Catnip Anti-anxiety Tea ❖ Hops Anti-anxiety Tea ❖ Calming Tea for Insomnia ❖ Sleep Pillow ❖ Herbal Milk Bath for Sleeplessness ❖ Relaxing Aromatic Bath ❖ Invigorating Oil for Fatigue ❖ Energy Tea for Fatigue

Healthy Home Remedies

In a time of increasing health-care costs, it is comforting to know that you can often successfully treat many everyday health problems with homemade remedies.

As you use the recipes on the following pages, you will be happy to discover that they can make a real difference to how you or a family member feels and to when you start to improve without spending a small fortune at the chemist.

From heartburn and motion sickness to constipation, colds and sore throats to sprains and muscle aches, and many more conditions, there are effective home remedies in this chapter that you can make and apply yourself.

Many of these homemade recipes use herbs and other natural ingredients that were known to our ancestors and have an honourable place in the history of healing. In many cases, modern medicines were discovered when scientists took plants that were recognised by herbalists as having special healing properties to the lab. The healing ingredients were then extracted and tested, and later manufactured. So with many of these recipes, you are simply going back to the original natural source. However, if any symptoms persist, you should always seek medical treatment.

Digestive Distress

Soothing Tea for Heartburn

1 cup (250 ml) water
1 teaspoon grated liquorice
  root
1 teaspoon chopped fresh
  ginger
1 teaspoon dried chamomile
  flowers

Liquorice, ginger and chamomile are traditional, easy-to-make and inexpensive digestive tract soothers that still work wonders for occasional flare-ups of heartburn.

1 In a small pan, bring the water to a boil. Add the liquorice and ginger. Simmer for 15 minutes. Remove from heat and add the chamomile. Cover and steep for 10 minutes.
2 Strain into a teacup and drink.

Stomach-calming Tea

1 cup (250 ml) boiling water
1 teaspoon dried peppermint
1 teaspoon dried chamomile

If you have indigestion, this therapeutic infusion will help to tame your outraged stomach.

1 In a small pot, pour the boiling water over the dried peppermint and chamomile. Cover and steep for 10 minutes, then strain into a teacup.
2 Drink up to 3 cups a day to help ease intestinal cramps.

Quick antacid from your spice shelf

Some common kitchen spice seeds contain oils that soothe spasms in your stomach and relieve nausea – without costing too pretty a penny. Just chew 1 teaspoon of aniseed, dill or caraway seeds for 1 minute, then spit them out without swallowing any of them. Repeat 3 times a day.

Settler for Motion Sickness

juice of 1 lemon
1 cup (250 ml) boiling water
1 teaspoon honey
1 crushed sprig spearmint
  or peppermint

While over-the-counter motion-sickness remedies can make you sleepy, ours just helps to take away the sick feeling. This is a tummy-soothing drink.

1 In a large cup, combine the lemon juice, boiling water and honey. Stir to mix and add the spearmint or peppermint.
2 Sip as needed. Keep warm in a thermos when travelling.

Chew ginger to settle your stomach

Ginger is a traditional stomach settler for motion sickness, and crystallised ginger may save you a trip to the chemist. Just chew on a lump of crystallised ginger as needed. Keep a packet in the car or your purse so you always have it handy.

Hiccup Reliever

2–3 teaspoons sugar or dry drink mix (such as chocolate milk drink granules)

You can't even find a remedy for hiccups in the chemist, but you can make one yourself.

Swallow the dry sugar or drink mix, which isn't easy. Trying to get it down may short-circuit the hiccups.

Anti-diarrhoea Tea

2 teaspoons dried raspberry and/or blackberry leaves
boiling water

This tea settles the digestive system. If your diarrhoea persists for more than 24 hours, however, see a doctor.

1 In a teacup, steep the berry leaves in freshly boiled water for at least 10 minutes. Strain.
2 Drink a small cup 3 times a day along with other fluids to prevent dehydration.

Electrolyte Drink

1 cup (250 ml) apple juice
2 cups (500 ml) water
½–1 teaspoon salt
juice from 1 lemon or 1 lime

Diarrhoea can drain your body of fluid and electrolytes quickly and quite dangerously. This juice drink helps maintain your body's equilibrium. If your diarrhoea persists for more than 24 hours, however, see a doctor.

1 In a jug, combine the apple juice, water, salt and the lemon or lime juice. Store in the refrigerator.
2 Drink throughout the day to maintain hydration and proper balance of electrolytes.

Making an infusion

Making an herbal infusion is similar to making a cup of tea. Place 3 rounded teaspoons (15 g) fresh herb leaves or 1 rounded teaspoon dried herb leaves in a teacup. Pour ½ cup (125 ml) boiling water over the leaves, cover with a saucer, and let steep for 5 or 10 minutes. Strain the drink while still hot – or let it cool if you're going to use it as part of a lotion or gargle with it. Infusions may be stored in the refrigerator for up to 24 hours.

Laxative

1–3 teaspoons psyllium husks
1 cup (250 ml) warm water

You don't have to buy expensive psyllium husk fibre supplements to treat temporary constipation.

1 Stir the psyllium husks into the warm water and drink once a day. Follow with a glass of plain water.
2 Drink 6 to 8 additional glasses of water throughout the day.

Grandma's always ready laxative

Here is an old-fashioned penny-pincher's remedy for constipation – it sounds simple because it is. Just take 1 to 2 teaspoons castor oil on an empty stomach. It should get things moving within 8 to 10 hours.

Herbal Tea for Flatulence

1 teaspoon dried chamomile
½ teaspoon dried peppermint
1 teaspoon dried catnip
1 teaspoon dried basil
2 crushed fennel seeds
½ teaspoon dried marjoram

It's embarrassing to have flatulence and embarrassing to have to buy something to treat it. Instead, make the following tea in the privacy of your home.

1 In a large cup, mix the herbs. Pour in ¾–1 cup (180–250 ml) boiling water and steep, covered, for 10 minutes. Strain and drink tea.
2 Drink 3 or more cups a day.

Haemorrhoid Pads

30 ml witch hazel
5 drops cypress essential oil
3 drops geranium essential oil
5 drops lavender essential oil
2 tablespoons aloe vera gel
cotton cosmetic pads

These pads are cool and soothing.

1 In an open-mouthed jar with a tight-fitting lid, combine the witch hazel, essential oils and aloe vera gel. Saturate several cotton cosmetic pads with the liquid and refrigerate for at least 1 hour.
2 Use a pad on the affected area when it burns and after each bowel movement. Store in the refrigerator for several days.

Colds, Congestion and Fever

Chest Rub

30 drops massage or carrier
oil such as almond, jojoba
or avocado oil
5–10 drops eucalyptus or
wintergreen essential oil

The essential oils in this rub are therapeutic. Cover them with flannel and a hot pad to warm your chest and help you absorb the essential oil.

1 In a small bowl, mix the carrier oil with the essential oil. Rub the mixture onto your chest.
2 Cover your chest with a cotton towel or piece of flannel, then put a heating pad or hot-water bottle on top of the flannel and snuggle under the blankets.

Chest Compress

a handful of dried, chopped
mullein (lungwort) or dried,
chopped lobelia
1–2 cups (250–500 ml) boiling
water

This warm, soothing compress will make you relax while it helps you to breathe.

1 In a bowl, steep the mullein or lobelia in boiling water for 10 minutes.
2 Saturate a hand towel in the warm liquid, wring it out, and place on your chest. Cover with a warm towel and place a heating pad on top of that.

Mustard Seed Plaster

30–45 ml olive oil
⅓ cup (70 g) mustard seed
20 g grated beeswax
cloth to cover chest

It's old-fashioned, but sometimes it's these kinds of remedies that are the best. And you are not risking the family fortune to try it.

1 Blend 30 ml olive oil and the mustard seed in a blender. Continue adding olive oil until you have a nice, thick liquid.
2 Pour the mixture into the top of a double boiler over low heat; add the beeswax and heat, stirring, until the wax melts. Spread the cloth on a flat surface. Once the mustard-wax mixture is warm and can be spread, apply it to the cloth and let it cool to room temperature.
3 Place the cloth, salve side down, on your chest and cover with a T-shirt or old flannel, then apply external heat on top with a heating pad or hot-water bottle. You should start to feel warmth seeping into your chest in about 10 to 15 minutes. Leave on for another 15 minutes. You can store the plaster in the fridge for several days; when needed, remove and let warm to room temperature before using.

Mustard Powder Plaster

3 teaspoons mustard powder
20 g flour

You can make an inexpensive, effective mustard plaster using a strong mustard powder.

1. In a small bowl, mix the mustard powder with the flour. Add enough water to make a paste.
2. Spread the paste over half of a tea towel. Then fold the towel in half, covering the paste, and apply to chest. Don't apply the mustard paste directly onto the skin. Check chest skin often and remove the mustard plaster if there are signs of irritation.

Cough Suppressant Tea

4 fresh sage leaves or
 1 teaspoon dried
boiling water

Here's a nicer, cheaper alternative to commercial cough syrups, which may help you cope with a nagging cough.

In a standard teacup, steep the sage leaves in freshly boiled water for at least 20 minutes. Strain and drink hot or cold.

Cough Suppressant

1 large onion, finely diced
2 garlic cloves, finely diced
50 g finely diced fresh ginger
honey

Gain a new appreciation of onions, garlic, ginger and honey after they conspire to stop your coughing.

1. In a small saucepan, combine the onion, garlic and ginger. Add honey to cover and cook over very low heat for 30 minutes. Then mash together and let cool. Strain and store in a clean jar with a tight-fitting lid in the refrigerator.
2. Take 1 teaspoon every 15 to 30 minutes.

Steam Cough Relief

4 cups (1 litre) water
2 drops thyme essential oil
4 drops eucalyptus essential oil
2 drops hyssop essential oil

Make your own herbal steam treatment to help relieve the symptoms of a persistant cough.

1. In a saucepan over medium heat, heat the water until nearly boiling (but don't boil). Pour into a heat-safe bowl and add the essential oils.
2. Hold your head about 20 cm above the water, drape a towel over your head and the bowl to make a tent, and breathe in deeply until the water cools. Make sure that you keep your eyes closed throughout.

Cough Drops

60 g dried or 170 g fresh
  horehound leaves
3½ cups (800 g) firmly packed
  soft brown sugar
20 drops eucalyptus
  essential oil
20 drops tea-tree essential oil

Do a little steeping and straining, boiling and stirring, rolling and cooling. Voilà! Your very own cough drops at a fraction the price of commercial ones. You need a sugar thermometer to make these.

1 In a saucepan, pour 3 cups (750 ml) boiling water over the horehound leaves and steep for 30 minutes over low heat. Strain into another saucepan and add the brown sugar; stir until the sugar dissolves.
2 Bring the mixture to a boil and boil until it reaches 146°C on a sugar thermometer. Stir in the eucalyptus and tea-tree oils. Let cool slightly, then, using buttered hands, roll into small balls and let the balls harden on wax paper. Wrap them individually in plastic wrap and use as needed.

Pepper spray for a raw throat

This quick and easy spray is an antiseptic and a painkiller that costs almost nothing to make. In a clean 250 ml spray bottle, combine 3 teaspoons of ground cayenne pepper with just enough water to almost fill the bottle. Shake well and use as a spray to numb the back of your throat. You can also use it for gargling. Use the spray sparingly and don't get it near your eyes. Keep out of reach of children.

Gargle Solution

40 g brown sugar
½ teaspoon salt
¼ teaspoon bicarbonate of soda
4 cups (1 litre) warm water

This old-fashioned gargle will make your throat feel much better, and it costs very little.

1 In a jar with a tight-fitting lid, combine all the ingredients. Shake well before using.
2 Gargle with up to ½ cup (125 ml) of this solution as often as needed.

Slippery Elm Tea

2 teaspoons powdered slippery
  elm bark
2 teaspoons powdered
  marshmallow root
⅔ cup (170 ml) boiling water

The combination of slippery elm and marshmallow root is soothing for a sore throat.

In a cup, place the slippery elm and marshmallow root. Pour in the boiling water and steep until cool. Strain into a teacup and drink. Store in the refrigerator and gently reheat as needed.

Steam Treatment

15 g finely chopped fresh thyme, sage, peppermint, eucalyptus or pine needles
boiling water

Aromatic herbs and humidity can do wonders for a stuffed-up head – the results can be priceless!

1 Put the herbs in a medium bowl and add boiling water.
2 Drape a towel over your head and the bowl, lean over and inhale for 10 minutes. Repeat 2 or 3 times a day as needed.

Sore-throat Lozenges

¼ cup (about 5 g) dried violet petals
¼ cup (about 5 g) dried rose petals
honey or maple syrup
1 teaspoon powdered marshmallow root
icing sugar (optional)

These lozenges are made with dried plant ingredients. They are cheap, easy to make and very effective.

1 With a mortar and pestle, crush the violet and rose petals until you get a fine powder. Mix with just enough honey or maple syrup to form a ball and add marshmallow root. Add more herbs or icing sugar until the mixture can hold its shape.
2 Form into pea-sized balls and place on a greased biscuit tray. Leave for 24 to 48 hours or until they harden, then wrap each individually in plastic wrap and store in a cool, dry place.

Decongestant Salve

½ cup (125 ml) olive oil
15 ml peppermint essential oil
15 ml eucalyptus essential oil
15 ml wintergreen essential oil
15 g grated beeswax
4 drops tincture of benzoin

This decongestant rub can be rubbed on the chest or under the nose for warm relief.

1 In the top of a double boiler over low heat, heat the oils. Add the beeswax and tincture of benzoin and stir until the beeswax is melted and the oils are well mixed.
2 Pour into a clean, wide-mouthed jar with a tight top and allow to cool. Put under your nose or rub on your chest. Keep this mixture in a cool, dark place for up to 2 weeks.

A quick decongestant to carry with you

The good news about this decongestant is that it doesn't come with a list of warnings! Just put 1 drop of tea-tree, peppermint or rosemary essential oil on a clean handkerchief and carry the handkerchief with you. Inhale as needed.

Herbal Inhalant

¼–½ teaspoon rock salt
2–4 drops peppermint
 essential oil
2–4 drops each eucalyptus and
 wintergreen essential oils

Make your own quick inhalant for a blocked nose.

1 Put the rock salt in the bottom of a small glass bottle or jar with a tight-fitting lid. Add the oils.
2 Carry with you and sniff as needed.

Humidifier Booster

2–4 drops peppermint
 essential oil
2–4 drops eucalyptus
 essential oil
2–4 drops wintergreen
 essential oil
cotton ball

Getting a good night's sleep is probably the best thing you can do for a cold. This recipe will help you to breathe and sleep through the night.

1 In a small bowl, mix the oils. Dip a cotton ball into the mixture and put it near the vent of a steam humidifier.
2 Place the humidifier and the cotton ball near your bed when you have a cold.

Saline Spray for Sinuses

¼ teaspoon table salt
1 cup (250 ml) distilled water,
 warmed to a comfortable
 temperature

Why pay good money for something that is essentially salt and water? Make your own saline spray.

1 Add the salt to the distilled water and stir until it dissolves.
2 To get the solution into your nose, use an ear bulb syringe (available from pharmacies). Flush your nasal passages 2 to 3 times a day.

Drops for Earache

1 garlic clove, crushed
5 g fresh or dried mullein
 (lungwort) flower
½ cup (125 ml) olive or
 almond oil

In winter weather, when earaches are more prevalent, keep these bargain ear drops close to hand in the refrigerator for emergencies. Always consult a doctor if earache persists.

1 In a clean jar with a tight-fitting lid, combine the garlic and mullein flower. Cover with the oil, seal the top and shake to blend. Store in a cool, dark place and shake daily.
2 Make sure the herbs remain under the oil for 2 weeks, then strain and store the oil in a clean jar with a tight-fitting lid in the refrigerator.
3 To treat an earache, let the oil come to room temperature or run it under warm water. Dispense 2 or 3 drops at a time with a sterile eye dropper. Gently massage the ear to help the oil make its way through the ear canal.

Fever Tea

yarrow
linden flowers
chamomile
spearmint
elder flowers
1 cup (250 ml) boiling water

Sip this tea to help reduce the symptoms of mild fever.

1 In a small bowl, mix equal amounts of dried, crushed yarrow, linden flowers, chamomile, spearmint and elder flowers.
2 Combine 3 teaspoons of this mix in a large cup and add boiling water.
3 Cover and steep for 10 to 15 minutes. Strain and drink hot. After drinking, get under the covers to induce sweating.

Spray for Fever

¼ cup (60 ml) methylated spirits
¼ cup (60 ml) witch hazel
3 drops peppermint essential oil
2 drops lavender essential oil

Spraying pulse points with a cool, soothing solution is said by many to help bring down a fever. It certainly feels great when you are hot and feverish. Pulse points are the places on the body where you can feel your heart rate when you touch them with your fingers – typically inside your wrists, just under each side of the jaw and the back of the knees.

1 In a clean spray bottle, combine the methylated spirits, witch hazel and essential oils. Shake the bottle to mix and then chill in the refrigerator.
2 Spray onto pulse points to reduce fever, taking care to avoid eyes and mouth.

Bug Bites, Hives and Itching

Insect Repellent

15–20 drops eucalyptus essential oil
15–20 drops lemon essential oil
15–20 drops lemongrass essential oil
15–20 drops citronella essential oil
30 ml carrier oil (olive oil or any massage oil)

The best way to treat bites is to avoid getting bitten in the first place. But forget spraying poisons on yourself. The essential ingredients of this insect repellent have been shown in studies to keep away stinging insects – notably, mosquitoes. Keep in mind, however, that if you live in an area with a high rate of mosquito-transmitted diseases, you may need stronger protection.

1 In a small jug, mix the essential oils with the carrier oil.
2 Put into a spray bottle and use as needed. Do not use on small children or infants.

Soothing Gel for Insect Bites

10–20 drops of a combination of lavender, tea-tree, chamomile, cedarwood and/ or eucalyptus essential oils

30 ml aloe vera gel or chamomile or calendula cream

Once you've been bitten, you need something to soothe the itch. This easy, inexpensive mixture will help.

1 In a small bowl, mix the essential oils into the gel or cream.
2 Smooth over itchy/painful area. If you make more than you need, you can store the mixture in a clean jar in a cool, dark place for 1 week.

Essential Oil Itch Soother

1 drop lavender, rose, chamomile or tea-tree essential oil

cold water

Instead of messy, expensive anti-itch salves, try this homemade soother, which can be made cheaply.

1 Fill a bowl with enough cold water to moisten a small washcloth or cotton pad. Swirl the essential oil through the water, then soak the cloth or pad.
2 Squeeze gently to remove any excess water and apply the cloth to the skin. Hold in place with your hand for as long as possible, or cover with plastic wrap and leave in place for about 1 hour.

Sandfly Bite Lotion

½ teaspoon salt
½ cup (125 ml) water
green (bentonite) clay powder
12 drops lavender essential oil
12 drops peppermint essential oil

The key to healing sandfly bites is to dry them up. To make the process less annoying, a coating of a heavy lotion keeps them from itching. This may be just as messy as calamine lotion, but it is a lot cheaper.

1 In a small bowl, dissolve the salt in the water and add enough bentonite clay to make a creamy mixture. Stir in the lavender and peppermint essential oils.
2 Spread over the affected area.

Bicarb soda paste for itches

Here is an incredibly easy itch reliever that costs almost nothing. In a small bowl, mix ¼ teaspoon bicarbonate of soda with a little iced water to make a paste. Then spread the paste over the bite area. Repeat as necessary.

Skin Rash Drying Paste

green (bentonite) clay powder
   or finely ground oatmeal
10 drops of lavender,
   chamomile, cypress and/or
   geranium essential oils
water

This easily made, inexpensive paste will coat and stick to the skin, soothing skin rashes caused by exposure to stinging and itching plants, such as nettles.

1 In a small bowl, put enough bentonite clay or finely ground oatmeal to cover the affected area. For every 3 teaspoons of powder, stir in 10 drops of one or more of the essential oils. Moisten the mixture with water to allow for easy application and spread over the affected area.
2 Cover loosely and allow to dry. Then rinse off and reapply as needed.

Healing Oil Bath

6–8 drops pine, geranium
   or lavender essential oils

Dry, irritated skin is the greatest culprit with either eczema or dermatitis. Try a fragrant herb oil bath for simple relief.

1 Add essential oil to a hot bath. Swirl to disperse the oil, then get in and soak for about 10 minutes.
2 Carefully get out of the bath (it will be slippery) and massage in any oil still left on the skin. Don't take this bath more than once every 24 hours.

Healing Calendula Lotion

calendula flower petals

Be sure you have *Calendula officinalis* flowers from your garden or a health-food shop when making this lotion for treating eczema or dermatitis; they are the ones with the therapeutic effect.

1 Crush several calendula flower petals between your fingers (or with a mortar or pestle) until the petals are juicy.
2 Rub both petals and juice onto the skin.

Salve for Eczema or Dermatitis

30 g grated beeswax

1 cup (250 ml) untoasted
sesame oil

½ teaspoon tincture of
goldenseal

½ teaspoon tincture of
barberry root

8 drops tea-tree essential oil

8 drops chamomile essential oil

Here is another treatment for rough, dry, irritated skin
that is gentle and natural.

1 In the top of a double boiler over low heat, melt the beeswax,
stirring occasionally. Stir in the sesame oil.

2 In a small dish, mix tincture of goldenseal and barberry root.
Add the tea-tree and chamomile essential oils.

3 Stir this mixture into the beeswax-oil mixture. Apply as needed.

Honey Ointment

30 g grated beeswax

1 cup (250 ml) untoasted
sesame oil

⅓ cup (115 g) honey

1 capsule vitamin E, 500 IU

60 drops rose, geranium,
chamomile, lavender or
bergamot essential oils
in any combination

The honey in this ointment serves as a humectant
to draw in moisture, which helps to ease the skin
irritation produced by eczema and dermatitis.

1 In the top of a double boiler over low heat, melt the beeswax,
stirring occasionally. Stir in sesame oil. Remove from heat and
let cool slightly, then add honey. Pierce the vitamin E capsule
and squeeze in contents. Add up to 60 drops of essential oils.

2 Pour the mixture into a clean jar or jars with tight-fitting lids
and use as needed to keep skin smooth and hydrated.

Anti-itching Solution for Hives

20–30 drops lavender
essential oil

bowl of cold water

You can buy pricey salves at the chemist to tame the
itching of hives, but this easy solution is also effective.

1 Stir the lavender essential oil into the bowl of cold water.

2 Dip a cloth into the liquid and apply directly to the hives
to reduce inflammation.

Oatmeal Bath for Hives

1 handful rolled oats

½ handful dry milk powder

½ handful chamomile

¼ handful calendula and/or
lavender

double-layer square of muslin
(cheesecloth)

Oatmeal bath products are famously good for soothing
the skin. Now you can make your own.

1 Place the oats, milk, chamomile and calendula or lavender
on the muslin (cheesecloth) square. Tie the ends together
to make a bag.

2 Run a warm (not hot) bath. Put the bag under the spout while
the water is running. Leave it in the bath and allow the water
to cool. (If the water is too hot, it will make the hives worse.)

3 Get into the tub and soak, squeezing the bag over your skin
to reduce itching.

Using essential oil to soothe rashes

Lavender and tea-tree essential oils have soothing properties that can alleviate as well as heal some rashes. Try this simple solution before buying expensive ointments. Put 1 drop of lavender or tea-tree essential oil directly on the rash, gently smoothing it over the surface. To treat a large area, apply a blend made by mixing 3 drops of either essential oil in 2 teaspoons light olive oil.

Anti-itch Wrap

¼ cup (60 ml) apple cider vinegar
¼ cup (60 ml) witch hazel
2 cups (500 ml) cold water
4 drops lavender essential oil
2 drops chamomile essential oil
2 drops bergamot essential oil
2 teaspoons bicarbonate of soda
clean cloths

This herbal wrap solution will soothe irritating rashes. It will also help to relieve the itching associated with chicken pox.

1 In a large bowl, mix the vinegar, witch hazel and cold water. In a separate small bowl, mix the essential oils with the bicarbonate of soda. Stir the bicarbonate of soda mixture into the water mixture.
2 Soak a cloth in the cool solution and wrap it over the itchy area for 20 minutes at a time or until the cloth begins to dry. Keep the solution chilled in the refrigerator for up to 2 weeks.
3 May be repeated 3 times a day.

Skin Outbreaks

Acne Facial Scrub

2 cups (200 g) rolled oats
½ cup (80 g) almonds
5 g dried lavender
3 teaspoons dried peppermint
3 teaspoons calendula leaf
½ cup (75 g) green (bentonite) clay powder

For a homemade version of an acne-relieving exfoliant that won't break the bank, try this. For more information on green clay powder, see Green Clay Purifying Face Mask, page 246.

1 In a coffee grinder or blender, grind the oats, almonds, lavender, peppermint and calendula leaf.
2 Add the clay and mix thoroughly, then put in a clean covered container and keep in a cool place. You can keep this scrub for up to 3 months.
3 To use the scrub, in a small open dish, make a paste by mixing 1 teaspoon of the mixture with water. Massage the paste onto your skin. Let dry, then rinse well.

Cleansing Liquid for Acne

1 cup (250 ml) distilled water
1 teaspoon dried thyme
1 teaspoon dried calendula
   flowers
1 teaspoon dried lavender
1 teaspoon dried yarrow
¼ cup (60 ml) witch hazel
5–10 drops tea-tree essential oil

Toners are primarily just water with a few other ingredients, yet they can cost far more than they should. Instead, make your own (see Making an Infusion, page 277). Dab an affected area 3 times a day, or use over your whole face after washing.

1 In a small pan, bring the distilled water to a boil. Add the thyme, calendula, lavender and yarrow. Remove from heat and steep, covered, until cool.
2 Strain and then mix the strained liquid with the witch hazel. Add the tea-tree essential oil, shake and apply to affected areas with a cotton pad.
3 Store the leftover liquid in the refrigerator and use within 2 weeks.

Acne Cleansing Pads

2 cups (500 ml) distilled water
3 teaspoons dried yarrow
3 teaspoons dried chamomile
15 drops tincture of benzoin
6 drops peppermint or
   wintergreen essential oil
cosmetic pads

Forget those high-priced acne pads that come impregnated with the medicine. Just make your own!

1 In a small pan, bring the distilled water to a boil. Then add the yarrow and chamomile. Remove from heat after 2 to 3 minutes and steep, covered, for half an hour. Strain and add tincture of benzoin and peppermint or wintergreen essential oil. Mix well and pour into a sterilised jar with a tight-fitting lid.
2 Put several cosmetic pads in with the liquid. Refrigerate and use as needed.

Overnight Acne Cream

4 drops tea-tree oil
1 teaspoon cosmetic clay

Antibacterial tea-tree oil is the active ingredient in this easy homemade paste.

1 In a small dish, mix the tea-tree oil and the cosmetic clay. Add just enough water to make a thick paste.
2 Dab onto blemishes and leave on overnight.

Hot Compress for Boils

20 ml hot water
2 drops lavender, lemon,
   tea-tree, sage or clove
   essential oil
1 cotton ball or gauze pad

This gentle treatment will help relieve the boil in a lovely, aromatic way.

1 In a bowl, pour the hot water. Swirl your chosen essential oil through the water, then soak the cotton ball or gauze pad in the solution.
2 Gently squeeze out excess liquid and apply the cotton ball or pad directly to the area of the boil. Cover with plastic wrap and secure with a bandage or tape. Leave in place for at least 1 hour. Repeat twice a day.

Antibacterial Drawing Paste

5 drops (in total) tea-tree,
   lavender and/or spikenard
   essential oils
slippery elm powder or green
   (bentonite) clay powder

This therapeutic paste works best if it is applied after putting a hot compress (above) on the boil for 15 minutes.

1 Mix the essential oils with enough slippery elm powder or green clay powder to cover the affected area generously.
2 Apply the moist powder to the boil and cover with a bandage for 24 hours.

Antibacterial Oil

3 teaspoons carrier oil
20 drops tea-tree essential oil
20 drops lavender essential oil
10 drops thyme essential oil

You don't want a boil to get infected; this antibacterial oil will help to protect you from that. You should, however, test it on a small area of normal skin first to make sure it's not irritating to your skin.

1 In a small bowl, combine the carrier oil with the essential oils. Mix well.
2 Hold a hot compress (above) on the boil for 10 minutes, then apply a small amount of the antibacterial oil and cover with a dressing. Repeat every few hours.

Ringworm Paste

3 teaspoons mustard seeds
water
1-2 drops sage and/or thyme
   essential oil

Try this antifungal paste on ringworm. If it's not better in a week, however, see a doctor.

1 Crush the mustard seeds with a mortar and pestle. Stir in enough water to make a paste, then add essential oil or oils.
2 Apply to the affected area and cover with a light bandage. Reapply once a day until the infection clears.

Dandelion Wart Treatment

freshly cut dandelion stalks
    or fig leaves

Here's an easy wart treatment straight from the backyard that won't cost you a thing. All you need are dandelion stalks or fig leaves.

1 Use the milky sap that exudes from the dandelion stalks or fig leaves and apply directly to the wart once or twice a day for several days, or until the wart pulls away from the skin. Keep the sap away from the skin around the wart and from sensitive areas such as the eyes.
2 If you are using this treatment on a child, cover the wart area with a bandage to prevent spreading the sap to sensitive skin.

Herbal Wart Treatment

1 drop tea-tree, lemon, clove, thuja or thyme essential oil
1 drop almond or olive oil
1 strip bandage

Warts are mysterious – they come and go seemingly without reason. You usually don't need a dermatologist or an expensive medicine to make them disappear.

1 Soak the wart in warm water for 15 minutes. Towel dry.
2 In a small dish, combine the essential oil with the almond or olive carrier oil. Test this oil mixture on a patch of skin to make sure it isn't irritating.
3 Apply the oil mixture to the wart and cover with the strip bandage. Reapply every 24 hours.

Cuts, Bruises and Burns

First-aid Antiseptic

60 g Calendula Ointment
    (page 292)
40 drops lavender essential oil
20 drops tea-tree essential oil
10 drops chamomile essential
    oil
10 drops lemon essential oil

Here is a natural solution with germ-killing properties that will help soothe a minor cut or abrasion. Be sure to wash the affected area well before applying it.

1 In a small sterile jar with a tight-fitting lid, combine the calendula ointment with the essential oils, mixing thoroughly.
2 Apply a small amount to the cleaned injury. Keep the remainder in a cool, dark place for up to 2 weeks.

Calendula Ointment

15 g fresh calendula petals
⅓ cup (80 ml) light olive oil
20 g chopped beeswax
1 capsule vitamin E, 500 IU

Use calendula flowers (*Calendula officinalis*) for this old-fashioned therapeutic salve that has many uses.

1 Put the calendula petals in a double boiler and crush slightly with the back of a spoon. Add the olive oil and simmer for 2 hours over low heat.
2 Strain the liquid into a bowl, pressing against the strainer with the back of a spoon to extract all the oils.
3 Return the liquid to the double boiler. Over medium heat, add the chopped beeswax and stir until it melts. Remove from the double boiler and beat the mixture until it cools and becomes creamy and thick. Pierce the vitamin E capsule with a needle, squeeze in the contents, and mix.
4 Spoon into a sterilised 120 g jar with a tight-fitting lid, seal and keep in a cool, dark place for up to 2 weeks.

Healing Ointment

30–45 g grated beeswax
1 cup (250 ml) olive or almond oil
2 capsules vitamin E, 500 IU
30 drops tea-tree essential oil
20 drops spike lavender or French lavender essential oil
10 drops chamomile essential oil
10 drops fir essential oil

You can have this ointment on hand to treat everyday cuts and scrapes as they arise, just as you would a tube of commercial antiseptic.

1 In the top of a double boiler over low heat, melt the beeswax. Stir in the olive or almond oil. Remove from the heat. Pierce each vitamin E capsule with a needle and squeeze the contents into the mixture. Then stir in the essential oils.
2 Pour into a small sterilised jar with a tight-fitting lid and store in a cool, dark place. Use as needed on wounds. This ointment should last 1 year.

Cleansing Soap

liquid castile soap
lavender essential oil
rosemary essential oil
tea-tree essential oil

Here is an antiseptic soap which will help to clean wounds properly and stave off infections. It smells good and costs very little.

1 To the bottle of castile soap, add the lavender, rosemary and tea-tree essential oils (10 drops total per 60 ml of soap). Dilute the mixture with more soap if skin is especially sensitive to any of the essential oils.
2 Use to clean cuts and abrasions.

Compress for Bruises

¼ cup (60 ml) water
¼ cup (60 ml) witch hazel or
cider vinegar
2 drops lavender essential oil
2 drops rosemary essential oil
2 drops peppermint or juniper
essential oil

A wet compress can relieve some of the pain of a bruise and help the healing process. This simple formula should have you feeling better in no time.

1 In a bowl, mix the water, witch hazel or vinegar and the essential oils. Soak a flannel cloth in the liquid, wring it out until nearly dry, and then place over the injured area.
2 Cover with plastic wrap so the skin absorbs the essential oils and cover the whole thing with a towel. Apply the compress for 30 minutes up to 3 times daily.

Anti-bruising Oil

30 ml arnica oil
10 drops rosemary
essential oil
10 drops peppermint
essential oil
10 drops juniper essential oil

Use this rub very, very gently on bruises to help in the healing process.

1 In a small bowl, mix the arnica oil with the essential oils.
2 Massage the mixture gently into bruised areas every 2 hours or apply to gauze and lay over the bruises.

Two quick treatments for burns

Aloe vera gel is an effective burns salve. Pull a leaf off the plant and scoop out the clear gel. Apply directly to the burn.

Lavender essential oil also provides relief from minor burns, such as sunburn. Apply several drops of oil directly to the burn.

Oil Rub for Burned Skin

1 drop tea-tree essential oil
¼ cup (60 ml) organic olive oil

This mixture gives relief to superficial burns and sunburn. You can safely use it several times a day.

1 In a small dish, dilute the essential oil with the olive oil.
2 Gently massage the mixture over the burned area.

Soothing Oil for Mild Burns

2 capsules vitamin E, 500 IU
5 drops lavender essential oil

If the burn area is large, you may need to double the ingredients for this soothing oil.

1 Pierce each vitamin E capsule with a needle and squeeze the contents into a small dish. Stir in the lavender essential oil.
2 Gently massage into the skin.

Burn Spray

30 ml iced water
30 ml aloe vera gel
25 drops (in total) lavender,
  chamomile, spearmint and
  yarrow essential oils
1 capsule vitamin E, 500 IU

Applying a spray doesn't hurt the burn the way that massaging in an oil might. This cool mixture offers relief at very little cost.

1 In a small spray bottle, mix the iced water, aloe vera and essential oils. Pierce the vitamin E capsule with a needle, squeeze its contents into the mixture, and chill.
2 Shake before use and spray over burned area. Keeps in the refrigerator for several days.

Growing your own aloe vera

You can buy an aloe vera plant at any garden shop or nursery. Aloes like warmth, so in colder areas, it is safer to keep the plant potted and place it near a sunny window than to plant it outdoors. (You can move the pot outdoors during the summer months.) Repot an aloe vera in a wide rather than a deep pot; it has shallow, spreading roots. Use one with a drainage hole and fill it with General Purpose Potting Mix (page 383) plus extra perlite. Don't overwater this succulent plant. Let its soil dry completely between soakings. Fertilise it yearly, in the spring, with a half-strength fertiliser mixture. When you need some aloe vera gel, just cut a lower leaf off the plant and squeeze it.

Antiseptic Lotion for Burns

1 handful dried plantain
  leaves
½ cup (125 ml) hot water
10 drops tea-tree essential oil

Nobody wants a burn to become infected. Here's a quick and inexpensive remedy with antiseptic properties.

1 In a blender, add a handful of dried plantain leaves to about ½ cup (125 ml) hot water. Begin blending, slowly adding water or plantain leaves as necessary until the mixture becomes thick, like porridge. Mix in the tea-tree oil.
2 Spread the mixture over the affected area. You can refrigerate the remainder for several days.

Sunburn Cooler

3 tea bags or 15 g loose tea
boiling water

For this recipe, you simply brew a pot of regular tea (any plain black leaf tea will do fine). The tannins in the tea help soothe the burning feeling.

1 In a teapot, place the tea. Pour in boiling water, cover and steep for 5 minutes. Cool.
2 Use a cloth or cotton ball to dab the sunburn with cooling tea.

Foot Care Products

Antifungal Foot Powder

½ cup (75 g) arrowroot or
   cornflour
20 g white cosmetic clay
10 drops cypress essential oil
10 drops lavender essential oil
3 drops clove essential oil
5 drops tea-tree essential oil
5 drops thyme essential oil

This easy-to-make antifungal foot powder can also be used to soothe the symptoms of jock itch.

1 In a small container with a tight-fitting cover, mix the arrowroot or cornflour with the cosmetic clay. Add the cypress, lavender and clove essential oils and mix. To make the powder antiseptic, add the tea-tree and thyme essential oils.
2 Let the powder sit for a couple of days to absorb the oils, then dust on your feet once or twice a day. Keep in a dry, covered container. It should last for several weeks.

Antifungal Foot Ointment

45 ml organic light olive oil
10 g finely chopped beeswax
50 drops of tea-tree, geranium,
   lavender, pine, myrrh or
   peppermint essential oils
   (in any combination)

Treating a fungus with your own aromatic homemade ointment is much more pleasant than paying more for a commercial antifungal ointment. Organic, light olive oil is available in health-food shops and supermarkets.

1 In the top of a double boiler, warm the oil over simmering water. Add the beeswax to the warmed oil and stir until it melts. Remove from the heat and stir until it cools. Then beat in the essential oils.
2 Spoon the ointment into a small, sterilised, wide-mouthed jar with a tight-fitting lid. Keep in a cool, dark place. Massage a small amount into the affected area twice a day. The ointment should keep for several weeks.

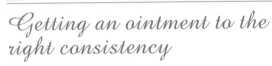

Getting an ointment to the right consistency

When making ointments, if the salve is too watery, reheat and add more beeswax. If it's too thick, reheat and add more oil.

Antifungal Solution

5–10 g dried thyme
5–10 g dried eucalyptus
5–10 g dried lavender

Use this solution to wipe down areas affected with fungal outbreaks twice a day. It's effective and inexpensive. Before applying this solution, wash the affected area with tea-tree soap (available in health-food shops).

1 In a large cup, combine the herbs. Cover with 1 cup (250 ml) boiling water and steep, covered, for 10 to 15 minutes. Strain solution and cool.
2 Soak a clean cotton cloth in the solution and apply twice daily to the skin (after your shower in the morning and before bed). You can also use this solution to soak your feet.

A quick and cheap antifungal footbath

Here's a quick and easy footbath to make up in a hurry. Fill a basin with warm water and add 2 or 3 drops of mustard oil or 1 teaspoon of hot mustard powder.

Soak your feet for at least half an hour. The mustard helps kill the fungus. Rinse your feet and dry thoroughly.

Corn Plaster

1 banana skin or fig skin, or pulp of a squeezed lemon
1 small dandelion leaf or garlic clove, crushed

This homemade corn plaster is very effective and costs only spare change to make.

1 Scrape the inside of the banana or fig skin until you have about 1 teaspoon of the pulp. Alternatively, you can use the flesh of a squeezed lemon.
2 In a small dish, mix the pulp with the dandelion or garlic to make a paste. Apply the paste directly to the corn, binding it in place with a small adhesive bandage.
3 When the skin is soft, gently rub the top layer of the corn away with an emery board.
4 Repeat the entire process daily until the corn disappears. For several days after the corn is gone, massage the area with a small amount of Calendula Ointment (page 292).

Salicylic Acid Corn Remover

5 aspirin tablets, 325 mg
  (adult)
½ teaspoon lemon juice
½ teaspoon water

Many commercial corn removers have salicylic acid as their main ingredient – the same active ingredient in aspirin. Here's how you can make your own salicylic acid corn remover.

1 In a small bowl, with the back of a spoon, crush the aspirin into a powder. Add the lemon juice and water and stir until the mixture forms a paste.
2 Dab the paste onto the corn and cover with plastic wrap, then place a heated towel over the wrap to help the paste penetrate more deeply. It will take several applications over several days before the corn falls off.

Lips and Mouth

Balm for Chapped Lips

¼ cup (60 ml) almond oil
3 teaspoons grated beeswax
1 teaspoon honey
1 capsule vitamin E, 500 IU
10 drops chamomile
  essential oil
10 drops orange essential oil
10 drops wintergreen
  essential oil
5 drops lavender essential oil

During winter, this homemade lip balm will keep your lips from cracking and peeling, if you use it faithfully. With its lovely smell, it is a true bargain.

1 In the top of a double boiler, warm the oil, beeswax and honey over low heat until the wax melts. Remove from the heat. Pierce the vitamin E capsule with a needle and squeeze its contents into the mixture.
2 Stir in the essential oils. Store in a cool, dark place and use by dipping a finger into the balm and smoothing it on your lips.

Cold Sore Ointment

5 drops lemon balm
  essential oil
1 drop lavender essential oil
1 drop chamomile essential oil
1 drop bergamot or rose
  essential oil
10 drops jojoba oil

This is more of a liquid than an ointment, but it is just as soothing. The jojoba oil serves as a carrier oil.

1 In a small, clean jar with a tight-fitting lid, dilute the lemon balm, lavender, chamomile, bergamot or rose essential oils in the jojoba oil.
2 Smooth over the affected area several times a day.

Quickly soothe a mouth ulcer with aloe vera

Instead of buying balm in the chemist to coat that painful mouth ulcer, make your own instantly. All you need are a cotton bud and an aloe vera leaf. Dry the sore area with a cotton bud, then squeeze a bit of gel from the aloe vera leaf over the area. Repeat as often as necessary.

Mouthwash for Mouth Ulcers

¾ cup (185 ml) water
3–4 drops clove or tea-tree essential oil

This is a simple, certainly inexpensive, mouthwash that helps to soothe annoying mouth ulcers.

1 In a clean jar with a tight-fitting lid, mix the water with the essential oil.
2 Swish the mixture in your mouth for 30 seconds, then spit it out. Cap the bottle and keep the mixture near the basin. Repeat mouthwash several times a day.

A fast cold sore preventive

The best time to prevent a cold sore outbreak is at the first tingle stage. If you feel one coming on, here's what to do. Apply 1 drop of lavender or lemon balm essential oil to the area where you feel the cold sore forming. Then hold an ice cube on top of the area for 10 minutes. This can sometimes prevent the outbreak altogether or at least reduce its severity. Repeat the whole procedure several times a day.

Cold Sore Paste

1 teaspoon finely chopped liquorice root or rhizome
90 ml distilled water
slippery elm powder, as needed
goldenseal powder, as needed

This soothing, not-so-costly paste smothers the irritation of a cold sore and may help to heal it.

1 In a small saucepan, combine the liquorice root and distilled water. Bring to a boil, then simmer for 10 minutes. Strain into a clean bowl. This makes a strong liquorice decoction.
2 In a small, clean container with a tight-fitting lid, mix equal amounts of slippery elm and goldenseal powder, and moisten with the liquorice decoction.
3 Apply the paste to the sore area to control pain and promote healing. Store the extra paste in the refrigerator or dilute with water and use as mouthwash.

Dental Care

Mouthwash

1 teaspoon glycerine
1 teaspoon aloe vera gel
10 drops peppermint,
    wintergreen or spearmint
    essential oil
1½ cups (375 ml) water

You don't need to spend good money on artificially flavoured mouthwash that is primarily alcohol.

1 In a clean jar with a tight-fitting cap, mix the glycerine and aloe vera gel with the essential oil you have chosen. Add the water and shake well. Use as a gargle.
2 Store in a covered jar and shake well before using.

Mints

1–2 fresh leaves spearmint,
    peppermint, fennel or
    parsley
¼ teaspoon fresh or dried
    caraway, cardamom or
    fennel seeds

Instead of sugary sweets, chew on breath-freshening herbs and spices.

Chew on the herb leaves and seeds for 2 or 3 minutes. Spit out and discard.

Toothpaste

2 tablespoons bicarbonate
    of soda
water
9 drops tea-tree essential oil
9 drops peppermint
    essential oil

Although we can't say 4 out of 5 dentists recommend it, we do know this homemade version will cost you far less than any of the commercial brands that fill supermarket shelves. The tea-tree oil provides an additional antiseptic boost to help keep gums healthy.

1 In a small bowl, mix the bicarbonate of soda with just enough water to make a paste. Add the tea-tree and peppermint essential oils.
2 Use the paste to brush your teeth and tongue. Cover the remaining paste and use for the next couple of days.

Gum Tonic

1 eye-dropperful of goldenseal
    tincture (about 20 drops)
2 drops myrrh essential oil
30 ml hot water

This will help treat the inflammation of bad gums without running up your grocery bill.

1 In a glass, combine the goldenseal tincture and myrrh essential oil. Dilute with the hot water.
2 Swish around your mouth and spit. Do not swallow.

Antibacterial Mouthwash

2 cups (500 ml) distilled water
10 g green tea
10 g dried, crumbled
  peppermint, spearmint
  or rosemary
10 drops tincture of benzoin or
  1 teaspoon tincture of myrrh

When used regularly, this mouthwash can help kill many of the germs that cause gum disease.

1 In a saucepan, bring the water to a boil. In a 600 ml jar with a tight-fitting lid, mix the green tea and peppermint, spearmint or rosemary. Pour in the boiling water, let cool, cover and steep overnight in the refrigerator.
2 Strain into a clean bottle with a tight-fitting lid. Add the tincture of benzoin or the tincture of myrrh and shake to mix.
3 Use 30 ml at a time as a mouthwash for sore and/or bleeding gums. Swish and spit without swallowing.

Super Dental Floss

10 drops goldenseal tincture
3 drops myrrh essential oil
2 drops tea-tree essential oil
dental floss

Save money by making your own antiseptic dental floss.

1 In a small container, combine the goldenseal tincture and the myrrh and tea-tree essential oils. Cut off enough dental floss to clean between your teeth and dip it into the mixture.
2 Use the dipped floss to clean between your teeth. Make a fresh batch every time you want to floss your teeth.

Toothache-relieving Rinse

1½ teaspoons whole cloves
1 cup (250 ml) boiling water

To quell the pain until you can get to a dentist, try this inexpensive rinse.

1 Put the cloves in a small pot. Pour in the boiling water and steep for 10 minutes. Strain into a glass.
2 Rinse your mouth with the warm infusion.

Fast toothache relief with clove oil

Until you can get to the dentist for your toothache, try this quick numbing trick. Put 1 drop of oil of cloves on a cotton bud, dip the swab in water, and then rub on the aching tooth and gum area.

Toothache-relieving Dental Paste

20 g ground ginger
20 g ground cayenne pepper
water

Some people don't like cloves and need another way to relieve dental pain without using expensive pain pills with lots of side effects. Try this.

1 In a small dish, mix the ground ginger and cayenne pepper with enough water to make a paste.
2 Saturate a cotton ball with the paste and put on the painful tooth. Keep the paste off your gums, because it may be irritating to them.

Joints and Muscles

Hot Pepper Rub

20 g ground cayenne pepper
½ cup (125 ml) Green
    Aloe Moisturising Lotion
    (page 258) or any
    commercial moisturising
    lotion

The capsaicin in hot chillies (peppers) has begun to be appreciated as a pain reliever even by commercial drug companies. Make your own for much less.

1 In a small bowl, combine the cayenne pepper with the moisturising lotion.
2 Massage the mixture into the painful area, being careful to wash your hands afterwards before touching your face or eyes.

Massage Cream

2 teaspoons grated beeswax
3 teaspoons coconut oil
¼ cup (60 ml) cayenne-infused
    oil
10–15 drops wintergreen
    essential oil
30 ml ginger tincture
30 ml water
30 ml aloe vera gel
½ teaspoon borax
¼ teaspoon powdered
    vitamin C

This soothing massage cream will help to take care of sore muscles and your bank balance.

1 In the top of a double boiler over low heat, mix the beeswax and coconut oil and stir until the beeswax has melted. Stir in the cayenne-infused oil and the wintergreen essential oil.
2 In a separate pan, heat the ginger tincture to evaporate as much alcohol as possible, then add the water, aloe vera gel, borax and vitamin C, and bring to 70°C to 80°C on a sugar thermometer. Place the ginger tincture mixture in a blender and whirl at high speed as you add the beeswax-oil mixture. Pour the resulting cream into a clean jar with a tight-fitting lid.
3 Massage the cream into sore joints as needed. Keep refrigerated for 4 to 6 weeks.

Quick-and-dirty Muscle Rub

5 drops cayenne-based hot sauce

3–5 drops peppermint essential oil

15 drops massage oil or olive oil

Again, capsaicin comes to the rescue of tense and tired muscles that need a good massage in a hurry without costing an arm and a leg.

1 In a clean small jar, combine the hot sauce, peppermint essential oil and massage or olive oil, and mix thoroughly.
2 Rub the mixture into the affected area by hand or with a cotton ball. This may initially irritate the skin, but the irritation will disappear as the painkilling becomes more effective.
3 Clean your hands with soap and water after each application and avoid touching your eyes.

Muscle Soak

½ cup (140 g) bicarbonate of soda

10–20 drops of eucalyptus, peppermint, juniper or pine essential oils

½ cup (125 g) Epsom salts

3 teaspoons juniper berries

3 teaspoons dried rosemary leaves

3 teaspoons dried chamomile flowers

3 teaspoons dried eucalyptus leaves

2 teaspoons dried lemon balm leaves

2 teaspoons dried peppermint leaves

double-layer square of muslin (cheesecloth)

A luxurious hot soak with beneficial herbs is priceless for relieving tight muscles and joints. You can make your own bag of just the right herbs.

1 In a small dish, place the bicarbonate of soda and add the essential oils; mix until the bicarbonate of soda has absorbed the oils. In a bowl, combine the Epsom salts, herbs and the soda mixture. Place in the middle of the muslin (cheesecloth) and tie up the ends to make a bag.
2 Hold beneath the running water until the tub fills, then massage your body with the bag and let it float in the tub. Soak until the water cools.

Liniment

4 teaspoons castor oil
30 ml glycerine
30 ml aloe vera gel
30 ml cayenne tincture
20 drops wintergreen
  essential oil

This is a traditional home remedy for the athletes in your family, helping to loosen tight joints and offering relief to tired and aching limbs.

1 In a clean glass bottle with a tight-fitting stopper, combine the castor oil, glycerine, aloe vera gel, cayenne tincture and wintergreen essential oil. Shake well.
2 Massage over sore joints as needed. Refrigerate the liniment for up to 6 weeks.

Cold Pack for Strains and Sprains

3 parts water
1 part methylated spirits
1 plastic self-sealing
  freezer bag

There are all kinds of clever products on the market to use as cold packs. This one is flexible, reusable and very, very inexpensive.

1 Combine the water and methylated spirits in the freezer bag and freeze.
2 Wrap the frozen pack in a towel and apply to the hurting joint. The methylated spirits keeps the pack flexible.

Castor Oil Rub for Back Pain

5 drops ginger essential oil
5 drops peppermint or
  wintergreen essential oil
2 drops camphor essential oil
2 drops rosemary essential oil
30 ml castor oil

You don't have to pay for a special tube of rubbing cream for back pain. Instead, try this easily made rub.

1 In a small bowl, mix together the essential oils and castor oil.
2 Rub into the painful area and cover with a piece of flannel or an old T-shirt, then put a heating pad over the cloth for 15 to 20 minutes to help the rub soak in. You can double the recipe for larger areas.

Women's Problems

Muscle Relaxant for Cramps

½ teaspoon valerian tincture
½ teaspoon cramp bark
  tincture

Instead of taking a pill, try this less expensive, easy-to-make remedy. These tinctures are available in natural food shops or online.

Take a dose of valerian tincture and a dose of cramp bark tincture every 1 to 2 hours. These are both natural muscle relaxants.

Hot Compress for Cramps

30 ml castor oil
10 drops ginger essential oil

You can enhance the help of a heating pad by using a touch of ginger and oil.

In a small dish, mix the castor oil and ginger essential oil. Spread the oil mixture over your abdomen, cover with a cotton or wool flannel cloth, then apply a heating pad for 20 to 30 minutes.

Anti-cramp Tea

1 cup (250 ml) boiling water
¼ teaspoon dried raspberry
  leaves
¼ teaspoon dried chamomile
  flowers
¼ teaspoon crushed fennel
  seeds
¼ teaspoon dried spearmint
  leaves

This combination of herbs will help to relax cramps and reduce your discomfort.

1 In a large cup, pour 1 cup (250 ml) boiling water over the raspberry leaves, chamomile, crushed fennel seeds and spearmint. Steep for 10 minutes and strain into a teacup.
2 Drink for relief when the cramps hit.

Ginger Tea for Morning Sickness

1 cup (250 ml) boiling water
½ teaspoon minced fresh
  ginger

A simple preparation that may help to calm your stomach in the morning and reduce nausea without making you sleepy.

1 In a large cup, pour the cup of boiling water over the ginger. Steep for 10 minutes, strain into a container and refrigerate.
2 Sip in the morning when you wake.

PMS Tea

3 teaspoons chopped dried
   dandelion roots and/or
   leaves
3 teaspoons chopped dried
   burdock root
4 cups (1 litre) water
1 teaspoon chopped dried
   black cohosh rhizome or root
1 teaspoon dried cramp bark
1 teaspoon grated orange peel
1 teaspoon chopped dried
   liquorice root

This tea is designed to help regulate hormone levels for all types of premenstrual syndrome without harming your stomach or liver.

1 In a pot, combine the dandelion roots and/or leaves and burdock root with the water. Add the black cohosh, cramp bark, orange peel and liquorice root. Bring to a boil, reduce heat and simmer, uncovered, for 40 minutes. Cover and steep for 15 minutes.
2 Strain into a clean container with a tight-fitting lid.
3 Drink ½ to 1 cup (125–250 ml) of the tea hot or cold as needed throughout the day. Refrigerate the remainder.

Yeast Infection Cream

1 capsule acidophilus bacteria
45 g plain organic yogurt with
   active cultures

You don't have to pay for expensive over-the-counter remedies for yeast infections. You can make this in no time and for very little money. Buy acidophilus bacteria capsules – the bacteria used to make yogurt – in health-food shops.

1 Open the capsule and place the bacteria in a small dish. Then mix in the yogurt.
2 Apply inside the vagina with a medicine syringe at night and wear a pad to prevent leakage.

Headaches

Headache Compresses

enough chilled lavender toilet
   water to soak 2 washcloths
2 washcloths

To ease a tension headache after a hard day, try this cool compress.

1 In a small bowl, pour in the toilet water. Soak both washcloths in the toilet water and squeeze out the excess.
2 Lie down with a towel behind your neck. Place a wet washcloth on your forehead with the other at the base of your skull. Relax for at least 15 minutes, preferably in a darkened quiet room.

Chamomile Tea

3 teaspoons dried chamomile
1 cup (250 ml) boiling water
1 teaspoon honey (optional)

Taking a break can relieve some of the tension that causes many headaches. Inexpensive chamomile tea is particularly soothing to frazzled nerves.

1 In a small pot, place the chamomile. Pour in the boiling water and steep for 5 minutes. Strain into a teacup.
2 Sweeten with honey, if desired. Then take a few minutes to sip the hot tea slowly while sitting in a quiet spot.

Lemon Balm Tea

3 teaspoons dried lemon balm
1 cup (250 ml) boiling water
1 teaspoon honey (optional)

Lemon balm is another soothing tea herb that can relax away headaches with little fuss for small change.

1 In a small pot, place the lemon balm. Pour in the boiling water and steep for 5 minutes. Strain into a teacup.
2 Sweeten with honey, if desired. Then take a few minutes to sip the hot tea slowly while sitting in a quiet spot.

Migraine Tea

2½ cups (625 ml) water
15 g dried lady's mantle leaves
3 teaspoons dried mint leaves

This inexpensive tea, served in a quiet, darkened room, can be very calming, but if any headache persists, seek medical advice.

1 In a saucepan, bring the water to a boil. Add the herbs and boil for 20 minutes. Remove from heat and steep for 10 minutes. Strain into a teacup.
2 Drink 1 cup (250 ml) slowly in a quiet, darkened room.

Headache Massage Oil

10 drops massage oil
3 drops peppermint
   essential oil
2 drops lavender essential oil
1 drop lemon, orange or lime
   essential oil

This fragrant aroma and gentle massage can bring a throbbing head back to health without jeopardising your stomach or liver. If pain persists, seek medical advice.

1 In a small bowl, mix the massage oil and the essential oils.
2 Dip your fingers into the oil and then massage the oil into the temples, along the hairline, and along the base of the skull, being careful not to get any oil in the eyes.
3 Wash your hands thoroughly after each application.

Headache Oil with Vitamin E

15 drops lavender essential oil
7 drops wintergreen
   essential oil
25 ml almond or olive oil
1 capsule vitamin E, 500 IU
hot water

Here is another aromatic solution for safely massaging away a headache. Wash your hands after applying.

1 In a small dish, combine the essential oils with the almond or olive oil. Pierce the vitamin E capsule with a needle and squeeze the contents into the dish.
2 Warm the oil mixture by putting the dish in a bowl of hot water before using. Dab your fingers into the fragrant oil and gently massage your temples and the back of your neck.

Anxiety and Fatigue

Catnip Anti-anxiety Tea

2 teaspoons dried catnip
1 cup (250 ml) boiling water

Catnip tea has a calming effect, and it may help relieve stress and combat anxiety. Sip a cup several times a day.

1 In a teapot, steep catnip in boiling water for 5 to 7 minutes.
2 Strain and drink. Serve yourself catnip tea 3 times a day.

Hops Anti-anxiety Tea

2 teaspoons dried hops
1 cup (250 ml) boiling water

Your cat is casting jealous glances at your catnip tea. So try hops, the critical ingredient in beer, instead.

1 In a teapot, steep hops in boiling water for 5 to 7 minutes.
2 Strain and drink. Serve yourself hops tea 3 times a day.

Calming Tea for Insomnia

boiling water
3 teaspoons dried chamomile
or lemon balm

Many over-the-counter sleep aids may be just repackaged antihistamines. Instead, try this natural alternative.

In a small pot, pour boiling water over the chamomile or lemon balm. Steep for 10 minutes, strain and drink 1 hour before bed.

Lavender rub for insomnia

Massage a single drop of lavender essential oil into each temple before going to bed.

Sleep Pillow

20 g sweet woodruff
10 g lemon balm
10 g lavender
3 teaspoons chamomile
3 teaspoons hops
3 teaspoons rosebuds
10–15 drops each chamomile,
lavender, clary sage and
marjoram essential oils
3 teaspoons powdered or
freshly grated orris root
1 small zippered pillowcase

This aromatic small pillow will work its wonders – with no side effects – on your sleep habits.

1 In a large bowl, mix the woodruff, lemon balm, lavender, chamomile, hops and rosebuds. In a separate small bowl, mix the essential oils with the orris root. Stir this mixture into the large bowl.
2 Fill the pillowcase, zip it and add it to your bed pillows for sweet dreams.

Herbal Milk Bath for Sleeplessness

½ handful lavender
½ handful chamomile
½ handful rose petals
½ handful dry milk powder
double-layer square of muslin
  (cheesecloth)

What is more relaxing than a nice soak in a soothing herbal bath?

1 Place the lavender, chamomile, rose petals and milk powder on the muslin (cheesecloth) and tie the corners to make a bag.
2 Place under the tap while the water is running. Start with warm water but allow it to cool before getting in. Cool water helps lower your body temperature, which is important for sleep.
3 Soak for 15 minutes while listening to relaxing music or a relaxation tape.

Relaxing Aromatic Bath

10 drops lavender, rose,
  geranium and/or bergamot
  essential oil

Here's another way to get sleepy or reduce stress without any pills. Keep the water relatively cool to maintain a low body temperature, important for sleep.

1 Add the essential oils to a cool bath.
2 Soak for 15 minutes while listening to relaxing music or a relaxation tape.

Invigorating Oil for Fatigue

2 parts eucalyptus essential oil
2 parts juniper essential oil
2 parts grapefruit essential oil
1 part clary sage essential oil
1 part ginger or peppermint
  essential oil
2 parts rosemary essential oil

These essential oils have fragrances that help to stimulate you and keep your mind alert.

1 In a clean small spray bottle, add essential oils. Shake to mix.
2 You can use this spray in a variety of ways: spritz an entire room when you feel tired and need to keep reading. Spray a cloth, hold it up to your nose and breathe deeply. Rub into your hands. Use in a diffuser or humidifier.

Energy Tea for Fatigue

1 teacup (200 ml) boiling
  water
½ teaspoon dried rosemary
  leaves
½ teaspoon dried ginseng root
honey (optional)

This energising tea is a real homemade pick-me-up that tastes good as well.

In a teacup, make an infusion of boiling water, dried rosemary leaves and dried ginseng root. Sweeten with a bit of honey, if you like, and drink as often as necessary.

Dog Food

Calcium-rich Dog Food ❖ Low-fat Chicken and Rice Dog Dinner ❖ Delectable Dog Biscuits ❖ Doggie Salad ❖ Lucky Liver Treats ❖ Sweet Breath Dog Treats ❖ Doggie Birthday Cake

Dog Care Products

Brush-and-go Dry Dog Shampoo ❖ Deodorising Minty Dog Wash ❖ Cocktail Flea Dip ❖ Flea-be-gone Bandanna ❖ Flea Powder ❖ Ear Mite Oil ❖ Firm Stool Fix

Cat Food

Wholesome Kitty Dinner ❖ Tuna Treats ❖ Catnip Crackers ❖ Quick Fish Stick Treats Sardine Balls ❖ Melon Squares ❖ Cat Grass Buffet

Cat Care Products

Baby-fresh Litter ❖ Dry Cat Shampoo Fragrant Flea Treatment ❖ Tick Removal from Cats

Treats for Birds

Pet Bird Honey Treats ❖ Pet Bird Snacking Salad ❖ Sweet and Crunchy Bird Muffins ❖ Finch and Canary Treat ❖ Wild Bird Food ❖ Parrot Pops ❖ Premium Wild Bird Mix ❖ Healthy Honeyeater Nectar

Food for Other Pets

Guinea Pig Salad ❖ Hamster Fruit Cup ❖ Gerbil and Rabbit Salad ❖ Pet Rodent Tabbouleh ❖ Turtle and Reptile Treat ❖ Aquarium Fish Treats

Natural Pet Care Products

Our animal companions provide us not only
with comfort and amusement, but also with an
uncritical devotion and loyalty that is difficult
to obtain elsewhere.

A loving pet provides therapy that instantly lifts its caretaker's
spirits. So all of us who love pets tend to enjoy buying them
expensive treats and toys. As this chapter will show you, however,
you don't have to spend a fortune to keep your pet – dog, cat,
bird, guinea pig, gerbil, rat, turtle or fish – well fed, healthily
groomed and happily occupied.

Indulge your pets with nutritious meals that they will gobble
up eagerly, and healthy treats that they can enjoy without
jeopardising their health and well-being. None of these foods
will strain your budget and most are actually fun to make. And
it is always reassuring to know exactly what goes into your pet's
food. In the recipes that follow, you will find not only healthy
everyday foods and rewards, but also special-occasion treats
such as a dog's birthday cake, catnip crackers for your cat and
honey treats for your pet bird.

You will also find great recipes for natural wet
and dry shampoos, flea dips and breath-saving
dog biscuits. For backyard bird lovers, there are
recipes for inexpensive seed combinations
you can mix to feed wild birds outside your
window. And for young families, there are
salads and treats for guinea pigs, hamsters,
turtles and other childhood friends.

Dog Food

Calcium-rich Dog Food

500 g minced chicken or beef
4 cups (about 750 g) cooked
    oatmeal or brown rice
½ cup (50 g) dry breadcrumbs
¼ cup (60 ml) vegetable oil
3 teaspoons bonemeal
    (available at garden centres)
1 dog vitamin, crushed
½ cup (60 g) grated cheddar
    cheese

Makes 6 servings, 1 cup
(about 240 g) each

This easy-to-make recipe will appeal to dogs and help to strengthen their bones. Although it is not inexpensive, it costs less than many canned dog foods and you can vouch for the quality of its ingredients.

1 In a frying pan over medium heat, brown the meat, stirring frequently. Remove from the heat.
2 Stir in the other ingredients and enough water to keep the mixture from being crumbly.
3 Cool and store in the refrigerator for 1 week or in the freezer for up to 3 months.

Note: Feed according to the weight of your dog. Feed a 5 kg dog 1 cup (about 240 g) daily; add 1 cup for every 5 kg of body weight. Monitor your dog's weight – you may need to adjust portions to avoid obesity.

Low-fat Chicken and Rice Dog Dinner

1.4 kg chicken, with skin
    and bone
1½ cups (280 g) cooked
    oatmeal or brown rice
1 dog vitamin
500 g fat-free cottage cheese

Makes 6 servings, 1 cup
(about 360 g) each

If you want a nutritious beef-and-wheat-free diet for your pet, this combination will satisfy its appetite and may even keep its weight under control. This is also an economical dog food with fresh ingredients.

1 Poach, bake or microwave the chicken until well done. Cool and cut into cubes. Drain and reserve pan juices to use as soup stock. Discard the bones.
2 In a large bowl, mix together the cubed chicken and oatmeal or rice. Crumble the vitamin and stir it in. Drain the cottage cheese and fold it into the mixture.
3 Store in a covered container in the refrigerator for up to 1 week.

Note: Feed according to the weight of your dog. Feed a 5 kg dog 1 cup (about 360 g) daily; add 1 cup for every 5 kg of body weight. Monitor your dog's weight – you may need to adjust portions to avoid obesity.

Delectable Dog Biscuits

900 g Calcium-rich Dog Food
   (opposite) or canned dog food
¼ cup (35 g) wholemeal flour
¾ cup (110 g) oat bran
1 cup (100 g) rolled oats
1 dog vitamin, crushed
   (optional)
¼ cup (25 g) grated parmesan
   or cheddar cheese (optional)
½ cup (125 ml) vegetable oil

Makes 16 medium biscuits

The combination of dog food and oatmeal makes these biscuits a healthy and tasty treat for your dog. You are assured of good ingredients and a better price than commercial dog biscuits. For a nutritional boost, add a crumbled dog vitamin.

1 Preheat the oven to 120°C (Gas ½).
2 Mix the dog food, flour, bran, rolled oats, vitamin (if desired) and cheese (if desired for a flavour boost).
3 Add the oil slowly, mixing the dough to a consistency that can be rolled and cut with a cookie cutter.
4 Roll and cut or mould the biscuits; place on an ungreased baking sheet. Bake for 3½ hours, or until hard.
5 Cool and store in a covered canister in the refrigerator for 1 week, or in a freezer for up to 1 month.

Homemade comforts for a new puppy

Puppies suffer from separation anxiety when they first leave their mother.
❖ To ease the transition, ask the breeder to put an old towel, T-shirt or other piece of clothing into the puppy's box for a few days. When you bring the puppy home, bring along the towel or clothing with the smells it recognises and put it into the puppy's new bed.
❖ Along with this security blanket, add something that smells of you, so that the pup will soon get used to its new home and associate your smell with comfort and safety.
❖ Another helpful transition aid is an old-fashioned ticking alarm clock, which emulates the mother's heartbeat.
❖ Also try filling an old sock with dried beans and microwaving it for a few seconds to create a soft, warm 'body' for the puppy to snuggle up to.

Doggie Salad

1 cup (155 g) grated carrots,
   raw
⅓ cup (60 g) cooked brown rice
½ cup (125 g) fat-free plain,
   live-culture yogurt
¼ cup (60 ml) vegetable oil

Makes 4 servings

Here's a delicious dietary supplement for your dog. Making your own costs very little and is much fresher. Dogs like carrots, which aid in digestion, freshen breath and provide vitamins. The yogurt is digestion-friendly.

1 Mix the carrots and rice in a bowl and set aside. In a second bowl, stir together the yogurt and salad oil. Pour this mixture over the carrots and rice and toss.
2 Store salad in a covered container in the refrigerator for up to 3 days. Serve ¼ cup (about 100 g) every day along with meals or as a treat.

Lucky Liver Treats

500 g beef or chicken livers
1 egg
1 cup (150 g) flour
¼ cup (20 g) unprocessed bran
  (wheat or oat)
¾ cup (110 g) polenta
  (cornmeal)
3 teaspoons garlic powder

Makes 117 liver treats

The secret of many successful show and obedience trainers is nothing more than a little baked chewy liver nibble that dogs can't resist. Try it – your pet will jump through hoops for this homemade treat.

1 Preheat the oven to 200°C (Gas 6). Chop the raw livers, and then liquefy them in a blender. Add the egg, pulse to blend, and then pour the mixture into a mixing bowl. Stir in the flour, bran, polenta and garlic powder.
2 Spread the mixture evenly into a greased 23 x 33 cm slice tin and bake for 15 minutes.
3 While still warm, cut the mixture into 2–3 cm squares. Turn the squares out onto a baking rack to cool and harden.
4 Store the cooled treats in a plastic self-sealing bag in the freezer to preserve freshness for up to 3 months. Serve either frozen or at room temperature.

Sweet Breath Dog Treats

3 teaspoons activated charcoal
  (available in fish section of
  pet shops)
½ cup (75 g) wholemeal flour
1 cup (150 g) white flour
¼ cup (20 g) bran cereal
½ cup (75 g) polenta (cornmeal)
¼ cup (60 ml) vegetable oil
1 egg
½ cup (30 g) chopped fresh
  basil, wintergreen or mint
½ cup (30 g) chopped fresh
  rosemary or thyme
1 cup (250 ml) acidophilus
  milk

Makes 24 medium biscuits

Here is a specialty dog biscuit that you don't have to shell out a fortune for at a pet shop. Puppies often have 'puppy breath' that they naturally outgrow by the age of 6 months. If an adult dog has occasional bad breath, this tasty recipe will combat the problem. If bad breath persists, however, it may be a sign of dental or digestive problems that a vet should treat.

1 Preheat the oven to 200°C (Gas 6). Process the charcoal in a coffee grinder until finely ground. Mix the flour, bran, polenta and charcoal together in a bowl. Stir in the other ingredients.
2 Form into bite-sized patties and place on a greased biscuit tray. Bake for 20 minutes, or until dry and hard.
3 Store in a covered container in the refrigerator for 1 week, or in the freezer for up to 3 months.

A quick water bowl for dog walkers

Pick up an inexpensive plastic shower cap to use as a portable pet water bowl. Stick it in your pocket when you're out walking your dog and, when needed, pull it out and fill it from a water bottle, the nearest tap or a drinking bubbler.

Doggie Birthday Cake

⅓ cup (50 g) flour
⅓ cup (50 g) polenta
  (cornmeal), bran
  or rolled oats
1½ teaspoons baking powder
½ teaspoon garlic powder
500 g minced chicken
30 ml honey
1 large egg
¼ cup (60 g) live-culture plain
  yogurt
4 teaspoons vegetable oil
1 container (125 g) spreadable
  cream cheese
Delectable Dog Biscuits, as
  needed to decorate cake
  (page 313)

Makes 1 cake with 4 to
6 servings

People do like to make a fuss over their dogs. For a birthday or adoption anniversary, you can go to a very fancy pet shop and spend a lot of money on a cake or you can make up this nutritious treat (to be meted out during the week) for much less. Here's a cake that you can feel good about offering your dog.

1   Preheat the oven to 180°C (Gas 4). In a medium bowl, stir together the dry ingredients. Make a well in the centre and add the chicken, honey, egg, yogurt and oil. Stir just until mixed.
2   Pour into a greased cake tin and bake for 25 minutes or until the chicken is done and a toothpick inserted in the centre of the cake comes out clean.
3   Turn out onto a cake rack to cool.
4   Ice the cake with cream cheese (thin cheese, if needed, with a little milk) and decorate with the dog biscuits. Refrigerate in a covered container for up to 1 week.

Dog Care Products

Brush-and-go Dry Dog Shampoo

1 box (500 g) bicarbonate
  of soda

Makes 1 or more shampoos,
depending on the size of dog

You can save heaps by substituting this single ingredient for a commercial dry pet shampoo. Although your pet will still need the occasional soap-and-water shampoo to remove ground-in dirt, dry shampoo will keep your dog clean and fresh smelling during cold weather or when you're travelling.

1   Test for sensitivity by rubbing a little bicarbonate of soda into your dog's coat between the ears (where it can't be licked off). Wait for 5 minutes and check for reddening or other signs of irritation. If there are none, proceed.
2   Rub the bicarbonate of soda into the dog's coat, working it in all the way to the skin. Be careful to avoid the eyes, nose, mouth and ears. Allow the soda to remain in the coat for a full minute to absorb oil and odour.
3   Brush the fur with a pet brush until all the bicarbonate of soda and debris are removed.

Deodorising Minty Dog Wash

1 large tube traditional-
   formula white toothpaste
   (coloured or gel pastes can
   discolour fur)
dog shampoo
¼ cup (60 ml) cider vinegar

Makes 1 treatment

When your dog rolls in something foul-smelling – as they
often do – confine it outdoors and run to the bathroom
supply cabinet for help.

1 Work the toothpaste into the dog's fur from head to tail, nose
   to toe. Allow the toothpaste to air-dry for 20 minutes.
2 Wet the dog and apply dog shampoo, working up a full lather.
3 In a large bucket, combine the vinegar with 4 litres of warm
   water. Rinse the dog with this solution (double it for a big dog)
   and dry as usual.
4 Repeat treatment as needed.

Cocktail Flea Dip

30 ml vodka or dry vermouth
825 ml water

Makes 1 treatment

To check for fleas, comb your pet over a sheet of white
paper: if black specks (flea dirt) drop onto the paper,
treat the animal at once with this dip (double recipe for
large pets). There are many expensive flea dips around
but this one does not contain harsh chemicals. To get rid
of flea eggs – and future infestations – wash the animal's
bedding and vacuum your house thoroughly.

1 In a large saucepan, stir alcohol into water and bring to a boil.
2 Remove from the heat, cover the pan, and allow the solution
   to steep for 2 hours.
3 Rub the cooled solution into your pet's fur, rinse and comb out.

Flea-be-gone Bandanna

1 cotton bandanna (colour
   and pattern of your choice)
1 small vial rose geranium
   essential oil
1 small vial lavender essential
   oil

Here's a safe, renewable, flea-repelling bandanna to make
for your dog. The active ingredients are essential herb
oils, which smell good to us, but fleas and mosquitoes
can't stand them. (Note that this is not a tick deterrent.
It should also not be considered adequate protection
against mosquitoes in heartworm areas.)

1 Sprinkle several drops of each oil on the bandanna.
2 Roll the bandanna and tie it loosely around your dog's neck.
3 Launder the bandanna; re-treat with oil when the scent fades.

Note: If your dog won't wear a bandanna, dab oil between its
shoulder blades where it can't be licked off. Don't get oil near
a dog's eyes, nose or mouth.

Natural ways to make fleas flee

Consider aromatic leaves, wood shavings and soap your first defence in your arsenal of flea repellents.

❖ Fill small drawstring bags (available at cooking supply and natural foods shops) with fresh or dried chamomile leaves, walnut leaves or cedar shavings and tuck them into your dog's bedding (where they can't be chewed) to repel fleas.

❖ Sprinkle garlic powder or mix a crushed garlic clove into your dog's food to ward off fleabites. Both garlic and chamomile are attractive flowering perennials, so for a free supply, try growing these herbs in your flower or vegetable beds.

❖ A sprinkle of brewer's yeast (buy from health-food shops) on your pets' food daily is also thought to help them repel fleas.

❖ Soap kills fleas on contact. When bathing your dog, begin by lathering the neck area first and then work your way towards the tail, because fleas tend to congregate around the neck.

❖ After rinsing, rub apple cider vinegar through the fur to help repel fleas, and add a teaspoon of cider vinegar to the dog's drinking water.

Flea Powder

1 box (500 g) bicarbonate of soda

10 drops in total peppermint, lavender, rosemary, cedar, eucalyptus or rose geranium essential oils

Makes 1 treatment

This inexpensive powder will leave your dog fresh smelling and helps to repel fleas. It is safe to apply as often as needed. Mix and match the oils according to your own scent preference.

1 In a mixing bowl, empty the box of bicarbonate of soda, sprinkle with your personal blend of oils, and stir to blend.
2 Work the treated bicarbonate of soda into your dog's fur, beginning at the neck (where fleas congregate) and working towards the tail. Keep the powder away from nose, mouth, eyes and ears.
3 Allow the powder to remain on the dog for 10 minutes, then comb or brush it out, along with dirt and fleas.

Note: If you have a large dog, you may need to make 2 or more recipes' worth.

Easy way to remove burrs and gum from fur

Burrs and chewing gum can be nearly impossible to comb or shampoo out of a pet's tangled fur. To make burrs easier to comb out, coat them with vegetable or mineral oil. Allow the oil to soften the burr for a few minutes, and then comb it out. To remove chewing gum, work creamy-style peanut butter into the gum until it dissolves, then comb out.

Ear Mite Oil

1 vitamin E capsule, 500 IU
¼ cup (60 ml) mineral oil

Makes ¼ cup (60 ml)

Ear mites can lead to serious infections and problems, including hearing loss in dogs. You can help to head off problems – and expensive vet bills – with this simple treatment. If you are too late and the problem persists, consult a veterinarian. It could be a yeast infection and not mites at all.

1 Pierce a vitamin E capsule with a needle and squeeze the contents into a small dropper bottle. Add the oil and shake. Store at room temperature.
2 To apply, hold the bottle in your hand for a few minutes to warm the oil. Put 2 or 3 drops of warm oil into the dog's ear canal and massage gently for a count of 10. Allow the dog to shake its head, then carefully swab oil and dirt from the ear. Repeat in the other ear.
3 Apply every other day for a full week.

Free pooper scoopers

❖ Save used self-sealing plastic sandwich and food storage bags to recycle as puppy toilet bags. To use a bag, turn it inside out and reach inside the clean side of the bag to grab the stool. Then pull the bag right-side-out, zip it closed and toss it in an outside bin.
❖ If you don't like the hands-on approach, you can relegate a cheap or decommissioned pair of scissors-style salad tongs to the status of pooper scooper – they work better than the real thing, and you can still make deposits into the self-sealing bags.

Firm Stool Fix

2 teaspoons mashed pumpkin
3 teaspoons cream cheese
¼ cup (7 g) cornflakes

Makes 1 treatment

If your pup or dog suffers occasionally from loose or runny stools, try this cheap and easy high-fibre remedy. If the problem persists, it could indicate internal parasites and you should consult a vet.

1 In a bowl, mix the pumpkin and cheese; roll the mixture into a ball and coat with the cornflakes.
2 Serve as a treat.

Cat Food

Wholesome Kitty Dinner

⅔ cup (180 g) minced chicken
 or beef
1 jar mixed vegetable baby
 food
1 cat vitamin, crumbled
 (optional)
⅓ cup (35 g) plain dry
 breadcrumbs

Makes 2 or 3 servings

This nutritious meat and vegetable meal will be a welcome change of pace for your cat. You know exactly what is in it, and it's budget-friendly, too.

1 In a small saucepan over medium heat, poach the minced meat in a small amount of water until medium–rare. Remove from heat and allow to cool.
2 Stir together the meat, meat juices, vegetables and vitamin, if using. Form into bite-sized balls and roll in breadcrumbs.
3 Serve as much as your cat will eat in one sitting. Store the rest in a covered container in the refrigerator for up to 3 days.

Tuna Treats

1 can oil-packed tuna
¼ cup (35 g) polenta
 (cornmeal)
¼ cup (20 g) bran cereal
1½ cups (225 g) wholemeal
 flour

Makes 24 or more depending
on size of treat

Cats are famous for loving tuna, and yours will jump for joy when you whip up these healthy treats that use a can of 'people' tuna and a few pantry staples. As a bonus, the oil-packed tuna may help prevent hairballs. You won't find fresh treats like this at any pet shop.

1 Preheat the oven to 180°C (Gas 4). In a large bowl, mix all the ingredients together.
2 Press the dough out on a floured board and cut into small cookies with a cookie cutter or pizza roller.
3 Place the treats on a greased biscuit tray and bake for 20 minutes or until light brown. Turn out onto a cake rack to cool. Store treats in a covered container in the refrigerator for up to 1 week or in the freezer for up to 1 month.

Trick your cat into taking medicine

Cats are choosy about what they eat, and often turn their noses up at the taste of medicine. If you have trouble getting yours to take its medicine, try smearing the medication on the back of a front paw – the cat will lick it off. If it is in pill form, crush and mix the pill with a little cream cheese to make it adhere to the paw.

Catnip Crackers

¾ cup (110 g) flour
½ cup (75 g) wholemeal flour
10 g dried catnip (available
   at pet shops and in the pet
   aisle of some supermarkets)
½ cup (125 g) yogurt
1 egg
3 teaspoons honey
45 ml vegetable oil

Makes 24 or more depending
on the size of crackers

Cats will go bonkers for these catnip crackers, so save them for rainy-day treats and special occasions.

1 Preheat the oven to 180°C (Gas 4). In a medium bowl, mix the flours and catnip together. Stir in the yogurt, egg, honey and vegetable oil.
2 Press out the dough on a floured surface and cut into tiny treats using a cookie cutter or pizza wheel. Place on a greased biscuit tray and bake for 15 minutes or until golden brown.
3 Store in a covered container in the refrigerator for 1 week or in the freezer for up to 3 months.

Quick Fish Stick Treats

1 box frozen, crumbed fish
   fingers
½ teaspoon garlic powder

Makes approximately 36 treats

Cats and their human companions alike will love these instant treats made from inexpensive frozen fish fingers. Adding a sprinkle of garlic powder will help your cat to repel fleas.

1 Empty the box of frozen fish fingers onto a cutting board. Sprinkle with garlic powder and cut the frozen fingers into 2–3 cm squares.
2 Store the squares in a self-sealing plastic bag (along with the cooking instructions from the package) in the freezer for up to 3 months.
3 To serve, remove a square and microwave according to packet directions, cool, then serve at room temperature.

Sardine Balls

1 can (185 g) sardines, packed
   in oil
¾ cup (75 g) plain
   breadcrumbs

Makes 6 or 8 treats

Cats will meow for the fishy flavour of these wholesome little fish balls. They're easy to make, kind on the budget, and the oily fish may help keep hairballs from forming.

1 Empty the can of sardines into a mixing bowl. Mix in ½ cup (50 g) breadcrumbs. Roll the mixture into bite-sized balls. When all balls are made, roll them in the remaining breadcrumbs to coat.
2 Store in a sealed container or self-sealing plastic bag in the freezer for up to 3 months.
3 To serve, thaw a ball to room temperature and place in your cat's food bowl.

Make your own cat toys

Cats love toys, and are especially fond of small, light, flexible and sparkly items. Avoid a costly trip to the pet shop by offering these found toys to your pet.

❖ Save the foil wrappers from chewing gum and other snacks and roll them into little balls for your cat to bat around.

❖ Twist a foil wrapper into a little 'bow tie' and fasten it on the end of a piece of string, then dangle it for your cat to play with.

❖ Tie these string foil-wrapper toys to doorknobs throughout the house. Your cat will love hiding behind the door and reaching around to pounce and bat at them.

❖ Create little rolling noise-makers by filling film canisters with non-toxic items, such as pieces of breakfast cereal and chopped nuts. Your cat will spend many happy hours rolling and chasing these toys.

Melon Squares

½ orange-fleshed melon
½ green-fleshed melon

Some cats love the flavour of melon. If yours is among them, keep some of these mixed melon treats on hand.

1 Peel and cube the melon flesh as you would for a salad.
2 Store melon cubes in a sealed container in the refrigerator for up to 1 week.
3 Serve 1 or 2 cubes as a treat daily.

Cat Grass Buffet

1 cup (180 g) whole oat grains
½ cup (90 g) wheat grains
½ cup (90 g) barley seeds
¼ cup (45 g) alfalfa seeds
¼ cup (45 g) rye grass seeds

Makes four 10 cm flowerpots of grass

House cats like green 'grass' to nibble on, and this recipe offers your cat long-lasting variety for little money. You can buy untreated sprouting grains inexpensively at health-food shops or even cheaper at feed mills. Keep grains in sealed plastic containers in the refrigerator. Save an empty parmesan shaker to fill with seed mix: it makes sowing easier.

1 Put the grains into a sealed plastic container and shake to mix. Fill shallow, tip-resistant pots with potting soil and moisten with tepid water.
2 Sprinkle the grains thickly over the top of the soil and cover grains with a sprinkling of soil. Set the pots in a sunny window and water as needed to keep the soil as moist as a wrung-out sponge. When the grass is about 2–3 cm tall, set a pot beside your cat's dinner dish and watch the fun.
3 For an ongoing supply, start a fresh pot of cat grass every other week.

Cat Care Products

Baby-fresh Litter

cat litter to cover bottom of litter box
⅓ cup (60 g) baby powder

Makes filler for 1 litter box

The most effective way to prevent cat litter odour is also a money saver: instead of throwing money away by filling the litter box to the top, just pour in a shallow layer. Use only 5–8 cm so that the litter can air-dry rapidly. Between litter changes, you can keep even the cheapest brand of litter smelling fresh with this simple, baby-safe recipe.

1 Pour the litter into a litter box to a depth of 5–8 cm.
2 Sprinkle the baby powder over the top of litter and stir to blend. For best results, change the litter at least once a week.

Dry Cat Shampoo

⅓ cup (25 g) unprocessed bran
⅓ cup (50 g) polenta (cornmeal)
⅓ cup (35 g) rolled oats

Makes 1 shampoo

Take the stress out of bath time for your cat by bathing it with this soothing, dry shampoo. As an added bonus, you'll save some pocket change because it's made from common pantry staples.

1 Pour the grains into a microwave-safe plastic container, seal and shake to combine. Warm in the microwave set on low for 10 seconds.
2 Rub the warm grains into your pet's fur. When finished, brush the grains out along with oil, dirt and dander.

Clever cat litter storage

If you keep your litter box in the laundry, bathroom or a walk-in wardrobe, try storing new kitty litter in an open bag at the bottom of your clothes hamper, the corner of a wardrobe, or near the washing machine. Not only will the kitty litter absorb odours and help keep these rooms smelling fresh, but you'll also be reminded to change the litter every time you change clothes.

Fragrant Flea Treatment

6 drops lavender essential oil
3 teaspoons mineral oil, or
   baby oil

Makes 1 treatment

Cats can be sensitive to any flea treatment, particularly toxic commercial flea powders. So try this mixture on a small patch of skin on the cat's stomach and wait for a day to see if there is a reaction. You must also wash the cat's bedding and vacuum the house thoroughly to get rid of flea eggs.

1 Drop the lavender essential oil and the mineral or baby oil into a small bottle and shake to combine.
2 Warm oil by holding the bottle in your hands for a few minutes.
3 Massage the warm oil into the neck area and the base of the tail where fleas congregate, then all parts of the cat, being careful to avoid contact with the cat's ears, eyes, nose and mouth. Repeat treatment when the scent is no longer detectable.

Free disposable cat litter boxes

Why clean a smelly plastic litter box when you can get bio-friendly ones for free and toss them out, dirty litter and all? Make a habit of stopping by your local convenience store or bottle shop (off-licence) and asking for their empty plastic-wrapped, shallow boxes – the kind that hold a dozen cans of soft drink. Keep the plastic on the box while in use, then pull it off and toss in the recycle bin before dumping the litter-filled box into the rubbish bin. They also make convenient toss-and-go litter boxes for travelling with your cat.

Tick Removal from Cats

petroleum jelly
hydrogen peroxide

Makes 1 treatment

Cats are sensitive to many kinds of medications and herbal treatments, including tick repellents, that are safe to use on dogs. Your best bet is to watch for ticks, especially around the face, ears and neck, and remove them according to the following recipe. However, if your cat is showing any signs at all of tick poisoning, seek veterinary advice immediately.

1 Coat the tick and surrounding skin with petroleum jelly applied with a cotton swab.
2 After the tick smothers, gently pull it, with the head intact, from the cat's skin.
3 Swab the area with hydrogen peroxide to disinfect it.

Treats for Birds

Pet Bird Honey Treats

⅓ cup (50 g) polenta
   (cornmeal)
½ cuttlefish bone, finely
   ground (in coffee grinder
   or mortar and pestle)
¼ teaspoon fine bird grit
¼ cup (40 g) mixed parakeet,
   finch or canary seeds
1 piece millet spray, crumbled
30 ml honey
¼ cup (25 g) wheatgerm
1 egg

Makes approximately 12 treats

Parakeets and songbirds like sweets. This calcium-rich, sweet treat is an inexpensive, wholesome snack. Most of the ingredients are already in your kitchen. You can find cuttlefish bone and bird grit at most pet shops or in the pet aisle of your supermarket.

1 Preheat the oven to 180°C (Gas 4). Place all the ingredients into a bowl and mix well. If the mixture is too thick to mould, add a little water. Press with your hands into small logs onto a greased and floured biscuit tray.
2 Bake for 30 minutes or until lightly browned.
3 Remove from the oven and turn logs out onto a cake rack to cool. Store, covered, in the freezer for up to 3 months.
4 To serve, thaw a log and fasten to cage bars with a treat clip. Renew when well nibbled.

Pet Bird Snacking Salad

3 leaves leaf lettuce, chopped,
   or ½ cup (20 g) chopped
   fresh spinach
½ cup (30 g) fresh or frozen,
   thawed, broccoli florets
½ cup (75 g) frozen and
   thawed whole kernel corn
½ apple, diced
½ segmented orange, diced
¼ cup (35 g) dried currants
½ cup (80 g) unsalted peanuts
   (for large birds only)

Makes about 6 servings

For optimum health, offer your bird fresh or thawed frozen fruits and vegetables daily. Forget expensive dried treats from a pet shop – they can't compare in freshness, flavour or vitamins. This salad appeals to all bird species, and is easy to put together by saving a little here and there from your meal preparations. Modify it as needed: you will learn quickly which ingredients your bird devours and which ingredients it leaves uneaten.

1 Toss all the ingredients in a covered bowl and store in the refrigerator for up to 5 days.
2 To serve, put a handful of salad in a shallow bowl or pottery flowerpot saucer in the cage. Offer daily and make new salad as needed.

The easy way to trap bird ticks

If your bird has ticks, hang a disposable white cloth (or a paper towel) on one side of its cage. The ticks are attracted to the bright object. After the ticks congregate on the cloth, remove and dispose in a sealed plastic bag.

Sweet and Crunchy Bird Muffins

1 small packet of commercial
   corn, bran or oatmeal
   muffin mix
⅓ cup (80 ml) milk
1 egg
¼ cup (65 g) apple sauce
½ cup (95 g) mixed dried
   fruits, unsweetened
½ cup (80 g) birdseed mix
   (appropriate to the species
   of bird)
1 bird vitamin, crumbled
   (optional)

Makes 6 muffins

Small-quantity corn, bran and oatmeal muffin mixes are sold cheaply in supermarkets – using them as a basis for these yummy bird treats lets you whip up treats faster than you could make them from scratch – but you can substitute your favourite muffin recipe (omit salt, which can harm birds). Plus, this all-in-one treat takes the place of several pricey commercial single-ingredient treats. For variety's sake, make all three flavours at the same time and alternate the flavours you offer your bird each day.

1 Preheat the oven to 190°C (Gas 5). Prepare the muffin mix according to packet directions, substituting the apple sauce for oil. Stir in the dried fruit, seed and bird vitamin, if using.
2 Pour the batter into greased muffin tins and bake according to packet directions, baking for 20 minutes or until golden brown.
3 Store in a sealed container in the freezer for up to 3 months.
4 To serve, thaw a muffin and place part or all of it in the bird's cage. You can refrigerate unused portions for up to 1 week.

Finch and Canary Treat

¼ cup (60 g) crunchy Peanut
   Butter (page 33) or crunchy,
   unsweetened, low-salt
   commercial peanut butter
½ cup (80 g) high-quality finch
   seed mix
¼ cup (25 g) wheatgerm

Makes 8 treats

Here's a bite-sized nutritious treat that's easy to make for small songbirds, such as finches and canaries. It is fresher and far less expensive than shop-bought treats.

1 In a medium bowl, mix the peanut butter and seeds together, adding more seeds if needed to make a stiff batter.
2 Pour wheatgerm into a shallow saucer. Form the peanut butter mix into small balls and roll the balls in wheatgerm to coat.
3 Serve 1 ball as a treat, in a bird-proof bowl. Store leftovers in a covered container in the refrigerator for up to 1 month, or freeze for up to 3 months.

Wild Bird Food

½ cup (60 g) sunflower seeds
½ cup (60 g) cracked corn
½ cup (60 g) raisins
½ cup (125 g) crunchy Peanut
   Butter (page 33)

Makes 2 cups

Watching backyard birds brings hours of enjoyment to adults and teaches children valuable nature lessons. This easy and inexpensive recipe – better than a bought packet of birdseed – will help to attract a wide variety of colourful and interesting birds to your garden.

1 Mix all the ingredients together in a bowl. Press the mixture into an empty bird feeder or small string bag.
2 Hang the feeder in a tree.

Homemade toys for parakeets and parrots

Parrots love toys, but they can be pricey and the bigger birds can destroy them quickly. Try these time-tested and inexpensive homemade toys.

❖ Parakeets love to preen in a mirror. So, instead of paying for a fancy bird mirror, just remove the hinge from an old compact and fasten the mirror securely to the cage bars near a perch.

❖ Parrots love to climb. Satisfy this urge by tying knots along a sturdy cotton rope and hanging it from the top of the cage.

❖ Parrots also love to bite and chew, and a dog-chew toy is often less expensive and just as long lasting as a parrot chew toy. Try a rawhide 'bone' or one made from nylon.

❖ Both parakeets and parrots like colourful toys, so string big wooden beads onto cotton rope and hang it for them to bat around and chew.

Parrot Pops

1 cup (125 g) high-quality mixed commercial parrot treats
½ cup (20 g) round oat cereal pieces
1 cup (185 g) dried mixed fruit, unsweetened
1 cup (160 g) unsalted peanuts
½ banana, mashed
1 eggwhite
6 craft or iceblock sticks (available at craft or kitchen supply stores)
½ cup (175 ml) honey

Makes 6 treats

These chewy sweet treats will keep your parrot happily occupied for hours. Whip them up inexpensively, then sit back and watch the fun.

1 Preheat the oven to 40°C. In a medium bowl, mix together the parrot treats, oat cereal, dried fruit and peanuts. Add the banana and eggwhite and stir to coat.
2 Spray muffin tin with non-stick spray, fill with mixture, insert a stick in each and press to compress. Bake for 2 hours, or until very hard. Remove pops from pan, coat each pop with honey, place on a greased baking sheet, return to oven, and bake for another 10 minutes or until honey is dry.
3 Serve 1 treat at a time. Remove and discard uneaten parts after 4 hours. Store in a sealed container in the refrigerator for up to 1 month or in the freezer for up to 3 months.

Premium Wild Bird Mix

500 g striped sunflower seeds, hulls on
500 g black-oil sunflower seeds, hulls on
500 g raw peanuts
500 g raisins, dried blueberries, apples or other dried fruits, chopped
500 g cracked corn
1 small carton live mealworms

Makes 2.5 kg

Avoid high-priced, and often inferior, wild birdseed blends. Individual seeds are available at stock-feed, health-food and pet shops. Adding live mealworms to your mix will entice insect-eating birds to your garden.

1 In a rodent-proof metal container with a tight lid, mix together the striped sunflower seeds, black-oil sunflower seeds, peanuts, fruit and cracked corn and store in a cool area, such as the cellar or garage. Store mealworms in the refrigerator according to packet directions.
2 Spread 1 or 2 scoops of the seed mixture onto a tray-type feeder and sprinkle with mealworms.

Healthy Honeyeater Nectar

2 cups (500 ml) water
½ cup (110 g) white sugar

Makes 2½ cups (625 ml)

Why buy expensive honeyeater nectar when you can make your own for next to nothing? This nectar will attract honeyeaters and lorikeets. Choose a feeder with a red base to attract the birds, so there's no need to use potentially harmful red food colouring. To prevent fermentation in hot weather, empty your feeder every 3 days and sterilise it by rinsing with boiling water.

1 In a small saucepan over medium heat, bring the water to a boil and then stir in the sugar until it dissolves. Return the solution to a boil. Remove from heat and cool, uncovered.
2 Store the nectar in a clean, tightly capped jar in the refrigerator for up to 1 month.
3 Sterilise the feeder by rinsing it with boiling water. Fill with fresh nectar and hang in the shade, at eye level.

Food for Other Pets

Guinea Pig Salad

½ cup (25 g) chopped fresh spinach
¼ cup (40 g) grated carrot
½ cup (90 g) chopped strawberries
¼ cup (60 ml) orange juice

Makes 2 servings

Fresh vegetables and fruits should be essential parts of a guinea pig's diet. The dried treats sold in pet shops are good in a pinch, but they're expensive and a poor substitute for fresh treats. This is a vitamin-rich fresh salad that's easy to make and good enough to share with your guinea pig.

1 In a bowl, toss the spinach, carrots and strawberries with the orange juice.
2 Serve in a feeding bowl. Remove and discard uneaten salad after 4 hours. Store leftovers in a sealed container in the refrigerator for 1 day.

Hamster Fruit Cup

½ banana
¼ cup (40 g) grated carrot
lemon juice
3 teaspoons raisins
1 teaspoon honey

Makes 2 servings

Experts agree that dried hamster pellets and treats do not provide a complete diet and pet shops don't include a salad bar, but your hamster can scurry to its bowl for this budget-friendly sweet treat that you can whip up in no time, using fresh fruits and vegetables.

1 Slice the banana and toss with the grated carrot in a bowl, adding a sprinkling of lemon juice to keep them from discolouring. Drain the juice from the bowl; add the raisins and honey and mash with a fork.
2 Serve half in a treat bowl and store the remainder in a covered container in the refrigerator for 1 day. Remove and discard uneaten treats after 4 hours.

Gerbil and Rabbit Salad

¼ cup (15 g) finely chopped
  spinach or leaf lettuce
¼ cup (40 g) grated carrot
1 teaspoon sunflower or
  pumpkin seeds, unsalted

Makes ½ cup (about 60 g)

It's important to offer pet rodents vitamin-rich fresh fruits and vegetables, and your gerbils and bunnies will welcome this healthy salad. For budget-boosting ingredients, ask for discarded outer leaves (which are more vitamin rich than inner leaves) at your greengrocer's, farmers' market or a restaurant salad bar. For variety, alternate seed toppings.

1 Toss the vegetables together in a bowl, top with the seeds, and serve in a small treat bowl. Store leftovers in a sealed container in the refrigerator for 1 day.
2 Remove and dispose of uneaten fresh foods after 4 hours.

Pet Rodent Tabbouleh

1 cup (175 g) burghul (bulgur),
  uncooked
30 ml boiling water
¼ cup (45 g) brown rice,
  cooked
¼ cup (25 g) rolled oats,
  cooked
¼ cup (30 g) parrot seed mix
¼ cup (90 g) dark molasses
1 rodent vitamin, crushed
  (optional)
¼ cup (25 g) wheatgerm

You just can't substitute dried pellets or grains from the pet shop for fresh foods when it comes to feeding a balanced diet to rodents. This is a nutritious treat recipe for pet mice and rats. You can make it easy by saving plain, leftover grains from the family table.

1 Put the burghul in a bowl, add boiling water and allow to stand for 5 minutes. Stir in the remaining ingredients, except wheatgerm, to make a thick, crumbly mixture.
2 Form into small balls and roll in a saucer of wheatgerm to coat.
3 Serve 1 ball daily as a treat. Discard uneaten treats after 4 hours. Store extra treats in a sealed container in the refrigerator for up to 1 week, or in the freezer for up to 1 month.

Rodents have a never-ending need to chew, and they can rapidly demolish expensive shop-bought toys. Save your wallet by collecting household 'chew toys' for mice, rats, guinea pigs and bunnies, such as

empty cardboard egg cartons, rolls from paper towels, food wrap and toilet paper, as well as small blocks of wood left over from woodworking projects.

Turtle and Reptile Treat

½ cup (80 g) grated carrot
½ cup (25 g) chopped lettuce
  or spinach
1 stalk celery, chopped
1 calcium tablet, crushed
1 teaspoon alfalfa sprouts
  (available at pet or
  health-food shops)
¼ cup (35 g) chopped melon
  or strawberries

Makes 2 servings

To give your pet turtle a calcium boost, try this fortified daily vegetable medley. And with a few additions, this treat will also benefit lizards and other cold-blooded vegetarian pets. Reptiles have very specific dietary needs and must be housed at the proper temperature to induce an appetite.

1 For a turtle snack, place the vegetables into a bowl, sprinkle with calcium and toss. For lizards and other reptiles, add the alfalfa and fruit.
2 Serve half in a chew-proof bowl. Store the remainder in a covered container in the refrigerator for 1 day.

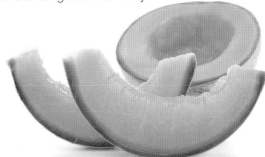

Aquarium Fish Treats

¼ cup (15 g) puréed spinach
1 earthworm, finely chopped
6 crickets
6 mealworms
6 bloodworms
¼ cup (25 g) raw beef liver,
  blended
1 raw prawn, blended

The best food for your aquarium fish is a high-quality commercial fish food formulated for the species of fish, but, for variety, they enjoy fresh or fresh-frozen live food and fresh vegetables. Experiment with the treats listed here. Crickets, mealworms and bloodworms are sold at pet shops.

1 Mix the spinach plus any two other ingredients. Store a week's worth of the mix in a sealed container in the refrigerator. Freeze the rest for up to 1 month.
2 To serve, drop a piece of the mix the size of a pencil eraser into the aquarium. Continue until fish stop feeding. After 5 minutes, remove uneaten food from the bottom of the aquarium, using a siphon or cooking bulb baster.

Part 3

Around the House

General Housecleaning

Basic Window and Glass Cleaner ❖ Super Window and Glass Cleaner ❖ Citrus Disinfectant ❖ Tough Multipurpose Cleaner ❖ Fresh-smelling Multipurpose Cleaner ❖ Wall and Cabinet Cleaner ❖ Interior Wall Cleaner ❖ Herbal Carpet Freshener ❖ Pine Floor Cleaner ❖ Spicy Carpet Freshener

Air Fresheners

Room Freshener Spray ❖ Spicy Room Freshener

Furniture Polishes

Lemon Oil Furniture Polish ❖ No-fuss Furniture Polish ❖ Cabinet Polish

Mould and Mildew Removers

Spot Mould and Mildew Remover ❖ Paint and Tile Mould and Mildew Remover ❖ Mould Remover for Leather and Luggage

Metal Polishes

Brass and Copper Paste Polish ❖ Cut-lemon Brass and Copper Polish ❖ Ketchup Copper Polish ❖ Chrome and Stainless Steel Polish ❖ Quick and Easy Silver Shine

In the Kitchen

Automatic Dishwasher Detergent ❖ Dishwashing Liquid ❖ Microwave Oven Cleaner ❖ Basic Oven Cleaner ❖ Lazy Person's Oven Cleaner ❖ Oven Floor Cleaner ❖ White Goods Cleaner ❖ Scouring Powder ❖ Homemade Scrub Powder ❖ Steel Wool Soap Pads

In the Laundry

Fabric Softener ❖ Laundry Soap ❖ Stain Remover

In the Bathroom

Multipurpose Disinfectant Cleaner ❖ Soft Scrub ❖ Eucalyptus Tile Cleaner ❖ Non-toxic Bathroom Cleaner ❖ Showerhead Cleaner ❖ Non-toxic Rust Remover ❖ Non-toxic Toilet Bowl Cleaner ❖ Tougher Toilet Bowl Cleaner ❖ Drain Opener ❖ Septic Tank Activator

Cleaning the Car

Basic Car Wash ❖ Upholstery Shampoo ❖ Windscreen Cleaner ❖ Vinyl and Leather Interior Cleaner

Clever Solutions Cleaning Products

Advertisements for 'new and better' cleaning supplies fill home magazines, and there is a vast and competitive industry dedicated to making you think you can't exist without the latest product.

Many of these highly touted products do have seemingly miraculous ingredients that can make dirt vanish, but many actually contain traditional cleaning compounds that you can make yourself. As the recipes here show, there are lots of safe ways to clean everything in your house, using simple mixtures of inexpensive, everyday staples that you probably already have in your pantry or store cupboard.

Homemade cleaning solutions not only get the job done easily and inexpensively, but they do it without harming you or your possessions – because you know exactly what is in them. Most of these products have a long and honourable history – your grandmother probably used many of them. As you might expect, you'll see recipes that use many traditional ingredients, such as bicarbonate of soda, vinegar and lemon juice. But you may be surprised to learn that you can still buy borax and washing soda at your local supermarket, and even more surprised to find that tomato ketchup is a fine copper polish.

These homemade cleaning products are all very economical. White vinegar and bicarbonate of soda, for example, are much cheaper than commercial fabric softeners for keeping lint off your clothes and stopping static electricity. Old newspapers are cheaper than paper kitchen towels for cleaning windows. And dried spices refresh your house far more inexpensively than any commercial room deodoriser.

General Housecleaning

Basic Window and Glass Cleaner

½ cup (125 ml) white vinegar
10 cups (2.5 litres) water
1 clean 4 litre container
1 clean 1 litre spray bottle
old newspapers

Forget about all of those shop-bought window cleaners. Your windows can get a professional shine for next to nothing. This recipe will clean a lot of windows. You can make a smaller batch in a 1 litre spray bottle by mixing ¼ cup (60 ml) vinegar with enough water to fill the container.

1 Mix the ingredients in the 4 litre container.
2 Fill the spray bottle and spray on windows and glass items as needed. (Save the remaining cleaner for another day.)
3 Dry the glass with crumpled newspaper for added brightness.

Super Window and Glass Cleaner

⅓ cup (80 ml) white vinegar
¼ cup (60 ml) methylated spirits
3¼ cups (810 ml) water
1 clean 1 litre spray bottle
old newspapers

The alcohol in this formula helps prevent streaking.

1 Mix all the ingredients in the spray bottle. Shake the bottle well before using.
2 Spray on a dirty windowpane or other glass surface.
3 Dry with crumpled newspaper.

Citrus Disinfectant

zest from 1 orange, grapefruit, lemon or lime
3 cups (750 ml) white vinegar
1 clean 1 litre container with lid
1 clean 1 litre spray bottle

If you like commercial orange cleaners, you'll love this fresh citrus-scented vinegar spray that is easy to make and costs very little. You can also deodorise a room by setting out a small bowl of citrus vinegar.

1 Combine the citrus zest and vinegar in the 1 litre container. Fasten the lid on the container and store the mixture in a cupboard for 2 weeks, giving it an occasional shake.
2 Remove the zest from the container, then strain the vinegar and return it to the container.
3 To use as a spray cleaner, pour 1 cup (250 ml) of citrus vinegar into the spray bottle and fill with water.
4 To clean linoleum floors, add 1 cup (250 ml) citrus vinegar to 8 litres water.

Tough Multipurpose Cleaner

3 cups (750 ml) water
⅓ cup (80 ml) methylated
  spirits
1 teaspoon clear household
  ammonia
1 teaspoon mild dishwashing
  liquid
½ teaspoon lemon juice
1 clean 1 litre spray bottle

When it comes to cleaning non-wood surfaces around your home, this cleaner is tough to beat. And it costs almost nothing.

1 Combine the ingredients in the spray bottle and shake well before each use.
2 Spray on benchtops, kitchen appliances and fixtures, and tile or painted surfaces.
3 Wipe down with a clean cloth or damp sponge.

Fresh-smelling Multipurpose Cleaner

3½ cups (875 ml) hot water
½ cup (125 ml) white or apple
  cider vinegar
1 teaspoon borax
1 teaspoon washing soda
1 teaspoon liquid castile soap
1 clean 1 litre spray bottle

This formula has a clean smell and works hard, despite its inexpensive ingredients. You can buy liquid castile soap at health-food shops.

1 Fill spray bottle first with hot water; then add vinegar, borax, washing soda and liquid castile soap. Shake well before using.
2 Spray on benchtops, kitchen appliances and fixtures, and tile or painted surfaces.
3 Wipe down with a clean cloth or damp sponge.

Wall and Cabinet Cleaner

1 cup (250 ml) clear household
  ammonia
1 cup (250 ml) white vinegar
¼ cup (70 g) bicarbonate of
  soda
4 litres warm water

If you have dingy cupboards, this cleaning solution will deodorise them as well as wiping up the dust and dirt.

1 Combine the ammonia, vinegar and bicarbonate of soda in a large bucket, add water and give it a few stirs.
2 Use a sponge or cloth rag to wash walls, ceilings, floors or cabinets with the cleaner.
3 Wipe up the excess liquid with a clean cloth and allow to dry thoroughly before replacing contents.

Use bread to spot-clean wallpaper

Cut the crusts off a slice of white bread and roll it up into a ball. Once the bread starts to feel slightly doughy, roll it over the bad spots on the wallpaper to lift off the dirt or fingerprints. Test the bread ball first on an inconspicuous corner.

Interior Wall Cleaner

½ cup (120 g) borax
1 tablespoon clear household
 ammonia
¼ cup (60 ml) white vinegar
4 litres warm water

Those scuff marks and stains on your painted walls seem to appear out of nowhere. This potent cleaner will remove them without harming your paint job.

1 In a large bucket, mix all the ingredients.
2 Apply the solution to the wall with a clean sponge. Use a second clean sponge to rinse the wall with plain water.
3 To minimise streaking, start at the bottom of the wall and work up.

Herbal Carpet Freshener

large handful fresh lavender
 flowers
1 cup (280 g) bicarbonate
 of soda

Many commercial air and carpet deodorisers simply mask odours. To truly freshen carpets around your home, try this inexpensive natural formula instead. (If you don't like the smell of lavender, you can also freshen up carpets with plain bicarbonate of soda.)

1 In a large bowl, crush the lavender flowers to release scent.
2 Add the bicarbonate of soda and mix well. Pour the mixture into a cheese shaker or a can with holes punched in the lid.
3 Sprinkle liberally on the carpet. Wait 30 minutes, then vacuum.

Pine Floor Cleaner

½ cup (50 g) pure soap flakes
¼ cup (70 g) washing soda
1 cup (225 g) salt
2 cups (500 ml) water
2 teaspoons pine oil
1 clean 500 ml plastic bottle
 with a tight-fitting lid
1 cup (250 ml) white vinegar

You shouldn't have to spend a small fortune to give your no-wax floors a pine-fresh smell. This excellent cleaner will do the job for only small change. If you can't find pure soap flakes, you can make your own by grating a bar of soap.

1 If you are making your own soap flakes, grate the soap on a coarse kitchen grater.
2 In a saucepan over low heat, combine the soap, washing soda, salt and water and stir until soap, soda and salt have dissolved.
3 Remove from the heat and allow the mixture to cool until it is lukewarm. Add the pine oil. Stir well, pour into the plastic bottle, and secure the top.
4 To use, pour 2 or 3 tablespoons of the cleaner into a half-bucket of hot water, stirring well. For large areas, you may need to double the amount.
5 After cleaning, add the vinegar to a half-bucket of clean water and rinse the floor.

Spicy Carpet Freshener

1 cup (280 g) bicarbonate
   of soda or cornflour
7–10 drops essential oil
   in your favourite scent
   (eucalyptus or rosewood,
   for example)

Add a nice smell to your rooms while you freshen the carpets with this simple mixture.

1 In a large bowl, combine the bicarbonate of soda or cornflour with the essential oil. Break up any clumps with a fork and stir well. Pour the mixture into a parmesan shaker or a can with holes punched in the lid.
2 Sprinkle liberally on the carpet. Wait 30 minutes, then vacuum.

Air Fresheners

Room Freshener Spray

1 clean 375 ml spray bottle
¼ cup (60 ml) methylated
   spirits
25 drops bergamot essential oil
8 drops clove essential oil
5 drops lemon essential oil
1 cup (250 ml) distilled water

Why waste your money on commercial air fresheners when it's so easy to make your own favourite scents? Use this spray judiciously, however. A room should have a hint of the spicy scent, not an overpowering perfume. You can combine up to three different essential oils to create a fragrance that suits you. Other choices include eucalyptus, lavender, geranium, grapefruit, orange, peppermint, pine, juniper, rose and spearmint.

1 In the spray bottle, combine the methylated spirits and the essential oils and shake well to disperse the oil. Add the water and shake for a minute or two more to blend all the ingredients thoroughly.
2 Let the mixture sit for a few days before using to allow the fragrance to blend and mature. A quick spritz is all that's needed to freshen a room.

Spicy Room Freshener

3 cups (750 ml) water
6 cloves
1 cinnamon stick
6 pieces dried orange peel

This fragrant mixture makes you think an apple pie is in the oven; real estate agents sometimes suggest putting this mixture on the stove before prospective buyers come to see the house.

In a small saucepan, combine all the ingredients and bring to a boil over medium heat. Reduce the heat and simmer, uncovered, until your home is filled with a fresh, spicy scent. (Don't let the water boil away.)

Furniture Polishes

Lemon Oil Furniture Polish

1 cup (250 ml) olive oil
⅓ cup (80 ml) lemon juice
1 clean 500 ml spray bottle

Shine up your wood furniture, panelling and knick-knacks with this natural polish that will take you only a minute to prepare, and costs very little. Discard any leftovers and make up a fresh batch each time you want to polish your wood treasures.

1 Combine the oil and lemon juice in the spray bottle. Shake well before using.
2 Apply a small amount of the mixture to a soft flannel cloth or chamois and apply it evenly over the wood surface.
3 Use a clean, dry flannel cloth to buff and polish.

No-fuss Furniture Polish

¼ cup (60 ml) boiled linseed oil
30 ml vinegar
30 ml whisky
1 clean 500 ml spray bottle

How would you like a furniture polish that you can just wipe on and forget? Well, your prayers have been answered – and for a lot less than you might expect!

1 Combine all the ingredients in the bottle. Shake well.
2 Apply a small amount of polish to a clean, soft cloth and wipe on. No need to buff; the dullness evaporates along with the alcohol.

Cabinet Polish

1 teaspoon lemon juice
1 teaspoon olive oil
2 cups (500 ml) warm water

Why burn through your household budget on furniture polish for those large wood kitchen cabinets, bookshelves or wardrobes around your home? This is the perfect polish to use on big jobs – and it costs almost nothing to make. Be sure to mix up a fresh batch for each use.

1 Combine the ingredients in a bowl or container.
2 Dip a soft flannel cloth into the solution and wring it out. Wipe over the wood.
3 Buff and polish with a soft, dry cloth.

Mould and Mildew Removers

Spot Mould and Mildew Remover

½ cup (125 ml) white vinegar
3 teaspoons borax
2 cups (500 ml) hot water
1 clean 1 litre spray bottle

Mix up a batch of this powerful but benign-smelling disinfectant to get rid of small patches of mould and mildew that breed in bathroom medicine cabinets, windowsills and other surfaces around your home.

1 Combine the ingredients in the spray bottle. Shake well.
2 Spray on surfaces where mould or mildew is forming. Wipe off mildew, but leave the cleaning solution residue to keep mildew from returning.

Paint and Tile Mould and Mildew Remover

¼ cup (60 ml) chlorine bleach
3 teaspoons borax
1½ cups (375 ml) water
1 clean 500 ml spray bottle

This formula will take mould and mildew off painted and tile surfaces for the cost of your small change. Be sure the room is well ventilated as you work.

1 Combine the ingredients in the spray bottle and shake to mix.
2 Spray the painted or tile surface and wipe off mildew and mould with a clean cloth. Rinse the surface with clean water and dry with clean cloths.

Mould Remover for Leather and Luggage

½ cup (125 ml) methylated spirits
¼ cup (60 ml) water
1 clean 250 ml spray bottle

If you discover mould on your expensive luggage, handbag or leather jacket, don't just race to the dry cleaners. Instead, remove the offending growth with this simple, inexpensive mould-removal recipe. Test on a small area first.

1 Combine the ingredients in the spray bottle and shake well to mix.
2 Spray affected area. Let the solution sit for 10 to 20 minutes, then wipe off mould with a clean rag and allow the item to thoroughly air-dry.

Metal Polishes

Brass and Copper Paste Polish

¼ cup (35 g) flour
¼ cup (55 g) salt
¼ cup (60 ml) vinegar
¼ cup (60 ml) hot water
1 teaspoon lemon juice

Use this simple, non-toxic – and very inexpensive – polish to brighten up all your tarnished unlacquered brass and copperware. (Lacquered items only need dusting.)

1 In a small bowl, combine all the ingredients to form a paste.
2 Using a soft cloth, rub the mixture onto the metal surface.
3 Rinse the object thoroughly in warm water (remember that salt is corrosive).
4 Dry with soft, clean cloths and then buff to a shine with a soft flannel cloth or chamois.

Cut-lemon Brass and Copper Polish

½ cup (125 ml) white vinegar
2 tablespoons salt
½ lemon

Here's an even easier way to shine up unlacquered brass or copper objects – and a useful way to use up leftover half lemons.

1 In a saucepan over medium heat, heat the vinegar for 5 minutes, then pour it into a small bowl and stir in the salt.
2 Dip the lemon into the mixture and rub it over the object, concentrating on the most heavily tarnished areas.
3 Thoroughly rinse the object in warm water and dry with soft, clean cloths. Buff to a shine with a soft cloth.

Ketchup Copper Polish

½–1 cup (125–250 ml) tomato
  ketchup
¼–1 lemon, juiced

This simple polish can be a bit messy, but it works like a charm on unlacquered copper – and it's completely non-toxic. Can your old copper polish say that?

1 In a small bowl, combine the ketchup and lemon juice and stir to mix. How much you need of each ingredient depends on the size of the object you want to polish, but keep the ratio of ketchup to lemon juice about 8:1.
2 Spread out some old newspapers on your work surface. Rub the mixture over the copper piece's surface. Let it sit for 5 to 10 minutes.
3 Thoroughly rinse the copper piece in warm water and dry with soft, clean cloths. Buff to a shine with a soft cloth.

Chrome and Stainless Steel Polish

¼ teaspoon baby oil
½ cup (125 ml) soda water

Baby the chrome and stainless steel finishes around your home with this simple one-two set of cleaners. They remove stains as well as dirt and fingerprints cheaply and quickly.

1 Apply a few drops of baby oil to a soft cloth or piece of flannel and wipe down the chrome or stainless steel surface. Moisten the second soft cloth with soda water, and rinse off the oil.
2 Dry and buff with a soft, dry cloth.

Quick and Easy Silver Shine

4 cups (1 litre) hot water
3 teaspoons bicarbonate of soda or washing soda
3 teaspoons salt
1 sheet aluminium foil

Want a really easy, inexpensive and amazingly effective way to polish your silver without any smelly chemicals or commercial products? This is easier than using a silver dipping cleaner.

1 Fill the kitchen sink with about 4 cups (1 litre) hot water.
2 Dissolve the bicarbonate of soda or washing soda and salt in the water, then place the sheet of aluminium foil at the bottom of the sink.
3 Rest the tarnished silver on the foil for 10 seconds. Remove and dry with a soft flannel cloth.

Potato rust remover for tin pans

Tin pie plates and other kitchen utensils are subject to rust if they are not dried carefully after each washing. Here, for little more than the price of a potato, is a way to restore your tinware without harsh chemicals. Peel a potato and cut it into easy-to-handle pieces. Put some bicarbonate of soda or salt in a saucer. Then dip a cut piece of potato in the soda or salt, and rub it over the rust spots. Rinse the tin utensil and dry thoroughly.

In the Kitchen

Automatic Dishwasher Detergent

2 cups (480 g) borax
2 cups (560 g) washing soda
1 clean 1 kg plastic container
   with cover

Even if you live in a hard-water area, this simple, inexpensive detergent recipe will help keep your dishes shiny and spotless.

1 Combine the borax and washing soda in the container and seal it tightly for storage.
2 For each load of dishes, put 2 tablespoons of the mixture in the dishwasher soap dispenser.

Fast, cheap rinsing agent for your dishwasher

Here's an easy way to get those dishes sparkling in your automatic dishwasher without using any chemical rinsing agents. Just stop the dishwasher during its rinse cycle and add 1 to 1½ cups (250–375 ml) white vinegar. Or pour the vinegar into the rinse compartment beforehand (being careful not to overfill). Then wash the dishes as usual.

Dishwashing Liquid

¼ cup (25 g) pure soap flakes
   (or a bar of pure soap,
   for grating)
1½ cups (375 ml) hot water
¼ cup (60 ml) glycerine
½ teaspoon lemon oil
1 clean 500 ml squirt bottle

This dishwashing soap for washing dishes by hand is inexpensive and really gets your dishes clean. It's mild on your hands, too.

1 If you are unable to find pure soap flakes, lightly grate a bar of pure soap on a coarse kitchen grater.
2 In a medium jug, pour the soap flakes into the hot water and stir with a fork until most of the soap has dissolved. Let the solution cool for 5 minutes.
3 Stir in the glycerine and lemon oil. A loose gel will form as it cools. Use the fork to break up any congealed parts and pour the liquid into the squirt bottle. Use 2 to 3 teaspoons per sink or washing up bowl of hot water to clean dishes.

Microwave Oven Cleaner

1½ cups (375 ml) water
3 tablespoons lemon juice or
  3 tablespoons bicarbonate
  of soda or 2 cups (500 ml)
  white vinegar

You don't need harsh cleansers and lots of elbow grease to clean your microwave. For the price of a lemon, some bicarbonate of soda or some white vinegar, you can just wipe away the splatters and stains inside.

1 In a microwave-safe bowl, combine the water and lemon juice or bicarbonate of soda, or just pour the vinegar. Place the uncovered bowl inside the oven, and run the microwave on high for 3 to 5 minutes, allowing the liquid to condense on its inside walls and ceiling.
2 Carefully remove the bowl with a towel or pot holder (it will be very hot!), and wipe the interior of the oven with a tea towel or paper towel.

Basic Oven Cleaner

30 ml liquid soap
2 teaspoons borax
2 cups (500 ml) warm water
1 clean 500 ml spray bottle
½ cup (140 g) bicarbonate of
  soda in an open bowl

Try this odourless recipe the next time you need to clean your oven, and leave those caustic chemical-based oven cleaners where they belong – on the shop shelf.

1 Pour the soap and borax into the spray bottle and add the warm water. Shake well to dissolve the borax.
2 Spray the solution on the oven's surfaces, giving special attention to dried, cooked-on spills.
3 Let the mixture sit for 30 minutes to 1 hour, then scrub the oven surfaces with a damp scrub pad dipped in the bicarbonate of soda. Rinse with clean water.

Lazy Person's Oven Cleaner

¾ cup (185 ml) clear household
  ammonia
1 cup (280 g) bicarbonate of
  soda in a wide-mouthed dish

Here is the recipe for a cheap, almost effortless oven cleaner that is still very effective.

1 Pour the ammonia into a small bowl and leave it overnight in a closed, cool oven.
2 The next day, remove and discard the ammonia and wipe down the oven's interior surfaces with moistened paper towels or damp sponges dipped in bicarbonate of soda.

Oven Floor Cleaner

½ cup (125 ml) water
1–2 cups (280–560 g)
  bicarbonate of soda
1 teaspoon liquid detergent

This recipe is for cleaning up the oven floor after a sticky sweet pie or a too-full casserole has spilled over and caused a real mess. You don't need expensive, caustic commercial oven cleaners to deal with it. You probably already have everything you need on hand.

1 Sprinkle water along the bottom of the oven.
2 Spread enough bicarbonate of soda over the surface to coat it entirely, and sprinkle more water on top of it.
3 Let the paste sit overnight. The next morning, the grease and grime will be loosened enough for you to wipe it up with damp paper towels or tea towels.
4 Once you've wiped up the core of the mess, use the liquid detergent on a damp sponge to remove any remaining residue. Rinse with water and let dry.
5 Repeat if necessary.

White Goods Cleaner

40 ml dishwashing liquid
20 g cornflour
1 cup (250 ml) water
1 cup (250 ml) white vinegar
a few drops herbal essential oil

Regular wiping with this solution will remove grubby fingermarks and leave the surfaces of freezers, refrigerators and washing machines looking like new without scratching them.

1 Put all the ingredients in a plastic spray bottle and shake gently to combine.
2 Spray a fine mist of the mixture over the grubby surface and wipe clean with a soft cloth.

Scouring Powder

1 cup (280 g) bicarbonate
  of soda
1 cup (240 g) borax
1 cup (225 g) salt
1 clean 1 kg plastic container
  with cover

You don't need chlorine bleach to clean stains off the non-porous surfaces in your kitchen and bathroom. This scouring powder is very effective, a lot safer to use and far more economical.

1 Combine the ingredients in the container and mix well. Close the container tightly to store.
2 To clean a stained surface, sprinkle some of the powder onto a damp sponge or directly on to the surface to be cleaned. Scour, rinse and dry.

Homemade Scrub Powder

2½ cups (700 g) bicarbonate
  of soda
1½ cups (335 g) salt
30 g cream of tartar
1 clean 1.5 kg plastic container
  with lid

Use this mixture to scrub off grease and grime from your stainless steel and enamelled cookware. (If you use bicarbonate of soda on aluminium cookware, it may cause darkening.)

1 Mix all the ingredients well, and store in a tightly sealed plastic container.
2 To use, pour 2 to 3 tablespoons of powder onto cookware and scrub with a brush or nylon scrubber that's been slightly moistened with water. Rinse well and dry with a soft cloth.

Steel Wool Soap Pads

1 bag steel wool pads (available
  at hardware stores)
60 g Homemade Scrub Powder
  (above)

Those popular pre-packaged steel wool soap pads are great for getting tough stains and cooked-on foods off your pots and pans, but they can be rough on your hands. These homemade steel wool pads work just as well, and are easier on both your wallet and your skin.

1 If you've purchased large pads, use sharp scissors or shears and carefully cut them into rectangles approximately 8 cm long by 5 cm high.
2 Spread a layer of scouring powder over the cooking surface, moisten the steel wool pad with warm water, and scrub away stains. Rinse well with water. Dry with a soft, absorbent towel.
3 To make your pads last longer, squeeze out remaining water and keep them in a bowl lined with aluminium foil.

In the Laundry

Fabric Softener

¼ cup (70 g) bicarbonate
  of soda
½ cup (125 ml) white vinegar

Here's a simple recipe for keeping your fabrics soft and fluffy. It's gentle on your clothes and much easier on your wallet than commercial fabric softeners.

1 Fill the washing machine with water.
2 Add the bicarbonate of soda and then the clothing.
3 During the final rinse cycle, add the vinegar (pouring it into the softener dispenser if your washing machine has one).

Laundry Soap

½ cup (50 g) pure soap flakes
(or a bar of pure soap)
½ cup (140 g) bicarbonate
of soda
¼ cup (70 g) washing soda
¼ cup (60 g) borax
1 clean 500 g plastic container
with lid

This basic laundry soap gets clothes just as clean as commercial cleaners; it just costs a lot less.

1 If you cannot find soap flakes, lightly grate a bar of pure soap on a coarse kitchen grater.
2 In a large bowl mix all the ingredients together. Store in a tightly sealed plastic container.
3 Use about ½ cup (110 g) of the mixture instead of detergent in each load of laundry.

Stain Remover

⅓ cup (80 ml) clear household
ammonia
½ cup (125 ml) white vinegar
¼ cup (70 g) bicarbonate
of soda
30 ml liquid castile soap
6 cups (1.5 litres) water
1 clean 2 litre recycled plastic
container
1 clean 500 ml spray bottle

Stains are always easier to get out if you treat them before they set (soda water is effective for lifting many stains before they dry). You can use other ingredients found around your home to remove many common types of stains (see Removing Common Stains, below).

1 Mix all the ingredients in the 2 litre container. Pour some of the solution into the spray bottle. Shake well before each use.
2 Spray liquid onto the stain and leave for 3 to 5 minutes. Launder as usual.

Removing common stains

❖ **Automotive Oil and Grease Stain Remover**
   4 cups (1 litre) cola soft drink
For severe stains, soak garment in cola overnight. Rinse and launder the next morning.

❖ **Grass and Bloodstain Remover**
   1 teaspoon 3% hydrogen peroxide
   ¼ teaspoon clear household ammonia
Mix the ingredients in a small bowl. Rub the mixture on the stain. As soon as the stain fades, rinse and launder.

❖ **Perspiration Stain Remover**
   1 cup (250 ml) white vinegar
   ¼ cup (55 g) salt
   8 cups (2 litres) warm water
Mix the ingredients in a bucket and soak the garment for 1 hour before washing.

❖ **Red Wine Remover**
   3 teaspoons borax
   2 cups (500 ml) warm water
Mix the ingredients together in a small bowl. Dip the garment in the solution, let it soak for 1 minute, then launder.

❖ **Tomato Sauce Remover**
   ½ cup (125 ml) 3% hydrogen peroxide
   3 cups (750 ml) water
Mix the ingredients in a washing up bowl or bucket. Soak the garment in the solution for 30 minutes before laundering.

❖ **Whitening Yellowed Whites**
   ½ cup (125 ml) white vinegar
   6 cups (1.5 litres) warm water
Mix ingredients in a washing up bowl or bucket. Soak clothes in the solution overnight and launder the next morning.

Vinegar: fabric softener plus

Who would have guessed that a single cup of an everyday staple – white vinegar, which costs almost nothing – could do everything that many people use a fabric softener, a colour setter, a disinfectant and a bleach to do? Just add 1 cup (250 ml) distilled white vinegar to your washing machine's rinse cycle, and it will help to kill any bacteria in the wash, set the colour of newly dyed fabrics, keep clothes lint- and static-free, brighten small loads of white clothes and eliminate the need for fabric softeners.

In the Bathroom

Multipurpose Disinfectant Cleaner

2 teaspoons borax
½ teaspoon washing soda
30 ml lemon juice
¼ cup (60 ml) white vinegar
3 cups (750 ml) very hot water
1 clean 1 litre spray bottle

Here's a good all-purpose disinfectant that is easy to use and is much cheaper than commercial bathroom cleaners.

1 Combine the borax, washing soda, lemon juice and vinegar in the spray bottle.
2 Slowly add the hot water, then vigorously shake the bottle until the powdered ingredients have dissolved. Shake the bottle before each use.
3 Spray on tile and ceramic surfaces and wipe with a damp, clean cloth.

Soft Scrub

¼ cup (60 g) borax
½ teaspoon vegetable-oil-based liquid soap, such as castile
½ teaspoon lemon juice

You don't need to buy special cleaners for your vulnerable kitchen and bathroom surfaces. This homemade soft scrub gets out tough stains on surfaces that are easily scratched, including ceramic sinks and benchtops, and costs very little per cleaning job.

1 In a small bowl, combine the borax and liquid soap to make a smooth paste.
2 Stir in the lemon juice and mix well.
3 Place a small amount of the paste onto a clean, damp sponge, apply to the surface, then rinse off and dry the surface with a clean rag.

Eucalyptus Tile Cleaner

½ cup (50 g) pure soap flakes
  (or a bar of pure soap)
1 cup (125 g) chalk or
  diatomaceous earth
1 cup (280 g) bicarbonate
  of soda
1 teaspoon eucalyptus
  essential oil
1 clean recycled 500 g jar
  with metal top

This fresh, tangy powder will leave your kitchen and bathroom tiles shiny and clean for a fraction of the price of commercial cleaners.

1 If you cannot find soap flakes, lightly grate a bar of pure soap on a coarse kitchen grater. Then, in a small bowl, crush the soap flakes with the back of a spoon until powdered (or grind them in a blender).
2 Mix in the chalk or diatomaceous earth and the bicarbonate of soda, breaking up any lumps.
3 Sprinkle the essential oil over the surface of the powdered mixture and stir it with the spoon. Stir for several minutes to disperse oil throughout the mixture, then spoon the mixture into a screw-top jar or can with some holes punched in the lid.
4 Cover the holes with masking tape to keep the powder dry between uses. Let the mixture sit for 1 week before using to be sure the essential oil has been thoroughly absorbed. Sprinkle surface with powder, scrub with a damp sponge, and rinse with clear water. Dry with a soft towel.

Non-toxic Bathroom Cleaner

1⅔ cups (450 g) bicarbonate
  of soda
½ cup (125 ml) liquid soap
½ cup (125 ml) water
30 ml white vinegar
1 clean 500 ml squirt bottle
  with lid

This is a terrific deep-cleaning cleanser for any bathroom surface. It cuts through soap scum and mildew and costs very little to produce.

1 Mix the bicarbonate of soda and liquid soap in a bowl. Dilute with the water and add the vinegar. Stir the mixture with a fork until any lumps have been dissolved. Pour the liquid into the bottle. Shake well before using.
2 Squirt on area to be cleaned. Scrub with a nylon-backed sponge. Rinse off with water. Keep lid on between uses.

Showerhead Cleaner

¼ cup (70 g) bicarbonate
  of soda
1 cup (250 ml) vinegar
1 plastic sandwich bag
adhesive tape or a large
  bag tie

Use this 'explosive' mix to blast away mineral deposits blocking up your showerhead. You don't need a plumber to clean your showerhead when you can do it yourself.

1 Pour the bicarbonate of soda and vinegar into the bag over a sink. Wait a minute or two for the foaming to stop and then place the opened end of the bag over the showerhead, which should be submerged in the solution.
2 Secure the bag to the showerhead stem with the tape or bag tie. Let the showerhead soak in the solution 1 to 1½ hours. Wipe off the showerhead with a soft cloth.

Non-toxic Rust Remover

1 lime (a second one may
  be needed for some jobs)
¼ cup (55 g) salt

Commercial rust removers are among the most toxic compounds found around the home. But here's a completely safe and surprisingly effective way to give rust stains on bathtubs and sinks the brush-off.

1 Squeeze the lime over the rust spots, then cover the moistened area with salt.
2 Let the mixture sit for 3 to 4 hours.
3 Use a nylon scrubber to scrub the mixture off. The rust should be gone. Repeat for really stubborn stains.

Non-toxic Toilet Bowl Cleaner

1 cup (240 g) borax
½ cup (125 ml) white vinegar

Clean and sanitise your toilet bowl without harmful chlorine! For no-scrub convenience, simply pour in this mixture and leave overnight.

1 Flush the toilet to wet the sides of the bowl.
2 Sprinkle the borax around the toilet bowl, then liberally drizzle some vinegar on top. Let the toilet sit undisturbed for 3 to 4 hours before scrubbing with a toilet brush.

Tougher Toilet Bowl Cleaner

⅔ cup (160 g) borax
⅓ cup (80 ml) lemon juice

For tougher jobs, try this potent paste that still has no chlorine and costs much less than commercial toilet bowl cleaners.

1 In a small bowl, combine the ingredients to form a paste.
2 Apply the paste to the toilet bowl using a sponge or rag. Let the paste sit for 2 hours, then scrub off. Flush the toilet.

Drain Opener

½ cup (140 g) bicarbonate
  of soda
1 cup (250 ml) vinegar
1 teapot boiling water

Don't bother with those caustic commercial cleaners; try this simple, inexpensive and safe way to unclog drains instead.

1 Pack the drain with bicarbonate of soda, then pour in vinegar.
2 Keep the drain covered for 10 minutes, then flush it out with boiling water.

Fast and easy drain freshener

Here's an easy way to eliminate drain odours while maintaining the proper pH and health of your septic system. Run warm tap water for several seconds, then pour 1 cup (280 g) bicarbonate of soda into the drain. Wait an hour and flush with a teapot of boiling water. For best results, repeat once every 2 weeks.

Septic Tank Activator

2 cups (440 g) sugar
4 cups (1 litre) simmering
  water
2 cups (300 g) polenta
  (cornmeal)
two 7 g packets dry yeast

If you detect a persistent unpleasant odour from your septic tank, it's probably due to a 'die-off' of sewage-digesting bacteria. Before you call in your local septic tank specialist, try using this simple recipe to give the little beasties a boost.

1 Dissolve the sugar in a saucepan of simmering water and cool to lukewarm. Mix in the polenta and the yeast.
2 Once the solution has been mixed, flush it down the toilet (flush twice, if necessary). For best results, do this before turning in for the night, or when there will be no activity in the bathroom for several hours.

Cleaning the Car

Basic Car Wash

½ cup (125 ml) mild
  dishwashing liquid
½ cup (140 g) bicarbonate
  of soda
about 4 litres warm water

Taking your car to a commercial car wash can be a costly habit to maintain – and the results aren't as satisfying as when you do it yourself. This soap is tough on grime but gentle on your car's finish and your wallet.

1 Mix the ingredients in a clean 4 litre container. Shake until all the bicarbonate of soda is dissolved.
2 To use, mix 1 cup (250 ml) solution in a bucket of warm water.

Upholstery Shampoo

30 g pure soap flakes (or a bar
   of pure soap)
20 g borax
2 cups (500 ml) boiling water

Use this shampoo on a regular basis to freshen up
fabric interiors that get a lot of use. It's much cheaper
than commercial upholstery cleaners, and does the job
just as well.

1 If you cannot find soap flakes, lightly grate a bar of pure soap
   on a coarse kitchen grater.
2 In a large bowl, mix the soap flakes and borax together.
   Slowly add the boiling water, stirring well to thoroughly
   dissolve the dry ingredients.
3 Let the mixture cool, then whip into a foamy consistency
   with an eggbeater.
4 Brush dry suds onto the upholstery, concentrating on soiled
   areas. Quickly wipe off with a damp sponge.

Windscreen Cleaner

3 cups (750 ml) glycerine
1 cup (250 ml) methylated
   spirits
2 cups (500 ml) water
1 clean 1.5 litre spray bottle

You shouldn't have to buy commercial windscreen
cleaner. Keep a spray bottle of this solution in your boot
(along with some old newspaper to wipe off the grime).
Be sure to wipe off any solution that gets on rubber or
plastic gaskets or wipers with a damp cloth, because
prolonged contact with alcohol may damage them.

Combine the liquid ingredients in the spray bottle and shake
well before using.

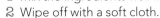

Vinyl and Leather Interior Cleaner

30 ml vegetable-oil-based soap,
   such as castile
¼ cup (60 ml) olive oil
1 teaspoon lemon essential oil

Put the life back into your car's vinyl or leather
interior with this fresh-scented polish without paying
auto-parts-shop prices.

1 Mix the ingredients well in a small bowl. Apply with a sponge.
2 Wipe off with a soft cloth.

Household Compounds

Fabric Paste ❖ Wallpaper Stripper ❖ Oil-paint Stain ❖ Varnish-based Stain ❖ Non-toxic Stain for Children's Wood Projects ❖ Furniture Finish Test ❖ Leaking Toilet Test

Craft-making Supplies

Craft Paste ❖ Pottery Glue ❖ Paper Glue ❖ Homemade Art Chalk ❖ Play Bubbles ❖ Vegetable Easter Egg Dyes ❖ Homemade Play Clay ❖ Simple Play Dough ❖ Finger Paints ❖ Basic Flower Drying ❖ Drying Medium for Preserving Flowers ❖ Potpourri Mixes ❖ Lemon-scented Potpourri ❖ Rolled Beeswax Candles

Household Pest Repellents

Citronella Mosquito Candles ❖ Cockroach Bait ❖ Homemade Flypaper ❖ Moth-repellent Cedar Sachets ❖ Pungent Moth-repelling Bundles ❖ Aromatic Moth-repelling Sachets ❖ Ant Traps ❖ Carpet Flea Remover

Garden Helpers

Spot Weed Killer ❖ Red Clay Stain Remover ❖ Rust Remover ❖ Fire Starters ❖ Whitewash ❖ Water Repellent for Exposed Wood

Garden Soil Care

Compost ❖ Green Manure Soil Conditioner ❖ Seaweed Soil Conditioner ❖ Wood-ash Potassium Boost ❖ Coffee Grounds Fertiliser

Garden Pest Deterrents

Blood and Bone Rabbit and Possum Repellent ❖ Repellent for Four-footed Pests ❖ Garlic Possum Repellent ❖ Soap Repellent ❖ Easy Earwig Trap ❖ Slug and Snail Trap ❖ Alcohol Insect Treatment ❖ Homemade Insecticide ❖ Aspirin Systemic Insecticide ❖ Antifungal Compost Tea ❖ Bicarb Soda Fungal Fix ❖ Bug Blaster Soap Spray ❖ Fruit Fly Trap ❖ Rhubarb Insect Solution ❖ Ammonia Plant Conditioning Spray ❖ Oil Spray Insecticide Concentrate ❖ Insect Repellent

Houseplants

Sterile Seed-starting Mix ❖ Lightweight Seed Mix ❖ Flowerpot Steriliser ❖ General Purpose Potting Mix ❖ Booster for Early Spring Flowers ❖ Repellent for Houseplant Pests ❖ Houseplant Food

Useful House and Garden Products

Running a household is a challenge. These days, just keeping a house operating smoothly takes money and ingenuity. But you can lessen the drain and strain with some of the easy-to-make products in this chapter.

Here you will find time-honoured recipes for wallpaper pastes and strippers, furniture stains and other useful household compounds. There are safe, natural ways to help keep your home pest-free, along with ideas for providing fun for children – and adults – with busy hands. And you can make them all with a minimum of money and a maximum of good results.

Keeping your outdoor space beautiful and productive without spending a fortune or using a lot of chemical compounds is also a concern of most householders. Here are recipes and formulas for helping to keep your garden weed-free without using expensive manufactured herbicides, and for making your own organic compost and natural soil conditioners and fertilisers. The many recipes for homemade garden pest deterrents will provide you with a choice of effective solutions to classic garden problems that neither cost very much nor taint the atmosphere. Simply by using ingredients that you already have in your kitchen, you can help to foil everything from black spot on your roses to slugs in the flower beds – and keep rabbits and possums out of your vegetable patch or shrubs. You will also discover some useful seed and potting mixes and other natural products that you can make to give your indoor plants a boost.

Household Compounds

Fabric Paste

fabric to cover the area
bottled liquid starch

Covering a less than perfect wall with attractive fabric is an old decorating trick that you probably already know. Using liquid starch as your glue may surprise you. It's now cheap and easy to add some colour to a wall, under the wainscoting or inside an alcove.

1 Select a fabric that is medium to light weight. Cut the fabric to the lengths needed and soak the cut pieces, one at a time, in a tub filled with liquid fabric starch. Press the fabric to the wall as you would if wallpapering, smoothing out wrinkles, and allow it to dry.
2 When you want to remove the fabric, simply pull it away from the wall and rinse away any starch that remains on the wall with a sponge or wet towel.

Wallpaper Stripper

wallpaper scoring wheel
    or wire-bristle brush
1⅓ cups (330 ml) very hot
    water
⅔ cup (170 ml) liquid fabric
    softener
sponge
paint roller
wallpaper scraper or putty
    knife

Removing old wallpaper is never fun, but you can make it easier by heating up your own homemade stripper. For a large room, make up batches of the stripper so that it always goes on hot.

1 Score the wallpaper lightly with a scoring tool or wire-bristle brush so that the stripper solution will be absorbed beneath the paper's water-resistant surface.
2 In a bucket, mix the hot water and fabric softener. Apply this stripper to small areas with a sponge. You can cover larger areas with a paint roller soaked in the hot solution.
3 Allow the stripper to soak into the wallpaper for 20 minutes, then scrape the paper off the wall with a wallpaper scraper or putty knife, being careful not to gouge any of the plasterboard or plaster underneath.
4 Reapply the stripper solution to stubborn spots, or if stripping multiple layers of paper. When the paper is removed, rinse the wall with a sponge and clean water, and allow it to dry before priming to paint or applying new paper.

Oil-paint Stain

artist's oil paints in tubes (one or more colours, as needed)
gum turpentine

This stain is perfect for colouring wooden picture frames because you can use the exact colours of a painting to make the artwork coordinate with the frame, thinning the pigment to allow the natural wood grain to show. If you want traditional wood colours, choose raw umber (equivalent to walnut), burnt umber (mahogany) and yellow ochre (golden oak).

1 Mix equal parts oil paint and turpentine in a clean, wide-mouthed jar. Test the hue and opacity of the stain on a scrap of wood. This flexible stain can be easily modified. If it is too opaque, add turpentine; if it is too transparent, add more oil paint. If you want a unique shade, mix paints as needed. Be sure to mix enough stain for the entire project, as it is hard to duplicate a custom stain if you run short.
2 Brush the stain on the wood and allow it to dry to the touch before varnishing. If you want more grain to show, wipe the freshly stained wood with a clean, lint-free cotton cloth (such as an old T-shirt) moistened with turpentine.

Fast fix for furniture scratches

You don't have to refinish a piece of wooden furniture, trim or floor just because it has a few scratches. (In the case of an antique, refinishing can actually reduce its value.) Here is an easy, inexpensive way to disguise a scratch. Get a children's crayon in a colour that closely matches the wood's finish. Burnt sienna, sienna and yellow ochre are among the most useful colours. Then just rub the sharpened crayon over the scratch and buff to blend it in. If you want permanent coverage, and the piece is less valuable, use a felt-tip marker instead; then apply some paste wax as directed to add sheen.

Varnish-based Stain

varnish
paint thinner
stain
1 varnish-quality natural-
   or nylon-bristle brush
extra-fine sandpaper
tack cloth (available from
   hardware stores)

Some wood species, such as maple, are so hard that they don't absorb stain satisfactorily. If you find that this is the case, you can still 'stain' a piece of furniture by tinting the sealer and varnish with the wood stain of your choice. This custom-tinted varnish recipe solves the problem, and is a little less than a commercial product.

1 Stir together 2 parts varnish, 2 parts paint thinner and 1 part stain in a wide-mouthed jar to create a tinted sealer coat. Stir slowly to avoid bubbling. Brush onto a smoothly sanded piece of wood and allow to dry overnight before varnishing.

2 Sand the sealed piece of furniture lightly and wipe down with a tack cloth. To deepen the stain colour, add stain, as desired, to tint the varnish in the can. When mixing colour, remember that the colour will deepen with each coat of varnish. Test the colour on a scrap of wood or inconspicuous part of the project before proceeding. When the colour is right (it should be transparent enough to allow wood grain to show through), brush the varnish onto the entire piece, taking care to avoid drips or streaks. Allow the varnish to dry overnight.

3 If a second coat of varnish is needed, repeat Step 2. Allow the varnished piece to dry for 2 days before using.

Non-toxic Stain for Children's Wood Projects

⅓ cup (60 g) powdered
   tempera paint
1 cup (250 ml) water
wide-mouthed 1 litre jar
paintbrush
non-toxic spray or brush-on,
   water-based varnish

If you have a child who is old enough for simple woodworking projects, or for painting pre-cut blocks and plaques, you'll want to try this recipe. It gives you brightly coloured, safe stains that cost very little compared to the name-brand counterparts.

1 Pour the powdered paint into the jar. Add the water, screw on the lid, and shake to mix.

2 Apply to wood with a paintbrush and allow the project to dry overnight.

3 Paint details and allow to dry overnight. Varnish the project with a water-based, non-toxic varnish, according to packet directions, to preserve the colour and add an attractive glossy surface. Dry as directed before using.

Four unexpected uses for vinegar

Shock Cure

If you have static electricity around the house in winter, try this simple, cheap vinegar cure.

1 Mix 1 cup (250 ml) white vinegar with 1 cup (250 ml) water in a 500 ml or larger spray bottle.
2 Spritz a dust cloth with the solution and wipe plastic tabletops, venetian blinds and upholstery to remove dust and discourage it from returning on static currents.

Glue Be-gone

You don't need to buy small bottles of expensive glue removers – you can wipe stubborn adhesive tags from shop-bought products with a little household staple.

1 Dip a clean cloth into white vinegar and rub it over glue spot until it loosens. Remove glue with a dry corner of the cloth. Use a plastic spatula to lift any stubborn spots.
2 Rinse the spot with a clean, damp cloth, and then polish with a dry cloth.

Hand Deodoriser

There is nothing more irritating than a strong fish, onion or garlic smell that sticks to your hands. Here's the cheap and easy answer.

1 Wash your hands with soap and water as usual, then pour vinegar over your clean hands and rub in for a few seconds.
2 Rinse and dry hands as usual.

Mineral Deposit Remover

If you live in an area with hard water, sooner or later you'll notice that your coffee maker takes longer to brew and the coffee doesn't taste as good, your carpet steamer doesn't work as well as it did, and your steam iron may stop steaming. Here's how to make them all like new again.

1 To clean coffee makers, steam-cleaning machines and steam irons, pour ½ cup (125 ml) white vinegar into the water reservoir (or more as needed to fill the reservoir), turn the machine on and allow it to run until all of the vinegar passes through.
2 Then fill the reservoir with clean water and run the entire reservoir of clean water through the machine to rinse out the vinegar residue. With coffee-makers, repeat rinsing stage, if needed.

Furniture Finish Test

nail-polish remover
cotton balls

With this simple process, you'll be able to determine the kind of finish used on a piece of furniture and the type of stripper you'll need to buy, saving both time and money. When working with chemical finish removers, use eye protection, wear rubber gloves that are designed for this use, and work in a well-ventilated place, such as a garage with opened doors.

1 Saturate a cotton ball in nail-polish remover and hold it briefly against an inconspicuous part of furniture, such as the bottom of a chair runner, side of a drawer or back of a table leg.
2 If the furniture finish becomes sticky or begins to dissolve, it is a lacquer-based finish, such as shellac or oil-based varnish, and you should buy a liquid furniture refinisher or methylated spirits to remove the finish.
3 If the finish is unaffected by the nail-polish remover, it is a plastic-based varnish, such as polyurethane, and you should strip it with paint remover.

Leaking Toilet Test

10 drops food colouring

Toilets can leak undetected, leading to an expensive waste of water and, sometimes, ruined floors. You don't need a plumber to find out. Here's how to test a toilet for leaks yourself.

1 Add food colouring to the cistern on the back of the toilet and leave it for 1 hour.
2 When the hour is up, examine the water in the toilet bowl. If coloured water has leaked into it, you need to replace the toilet-cistern ball. Buy a replacement at a hardware store and, following directions on the packet, put in the new ball.
3 If any coloured water has leaked onto the floor, you need to call a plumber.

Craft-making Supplies

Craft Paste

4 cups (1 litre) water
¼ cup (55 g) salt
1½ cups (225 g) white flour
   (more or less as needed)

Flour paste is a time-honoured favourite for paper crafts, like decoration making and papier-mâché. It is easy and cheap to make at home.

1 In a saucepan, bring the water to a boil, and then remove from heat.
2 Stir in the salt and add the flour a little at a time, stirring constantly to prevent lumping, until the mixture reaches the consistency of very thick gravy. Cool and use.
3 Store leftover paste in a sealed container in the refrigerator for up to 5 days. Discard paste if mould forms or if it smells spoiled.

Pottery Glue

1½ teaspoons glycerine
4½ teaspoons gum arabic
¼ teaspoon water
rubber bands (optional)
duct tape (optional)

Use this traditional homemade recipe to make durable glue for repairing broken pieces of crockery or china.

1 In a small bowl, mix the glycerine, gum arabic and water thoroughly and store in a small, sealed bottle.
2 Coat both sides of the surfaces to be glued with the mixture and clamp them together with strong rubber bands or duct tape until the glue dries (about 1 hour).
3 Wash mended objects carefully by hand; do not place them in a dishwasher or on the stove. Do not use for hot liquids.

Paper Glue

1 cup (125 g) cornflour
3 cups (750 ml) water
¼ cup (60 g) light corn syrup
   or glucose syrup
2 teaspoons white vinegar

This inexpensive homemade glue is more transparent than flour paste and is good for gluing pieces of paper together where looks count, such as scrapbooking or making greeting cards.

1 Mix and cook ½ cup (60 g) cornflour, 1½ cups (375 ml) water and all the corn syrup and vinegar over medium heat until thickened. Remove from heat.
2 In a separate bowl, stir together the remaining ½ cup (60 g) cornflour and ½ cup (125 ml) water. Blend into heated mixture. Store in a sealed container in the refrigerator for up to 2 months.

Homemade Art Chalk

cardboard toilet-paper tubes
   or plastic taper candle moulds
   (available at craft stores)
masking tape
baking paper
disposable milk or ice-cream
   carton
1½ cups (225 g) plaster of Paris
¾ cup (185 ml) water
paint stirring stick
8 teaspoons powdered tempera
   paint colour (or mix
   4 teaspoons coloured paint
   and 4 teaspoons white paint
   for pastel colours)

Whether you need an ongoing supply of chalk for the family blackboard or simply want to supply budding artists with an endless supply of pavement chalk, here is an easy and inexpensive way to make your own.

1 Cover one end of each mould (toilet-paper tubes for fat pavement chalk and taper candle moulds for blackboard-sized chalk) with masking tape to prevent leaks. Line the moulds with baking paper so that the finished chalk will release easily.
2 In a disposable container, stir the plaster of Paris and water together slowly with a paint stirring stick. Divide the solution into 2 or 3 containers if you are making more than one colour of chalk. Add the paint powder to each container and stir to distribute the colour evenly.
3 Sit the baking-paper-lined moulds upright on a flat surface, fill with the chalk mix and tap the sides of the mould to release any air bubbles. Allow the chalk to air-dry for 3 days before unmoulding. The chalk should slide out of the cardboard tubes or candle moulds.
4 Make up new batches as needed until all desired colours are made.

Play Bubbles

½ cup (125 ml) dishwashing
   detergent
1½ cups (375 ml) water
2 teaspoons sugar
1 teaspoon glycerine

Bubbles are a great party starter for kids of all ages, and this easy recipe makes lots of bubbles. Use your imagination – you can create bubble blowers out of open-ended cookie cutters and empty juice cans with both ends cut out. Instead of blowing bubbles, you can hold these blowers and whisk them through the air to release streams of bubbles.

1 In a medium bowl, slowly mix the ingredients, using a spoon or whisk to avoid foaming.
2 Pour the mixture into shallow bowls, dip blowers into the bowls, and wave them through the air to make big bubbles.

Vegetable Easter Egg Dyes

peels of 2 or more onions
½ cup (100 g) frozen spinach,
   thawed
1 fresh beetroot

You can make your own colourful natural Easter egg dyes very cheaply from vegetable juices. To make patterns on the already hard-boiled eggs, draw the design with a non-toxic wax pencil or crayon and then dip the eggs into hot dye long enough to colour the egg without melting the wax. For a lacy pattern, soak a piece of fabric lace in melted paraffin and wrap around an egg while the wax is still soft. Put the wrapped egg in a spoon and dip into hot dye just long enough to colour it. Remove the egg, and peel off the fabric to reveal a lacy coloured pattern.

1 For yellow eggshells: In a saucepan of water, boil the onion peels for 20 minutes or until the water turns yellow. Remove onion peels, add eggs and boil for 5 minutes. Remove eggs and set aside to cool.
2 For green eggshells: In a saucepan of water, boil the spinach for 20 minutes or until the water turns green. Strain out spinach and return green water to saucepan, add eggs and boil for 5 minutes. Remove eggs and set aside to cool.
3 For red eggshells: Cut the beetroot into small pieces and put in a saucepan of water, boil for 20 minutes or until the water turns red. Remove beetroot pieces, add eggs and boil for 5 minutes. Remove eggs and set aside to cool.

Homemade Play Clay

4 cups (600 g) plain flour
1 cup (225 g) salt
1½ cups (375 ml) water
food colouring kit

This simple, money-saving recipe is great for making children happy on a rainy afternoon, but it is also the basis of Christmas tree ornaments, beads and other sophisticated crafts. The recipe makes doughlike 'clay' that bakes hard in the oven, and can be painted and coated with a craft varnish for a permanent and professional finish.

1 Preheat the oven to 180°C (Gas 4). Mix ingredients together and knead for 5 minutes. You can divide the dough into portions and add drops of food colouring at this point, or model the white 'clay' and paint the finished piece. Put unused clay into sealed plastic bags and use within 4 hours of mixing.
2 Place finished pieces on a baking sheet and bake for 1 hour, or until hard.

Simple Play Dough

2 cups (300 g) plain flour
1 cup (225 g) salt
40 ml vegetable oil
4 teaspoons cream of tartar
2 cups (500 ml) water
food colouring or non-toxic
    powder paint

A perennial favourite, this inexpensive dough can be played with, then returned to the fridge and stored for another day. Why buy commercial play dough when it's cheap as chips to make?

1 Combine all the ingredients, except food colouring or powder paint, in a saucepan and stir over a medium heat for about 3–5 minutes until a stiff dough forms.
2 Cool, then divide into portions and add a different food colouring to each portion. Work the colouring thoroughly through the dough. Store in self-sealing bags in the fridge.

Finger Paints

½ cup (60 g) cornflour
2 cups (500 ml) cold water
6 small plastic containers
    with snap-on lids
food colouring kit

You can feel good about giving little artists finger paints that you make yourself from kitchen pantry staples that you know are safe – and washable.

1 In a small saucepan, combine the cornflour and water. Bring to a boil over high heat, stirring constantly until thickened. Remove from heat and let cool to room temperature.
2 Divide the cornflour mixture evenly among the containers. Put several drops of food colouring into each container and stir to distribute colours evenly.

Basic Flower Drying

selection of flowers, such
   as roses, hydrangeas,
   everlasting daisies, Queen
   Anne's lace or baby's breath
rubber bands
string

Dried flowers can make a very natural-looking floral arrangement that will last you a long time. And if you do the drying yourself, the cost is minimal. Some candidates can come from your own garden and others you can find elsewhere. If you like roses, for example, you can often get wilted ones from a florist at no cost. (They won't look wilted when they are dried.) Try to get a dozen or more flowers with stems.

1 Remove the leaves from the stems. Then bundle the stems together in groups of six with a rubber band. Hang the bundles upside down by string from a rod or a clothesline in a dry, warm place, such as a cupboard or the attic. The stems are hung upside down so that the flowers don't flop over during drying.
2 Leave bundles for a week or two or until the flowers are dry to the touch.

Drying Medium for Preserving Flowers

500 g borax
500 g polenta (cornmeal)
1½ teaspoons salt
flowers and flower buds
artist's brush with pointed tip

Many flowers dry better in a drying medium, which you can make yourself much more economically than if you buy it. Most flowers dry best and last longest when they are picked fresh and are just beginning to open. This drying medium will dry many kinds and colours of flowers and buds, although you must re-create their stems with floral wire and floral tape. To preserve their colour, display dried flowers out of direct sunlight.

1 Preheat the oven to 100°C (Gas ½). In an open casserole, mix the borax, polenta and salt. Bake uncovered for 30 minutes, stirring occasionally, to dry the contents completely.
2 Pour half of the drying mixture into a shoebox or plastic storage container. Set aside the remainder of the drying mixture.
3 Make a shallow well in the centre of the mix. Trim the stem of a bud or flower to 2–3 cm long. Hold the flower and trickle polenta mix between its petals to fill the blossom. Place the flower into the well in the container of mix, stem end down. Repeat with as many flowers as will fit in the container.
4 Pour the remainder of the mix over all flowers until they are buried. Set the container in a warm, dry, dark place, such as a wardrobe, for 2 weeks.
5 After drying, remove the flowers carefully from the polenta mix and brush the mix from the petals with an artist's brush. Fasten the flowers and buds for arrangements onto floral wire stems with floral tape. You can hot-glue the short stems to wreaths and gift packages.

Potpourri Mixes

3 cups dried flower petals,
   herb leaves and small pine
   cones (optional)
30 g dried orris root or orris
   root powder (available at
   craft or herb stores)
10 drops essential oil (one type
   or a blend of your choosing)

A bowl of fragrant, flowery potpourri can fill a room
with the essence of summer – even in the middle of
winter. Make potpourri to perfume your own home –
or as homemade gifts. If you don't have a garden, ask
your florist for past-their-peak flowers, such as lavender,
statice and roses, and lemon leaves that you can dry
(see Drying Medium for Preserving Flowers, opposite).

1 In a large bowl, mix together flower petals, herb leaves, small
   pine cones, if using, and orris root.
2 Sprinkle essential oils over the dry ingredients and stir to
   distribute the fragrance.
3 Display in an open bowl out of direct sunlight and add a
   couple drops of oil, as needed, to refresh the fragrance.
4 Store, or give as a gift, in a sealed glass or plastic container.

Lemon-scented Potpourri

1 cup (15 g) dried calendula
   flowers
1 cup (20 g) dried chamomile
   flowers
½ cup (10 g) dried lemon balm
½ cup (10 g) dried lemon
   verbena
½ cup (15 g) dried lemon thyme
½ cup (10 g) dried basil
½ cup (80 g) finely diced dried
   lemon peel
30 g orris root powder
½ teaspoon lemon verbena
   essential oil
6 drops chamomile essential oil

If you like a citrus scent, you'll love the fresh perfume
of this colourful mixture. If you have other lemon-
scented leaves, such as lemon-scented geranium or
lemon-scented tea-tree, feel free to add them.

1 Combine all the ingredients and mix well. Put in a sealed
   container and leave for a few weeks to mature.
2 To use, transfer potpourri to open bowls and stir gently
   to release the scent.

Rolled Beeswax Candles

sheets of beeswax (as many as the number of candles desired)
wicking

Candles rolled from sheets of beeswax are simple to make and long-burning. They make elegant gifts.

1 Cut wicking 8 cm longer than the sheets of beeswax.
2 Melt a small amount of beeswax in a double boiler over low heat. Soak the wicks to saturate in wax, remove and stretch out straight on a sheet of wax paper to cool.
3 Warm the beeswax sheets until malleable with an electric hair dryer set to its lowest setting. Lay a prepared wick on the edge of a sheet, placed on a flat surface. Roll the sheet tightly and evenly around the wick until it is as thick as desired.
4 Trim excess beeswax with a utility knife, and seal candle seam with a heated butter knife. Repeat steps for remaining candles.

Household Pest Repellents

Citronella Mosquito Candles

1 packet wicking
one 4.5 kg block paraffin
crayons (colours of your choice), roughly chopped
citronella essential oil
moulds
cooking spray
1 packet mould seal

Citronella is a natural mosquito repellent that you can use indoors or out. Mould the candles in containers that you already have, such as soup cans, or use terracotta flower pots and leave them in the mould. Buy wicking, paraffin and mould seal at craft shops.

1 Cut wicking 10 cm longer than the mould's height. Melt some of the wax in a double boiler over very low heat and soak the wicks until saturated. Lay out straight on baking paper to cool.
2 Lightly spray the inside of each mould with non-stick cooking spray, and seal with mould seal if it doesn't have its own.
3 Stick the wick to the bottom of the mould with a bit of mould seal. Tie the other end to a small stick or skewer, pull the wick taut and lay the stick across the mouth of the mould.
4 Melt the remaining wax in a double boiler, never letting it exceed 90°C (use a sugar thermometer to check). Use oven mitts to handle hot wax to prevent burns. Lower heat, add the crayons and a few drops of citronella oil and stir to distribute evenly.
5 Pour the wax into the moulds, stopping 1.5 cm from the top. Place the moulds in a pan of cold water (use pot holders), taking care not to splash water into the mould. Let cool for 1 hour.
6 When the mould is cool, remove the candle. Trim the wick and smooth the bottom of the candle by standing it in a pot of warm water. If you used a 2 part mould, trim any ragged seams with a paring knife.

Cockroach Bait

1 metal coffee can with
  plastic lid
1 old-style beer-can opener
  (that cuts V-notches)
20 g borax
3 teaspoons flour
3 teaspoons sugar

Cockroaches are attracted to damp areas, such as under the kitchen sink, but this inexpensive solution will kill them if they eat it. Remember to store pest treatments, such as this, in sealed and labelled bottles in a childproof cabinet.

1 Punch holes around the base of the empty coffee can, using the beer-can opener. Label the can with a sign that reads 'Cockroach Killer'.
2 In a small bowl, mix the ingredients together. Put the mixture in the coffee can, snap on the lid, and place it under the sink or wherever you've seen cockroaches. Lock the undersink cupboard if you have children or pets.
3 Refill the can, or create additional cans as necessary.

Homemade Flypaper

½ cup (110 g) corn syrup or
  glucose syrup
3 teaspoons brown sugar
3 teaspoons white sugar
6 strips brown paper (cut from
  a paper bag)

Why buy flypaper when you can make your own? All you need is a brown paper bag, a little bit of sugar and some corn or glucose syrup.

1 Combine the syrup and sugars in a shallow bowl.
2 Poke a hole at the top of each strip of brown paper. Soak the paper in the syrup mixture overnight.
3 Scrape the paper strips across the edge of the saucer to remove excess syrup and hang the finished flypaper strips near windows and doors.
4 Replace when the strips are covered with insects.

Moth-repellent Cedar Sachets

2 pairs colourful adult or baby
  socks
1 bag cedar shavings (often
  sold at pet shops as bedding)
satin or grosgrain ribbon
clothes hanger

You can have the benefits of a moth-repellent cedar wardrobe or cedar-lined drawers at a fraction of the cost of the real thing with these fragrant cedar sachets.

1 Fill the socks with cedar shavings – adult-sized for wardrobes and baby-sized for drawers.
2 Tie the tops of the socks closed with coordinating ribbon.
3 Tie large sachets to clothes hangers and hang in wardrobes to freshen air and repel moths. Tuck the little ones into lingerie and woollens drawers.

Pungent Moth-repelling Bundles

1 small bundle southernwood,
   camphor, tansy or sweet
   woodruff
1 rubber band
string
1 clothes hanger

Moths dislike the strong fragrance of certain herbs.
They also avoid cupboards that are regularly aired
out, so every once in a while leave your wardrobe or
chest of drawers cracked open for a day, and make
a herbal repellent.

1 Bind together a small bundle of fresh herbs (either one kind
   or a blend) by fastening a rubber band around the stems.
2 Tie a bundle to an empty clothes hanger and hang it in the
   wardrobe among woollen clothes, or tuck it under drawer-liner
   paper in a drawer containing woollens.

Aromatic Moth-repelling Sachets

25 m fine material, such
   as silk or nylon netting
dried lavender flowers
dried elder flowers

This sachet containing lavender and elder flowers makes
a lovely aromatic gift and will also keep your drawers
fragrant and moth-free.

1 Fold the fabric with right sides together and cut to create a
   20 x 20 cm square plus a 1.5 cm seam allowance on all 4 sides.
   Sew 3 seams.
2 Turn the pouch right side out and fill with flowers. Tuck the
   remaining seams inside and stitch the bag closed by hand.
3 Place in drawers or chests with woollens to repel moths.

How to keep pet food ant-free

Placed on the floor, pet food bowls are like a natural magnet for ants. Here's a simple, totally non-toxic way to keep ants away. Set an empty pie dish where you usually feed your pet. Fill the pet's bowl with food and set it into the pie dish. Pour water into the pie dish, filling it to the rim. Ants and other crawling insects cannot cross this 'moat' to reach the pet food.

Ant Traps

3 cups (750 ml) water
1 cup (220 g) sugar
4 teaspoons borax
3 clean 250 g screw-top jars
cotton balls
old-style beer-can opener
  (that cuts V-notches)

Here's an easy, inexpensive way to round up the ants that begin to invade your house each summer.

1 In a jug, mix the water, sugar and borax together. Loosely pack the jars half-full of cotton balls and saturate the balls with the solution.
2 Pierce jar lids with the can opener, making 2 or 3 holes just large enough to admit ants.
3 Place the baited jars where ants are active, but make sure jars are out of the reach of pets and children. Attracted by the lethal sugar and boric acid mixture, ants will crawl into the traps.

Carpet Flea Remover

3 mothballs
duct tape

If fleas hitchhiked indoors on your pet, try this simple, effective and cheap fix for freshening and debugging your carpets, using your vacuum. Wear rubber gloves when handling mothballs and be sure to keep pets and children away while you work.

1 Cut a small slit into the disposable vacuum bag liner and drop in mothballs. Seal the slit with a piece of duct tape. If you have a bagless vacuum, simply drop the balls on the floor and vacuum them up, or open the canister and drop them in.
2 Vacuum as usual. Fleas that are vacuumed up will be killed by the mothballs in the bag or canister. Drop in new mothballs when you change the disposable bag or empty the canister.

Garden Helpers

Spot Weed Killer

boiling water

Weeds that pop up between flagstones and in cracks of the footpath are hard to dig out of the small crevices. Control weeds in your terrace or walkway by dousing them with this very simple solution!

1 Boil a kettle full of water.
2 Douse weeds with the boiling water, wait 1 day and check for withering. If the weeds resist, repeat. Keep boiling water away from garden beds.

How to protect plants when spot-treating weeds

It's difficult to spot-treat weeds that sidle up to your favourite garden plants without killing the good plants. Here's how to keep the weed killer on the weed and off your prized peonies: Cut the bottom out of a large, 2 litre clear plastic soft drink bottle or 4 litre container and remove the lid.

To isolate a weed for treatment, set the bottomless bottle over it, stick the weed-killer spray applicator into the lid opening and spray. Be sure to label the bottomless bottle with the pesticide being used and to store it in a locked cabinet with other pesticide equipment.

Red Clay Stain Remover

table salt
vinegar

If you garden in an area with clay soil, you know all too well how its red colour stains your clothes. Set aside an old pair of jeans just to garden in. When they're caked with mud, use this simple recipe to keep stains off the clothes you wash them with.

1 Drape the muddy jeans over the back of a garden chair or lay them out on a picnic table and rinse vigorously with a garden hose.
2 In a small jar, add vinegar to the salt, a little at a time, to make a paste. Rub the paste into the mud stains, allow to sit for 20 minutes, then launder as usual.

Sure and safe weed controls

In the old days, gardeners had to outsmart weeds because there were no chemical weed killers. Take a few tips from them, save a trip to the garden centre, and keep your garden weed- and chemical-free.

1 Weed early and often to keep weeds from taking hold. Hold the hoe blade horizontal to the ground and scrape weed seedlings from the vegetable garden and in and around ornamentals. Avoid tilling deeply – it can bring buried seeds to the surface, where they will sprout. To save your back, use an ergonomic hoe with a gooseneck that lets you stand up straight.

2 Burn weeds that pop up in the driveway or between pavers with a small propane torch or kill them with boiling water.

3 Spread an 8 cm-deep layer of organic mulch, such as straw, wood chips or compost, around the base of plants to smother weeds and retain soil moisture.

4 Pull any weeds sprouting from potted nursery plants before planting them in your garden.

5 Apply granulated lime according to packet directions to lawns in the autumn, using a fertiliser spreader. Most lawn weeds can't thrive in alkaline soil.

Rust Remover

white vinegar
steel wool
paper towels

Use vinegar as a rust remover for old hinges, screws and metal garden furniture exposed to the elements.

1 Fill a wide-mouthed jar half-full of vinegar, drop in small rusty parts, screw the lid on and soak for a few days until rust loosens. Remove the objects, rinse and carefully dry.

2 Soak a paper towel in vinegar and lay it over furniture surfaces to loosen rust. If the rust is stubborn, cover the saturated towel with plastic wrap to keep the towel damp. Sit the piece out of direct sunlight for a few days. Remove the wrapping, steel-wool the spot smooth, rinse and dry. Paint, if desired.

Fire Starters

500 g paraffin wax
scraps of kindling wood
cake cooling rack

If you use this simple recipe to make your own fire starters, you'll never have to dash to the hardware store at the last minute when you'd rather be enjoying your outdoor fireplace or charcoal barbecue.

1 Melt the paraffin in the top of a double boiler over low heat or in a slow cooker set on low heat.

2 Dip wood scraps into the melted wax to cover completely, remove and arrange on the cooling rack to harden.

3 When the wax cools, store the waxed wood scraps in an old coffee can in a cool place. To use, place 1 or 2 scraps at the bottom of your fireplace or charcoal barbecue and stack logs or charcoal over them. Use a long-handled match to light the starters, which will act as long-burning igniters for your fire.

Whitewash

1 cup (225 g) table salt
2 cups (450 g) hydrated lime
4 litres water or milk

Whitewash is a wood coating that has been used for hundreds of years. In the days when paint was an expensive luxury, whitewash was popular for painting farm buildings and fences. Whitewash has no binders and will slowly wear away in rain, which is why it was routinely painted on greenhouse roofs to shade plants in summer. To finish a traditional project, or to shade your greenhouse, try this simple recipe. While whitewash must still be mixed by hand, the ingredients, including colour tints, are sold at concrete supply stores.

1 Stir the ingredients together slowly in a metal bucket, taking care not to splash. The ingredients will become warm as they are mixed. Add more lime or water as needed to achieve the colour and consistency of milk. For a more permanent paint, substitute fresh milk for water.
2 Allow the mixture to cool before painting on wood and allow it to air-dry.

Caution: Mix whitewash outdoors; wear protective eye goggles and old clothes. Be careful not to splash the mixture on your skin when mixing and rinse it off right away if any does get on your skin. Mix whitewash in a metal bucket, because it heats up as the ingredients combine and may affect a plastic container.

Water Repellent for Exposed Wood

1 litre exterior varnish (spar or polyurethane)
1 clean 4 litre paint can
1 cup (130 g) grated paraffin wax
1 stirring stick
mineral turpentine
paintbrush or roller

Try this recipe for a long-lasting, waterproof coating for decks, shutters and other wooden items that are exposed to the elements. If you plan to stain the wood, do so before applying the water repellent. If you want to paint or varnish, apply the water repellent first and allow it to dry before painting or varnishing.

1 Pour the varnish into the paint can. Add the wax and stir slowly until the wax dissolves.
2 Add mineral turpentine until the can is full and stir slowly to mix all the ingredients without creating air bubbles.
3 Brush or roll the treatment onto raw or stained wood and allow to dry for 4 hours before using, painting or varnishing.
4 If you want to paint the wood, prime with oil primer after the water repellent dries, allow the primer to dry as directed on packet label, then paint.

Garden Soil Care

Compost

6 parts dried (brown) plant material (dry leaves, straw, sawdust or paper)

1 part fresh (green) plant material (grass clippings, vegetable scraps, coffee grounds, horse, cow or chicken manure)

Compost is the best natural soil amendment you can use. It contains valuable plant nutrients and plant disease-fighting organisms, and it also makes soil moisture-retentive and easier to till. Best of all, compost is free when you make your own. You can make your compost in a bin (1 metre square is ideal) or simply pile the ingredients on the ground. If you turn the pile periodically, it will break down faster, but even if you pile it and leave it for a year, it will break down.

1 Put a layer of brown material directly on the ground, then add a layer of green material. Continue to layer brown and green material to a height of 1 metre. Water with a hose as needed to keep the pile as moist as a wrung-out sponge.

2 To speed up decomposition, use a hay fork to puncture and turn the pile to allow air into its centre. In rainy weather, cover the pile with a tarp to prevent saturating it.

3 If the pile becomes smelly, it is too wet – mix in more brown ingredients. When the pile looks like rich, crumbly black soil and has a sweet, earthy fragrance, it is ready to use in the garden or as mulch.

An inexpensive, very helpful soil test

A complete soil test costs much less than you'd think and is one of the best investments you can make in your garden. The test results will provide an exact prescription for fertilisation, liming and adding trace elements.

Knowing what your soil needs allows you to furnish your plants with ideal conditions with no wasted effort. For testing locations and to order a kit by mail, check your phone book or do an online search.

Green Manure Soil Conditioner

mixture of 'green manure' seeds (grasses and legumes)

Often called 'green manures', these are annual crops that thrive in cool weather, improving the soil and protecting garden soil from erosion and weeds. Use a combination of grasses and legumes. Check with your local nursery for a list of seeds to suit your area.

1 After clearing vegetables or annual flowers from a bed in autumn, sow green manure seeds in cleared beds according to packet directions.
2 In early spring, 3 to 4 weeks before planting time, dig the green manure into the soil, or harvest it at the lower stem and use it for mulch. As it decomposes, green manure adds humus to the soil and acts as fertiliser for the next crop.

Seaweed Soil Conditioner

seaweed

Seaweed is actually higher in nitrogen and potassium than most animal manures and is also a rich source of trace elements. Check with beachside municipalities if they are happy to have you haul it away.

1 To cleanse seaweed of salt, pile it where runoff will be directed to a storm drain, such as on your driveway. Allow several rains to rinse away the sea salt, then add the seaweed to your compost pile or dig it into garden beds in the autumn.
2 To make seaweed tea, steep an old pillowcase filled with seaweed in a bucket of water for 1 week. Remove and discard the bag, dilute the liquid to the colour of weak tea, and water your plants with it.

Waterwise gardening techniques

You can save water and still have a beautiful garden. All it takes is noting moist and dry areas of your property and choosing the right plant for the right place.

❖ **Target practice** Think of your yard as radiating outwards from your house like a bull's-eye target. The wettest areas are closest to the house – especially around outdoor taps where water drips, and the next wettest area is within reach of a 15 to 30 metre garden hose. Beyond the reach of your hose are the driest areas.

❖ **Plant with care** Grow water lovers, like ferns and annuals, near the house, and select drought-tolerant perennials with deep roots that can reach groundwater, such as echinacea (coneflower), rudbeckia and ornamental grasses, outside the reach of your garden hose.

❖ **Consider climate** If you live in a mild-winter climate, choose water-conserving garden plants that are native to drier regions. Or select plants that are native to your specific area, which are naturally adapted to your local soil and rainfall.

Fertiliser, free for the asking

Healthy plants are naturally resistant to insects and diseases, and natural fertilisers are the best way to ensure healthy plants and a balanced garden ecosystem. No matter where you live, good sources of fertiliser may be available, free for the hauling, at farms and from neighbours who have pet rabbits or chickens. All you have to do is ask for animal manure to enrich your compost.

Wood-ash Potassium Boost

wood ashes

Wood ashes from a fireplace or woodstove (not coal or charcoal ashes) are a free source of the plant nutrients potassium, calcium and phosphorus. They can also be used to decrease soil acidity, similarly to lime. Benefits of treating soil with ashes include improved hardiness and flavour of fruits. Be sure to apply in small amounts or compost well before applying, to keep the caustic ashes from burning plants. Water-soluble nutrients can leach from ashes, so be sure to use fresh ones that have not been exposed to rain.

1 Apply 750 g to 1.5 kg of ashes per 30 square metres of garden in the autumn.
2 To reduce soil acidity, use wood ashes as a substitute for ground limestone: see packet directions for limestone and apply up to twice as much wood ashes as it recommends. Allow ashes to weather over the winter before planting.

Coffee Grounds Fertiliser

coffee grounds

Acidic coffee grounds make an excellent soil conditioner or mulch for acid-loving plants such as conifers, azaleas and rhododendrons. You can often have as much of the used grounds as you need, free for the taking, from your local cafe.

1 Apply an 8 cm-thick mulch of coffee grounds around the base of acid-loving plants, leaving a 15 cm ring of bare soil around the trunk of the plant to discourage fungal collar-rot diseases and trunk-eating insects.
2 For a complete fertiliser, mix 4 parts coffee grounds with 1 part composted wood ashes, and work into soil in autumn.

Garden Pest Deterrents

Blood and Bone Rabbit and Possum Repellent

blood and bone fertiliser

They may be cute, but when rabbits and possums munch on your prized garden produce or gnaw the bark of young trees, they wear out their welcome. Blood and bone is an organic fertiliser that is high in nitrogen, the nutrient most needed by green plants. But more importantly, the rabbits and possums associate the smell of it with predators, and will avoid gardens treated with it.

1 Sprinkle the fertiliser over the soil around garden perimeters and in garden beds according to packet directions.
2 Reapply after heavy rains.

Use fencing to keep rabbits out

Use fence wire or shade cloth with holes small enough to discourage chewing and exclude the tiniest rabbit. Wrap young tree trunks with shade cloth to keep rabbits from gnawing the bark. To protect a vegetable garden, staple chicken wire that has small holes along the inside of your garden fence. For the most effective control, bury the fencing 30 cm deep to keep rabbits from digging under it.

Repellent for Four-footed Pests

water
ammonia
mothballs

Whether it's rats, stray cats or possums treating your rubbish like an all-you-can-eat buffet, or mice and rats looking for a holiday home in your barbecue, you can get four-footed pests to keep clear with a couple of inexpensive household products.

1 In a spray bottle, mix a solution of half water and half ammonia. Liberally spray the mixture on rubbish bins or other areas visited by animal pests. If rubbish bins sit outside, swab them out with full-strength ammonia after every emptying.
2 Place a handful of mothballs in a shallow dish or pan and set into an unused barbecue to repel mice, possums and rats. Remove mothballs when the barbecue is in use. Tuck a few mothballs into garden furniture cushions before storing them over the winter to repel nesting mice. Be sure to keep mothballs, which are toxic, out of the reach of children and pets.

Garlic Possum Repellent

8–10 cloves garlic, crushed
4 cups (1 litre) hot water

Possums can be a great nuisance in the garden, but they hate the taste of garlic. Whip up this brew and they'll soon be feeding elsewhere. You can also use ground fresh chillies or fish sauce in the solution instead of garlic.

1 In a bowl, mix the crushed garlic into the hot water and allow to stand overnight.
2 Strain the mixture into a spray bottle and spray foliage. Repeat every few days (or after rain) until the possums get the message.

Soap Repellent

several bars or scraps of
    deodorant bath soap (not
    floral scented)
long nail or drill with 3 mm
    bit, or old socks
string

This repellent works for some animals such as deer. Deer dislike the smell of deodorant soap. Collect soap scraps and tie them into an old sock for a long-lasting, environmentally safe protection for prized plants. Fresh bars of soap make an even stronger deterrent. One bar can protect a 2–3 square metre area, so space the bars as needed to protect vulnerable plants.

1 Remove the soap from the wrapper, make a hole in one end of a bar with the nail or the drill, and run a piece of string through the hole. If using soap scraps, drop them into the toe of an old sock and tie the open end closed with string.
2 Tie the soap (or soap-filled sock) to the branch of a shrub or tree with sting or attach to a stake in the garden bed. Replace when the soap is diminished by rain.

Easy Earwig Trap

several sheets of used
   newspaper
string

These fearsome-looking insects can be identified by the pincers at the ends of their tails. Although earwigs don't hurt people, these nocturnal feeders can nibble plants overnight. Try this non-toxic control made with recycled newspaper. This technique also works with slaters.

1 Roll several thicknesses of newspaper into a tight cylinder and secure with string. Dampen the rolled paper and place on the soil near eaten plants.
2 Check the newspaper roll each morning to see if earwigs are hiding inside. If so, dispose of them in a securely tied garbage bag and set out a new roll. Continue this routine until earwigs are under control.

Slug and Snail Trap

1 teaspoon dry yeast
1 teaspoon sugar
1 cup (250 ml) tepid water
stale beer (optional)
1 or more clear plastic
   drinking-water bottles
   and caps

Slugs and snails devastate prized garden plants by chewing round holes in the leaves, leaving telltale shiny slime trails. They climb up into plants like hostas and marigolds to feed after sundown and, in the morning, crawl down to hide in mulch or garden debris. Here's a non-toxic recipe for catching them.

1 Mix the yeast, sugar and water together and allow it to rest for 5 minutes. Pour just enough yeast solution (or stale beer) into an empty drinking-water bottle, so that when you lay it on its side the liquid does not run out.
2 Lay the bottle on its side under a plant that shows slug or snail damage or place under a vulnerable plant as a preventive measure. Slugs and snails will be attracted by the yeasty odour, crawl in and drown.
3 Check the bottle daily and, when full, replace the lid, throw it away and make a new trap. Make as many as you need – these traps may not be beautiful, but they look better than the skeletal remains of a slug-eaten plant in the garden.

A quick slug and snail barrier

When you don't have time to set elaborate traps for these garden pests, make an unbroken ring of wood ashes around your favourite flowers. Snails and slugs will turn away from caustic ashes. Make sure that you reapply the ashes after it rains.

Alcohol Insect Treatment

1 cup (250 ml) methylated
  spirits
1 cup (250 ml) water

Methylated spirits is a tried-and-true homemade treatment for soft-bodied garden pest insects such as aphids and mealybugs. Traditionally, it was advised that you dab it onto individual insects with a cotton bud, but this is a time-consuming task. Try this speedy spritz instead.

1 Combine the alcohol and water in a spray bottle and shake to combine.
2 Before treating, spray one leaf of the infested plant as a test to make sure there are no reactions, such as browning. If not, spray the entire plant, including undersides of leaves and flower buds. Avoid spraying open flowers, which may turn brown if treated with alcohol.
3 Repeat every other day for 3 days to kill hatchlings. Monitor plants and spray again as needed. Label the bottle and store it out of the reach of children and pets.

Homemade Insecticide

10 cloves garlic
3 teaspoons vegetable or
  mineral oil
3 cups (750 ml) hot water
1 teaspoon dishwashing liquid
  (not laundry or dishwasher
  detergent)

When aphids, whiteflies and other insect pests become a problem in the garden or on your houseplants, don't rush to the market for an expensive spray. Make your own from these kitchen-tested ingredients. Store all garden treatments, such as this, in a sealed and labelled bottle in a childproof cabinet.

1 In a blender, purée the garlic, skin and all, and oil.
2 Strain the mixture through a sieve into a 1 litre jar. Add water and dishwashing liquid. Close the jar and shake gently to mix.
3 Decant the mixture into a spray bottle (you can clean and reuse a cleaning product spray bottle). Spray infested plants, making sure to cover both sides of the leaves. Apply every 3 days for a week to control hatching insect eggs. Repeat as needed after rain or when problems arise.

Outsmarting stinging insects

You can avoid attracting stinging insects, such as bees, wasps and mosquitoes, by being careful about what you wear or how you smell while gardening or sitting on the patio. Here are some smart suggestions:

1 Stinging insects that strike during daylight hours are attracted to flower colours – red, pink, yellow, orange and purple – so wear clothes in cool shades of blue, green, black, grey or white for yard and garden work.

2 Many stinging insects are also attracted to floral and fruity scents, so forgo perfume, scented shampoo, scented hair conditioners and fragrant body lotions.

3 Stinging insects are often repelled by herbal scents. Wear a broad-brimmed hat in the garden and tuck sprigs of rosemary, chrysanthemum or marigold flowers into the brim to repel insects. Or, if you don't want to wear a hat, put the sprigs into the pocket of a T-shirt.

Aspirin Systemic Insecticide

1½ regular-strength aspirin
   (450 mg in total)
10 litres water

Plant experts have experimented successfully with watering plants with aspirin-water as a systemic insecticide and promoter of plant growth. Plants naturally produce some salicylic acid, which aspirin contains, as a natural protection. When watered with the aspirin solution, treated plants absorb extra salicylic acid, which helps them repel sucking insects, and they produce strong, healthy growth.

1 In a large watering can, stir the aspirin into the water until dissolved. Water plants as usual with treated water or put it in a spray bottle and use as a foliar spray.
2 Treat plants twice monthly with aspirin water.

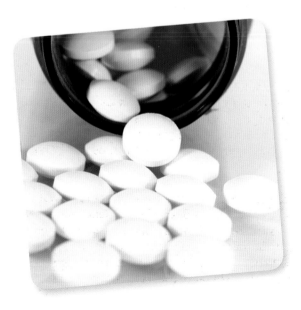

Antifungal Compost Tea

3–4 litre bag compost
1 empty hessian sack or
   old pillowcase
string
10 litres water

Compost is not just a great soil conditioner and fertiliser. It also contains beneficial organisms that resist soil-borne fungal diseases. To discourage the formation of fungus on plants, such as brown patch, sooty mildew and powdery mildew, make a 'tea' treatment using common garden compost.

1 Place compost in the sack, tie the bag shut with string and drop it into a bucket of water.
2 Set the bucket in a sunny spot, and steep the bag in the water for 2 or 3 days – until the water turns dark brown.
3 Remove the bag of compost (use the contents as mulch). Dilute the remaining solution with water to the colour of weak tea. Spray it on roses, zinnias, phlox and other plants that are susceptible to fungal infections. Repeat twice monthly during the growing season to prevent outbreaks.

Bicarb Soda Fungal Fix

1 teaspoon bicarbonate of soda
1 teaspoon dishwashing liquid
   (do not use laundry or
   dishwasher detergent)
4 cups (1 litre) warm water

When a bicarbonate of soda solution is applied to fungus-prone plants, such as roses, before signs of mildew appear, it can prevent diseases such as powdery and sooty mildew and black spot. This spray is cheap and easy to make – keep it on hand and apply as needed. To further discourage fungal diseases, keep plant leaves as dry as possible by watering the soil without splashing the leaves, and mulch plants with compost.

Pour the ingredients into a large spray bottle and shake to mix. Spray both sides of leaves and stems.

Bug Blaster Soap Spray

3 teaspoons dishwashing
   liquid (do not use laundry
   or dishwasher detergent)
3.75 litres water

Dishwashing liquid is harmless to the environment and is safe to use in the house. Outdoors it also makes an effective control for soft-bodied insects, such as thrips, caterpillars, aphids and mealybugs, because the soap breaks down their protective coverings, causing the pests to dehydrate.

1 Stir the dishwashing liquid into the water. Fill a spray bottle and test-spray 1 or 2 leaves of an infested plant. Wait a day, and if the leaves are not damaged, spray the entire plant. Be sure to coat the stems as well as both sides of the leaves.
2 Repeat the treatment twice a week until the pests are no longer visible. Then repeat as often as needed.

Fruit Fly Trap

1 litre plastic bottle with lid
bait, such as yeast spread,
    port wine or vanilla essence
    and sugar
methylated spirits

In many areas, fruit fly can completely ruin your home-grown crop. Instead of resorting to deadly sprays, hang a few of these simple traps in your trees to reduce the fruit-fly population.

1 Punch several 5 mm holes in the neck of the plastic bottle.
2 Put a little of your bait substance in the bottom of the bottle along with a few drops of methylated spirits.
3 Hang the trap in the fruit tree, just above the lower leaves. Replace the bait at least twice a week. Start using the traps about 6 weeks before harvest time and continue until the fruit has been picked.

Rhubarb Insect Solution

3 stalks rhubarb with leaves
3.5 litres water

Rhubarb is an attractive perennial plant that not only makes good pies but also makes an insecticide that is toxic to sucking insects. This recipe is for ornamental plants only. Do not spray on herbs, fruits or vegetables, because rhubarb leaves are toxic to humans and animals.

1 Chop the rhubarb leaves and stems. In a stockpot, combine the rhubarb and water. Bring to a boil, reduce the heat, and simmer, uncovered, for 1 hour.
2 Cool to room temperature and strain liquid into a spray bottle through a funnel. Spray mixture on infested plants at 3 day intervals for 10 days. Repeat as necessary.

Use scented mulch to keep insects away

Trimming herbs frequently, especially removing flower stalks, helps them maintain lots of tender, flavourful new growth. Sprinkle the sprigs and flowers that you don't use in the kitchen along garden paths as aromatic and insect-repelling mulch.

Ammonia Plant Conditioning Spray

1 part household clear
  ammonia
1 part dishwashing liquid
  (do not use laundry or
  dishwasher detergent)
7 parts water

Ammonia is a concentrated form of nitrogen, which is the nutrient most needed by green plants. You can make an inexpensive all-purpose fertiliser and insecticidal spray using ammonia and soap. The soap helps the ammonia stick to the leaves and also kills soft-bodied insects. Mix as much as you need for garden plants and lawns. Store all garden treatments, such as this, in a sealed and labelled bottle in a childproof cabinet.

1 In a large container combine the ingredients.
2 Fill a spray bottle and apply the mixture to stems and both sides of leaves for garden plants. Use a hose-end applicator to spray the lawn.

Oil Spray Insecticide Concentrate

3 teaspoons dishwashing
  liquid (do not use laundry
  or dishwasher detergent)
1 cup (250 ml) vegetable oil

Some plant pests and fungal infections are hard to eradicate because they have shells or waxy coatings that protect them from traditional treatments. You can, however, smother tough-shelled scale, the eggs of many insects and even mildew infections by coating them with oil. Store all garden treatments, such as this, in a sealed and labelled bottle in a childproof cabinet.

1 In a 500 ml container, combine the ingredients to form a spray concentrate. Store it in a sealed, labelled container.
2 To apply, mix 1 or 2 teaspoons concentrate with 1 cup (250 ml) water in a spray bottle and apply to stems and both sides of plant leaves. Reapply after it rains.

Insect Repellent

sprigs fresh rosemary
sprigs fresh basil
sprigs fresh thyme

This fragrant, herbal smoke will help to deter flies and mosquitoes at your next barbecue. However, it is a mild solution and extra protection should be used in areas with mosquito-transmitted diseases.

1 When you remove food from the barbecue, spread out a handful of pungent culinary herbs on the top rack where they will smoke, but not burn.
2 Allow the herbs to cook and release their fragrances.

Houseplants

Sterile Seed-starting Mix

1 part sifted garden soil
2 parts sphagnum peat moss
2 parts coarse sand
1 baking potato

Mature plants develop defences against many kinds of insects and diseases, but fragile seedlings can be wiped out by soil-borne diseases or insects. Use this money-saving recipe to make a sterile potting medium for sprouting garden seeds, and also for making potting soil to protect valued houseplants.

1 In a large container, mix the soil, peat moss and sand together.
2 To sterilise, moisten and place the mixture in a shallow baking pan with a baking potato and bake at 100°C (Gas ½) until the potato is done. This is a smelly process, ideal for doing on an outdoor barbecue. Discard the potato.

Lightweight Seed Mix

1 part vermiculite
1 part milled sphagnum moss
1 part perlite

This mix is made of sterile materials bought at a garden centre and does not need to be baked.

1 In a large container, mix all the ingredients together.
2 Moisten with warm water before using.

Flowerpot Steriliser

1 part household bleach
10 parts water

Just because a flowerpot is used and dirty, you don't need to toss it. Whether terracotta, plastic or ceramic, the pot can be superficially cleaned with a strong blast from a garden hose. If the pot has white, crusty mineral deposits, scrape them off with an old knife (scraping terracotta pots will sharpen the knife). When the pot is free of dirt and minerals, sterilise it to kill insect eggs and plant diseases.

1 Mix the bleach and water, making enough to fill a tub that is deeper than the largest pot you want to sterilise.
2 Place the cleaned pots in the tub and allow them to soak for 20 minutes.
3 Remove sterilised pots, rinse again with clear water and set them in the sun to dry. They are now ready for new plants.

General Purpose Potting Mix

1 part perlite
1 part finished compost
1 part topsoil

The compost in this mix contributes disease-fighting micro-organisms and nutrients to help mature indoor and outdoor potted plants thrive.

1 Mix all the ingredients together and store them in a waterproof, sealed container.
2 To modify this mix to suit succulents, cacti and other plants that need sharply drained soil, increase the perlite to 2 parts, or add 1 part builder's sand to the original recipe.
3 Before filling a large pot, invert several small plastic pots on the bottom of the larger pot, then fill with soil. The air space beneath the small pots will aid drainage and lighten the overall weight of the pot.

How to overwinter herbs indoors

To preserve culinary herbs for use thoughout the winter months, dig the plants from the garden towards the end of summer and transfer them to pots.

Place the pots on a sunny windowsill indoors. For the best results, select vigorous but compact plants and use 15 cm terracotta pots.

Booster for Early Spring Flowers

5.5 litres warm water
   (43°C to 46°C)
10 litre bucket
1 cotton ball
cloudy ammonia
1 plastic garbage bag

Get a jump on spring by forcing branches of flowering shrubs and trees to bloom early indoors. In late winter, watch for flower buds to swell on spring bloomers, such as quince and ornamental cherry trees. Prune enough branches to fill a tall vase.

1 Cut stems, crush the cut ends with a hammer, and place them in the bucket of warm water.
2 Saturate a cotton ball with cloudy ammonia and drop the ball into the bucket.
3 Put the bucket of stems in a clean garbage bag, tie it closed, and then leave it in a warm place indoors until the buds begin to open. Then arrange the stems in a vase of clean water and set them out in a room for a long-lasting bouquet.

Reblooming houseplants

When you receive a special flowering plant as a gift, it can be heartbreaking to have to throw it away after it finishes blooming, but it doesn't have to end this way. With a little effort, you can keep these plants from year to year, and get them to rebloom.

❖ **Hippeastrum (*Amaryllis*)** After blooming, set the plant in a sunny spot and water as usual, letting it die back naturally, as you would for any bulb. This will occur sometime between late summer and early autumn. Remove the withered foliage. Keep the plant in a cool (about 12°C), dark place over winter (such as a cellar or garage) and do not water it. At the end of winter, bring the plant out into the light and warmth. Water and fertilise it, and flowers should appear by early summer.

❖ **Poinsettia** As the length of the day increases in spring, poinsettias will stop blooming, but their foliage will remain fairly attractive. They can be placed outside in the warm months, but be sure to do a hard pruning in midsummer (cut stems back to 5 cm above the soil). During early autumn, put the plants on a strict light schedule: 14 hours of total darkness at night, 10 hours of bright light during the day. Any light at all during the dark period can disturb the cycle, which is why some people place the plants under garbage cans or in a cupboard at night. Once the flower heads have formed, you can bring the plants back into normal conditions.

Repellent for Houseplant Pests

1 large clear plastic
 dry-cleaning bag
6 mothballs
1 twist tie

If you have a houseplant that is bothered by aphids, mealybugs or other insect pests, you can banish them with this simple, no-mess recipe. Use rubber gloves when handling moth balls.

1 Put the infested plant, pot, saucer and all, into the dry-cleaning bag. Moisten the soil, drop mothballs into the bag, and tie the bag closed with a twist tie.
2 Set the bagged plant in a bright place that is out of direct sunlight for 1 week. At the end of the week, remove the plant and put it in its usual home, then dispose of the bag and mothballs. Repeat the treatment as needed until pests are gone.

Houseplant Food

2 bucketfuls fresh horse or
  cow manure or 1 bucketful
  poultry manure
1 hessian bag
rope
1 barrel or rubbish bin
water

For an easy organic food for houseplants, try this recipe for 'manure tea'.

1 Dump manure into the hessian bag. Tie the bag shut with one end of a long rope and place it in an empty barrel or rubbish bin.
2 Fill the barrel or rubbish bin with water and leave the bag to steep for a week, using the rope occasionally to jerk it up and down and mix the liquid.
3 Thin the 'tea' to the colour of weak tea and apply monthly to the soil around houseplant roots. Keep reserved tea in labelled jars with tight lids, out of the way of children and pets.

How to create a lush indoor garden

If you display your houseplants all in one area, you will get a lush visual effect, and the plants will benefit from the heightened humidity gained by grouping the pots of moist soil.

Arrange the potted plants on a water-proof covering, with the shorter ones at the front and rows of successively taller ones behind. For extra protection, set water-collecting saucers under each pot. To increase the humidity of the garden, include a few vases or decorative bowls filled with pebbles and water.

Index

PHOTO CREDITS